California's Criminal Justice System

Carolina Academic Press
State-Specific Criminal Justice Series

Criminal Justice Basics and Concerns
William G. Doerner, ed.

Alabama's Criminal Justice System
Vicki Lindsay and Jeffrey P. Rush, eds.

Arkansas's Criminal Justice System
Edward Powers and Janet K. Wilson

California's Criminal Justice System
Third Edition
Christine L. Gardiner and Georgia Spiropoulos, eds.

Florida's Criminal Justice System
Second Edition
William G. Doerner

Georgia's Criminal Justice System
Deborah Mitchell Robinson

Illinois's Criminal Justice System
Jill Joline Myers and Todd Lough, eds.

California's Criminal Justice System

Third Edition

Edited by
Christine L. Gardiner
&
Georgia Spiropoulos

CAROLINA ACADEMIC PRESS
Durham, North Carolina

The Library of Congress has cataloged the second edition as follows.
For the third edition listing, see the the Library of Congress website
at www.loc.gov.

Library of Congress Cataloging-in-Publication Data
California's criminal justice system / edited by Christine L. Gardiner
and Pamela Fiber-Ostrow. -- Second edition.
    pages cm -- (State-specific criminal justice series)
  Includes bibliographical references and index.
  ISBN 978-1-61163-509-6 (alk. paper)
  1. Criminal justice, Administration of--California. I. Gardiner,
Christine L., editor of compilation. II. Fiber-Ostrow, Pamela, editor
of compilation.

  KFC1102.G37 2014
  364.9794--dc23

                        2014011477

                CAROLINA ACADEMIC PRESS, LLC
                        700 Kent Street
                Durham, North Carolina 27701
                Telephone (919) 489-7486
                    Fax (919) 493-5668
                    www.cap-press.com

            Printed in the United States of America

Contents

Series Note

Carolina Academic Press' state-specific criminal justice series fills a gap in the field of criminal justice education. One drawback with many current introduction to criminal justice texts is that they pertain to the essentially non-existent "American" criminal justice system and ignore the local landscape. Each state has its unique legislature, executive branch, law enforcement system, court and appellate review system, state supreme court, correctional system, and juvenile justice apparatus. Since many criminal justice students embark upon careers in their home states, they are better served by being exposed to their own states' criminal justice systems. Texts in this series are designed to be used as primary texts or as supplements to more general introductory criminal justice texts.

Preface

We are delighted to present the third edition of this book, *California's Criminal Justice System*. Much has changed since the release of the second edition. While each region in the United States is faced with its own unique issues relating to criminal justice, the policies and practices in California are perhaps some of the most well-known and dramatic applications of criminal justice policy in the United States. California has one of the largest and most expensive criminal justice systems in the nation. A significant proportion of tax dollars are used to keep an estimated 128,000 people incarcerated in state prisons[1] and 75,000 in county jails[2] annually. Indeed, our projected state budget for 2017–2018 proposes over 16 billion dollars to be spent on criminal justice and court programs.[3] California's criminal justice system employs more than 210,000 individuals[4]—the majority of whom (118,000) work in law enforcement. In fact, California has more cops than any other state in the country.[5]

The way California has "done criminal justice" in the last 40 years has changed dramatically. While California was a leader in implementing the "tough on crime" ideology in the 1980s and 1990s, recent decades demonstrate a public and government that are coming to terms with the high costs of this strategy. The most notable "get-tough" policy in California, and perhaps one of the most well-known applications of a habitual offender law in the United States, was the three-strikes law. Enacted in 1994, it contributed to an increase in the state prison population to the point that California was successfully sued by inmates and ordered by the U.S. Supreme Court to reduce its prison population

---

1. http://www.cdcr.ca.gov/Reports_Research/Offender_Information_Services_Branch/Projections/S17Pub.pdf

2. http://www.bscc.ca.gov/downloads/4Q15%20JPS%20Full%20Report%206.24.16.pdf

3. http://www.lao.ca.gov/Publications/report/3539

4. http://www.cdcr.ca.gov/News/docs/2011_Annual_Report_FINAL.pdf and http://www.ppic.org/main/publication_show.asp?i=1081

5. http://www.fbi.gov/about-us/cjis/ucr/crime-in-the-u.s/2012/crime-in-the-u.s.-2012/tables/77tabledatadecpdf/table_77_full_time_law_enforcement_employess_by_state_2012.xls

(*Plata & Coleman v. Schwarzenegger*). In direct response, AB109 (Realignment) was enacted in 2011; it drastically changed the landscape of California's criminal justice system and successfully reduced the prison population.

California voters approved a number of initiatives aimed at reducing the quantity of people caught in the state's punitive policies even before the historic Realignment legislation. In particular, voters recognized that California's drug laws have also played a significant role in the massive growth of the state prison population. In 1996, for example, voters approved the use of medical marijuana (Proposition 215); they also voted to divert first-time drug offenders to treatment in 2000 (Proposition 36) and to legalize the recreational use of marijuana in 2016 (Proposition 64). Even our legislature felt comfortable reducing penalties for drug offenses, as evidenced by the passage of SB 1449 in 2010 (it made marijuana possession an infraction rather than a misdemeanor).

The easing of solely punitive policy not only applies to drug offenders; voters also approved legislation that limited the use of the three-strikes law in 2012 (also Proposition 36), reclassified low-level property and drug crimes from felonies to misdemeanors in 2014 (Proposition 47), and increased the use of parole for non-violent offenders and eliminated direct file of juveniles to adult court in 2016 (Proposition 57). Still, not all of California's criminal justice policies have been affected by the recent trend, as the state has some of the stiffest gang enhancements and the largest death row population in the nation.

The purpose of this book is to introduce the reader to California's criminal justice system in a comprehensive way. This book introduces the reader to California criminal justice by examining the state's crime rates, laws, legal structures, policing, courts, corrections, and other important areas. In addition, we highlight some of the unique policies and procedures that are distinctive to California and provide examples that have influenced the state's criminal justice system. Historically, California has been at the center of many key developments in criminal justice practices. Recent years have shown continued innovation in the face of change in terms of how the state does criminal justice. Indeed, a review of the issues facing California in this book can serve as an example for other states when they confront similar issues in criminal justice administration.

Organization and Contents of the Book

The book is divided into thirteen chapters that virtually cover the entirety of California's criminal justice system. Each chapter begins with learning objectives, an introduction to the issues, and a presentation of the basic themes of the subject. The chapter concludes with a discussion of the critical issues facing California's criminal justice system in the twenty-first century.

The first chapter presents the volume and characteristics of crime in California. It includes a discussion of the different data sources that are used to obtain crime rates and provides a comparison of crime both by time and geographic region.

Chapter 2 acquaints readers with the demographics of crime in California. Specifically, the first section examines the over-representation of racial and ethnic minorities in California's criminal justice system. The second section describes women's involvement in crime and the criminal justice system. Finally, the chapter concludes with a discussion of immigration and how immigrants are uniquely involved in California's criminal justice system.

The third chapter focuses on lawmaking practices in California. Beginning with a discussion of our federal and state constitutions, this section highlights how laws related to criminal justice issues are created as part of the legislative process. In particular, California has an unusual direct democracy model that has immediate, and substantial, implications for the criminal justice system.

Chapter 4 focuses on the twenty-nine different legal codes that make up the laws of the criminal justice system in California. These legal codes include the Penal Code, which highlights the definitions of criminal activities (for example, what distinguishes the charge of second-degree murder from the charge of manslaughter) as well as the punishments proscribed under the law. This chapter also highlights other legal codes that have an impact on criminal justice operations, such as the welfare and institutions code.

Chapter 5 introduces policing in California. The section begins with a discussion of the history of law enforcement in California and the significant contributions that our state agencies have made on the practice of policing both within the state and nationwide. The section then turns to a discussion of the organization of law enforcement, beginning with municipal agencies and the differing roles and responsibilities of county sheriffs' departments, up to the state-wide jurisdiction of the California Highway Patrol and the California Attorney General's Office. Finally, the chapter concludes with discussions of professionalization and training and ethics.

The sixth chapter focuses on the structure and functions of the California courts system. Beginning with a discussion of the organization of the courts by jurisdiction and general duties (Superior Court, Appellate Court, and the California State Supreme Court), this section continues with an introduction to the different actors within the courts system, ranging from the judges and prosecutors to defense attorneys and juries. The section concludes with a discussion of the use of specialty courts and reforms to the court system.

The seventh chapter highlights correctional policies and practices in California's criminal justice system. This chapter is organized into three broad sections. The first section presents a general examination of each key component of the correctional system. This begins with a discussion of regional correctional systems: county jails and the use of community corrections, such as probation, which allow offenders to remain in their communities while under the supervision of criminal justice agents. Next, the chapter presents a general review of the structure and organization of California's state prison system, followed by parole supervision and community reentry. The second section of the chapter examines the historical context of the growth in California corrections, including a review of changing sentencing practices and increasing prison populations. Finally, the third section of this chapter presents a detailed chronology of contemporary prison litigation and subsequent reform efforts. This consists of a close examination of the implementation and consequences of correctional Realignment, including a discussion of the reallocation of correctional populations across different correctional subsystems.

Chapter 8 highlights the application of the death penalty in California. Beginning with a discussion on the history of capital punishment, this chapter outlines the current practices related to the death penalty in the state. While California has the largest death row population, the number of modern-day executions is few. This chapter examines the practice of the death penalty and highlights why we carry out so few death sentences. The section concludes with a discussion of current issues related to the death penalty, such as the fiscal concerns of maintaining the death penalty and legal challenges to the execution process here in the state.

Chapter 9 focuses on the juvenile justice system in California. It begins with a brief history of juvenile justice and the implications of various policies on the state juvenile populations at different points in history. It describes juvenile crime, why juveniles commit crime, the juvenile court process, and juvenile corrections and chronicles the events that led to the adoption of distinct policies for juveniles, as well as describes the newest policies that are intended to reduce the number of juveniles in state institutions. It concludes with a discussion of California's use of evidence-based programs in juvenile justice.

The tenth chapter discusses California gangs. The chapter begins with a historical review on the emergence of the different gangs in California, both in the community as well as within the state's penitentiary system. The chapter then turns to a discussion on the prevention, intervention, and rehabilitation of gang members and highlights some of the unique programs and practices used by communities and the criminal justice system to address issues of gang violence.

The eleventh chapter introduces readers to important crime policies from a California perspective. The chapter starts with an introduction to gun policy in California and explains how our policies differ from federal policies. The second part of this chapter details the extent of drug crimes in California and then describes California drug policies, compares them to federal drug laws, and puts them into context with the rest of the United States. The final section of this chapter describes a wide variety of sex crime laws in California.

Chapter 12 highlights victim's rights and victim services in California. The chapter begins by presenting the evolution of the victims' rights movement. The chapter then provides a current description of the resources for victims of crime, such as rape crisis organizations and domestic violence shelters. Last, the chapter turns to a discussion of restorative justice practices within the state.

Chapter 13 concludes the book with a discussion of employment trends in criminal justice. Here, students will learn about the requirements for jobs in policing, courts, and corrections and how to apply for these positions. In addition, students will learn about the average salaries for these jobs (and how they compare to similar positions throughout the United States) as well as the projected growth for these fields.

Our hope is readers of this book gain a comprehensive understanding of California criminal justice after completing the book. As you will soon learn, California's criminal justice system is an important and dynamic system in the state that plays a significant role in the lives of its residents and serves as a unique model for criminal justice in the United States.

New in the Third Edition

- A new, easily accessible table that serves as a guide to California's most significant policies.
- Learning objectives added to each chapter.
- Updated information and statistics in every chapter.
- Updated policy changes passed by voters in November 2016 in every relevant chapter.
- Completely new chapter on corrections.

PREFACE

California Criminal Justice Time Line 1822–2017[1]

1822	End of Spanish Rule in California. Mexican control begins.
1836	1st vigilance committee formed in "Pueblo de Los Angeles"
1846	1st jury summoned by Walter Colton, first American alcalde, in Monterey
1848	Gold discovered at Sutter's Mill. Treaty of Guadalupe Hidalgo signed—Mexico cedes California to U.S.
1849	San Francisco Police Department 1st in state, Sacramento & San Jose PDs also formed. 1st CA constitution ratified. 1st state election (H. Burnett elected 1st Governor, Edward J.C. Kewen elected 1st attorney general, C.S. Hastings elected 1st Chief Justice of State Supreme Court).
1850	California granted statehood and admitted as 31st state. 20 sheriff's departments formed. 1st county election held in San Francisco.
1851	1st state prison, a ship named "Waban" opens. New CA law makes robbery & grand larceny punishable by imprisonment or death. 1st San Francisco Vigilance Committee formed.
1852	1st prison built on land, San Quentin, is founded.
1853	Legislature approves formation of California Rangers to track down Joaquin Murrieta.
1859	San Francisco Industrial School, the 1st house of refuge for juveniles in California, opened.
1872	Penal code becomes law.
1874	Construction begins on Folsom prison. When it opened in 1880 it was one of the first maximum security prisons in the nation
1879	California constitution of 1879 approved. State Board of Prison Directors established. Private prison industries abolished.
1884	Wells Fargo created its own investigative division (313 stagecoach robberies in prior 14 years)
1891	1st state-run juvenile institution opened in Whittier. State assumes responsibility for executions.

---

1. Adapted, with permission, from the California Department of Justice, Criminal Justice Statistics Center's "California Criminal Justice Time Line 1822–2000" which can be found at: http://oag.ca.gov/sites/all/files/pdfs/cjsc/glance/tl4pg.pdf

California Criminal Justice Time Line 1822–2017 (*continued*)

1893	1st parole law enacted.
1903	Law enables counties to establish juvenile courts. 1st probation programs in the state
1905	CA State Bureau of Criminal Identification created to maintain records on wanted persons and those in custody.
1909	Law requires counties to maintain separate juvenile detention facilities.
1910	Alice Stebbins Wells becomes the 1st police woman (with arrest powers) in CA.
1911	Law provides that no intoxicated person shall drive.
1914	Los Angeles County creates Office of the Public Defender—1st of its kind in U.S. Walton J. Wood becomes 1st public defender. U.S. Congress passed Harrison Act.
1916	August Vollmer develops 1st formal, academic law enforcement program at UC Berkeley.
1917	California adopts indeterminate sentencing system.
1920	Volstead Act (Prohibition) takes effect.
1926	1st female judge, Georgia P. Bullock, elected to Los Angeles Municipal Court.
1927	Division of Narcotic Enforcement created as part of State Board of Pharmacy.
1929	California Highway Patrol created.
1930	Bureau of Criminal Identification & Information (CII) created & begins collecting data. State Teachers College at San Jose (now SJSU) is 1st in nation to offer an A.A. degree in police training.
1931	CA becomes 1st state to establish statewide reporting system to provide crime data. Act regulating sale, possession, transportation of machine guns approved. CA legislature establishes Board of Prison Terms and Paroles.
1933	21st Amendment to U.S. Constitution repeals Volstead Act (Prohibition)
1935	Comprehensive Motor Vehicle Act distinguishes between drunk driving causing injury or death and all other types; also increases penalties for recidivism.

California Criminal Justice Time Line 1822–2017 (*continued*)

1938	1st lethal gas execution carried out in California.
1941	California Youth Authority created; 1st woman executed in San Quentin's gas chamber.
1942	Last official hanging occurs in California.
1944	Prison Reorganization Act restructures CA's penal system. State Departments of Justice and Corrections created.
1945	Bureau of Criminal Statistics (now Criminal Justice Statistics Center) formed to collect criminal justice data.
1959	CA established statewide standards for police officers & created 1st POST in nation.
1965	California establishes victims' compensation fund, 1st in nation to do so.
1969	California Legislature enacts "Use a gun, go to prison" statute.
1971	Keldgord Report calls for restructuring of corrections in California, with emphasis on community-based alternatives.
1972	Death penalty ruled unconstitutional by California Supreme Court.
1974	Public vote results in reinstatement of death penalty in California.
1976	Law decriminalizes marijuana (<1oz = misdemeanor). California invokes determinate sentencing. Death penalty again ruled unconstitutional.
1977	Death penalty reinstated.
1981	Law provides mandatory minimum penalties for drunk driving convictions.
1982	California voters approve Proposition 8, the "Victims' Bill of Rights."
1985	CA DOJ's Automated Fingerprint Identification System (AFIS) becomes operational (identifies Richard Ramirez as the "Night Stalker" serial killer).
1990	Coleman v. Wilson lawsuit filed by inmates alleging mental health violations in prisons. 1st boot camp in California opens for juveniles in Los Angeles County. Blue Ribbon Commission recommends expanded use of punishment options, particularly community based alternatives, in response to prison overcrowding. Crime Control Act of 1990 passed by Congress prohibiting importation & manufacture of semi-automatic weapons and establishing gun-free school zones.

California Criminal Justice Time Line 1822–2017 (*continued*)

1991	1st California drug court established in Alameda County.
1992	Jury acquits 4 LAPD officers in beating of Rodney King—results in 6 days of rioting, 54 deaths, 2,383 injuries, 13,000 arrests, and $700 million in property damage.
1994	CA's "Three strikes and You're Out" law signed into law. President Clinton signs Violent Crime Control and Law Enforcement Act of 1994 (including 1st Violence Against Women Act). Congress passes Brady Handgun Violence Prevention Act (CA law exceeds standards). Executions by lethal gas ruled unconstitutional by State.
1995	California State Police merge into California Highway Patrol. U.S. District Judge holds in Madrid v. Gomez that inadequacies in the mental and medical health care system, a pervasive pattern of excessive force against inmates, and the inclusion of seriously mentally ill inmates in security housing units at Pelican Bay State Prison violates the 8th Amendment.
1996	California voters approve Proposition 215, "Medical Use of Marijuana initiative." President Clinton signs "Megan's Law."
1997	Restorative Justice Program funded in Santa Clara County.
1998	CA voters passed Proposition 220, unifying municipal & superior courts in state. CA's Little Hoover Commission finds inadequate space in county jails & state prisons. CA DOJ implements Applicant LiveScan (allowing electronic submission of fingerprints and automated background checks). FBI announces the National DNA Index System (NDIS).
1999	1st mental health courts established in California Scandal erupts when former police officer Rafael Perez alleges widespread corruption in LAPD's CRASH Anti-Gang Unit housed at Rampart Station.
2000	USDOJ "consent decree," signed by Los Angeles mayor, calls for reforms and the appointment of a federal monitor in response to "Rampart Scandal." Voters approve Proposition 21, "Juvenile Crime Initiative," requiring more juveniles to be tried in adult court. Voters approve Proposition 36, "Substance Abuse and Crime Prevention Act of 2000," allowing certain drug offenders to receive treatment in lieu of jail. FBI creates the Internet Fraud Complaint Center to deal with new internet crimes.

California Criminal Justice Time Line 1822–2017 (*continued*)

2001	Plata v. Davis lawsuit filed by state inmates alleging constitutionally inadequate medical care in prisons
2003	Farrell v. Cate lawsuit filed alleging CYA failed to deliver state-mandated rehabilitation.
2005	California Department of Corrections (CDC) becomes California Department of Corrections and Rehabilitation (CDCR). California Youth Authority (CYA) closes and becomes the Division of Juvenile Justice within the newly reorganized CDCR.
2006	President Bush signs Violence Against Women Act of 2005. Executions halted in CA due to legal challenges surrounding lethal injection protocol.
2007	SB81 passed limiting juvenile offenders in state institutions to the most serious.
2008	California Legislature passed Marsy's Law, the Victims' Bill of Rights Act.
2009	Plata & Coleman v. Schwarzenegger Three Judge Panel requires prison reduction.
2010	SB 1449 reduced marijuana possession from a misdemeanor to an infraction.
2011	U.S. Supreme Court rules, in Brown v. Plata, that overcrowded prisons violate inmates 8th Amendment Rights. Governor Brown signs Criminal Justice Realignment legislation (AB109).
2012	Voters approve Proposition 36, changing the state's "three strikes law."
2013	LAPD no longer under the authority of a federal monitor.
2014	Voters passed Proposition 47 reducing some felonies to misdemeanors.
2016	Judge terminated Farrell lawsuit, finding CA had implemented most requirements to reform DJJ. Voters passed Proposition 57 eliminating direct file of juveniles to adult court and revamping parole rules, Proposition 63 extending background checks to ammunition and banning large-capacity magazines, Proposition 64 making recreational marijuana use legal, and Proposition 66 streamlining death penalty cases.
2017	Governor Brown signed criminal and juvenile justice reform legislation, including SB 395 which requires children under 16 to consult with an attorney before waiving their Miranda rights. He also signed SB 54 limiting local law enforcement officers' ability to enforce federal immigration laws.

Guide to Key California Criminal Justice Policies

Policy	Name	Effective Date	Summary	Chapter
AB971 (Proposition 184)	The Three Strikes and You're Out Law	1994	Significantly increased prison sentences for violent and serious offenders convicted of felonies.	7
Proposition 215	Medical Use of Marijuana Initiative (Compassionate Use Act)	1996	Allows patients and certain medical caregivers to possess and cultivate marijuana for medical treatment as recommended by a physician.	11
Proposition 21	Treatment of Juvenile Offenders	2000	Increased correctional penalties and reduced confidentiality for juveniles committing certain types of violent and sex crimes; reduced minimum transfer age to 14 for criminal court and introduced direct file of juveniles to adult court.	9, 10
Proposition 36 (2000)	Substance Abuse and Crime Prevention Act of 2000	2001	Allowed certain defendants convicted of nonviolent drug possession offenses to receive probation instead of incarceration.	11

Policy	Name	Effective Date	Summary	Chapter
Proposition 63	Income Tax Increase for Mental Health Services	2005	Levies an additional 1% tax on millionaires to fund mental health services; requires counties to provide wraparound services for at-risk offenders.	9
SB81	Juvenile Justice Realignment Bill	2007	Required states to transfer all non-violent juvenile offenders to county facilities and increased funding for the Governor's Gang Reduction and Prevention Program (CalGRIP).	9
Proposition 9	Marsy's Law (California's Victim's Bill of Rights)	2008	Expanded the legal rights of victims and restitution. It included 17 enumerated rights in the judicial process.	12
SB 1449	Marijuana: Possession	2010	Reduced possession of marijuana for personal use from a misdemeanor to an infraction.	9, 11
AB109/AB117	Public Safety Realignment	2011	Suspended counties from transferring non-serious, non-violent, and non-sexual offenders to the state prison system.	1, 7
Proposition 36 (2012)	Three Strikes Law. Repeat Felony Offenders. Penalties. Initiative Statute.	2012	Revised three-strikes law, particularly with regard to the imposition of life sentences.	7

Policy	Name	Effective Date	Summary	Chapter
Proposition 47	Reduced Penalties for Some Crimes Initiative	2014	Reclassified non-serious and non-violent drug and property crimes from felonies to misdemeanors.	1, 7
Proposition 57	Parole for Non-Violent Criminals and Juvenile Court Trial Requirements	2016	Increased parole and good behavior opportunities for non-violent felons and eliminated direct file of juveniles to adult court.	7, 9
Proposition 63	Background Checks for Ammunition Purchases and Large-Capacity Ammunition Magazine Ban Initiative	2016	Requires individuals and businesses to obtain licenses to purchase and sell ammunition. It also limited the exemptions to the large-capacity magazine ban.	11
Proposition 64	Marijuana Legalization Initiative	2016	Legalizes the recreational use of marijuana for individuals over age 18, levies its tax, and sets up parameters for its legal sale.	11
Proposition 66	Death Penalty Procedures Initiative	2016	Changes and streamlines the procedures governing state court appeals and petitions that challenge death penalty convictions and sentences.	8

About the Authors

Gregory C. Brown is an associate professor of criminal justice at California State University, Fullerton. Dr. Brown received his Ph.D. from the University of California, Irvine in social ecology, with an emphasis in criminology. His teaching and research interests include corrections, street gangs, prisons, punishment theory and practices, white-collar crime, and minorities and crime. He has published articles in several journals, including the *Journal of Contemporary Criminal Justice*, *Journal of Ethnicity in Criminal Justice*, *International Journal of Cyber Criminology*, *Police Practice and Research*, *Public Personnel Management*, *Journal of Medical Education*, and *Western State University Consumer Law Journal*.

Heather Brown is an adjunct lecturer at California State University, Fullerton where she teaches a class on sex, crime, and culture. She received her undergraduate degree in psychology from Loyola Marymount University and her J.D. from Pepperdine University School of Law. She has served as a senior deputy district attorney with the Orange County District Attorney's Office for the past 19 years and prior to that worked for the Los Angeles County Probation Department in their Narcotics Testing Unit and was a law clerk for the Los Angeles County District Attorney's Office. She specializes in sexual assault crimes and has worked in the Sexual Assault Unit for 10 years, prosecuting child molesters, rapists, and sexual deviants. She routinely trains local law enforcement agencies, FBI, CDAA, CAST, UC Irvine, and community service programs and presented a case study at the 2010 Crimes Against Children Conference. She was previously on the board of the Innocence Mission, which is a non-profit dedicated to the eradication of sexual crimes against children.

Robert F. Castro is a professor in the Division of Politics, Administration & Justice at the California State University, Fullerton. He holds a B.A. in criminology, law and society from University of California, Irvine, a Ph.D. in political science from the University of Michigan, Ann Arbor, and a J.D. from the UCLA School of Law, where he was in the inaugural class in the program in public interest law and policy (PILP). His work on immigration, law and the U.S.–Mexico borderlands has been published in several leading journals, such as *Law & Inequality*; *Journal of Hate Studies*; *Harvard Journal of Hispanic Policy*; *Harvard Civil Rights and Civil Liberties Law Review*; and the *Harvard Latino Law Review*.

Pamela Fiber-Ostrow is a professor of political science at California State University, Fullerton and also serves as the Moot Court director at CSU Fullerton. She earned her Ph.D. in American politics, policy and law from Claremont Graduate University. Her teaching and research interests include public law, gender and election law, fetal personhood, and gender and legislative behavior. Her research has been published in *California Journal of Politics and Policy*, *Journal of Women, Politics & Policy*, *Yale Journal of Health Policy, Law, and Ethics*, and *Duke Journal of Gender Law and Policy*.

Christine L. Gardiner is an associate professor of criminal justice at California State University, Fullerton. She received her Ph.D. in criminology, law, and society from University of California, Irvine, where she received a prestigious National Institute of Justice Dissertation Fellowship to support her research on Proposition 36. Her fields of expertise include policing, crime policy, and juvenile delinquency. She has edited several textbooks and authored *Policing for the 21st Century: Realizing the Vision of Police in a Free Society*. Her research has been published in *Criminal Justice Policy Review*, *Policing*, *Federal Probation*, and *Journal of Drug Issues*. She currently serves as a senior research fellow for the Police Foundation. Beyond her academic experience, she also has experience as a sheriff's department crime analyst, a police dispatcher, and an intern probation officer.

Philip L. Gianos is an Emeritus Professor of Political Science at California State University, Fullerton, where he served as chair of the Division of Politics, Administration, and Justice and Associate Dean in the College of Humanities and Social Sciences. His research and teaching interests are in U.S. national politics and political behavior, California politics, and film and politics.

Veronica M. Herrera is an assistant professor of criminal justice at California State University, Fullerton. She received her Ph.D. in psychology from the University of Arizona. Her research interests focus on violence against girls and women, the impact of exposure to family violence on youth risk behavior, and gender differences in pathways to delinquency. She teaches courses on women and crime, victimology, juvenile justice, and theories of crime and delinquency. She has published articles in several journals, including the *Journal of Developmental and Life Course Criminology*, *Journal of Research on Adolescence*, *Journal of Youth and Adolescence*, *Journal of Marriage and the Family*, *Journal* *of the American Academy of Child & Adolescent Psychiatry*, *Violence and Victims*, and *Child Abuse and Neglect*.

Dixie J. Koo is a professor of criminal justice in the Division of Politics, Administration, and Justice at California State University, Fullerton. She earned her Ph.D. in sociology from the University of Miami. Her research interests include areas of substance use, race/ethnicity, and violence and victimization.

Gary LoGalbo has been a part-time lecturer at California State University, Fullerton in the Division of Politics, Administration and Justice for the past 16 years. He has also been a full-time deputy district attorney with the Orange County District Attorney's Office for past 19 years. He has worked in many different assignments there, including the Gang, Domestic Violence and Career Criminal and Writs & Appeals Vertical Prosecution Units. Prior to that he was a police officer and investigator with the Placentia Police Department in Orange County, California, for 10 years. He holds a B.A. in criminal justice from CSU Fullerton and graduated cum laude. He also holds a J.D. from Western State University College of Law in Fullerton, California, and graduated cum laude there as well. He has previously published training materials, law review articles, and college-level book chapters on criminal justice topics.

Stacy L. Mallicoat is a professor of criminal justice and chair of the Division of Politics, Administration and Justice at California State University, Fullerton. Her research interests include issues of feminist criminology, criminal justice policy, and capital punishment. She is the author of several textbooks, including *Crime and Criminal Justice: Concepts and Controversies*. Her research has appeared in journals such as *Feminist Criminology*, *American Journal of Criminal Justice*, and various edited volumes.

Kristy N. Matsuda is a research specialist at the Center for Evidence-Based Corrections at the University of California, Irvine. She designs and conducts evaluation research studies on juvenile and adult correctional populations. The studies are designed to assist corrections officials make evidence-based policy decisions in California. She received her doctorate from the University of California, Irvine. Prior to her return to UC Irvine, she was an assistant research professor in the Department of Criminology and Criminal Justice at the University of Missouri—St. Louis, where she helped manage the National Evaluation of the Gang Resistance Education and Training (G.R.E.A.T.) Program. Her research interests include juvenile justice, corrections, gangs, and evaluation research. Her research has been published in *Justice Quarterly*, *Evaluation Review*, and *Crime & Delinquency*.

Monishia "Moe" Miller is an adjunct lecturer of criminal justice at California State University, Fullerton, where she teaches courses in juvenile justice, corrections, and foundations of criminal justice. She received her M.S. degree from California State University, Los Angeles, in criminal justice administration. She has worked and volunteered in the juvenile justice field for over twenty years.

Jill Rosenbaum is an emerita professor of criminal justice at California State University, Fullerton. Her research interests focus on issues of female delinquency and the victimization of women. She has participated in numerous local and statewide assessments of incarcerated delinquent girls, rape crisis organizations, services for victims of child abuse, and domestic violence. Her articles have appeared in several criminal justice and criminology journals, including *Women in Criminal Justice*, *Justice Quarterly*, *Crime & Delinquency*, *Youth and Society*, and *Feminist Criminology*. She is coauthor of *Implementing a Gender-Based Arts Program for Juvenile Offenders* (Elsevior, 2014).

Georgia Spiropoulos is an associate professor of criminal justice at California State University, Fullerton. Dr. Spiropoulos holds a Ph.D. in criminal justice from the University of Cincinnati. Her areas of expertise include evidence-based corrections and correctional rehabilitation, correctional program development and evaluation, and theories of behavior and behavioral change. Her published works are seen in the journals *Crime & Delinquency*, *Criminal Justice & Behavior*, *International Journal of Offender Therapy & Comparative Criminology*, and *Journal of Offender Rehabilitation*.

Stephen J. Stambough is a professor of political science and chair of the California State University, Fullerton Academic Senate. He received his Ph.D. in political science from the University of California, Riverside in 1997. He is the author of *Initiative-Centered Politics: The New Politics of Direct Democracy* and co-editor of *California Government in National Perspective*. His work on congressional elections, gubernatorial elections, and gender issues in campaigns has appeared in leading political science journals, including his most recent work on the impact of state legislative term limits on women's representation.

Jennifer Sumner is an assistant professor of criminal justice administration in the Department of Public Administration at California State University, Dominguez Hills. She completed her doctorate in criminology, law and society at the University of California, Irvine. Her research examines correctional policy, practice, and culture and the relationship between gender, sexuality, and the criminal justice system. She has obtained research funding from the National Science Foundation to examine correctional policy in international settings. Her research has been published in journals such as *Critical Criminology*,

Deviant Behavior, Journal of Crime and Justice, Justice Quarterly, and *Law & Social Inquiry* as well as in several edited volumes. She is also co-author of two reports to the California Department of Corrections and Rehabilitation on studies of violence and victimization in California prisons.

Brenda L. Vogel is a professor and the director of the School of Criminology, Criminal Justice, and Emergency Management at Long Beach State University. She received her Ph.D. in criminology, law, and society from University of California, Irvine. She has authored one book and numerous journal articles in the areas of criminological theory, the death penalty, and public perceptions of law enforcement. She is also a pretty groovy human and generally loves life!

Julius (Jay) Wachtel is an adjunct lecturer of criminal justice at California State University, Fullerton. A retired ATF agent, he earned a Ph.D. in criminal justice at the University at Albany in 1982. Jay's historical novel, *Stalin's Witnesses*, a fact-based account about the Moscow show trials, was published in December 2012. Jay blogs on law enforcement issues at www.policeissues.com.

Sigrid Williams is an adjunct lecturer in the Division of Politics, Administration and Justice at California State University, Fullerton and assistant professor of Administration of Justice at Norco Community College. She received her Ed.D. in educational leadership in 2017, a master's in public administration with a dual emphasis in criminal justice and human resource management in 2005, and has served as a deputy sheriff with the Los Angeles County Sheriff's Department. She currently volunteers as a member of the Riverside County Sheriff's Department Mounted Posse and is certified in search and rescue, emergency management, and large animal rescue. In 2015, she was inducted into the Honor Society of International Scholars. In 2011, she was awarded the Outstanding Part-Time Faculty Award by the College of Humanities and Social Sciences at California State University, Fullerton for her excellence in teaching. Sigrid enjoys her volunteerism and was awarded the Presidential Lifetime Medal in 2007 for her volunteer work, having documented over 10,000 certified hours of volunteer service. She has currently volunteered over 13,000 hours with a variety of non-profit organizations and continues to give of herself to others.

California's Criminal Justice System

Chapter 1

Crime in California

Georgia Spiropoulos

Learning Objectives

After reading the chapter, students should be able to:

- Identify how we count crime in America.
- Demonstrate an understanding of current crime rates and their characteristics in California.
- Recite recent and historical crime trends in California and compare them to that of the nation.

Introduction

The July 18, 2016, Republican National Convention was dedicated to the theme "Make America Safe Again." Accepting the nomination from his party, the then presidential hopeful Donald Trump proclaimed, "I have a message for all of you: the crime and violence that today afflicts our nation will soon come to an end. Beginning on January 20, 2017, safety will be restored" (Politico, 2016). Donald Trump was politically savvy to directly address Americans' fear of crime. Crime is a major concern of the American public. As has been true for decades, the majority of Americans believe that crime is higher today than it was a year ago (Gallup, 2016b). Fueled by that belief, for almost every year since 2000 more than half of Americans considered crime to be a very serious problem or extreme problem in America (Gallup, 2016b) and more than 70% of Americans annually said that they personally worried about crime and violence either a great deal or a fair amount of time (Gallup, 2016b). In 2016, our fear of crime reached a 15-year high as slightly more than half (53%) of Americans said they worried about crime at the highest level, a "great deal," (Gallup, 2016a). Moreover, a persistent sense of dissatisfaction pervades the public's perception of how the criminal justice system is combating crime. In 2016, only 5% of Americans were very satisfied with the nation's policies to reduce or control crime (Gallup, 2016b), and only 9% claimed that they had a great deal of confidence in the criminal justice system (Gallup, 2016b).

Together, these data suggest that many Americans believe that crime is chronically increasing and they are very fearful of crime, which may be potentially compounded by their mistrust of the criminal justice system. While the concept of fear of crime may be as important of an issue to address as the actual crime rate (Warr, 1994; Warr, 2000) and the statement that "one crime is too many" is true, this chapter is devoted to exploring whether the crime data can tell us whether crime levels are particularly high in California. To this end, this chapter provides the reader with an informed understanding of crime in California by examining official crime data.[1] This chapter is divided into three sections. The first section presents an overview of the crimes that occurred in California in 2015,[2] with note of the potential effects of *Realignment* and Proposition 47 on the crime rate. The second section examines more than 50 years of crime data in California, comparing these annual figures to national averages, and provides a detailed look at selected crime trends. The third section presents evidence to what is commonly known as the *crime drop* of the 1990s (as it relates to violent crime). Overall, two major points are made in this chapter. First, despite the fact that crime increased across the board (in most types of crime) in California this past year (from 2014 to 2015), it is too soon to be sure that a "real" *crime trend* is taking place.[3] Second, California's crime trends parallel the nation's from 1960, when crime levels were generally higher than the national average, until roughly a decade ago.

What Is Crime?

An old joke in criminal justice circles asks, *what causes crime?* The answer is *laws*. Laws are codified rules that pronounce to a population the behaviors

---

1. Official crime data only represent crime known to the police. In contrast, victimization data measures crimes reported by the victims themselves regardless of whether these crimes were reported to the police. The only publicly available victimization database is the National Criminal Victimization Survey (NCVS). Unfortunately, it is only a national-level database and cannot be disaggregated to specifically count California victimizations.

2. As of this writing (spring of 2017) the latest available crime data is from 2015.

3. Crime rates invariably fluctuate upwards or downwards year-by-year. In this work, a *crime trend* is a consistent increase or decrease in crime rates that lasts three years or more. Save the current year (2015), the crime rate last increased in California in 2012. But crime fell again in subsequent years (2013 and 2014). The 2012 increase is therefore not the start of a trending increase in crime.

that are permissible, required, and prohibited by the government. If no laws exist then, by definition, no crime would exist either. *Crimes* are considered behaviors or lack thereof that are in violation of laws.

The Uniform Crime Report (UCR) Program

An important task for any state criminal justice system is to track the amount of crime that occurs within its borders. The *Uniform Crime Report (UCR)* program provides one of the most common crime recording and reporting mechanisms in the country. The UCR program is housed within the Federal Bureau of Investigation (FBI) in the Department of Justice (DOJ). Since the UCR's creation in 1929, select crime counts have been sent to the FBI from almost all law enforcement agencies in the nation. Importantly, UCR data are not statistics obtained from a sample; they are actual counts of crime gathered across the nation by police agencies. The UCR collects these data and annually publishes the collection. The UCR does not count every type of crime. The most commonly tracked UCR data include only certain types of felonies called *Part I index crimes*. The Part I index crimes are murder (and non-negligent manslaughter), rape,[4] robbery, aggravated assault, burglary, larceny-theft, motor vehicle theft (MVT), and arson.[5] These data are commonly used to track crime levels and crime trends. All California jurisdictions report UCR data.

UCR data has limitations. First, UCR data reflect crime counts for Part I index crimes and not all of the crimes that happened in a geographic location over a given period of time. Second, the UCR only captures crimes reported to the police. The UCR does not capture crimes that were never reported to the police or those crimes that law enforcement officers discretionarily dismissed. Third, the UCR counts are sensitive to changes in police reporting procedures and definitions of crime, which can obscure crime counts. In the case of the former, California law enforcement procedures changed in 1985 to require

---

4. On January 6, 2012, Attorney General Eric Holder announced that the UCR would change the name and definition of rape. The name changed from *forcible rape* to *rape*. The "revised" definition went into effect with the UCR in 2013. California did not report the revised definition of rape, however, until 2014 (Criminal Justice Statistics Center, 2016, p. 63). In some cases, the "legacy" definition is presented in this work when looking at trends.

5. Arson is selectively presented in the first section of the chapter in the total California crime and property crime in 2015, but it is not discussed in detail.

officers to report domestic violence situations. This *procedural* change in police actions produced a 35% increase in the UCR count of aggravated assaults in 1986 (CJSC, 2010).

Fourth, UCR data only allows one crime to represent a criminal event even if several crimes were committed during the event. The *hierarchy rule* dictates that only the most serious crime is reported for that criminal event. So, if an aggravated assault and burglary occur together in one criminal event, only the aggravated assault is reported by the UCR since it is the more serious crime. Fifth, the definitions of crimes used by the UCR may omit certain criminal events from being counted. For example, up until 2012, the UCR defined rape as the "carnal knowledge of a female forcibly and against her will" (*legacy* definition) (FBI, 2004). This limited and dated definition of rape does not include events that most people would consider "rape." For example, this definition does not count male rape victims. The omission of men and boys as victims of rape is not a trivial matter. In the mid-1990s, the *National Violence Against Women Survey* estimated that 92,748 males are raped in a given year (Tjaden & Thoennes, 2000).[6] The changed definition of *rape* in the UCR to include (1) male and female victims, (2) any type of sexual penetration of the victim and (3) a clearer understanding of the incapacity to consent (White House Press Release, 2012) has produced what this author estimates is an average 29.2% higher count of rape over the last three years (2013–2015). This increase, however, does not represent an actual increase in the incidence of this crime; it represents better collecting and reporting of extant behavior. Despite these limitations, UCR data are the best crime data to use, because it is the only national and state public crime dataset available that counts crime over a long enough period of time to investigate important crime trends.

This chapter will report annual crime rates since 1960. It is important to note that crime rates inevitably fluctuate from year to year—they inevitably go up or go down. Generally, these fluctuations are small and inconsequential. When attempting to determine whether crime rates are actually changing enough to warrant calling such changes a *crime trend*, three or more years of similarly trending data are used in this work to signal a substantial and consequential trend in crime.

---

6. While UCR rape data still likely underestimates the actual number of rapes that annually occur despite the improved definition of the crime, this chapter is as much about relative differences in crime rates as it is about the absolute count of crime. Therefore, an assumption is made by the author that the underreporting of rape is constant over time, thus allowing relative differences to be examined.

What Are Crime Rates?

There were over 39 million people living in California in 2015 (CJSC, 2015).[7] It is one of the most populous states, accounting for approximately 12% of the nation's population.[8] Given the state's large population size compared to other states, one would expect crime counts in California to be naturally higher than those found in less populous states. For this reason, crime counts are commonly put into context in the form of *crime rates*. A crime rate is a crime count specified to a certain population size (most often per 100,000 population).[9] A crime rate is considered a *standardized* measure of crime, because the units of comparison, such as geographical or temporal units, are based on the same population size, which are 100,000 people in this work. So crime rates refer to the number of crimes for every 100,000 people in a geographical/temporal unit.

Crime in California in 2015[10]

A total of 1,190,416 crimes, or 3,047 crimes for every 100,000 people, were committed in California in 2015 (CJSC, 2015). Figure 1.1 shows the counts and percentages of the different Part I index crimes. There are several expected findings from Figure 1.1. First, the rates of crimes that involve property, called *property crime* (86%[11] of all crimes), by far exceeded crimes that involve harm to persons, called *violent crime* (14% of all crimes).[12] The most common crimes committed in California in 2015 were larceny/theft[13] (55% of all crime), followed

---

7. The California Department of Justice estimated based on the Demographic Research Institute, California Department of Finance estimates that the state's population in 2015 was 39,071,323 (CJSC, 2016).

8. The United States population was estimated to be 321,369,000 (U.S. Census Bureau, 2017).

9. The crime rate formula is [(# of crimes/population size) *100,000].

10. California's crime data in this section, Crime in California in 2015, is produced by the California Criminal Justice Statistics Center and provided by the California Attorney General's Office (AGO) versus the UCR directly. The state's data provide more detail about the crimes examined in this work. For a variety of methodological reasons, there are small differences in the counts and rates of crime between the state's AGO and the federal UCR.

11. All percentages are rounded to the nearest whole number.

12. Murder, forcible rape, robbery, and aggravated assault were combined to create the violent crime category, and burglary, larceny-theft, and motor vehicle theft were combined to create the property crime category.

13. California changed the way it counted larceny-theft in 2011 that caused a substantial increase in the count of crime. Prior to 2011, only larceny-thefts >$400 were counted by the

Figure 1.1. Percentage Crime By Crime Type, 2015

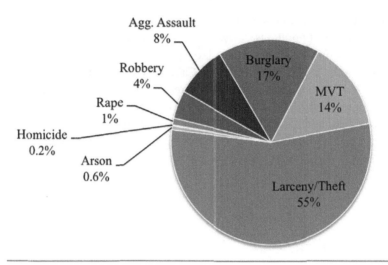

Note: Data taken from Crime in California, 2015, Table 1. Percentages may not add up to 100.0% due to rounding.

by burglary (17%) and motor vehicle theft (14%). The least common crimes were homicide (0.2%), rape (1%),[14] and arson (0.6%).

Figures 1.2 and 1.3 show the counts and percentages of crimes committed in California in 2015 disaggregated into violent and property crime. Crime is regularly disaggregated into violent and property crimes because (1) these crimes differ in target (i.e., violations to person or property) and (2) they can have different trends. Figure 1.2 shows a common and predictable pattern in violent crime where the rate of violent crime sequentially decreases according to the seriousness of the crime so that the more serious the violent crime, the less often its incidence. Murder ($n = 1,861$; 1%) and rape ($n = 12,793$, 8%) are the most serious yet the least frequent crimes that happened in 2015. Robbery ($n = 52,785$; 32%) and aggravated assault ($n = 99,149$; 59%) were less serious but more common violent crimes committed in 2015.

---

state. Since 2011 (because of Realignment), all larceny-thefts, regardless of dollar amount, are counted. To provide some perspective of this increase, the rate of larceny-thefts in 2010 was 525 (CJSC, 2010, p. 6) and in 2011 the rate was 1,590 per 100,000 population size (CJSC, 2011, p. 6). Since 2011, California adjusted their reporting of all annual larceny-thefts to total counts to allow for the examination of trends (Criminal Justice Statistics Center, 2016, p. 63).

14. Rape is counted using the *revised* definition.

Figure 1.2. Violent Crime Counts Disaggregated by Crime Type, 2015

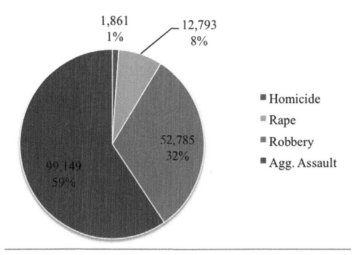

Note: Data taken from Crime in California, 2015, Table 1. Percentages may not add up to 100.0% due to rounding.

Property crime roughly followed the same incident-seriousness pattern found with violent crime. As seen in Figure 1.3, the least serious and the most frequently committed property crime in California in 2015 was larceny-theft ($n = 655,851$; 64%). In order of seriousness and incidence, the remaining property crimes were burglary ($n = 197,189$; 19%), motor vehicle theft ($n = 170,788$; 16%), and arson ($n = 7,380$; 1%).

California's Crime Increase of 2015

Crime increased in California in 2015 after years of trending downwards (save single-year increases such as in 2006, 2010, and 2012). This section presents the magnitude of the increase and examines whether this increase could be caused by recent policy changes in California such as Realignment and Proposition 47 by comparing the crime rate trends in California to the trends in adjacent states (Arizona, Nevada, and Oregon) and the national average from 2005 to 2015.

Two significant criminal justice policies were implemented in the last five years in California, both of which have been argued by their opponents to potentially cause an increase in crime. First, a process called *Realignment* changed California's corrections system in 2011. The *Public Safety Realignment Act* (As-

Figure 1.3. Property Crime Counts Disaggregated by Crime Type, 2015

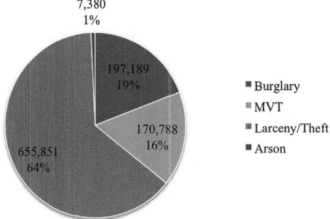

Note: Data taken from Crime in California, 2015, Table 1. Percentages may not add up to 100.0% due to rounding.

sembly Bills 109 & 117) shifted the responsibility for supervising specific adult offender populations from the state's California Department of Corrections & Rehabilitation to the local 58 counties of California. Specifically, the act requires counties to retain their offenders convicted of non-serious, non-violent, and non-sexual offenses (N3) rather than transfer them to state prison (Krisberg & Taylor-Nicholson, 2011). The legislation was created in reaction to the U.S. Supreme Court's affirmation directing California to reduce its prison population to constitutional levels (Rothfield, 2009). The supervision options available to the counties are county jail and a variety of intermediate sanctions. The Re-alignment Act gives counties considerable autonomy to supervise N3s as they see fit, ideally using an evidence-based approach to promote community-based corrections for low-level offenders such as home confinement/electronic mon-itoring, GPS tracking, work-release, residential treatment programs, day-reporting centers, community service, restorative justice, and intensive community supervision. Realignment should decrease state spending on criminal justice, reduce prison overcrowding, and improve upon a state correctional system that was in crisis (Krisberg & Taylor-Nicholson, 2011). Some suggested that Realignment could cause an increase in crime in California because, it was argued, a significant number of offenders would be released from prison. Research shows there was a slight increase in motor vehicle thefts (70 more auto thefts per 100,000 residents) in 2012 that may be attributable to Realignment, but there was no increase in violent crime (Lofstrom, Bird, & Martin, 2016).

Second, Proposition 47 is a voter initiative that reduces certain non-violent, non-serious crimes to misdemeanors unless the offender has a prior conviction for murder, rape, certain other sex offenses, and certain gun crimes. Enacted in November of 2014, crimes valued under $950 involving shoplifting, grand theft, receiving stolen property, forgery, fraud, writing bad checks, and the personal use of most illegal drugs are now considered misdemeanors. The law allows for the reclassification of offenders currently serving sentences. Proponents of the initiative claim that it prevents some offenders who are in prison from staying there. Opponents claim that it leaves offenders free to continue to commit crime with little punishment (Chang, Gerber, & Poston, 2015). As a result, opponents suggest that crime is likely to increase as a result of this measure.[15]

Table 1.1 shows the percentage change in crime rates in 2015 in California to the baseline years of 2005 and 2010 and the years that Realignment (2012) and Proposition 47 began (2014). The crime rate clearly increased in California from 2014 to 2015, 8.4% for violent crime and 6.6% for property crime. While some of this increase is due to the redefinition of rape,[16] the increase is substantial enough to require further examination. To do so, it is instructive to compare the percentage change in the 2015 crime rate with crime rates from prior years to get figures that show the magnitude of this recent increase. As seen in Table 1.1, California's violent crime rate in 2015 was still 19% lower than it was in 2005, 3% lower than it was in 2010 and a little higher (0.4%) than it was in 2012. A similar pattern was found with property crime. The property crime rate in California was 21% lower than in 2005, 0.4% lower than in 2010 and 6% lower than on 2012. Overall, these data suggest that while the crime rate increased from 2014–2015, it was still substantially lower than it was a decade ago and about even or a little lower than it was five years ago.

It is further instructive to see if the latest increase in crime is isolated to California. If California's policies are producing an increase in crime, one would expect the increase to be isolated to California. The percentage change in crime rates for adjacent states and the nation across the four time periods are given

---

15. It is important to point out that this work does not investigate any crimes that are not Part I index crimes with one exception. Larceny-theft is captured with no dollar value attached so these data do not distinguish between misdemeanor and felony theft.

16. The redefinition of rape (difference between the legacy and the revised definition) produced an estimated 29.7% increased rate of this crime in 2013, a 21.7% increase in 2014 and a 36.3% increase in 2015.

Table 1.1. Percentage Changes in Crime Rates in 2015 Compared to 2005, 2010, 2012 and 2014 for California, Adjacent States and the Nation

	California	Arizona	Nevada	Oregon	Nation
Violent Crime					
2014–2015	8.4	2.6	9.5	11.8	3.0
2012–2015	0.4	-4.3	14.3	5.1	-3.7
2010–2015	-2.9	-0.8	5.0	3.3	-7.9
2005–2015	-19.1	-19.9	14.5	-9.5	-20.6
Property Crime					
2014–2015	6.6	-5.1	1.6	2.4	-3.4
2012–2015	-5.5	-14.2	-5.2	-9.1	-13.0
2010–2015	-0.4	-14.2	-3.8	-3.1	-15.6
2005–2015	-21.1	-37.2	-37.2	-33.1	-27.5

Note: Percentage changes calculated on rates taken from Crime in California, 2015 for California and Uniform Crime Report data for the remaining states and the national average. The percentage change was calculated using the formula (year 2-year 1/year 1).

in Table 1.1. As seen in Table 1.1, the results are mixed. From 2014 to 2015 violent crime increased not only in California (8%) but also in Arizona (3%), Oregon (12%), Nevada (10%), and nationally (3%). So California, its neighboring states, and the nation (on average) experienced a violent crime increase from 2014–2015. Comparing the property crime rate in California to adjacent states and nationally provides a more complicated picture. Property crime increased in Nevada (2%) and Oregon (2%) but decreased in Arizona (5%) and the nation (3%). Compared to the national average and its adjacent states, California experienced the highest property crime increase from 2014–2015. Overall, these rates show that it is unlikely that policy changes within California produced an increase in violent crime but could have produced an increase in property crime.

If California's property crime rate increased disproportionately with its neighbors and the nation, does this mean that California has a particularly high property crime rate compared to its neighbors? What about California's violent crime rate? As shown in Figures 1.4 and 1.5, California's violent and

Figure 1.4. Annual Rates of Violent Crime in California Compared to
Adjacent States and the National Average, 2005–2015

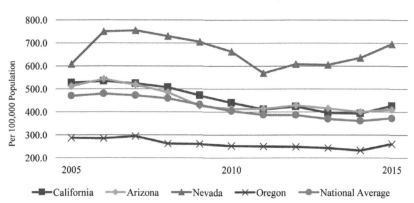

Source: Uniform Crime Report

property crime rates are not currently the highest or lowest in the region and
the trend in crime mirrors that of other states and the nation from 2005 to
2015. The violent crime rate has been similar to Arizona and the national
average for the last 10 years. The property crime rate was the lowest in the
region until recently, and with the recent increase, is similar to the rates found
with its neighboring states and the national average.

Figure 1.5. Annual Rates of Property Crime in California Compared to
Adjacent States and the National Average, 2005–2015

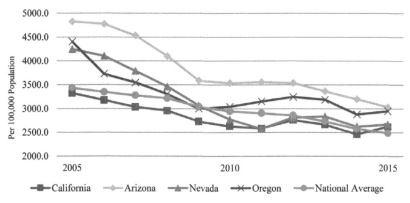

Source: Uniform Crime Report

Figure 1.6. Rates of Murder in California Compared to the
National Average, 1960–2015

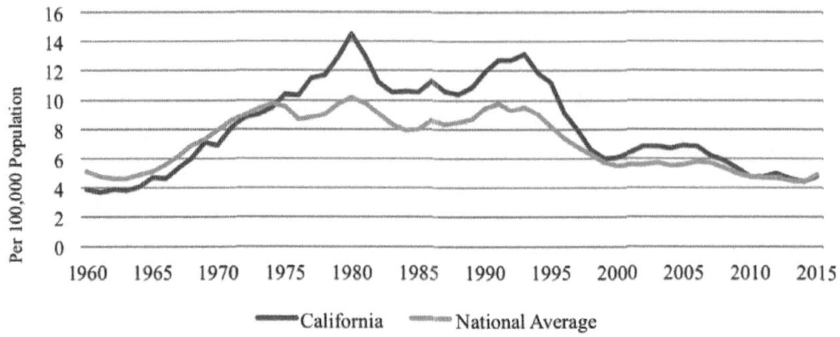

Source: Uniform Crime Report

Overall, there is some evidence that Realignment and Proposition 47 might
have increased the incidence of property crime in California, but violent crime
remains unaffected and on par with its neighboring states and the nation. Still,
putting the property crime increase in perspective, the property crime rate is at
a level similar to the rates found in Arizona, Nevada, Oregon, and the nation.

Crime Trends

If California's crime rate is currently fairly even with its adjacent states and
the national average, has this generally been the case? Specifically, how has
California's crime rate compared to the national average over the past 55 years?
In this section, a more detailed look at the Part I index crimes in California is
given in order to examine whether the state's crime levels since 1960 are trending
similar to the nation. Second, this section provides a detailed look at particular
characteristics related to California's Part I index crimes in 2015.

Murder/Non-Negligent Manslaughter

Murder is the purposeful or intentional killing of another person (FBI,
2004). The crimes of homicide and non-negligent manslaughter are typical
crimes of murder. Figure 1.6 shows the annual murder rates in California
and the average murder rates for the nation from 1960 to 2015. A visual comparison of murder trends in California and the nation shows that these trends

Table 1.2. Demographic Characteristics of Murder Victims in
California in 2015

	Number of victims	% of total victims	% demographic in population	Rate
Total	1,861	100.0	100.0	4.8 [a]
Gender				
Male	1,540	82.8	49.7	8.0
Female	321	17.2	50.3	1.6
Race/Ethnicity				
Hispanic	802	43.1	39.0	5.3
White	394	21.2	38.5	2.6
Black	526	28.3	5.7	23.5
Age				
Under 18	145	7.8	23.4	1.6
18-29	718	38.6	17.4	10.6
30-39	389	20.9	13.8	7.2
40 and over	601	32.3	45.4	3.4

Note: Data taken from Homicide in California, 2015, Tables 2, 3 & 4. The numbers and percentages may not add up to their respective totals due to the omission of 'other' and 'unknown' categories.
[a] This homicide rate is different than found in the federal UCR data as it is based on a slightly different population size (39,071,323).

were similarly patterned and can be divided in three parts: an increase in murders from 1960 to 1980, a noticeable dip and second peak of murders in the early 1990s, and a general decline in murders to 2015. Despite the trending being similar, California's yearly murder rates were, to varying degrees, higher than the national average from 1976 to 2009. California's current rate of 4.8 murders per 100,000 population size is the lowest it has been since the mid-1960s and just under the national average of 4.9 per 100,000 population size.

Who were the victims of murder in California in 2015? Table 1.2 provides the gender, race/ethnicity, and age of these murder victims in the form of the number and percentage of victimizations, the percentage in its given population demographic, and the rate of victimizations. Of the 1,861 murders committed in 2015, 83% ($n = 1,540$) of the victims were men; as is true every year, many more males (8 per 100,000 population size) than females (2 per 100,000 population size) were the victims of murder in 2015.

More Hispanics than any other ethnic group were victims of murder ($n = 802$; 43%) in California in 2015 (see Table 1.2). Blacks were disproportionate murder victims, however (as has been true for decades), because while they made up 6% of the state's population, they made up 28% of the murder victims in 2015 ($n = 526$). Whites, on the other hand, were under-represented in murder victimizations in 2015 (as usual). Whites made up about 39% of the population but they only accounted for 21% of the murder victimizations ($n = 394$). The murder rates illustrate the discrepancy in murder victimizations by ethnicity. The murder rates for whites and Hispanics were only 3 and 5 per 100,000 population size respectively while the murder rate for blacks was 24 per 100,000 population size.

Table 1.2 shows that most murder victims in California in 2015 were 18–29 years old ($n = 718$) representing 39% of all murder victims despite this age group only making up 17% of the population. A little less than a third of the remaining murder victims were 40 years old and over ($n = 601$; 32%), a fifth were 30–39 years old ($n = 389$; 21%) and the remaining were under 18 years old ($n = 145$; 8%).

By far, firearms ($n = 1,276$; 71%) were used to commit most murders in California in 2015 (see Table 1.3). The weapon most often used was a handgun ($n = 855$; 47%). Table 1.4 shows an important point about the victim-offender relationship for murders in California in 2015 and what is true about most murders in the United States. Most often murders happened between people who knew each other. In 2015, about 69% of murder victims knew their murderers as friends and acquaintances ($n = 485$; 47%) and part of the extended family unit [parent and child ($n = 81$; 8%), spouse ($n = 72$; 7%) or other relatives ($n = 65$; 6%)]. The murder of strangers only happened 31% of the time ($n = 321$). These data support the well-known assertion among criminal justice practitioners and researchers alike that murder is most often a personal crime.

The number and rate of murders varied widely by counties in California in 2015. In Table 1.5, two columns of county data are given. In the first column, counties with murder rates that surpass 50 victimizations per 100,000 population are listed. In the second column, counties with a murder rate above the average for the state (5 murders per 100,000 population) are listed in descending order. As seen the first column in Table 1.5, Los Angeles County had the highest number of murders in 2015 ($n = 592$, 32%). Alameda ($n = 119$, 6%) and San Bernardino ($n = 109$, 6%) also had high numbers of murders. The list of counties with the highest counts of murders in Table 1.5 does not provide par-

Table 1.3. Number and Percentage of Murders According to
Weapon Type in California in 2015

Weapon	n	%
Total	1,821[a]	100.0
Firearm	1,276	70.1
Handgun	855	47.0
All other firearms[b]	421	23.1
Non-Firearm	545	29.9
Knife	263	14.4
Blunt Object	97	5.3
Personal Weapon[c]	90	4.9
All other non-firearms[d]	95	5.2

Percentages may not add up to 100 due to rounding
[a] *n = 40 homicides had an unknown weapon type.*
[b] *The* all other firearms *category includes rifles, shotguns and other or unknown firearms.*
[c] *The* all other non-firearms *category includes ropes, drugs, arson, poison and drowning.*
[d] *Personal weapon includes hands and feet.*

ticularly surprising information given the population sizes of the counties (such as Los Angeles and San Diego counties). The second column takes these counts and coverts them into rates, thus standardizing the number of murders by the population size of the county. These rates offer a different and perhaps more informative look of the distribution of murders across the state. Notice that Los Angeles County has an above-average murder rate (6 per 100,000 population) but it was not nearly the highest in the state. The counties with the highest murder rates were Monterey (14 per 100,000 population), Merced (10 per 100,000 population), and Tulare (10 per 100,000 population).[17]

---

17. Caution is warranted when rating counties by crime counts and rates. Crime counts can fluctuate greatly year-to-year in counties. As important, counties with lower population sizes have more unstable rates where smaller changes in crime counts can cause large changes in crime rates.

Table 1.4. Number and Percentage of Murders According to
Victim-Offender Relationship in California in 2015

Victim-Offender Relationship	n	%
Total	1,024[a]	100.0
Friend & Acquaintance	485	47.4
Stranger	321	31.3
Parent & Child	81	7.9
Spouse	72	7.0
Other Relative	65	6.3

Note: Data taken from Homicide in California, 2015, Table 11.
Percentages may not add up to 100 due to rounding.
[a] n = 837 homicides have unknown victim-offender relationships

In summary, many murder victims in California in 2015 (by proportion) were male, ethnic, between 18–29 years old, and killed with a firearm by someone they knew. One-third of murder happened in Los Angeles County but, accounting for its population size, more murders per capita happened in 12 other counties, such as Monterey, Merced, and Tulare.

Rape

Until 2013, the UCR reported rape using the term *forcible rape* that counted crimes that involved "the carnal knowledge of a female forcibly and against her will" (FBI, 2004). Forcible rape counts had no age restriction on the female victim, and included completed and attempted rapes and rapes that were against the will of the victim due to the incapacity of the victim to give consent because of a temporary or permanent condition such as youthful age and mental disability. This definition did not include counts of statutory rape, incest, or sodomy unless force or threat of force was used against the victim (FBI, 2004). In 2013, the government changed the category name from *forcible rape* to *rape* and revised the definition to include "the penetration, no matter how slight, of the vagina or anus with any body part or object, or oral penetration by a sex organ of another person, without the consent of the victim" (The White House Office of the Press Secretary, 2012). This revised definition includes any gender of the victim or perpetrator, and instances of lack of

Table 1.5. Frequencies, Percentages and Rates of Murders by Select Counties in California in 2015

Number (> 50 murders)			Rate (> 5.0)	
County	n	%	County	Rate
Total	1,861	100.0	x-bar	5.0
Los Angeles	592	31.8	Monterey	13.8
Alameda	119	6.4	Merced	10.0
San Bernardino	109	5.9	Tulare	9.7
Sacramento	92	4.9	Humboldt	8.9
Riverside	87	4.7	San Joaquin	8.8
San Diego	84	4.5	Alameda	7.3
Kern	64	3.4	Kern	7.2
San Joaquin	64	3.4	Solano	7.2
Monterey	60	3.2	Stanislaus	7.2
Fresno	59	3.2	Sacramento	6.2
Orange	57	3.1	San Francisco	6.1
Contra Costa	57	3.1	Fresno	6.0
San Francisco	53	2.8	Los Angeles	5.8
			Contra Costa	5.1
			San Bernardino	5.1

Note: Data taken from Homicide in California, 2015, Table 14.
Percentages may not add to 100% due to rounding and not including counties in the table that did not meet the criteria

consent because of mental incapacity, influences of substance use, and age. Furthermore, lack of consent does not require physical resistance.

Figure 1.7 provides the rates of rape in California compared to the national average since 1960. It includes the legacy definition and the revised definition that began to be reported in 2013. The figure shows that the yearly rates of rape generally decreased in California since its peak in 1980 and in the nation since its peak in 1992. A visual comparison of the yearly volume of rape in

Figure 1.7. Rates of Rape in California Compared to the
National Average, 1960–2015

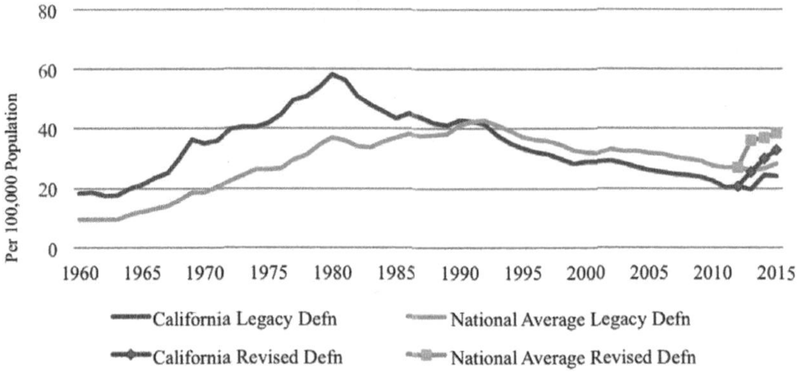

Source: Uniform Crime Report

California compared to the nation reveal that for many years (1960–1992) California had a higher rate of rape than the nation, but since then the rate of rape in California has been slightly below the national. California's legacy rape rate is currently the lowest it's been since the 1960s (21 per 100,000 population). Not surprisingly, the revised definition of rape shows a substantially higher level of rape than the legacy definition. In California, the annual rate of rape from 2013 to 2015 using the legacy definition was 19.5, 24.4, and 24.0 and the revised definition 25.3, 29.7 and 32.7. This represented 22%–36% higher annual reported rape.

Robbery

Robbery is the "taking or attempting to take anything of value from the care, custody or control of a person or persons by force or threat of force or violence and/or by putting the victim in fear" (FBI, 2004). Robbery is a type of serious larceny or theft that involves the perpetrator confronting the victim with force (or assault) or the threat of force in order to receive the desired property.

Figure 1.8 presents robbery rates in California and the nation since 1960. Yearly robbery rates show that robbery has been consistently higher in California than the nation. The trend lines show two patterns. Robbery rates steadily increased in California and the nation from 1960 to about 1980, fluctuated until 1992 and generally declined (despite marked fluctuations) since then. The relatively low rate of robbery in California (135 per 100,000 population size)

Figure 1.8. Rates of Robbery in California Compared to the
National Average, 1960–2015

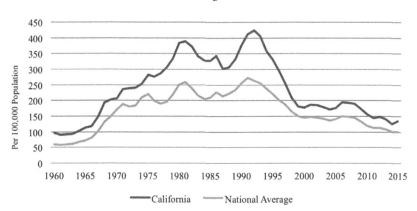

Source: Uniform Crime Report

has not been seen since the late 1960s but was higher than the national average (102 per 100,000 population size) in 2015.

Table 1.6 shows the number and percentage of robberies that happened in California in 2015 that involved weapons, including the type of weapons and the location where the robberies occurred. Slightly less than half (n = 25,385; 48%) of the robberies were committed with the use of a weapon. When weapons were used in the commission of a robbery, firearms were the most common (n = 14,706 total, 58%).

The greatest percentage of robberies in California in 2015 happened in public places such as streets, parks, and parking lots (n = 22,872; 43%). But many robberies also occurred in commercial places like gas stations and convenience stores (n = 13,669; 26%), "other" places such as churches, schools, and government buildings (n = 11,299; 21%), and residences (n = 4,283; 8%).

Aggravated Assault

Aggravated assault is described as the unlawful attack against another person using a weapon or other means to induce great bodily harm or death (FBI, 2004). The use of a weapon is not enough to elevate the crime of assault to that of aggravated assault. It is the high level of victim injury that distinguishes an aggravated assault from a simple assault (FBI, 2004).

The trend lines in Figure 1.9 show that California has generally had a higher rate of aggravated assault than the nation from 1960 until 2006 and has been

Table 1.6. Number and Percentage of Robberies According to
Weapon Type and Location in California in 2015

Weapon	n	%
Total	52,785	100.0
Armed	25,385	48.1
Strong-arm	27,400	51.9
Armed		
Knife or cutting instrument	5,028	19.8
Firearm	14,706	57.9
Other weapon	5,651	22.3
Location		
Highway[a]	22,872	43.3
Commercial properties[b]	13,669	25.9
Residences	4,283	8.1
Bank	662	1.3
Other[c]	11,299	21.4

Note: Data taken from Crime in California, 2015, Table 6.
Percentages may not add to 100% due to rounding
[a] Highway includes streets, parks, parking lots, etc.
[b] Commercial properties include gas stations and convenience stores, etc.
[c] Other properties include churches, schools, government buildings, trains, etc.

relatively even since then. The rate of aggravated assaults in California and the nation increased in the early 1960s and peaked in 1992. Since then the rates declined to varying degrees.[18] Aggravated assaults in California in 2015 (254 per 100,000 population size) were slightly higher than the national average (238 per 100,000 population size).

18. The increase in aggravated assaults in California in 1985 may be attributable to changes in law enforcement reporting procedures. In 1985, law enforcement agencies mandatorily reported domestic violence crimes, many of which were reported as aggravated assaults (CJSC, 2009). Yet, it is noted that the national average increased during this time as well.

Figure 1.9. Rates of Aggravated Assault in California Compared to the National Average, 1960–2015

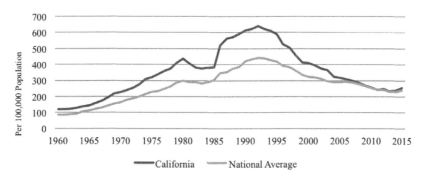

Source: Uniform Crime Report

Most of the aggravated assaults that happened in California in 2015 were accomplished with the use of weapons (n = 69,371; 70%) as shown in Table 1.7. Firearms (n = 18,286; 18%) and knives (n = 17,100; 17%) were regularly used but not as often as "other" dangerous weapons (n = 33,985; 34%).[19] Almost

Table 1.7. Number and Percentage of Aggravated Assault Crimes by Weapon Type in California in 2015

Weapon Type	n	%
Total	99,149	100.0
Firearm	18,286	18.4
Knife or cutting instrument	17,100	17.2
Other dangerous weapon	33,985	34.3
Personal weapon[a]	29,778	30.0

Note: Data taken from Crime in California, *2015, Table 7.*
Percentages may not add up to 100 due to rounding.
[a] Personal weapon *includes hands and feet.*

19. A description of these "other dangerous weapons" is not reported (CJSC, 2015, p. 10).

Figure 1.10. Rates of Burglary in California Compared to the
National Average, 1960–2015

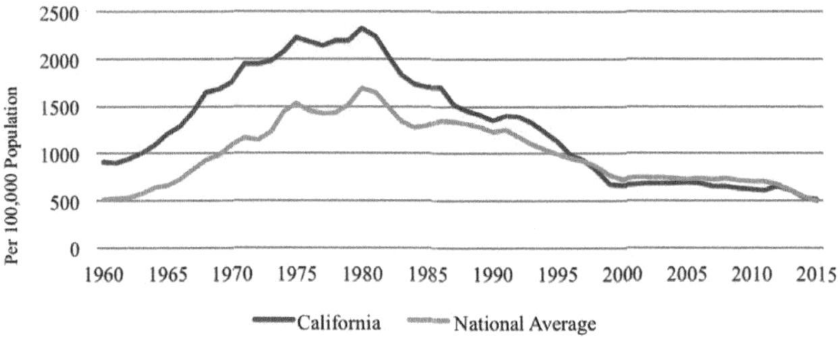

Source: Uniform Crime Report

a third of all aggravated assaults were committed by punching, kicking, and the use of other personal weapons (n = 29,778; 30%).

Burglary

Burglary is defined as the illegal entry into a structure with the intent to commit a felony or a theft (FBI, 2004). The UCR includes forceful, non-forceful, and attempted entries as burglaries. Structures included in this definition include both commercial properties and residential dwellings.

The yearly rates of burglary in California and the nation have been relatively similar since 2000 (see Figure 1.10). However, this hasn't always been the case. Burglary in California was substantially higher than the nation from 1960 to the early 1990s. Burglary rates declined in California and the nation until 2000. Burglary in California (505 per 100,000 population) was slightly higher than the national average (491 per 100,000 population) yet was approaching half of what it was in the 1960s (902 per 100,000 population).

Table 1.8 shows the location, the time of day, and the type of entry for burglaries that happened in California in 2015. A majority of them were committed in residences (n = 120,297; 61%) compared to non-residences (n = 76,892; 39%). A majority of burglaries happened during the daytime (n = 75,560; 38%) rather than the nighttime (n = 59,308; 30%).[20] Much of the time, force was used to gain entry into the structure (n = 115,641; 62%).

20. Of note, the time of day in which a large proportion of burglaries took place remains unknown (n = 62,321; 32%).

Table 1. 8. Location, Time of Day and Type of Entry for
Burglaries in California in 2015

Larceny-Theft Characteristics	n	%
Total	197,189	100.0
Location		
Residence	120,297	61.0
Non-residence	76,892	39.0
Time of Day		
Daytime	75,560	38.3
Nighttime	59,308	30.1
Unknown	62,321	31.6
Type of Entry[a]		
Force	115,641	62.1
No Force	70,535	37.9

Note: Data taken from Crime in California, 2015, Table 8.
Percentages may not add up to 100 due to rounding.
[a] The type of entry figures excluded attempted burglaries ($n = 11,013$)

Larceny-Theft

Larceny-theft is the "taking of property from the possession of another" (FBI, 2004). This count includes all such cases of larceny and theft except when the property stolen is a motor vehicle (this is called *motor vehicle theft*). The count does not include the crime of embezzlement, where the property is entrusted to another and then misappropriated (FBI, 2004). Examples of larceny-theft include pick-pocketing, purse-snatching, shoplifting, and thefts from open and public places.

Figure 1.11 shows larceny-thefts in California compared to national averages for the past 55 years. Larceny-theft rates were higher in California compared to the nation from 1960 to 1990, and then California larceny-thefts rates were lower than the national average from 1990 to 2012. California's highest rate of larceny-thefts happened in 1980. By contrast, the nation's larceny-theft rate did not peak until 1992. California's larceny-theft rate (1,679 per 100,000 population size) is currently lower than the national average (1,775 per 100,000 population size).

Figure 1.11. Rates of Larceny/Theft in California Compared to the National Average, 1960–2015

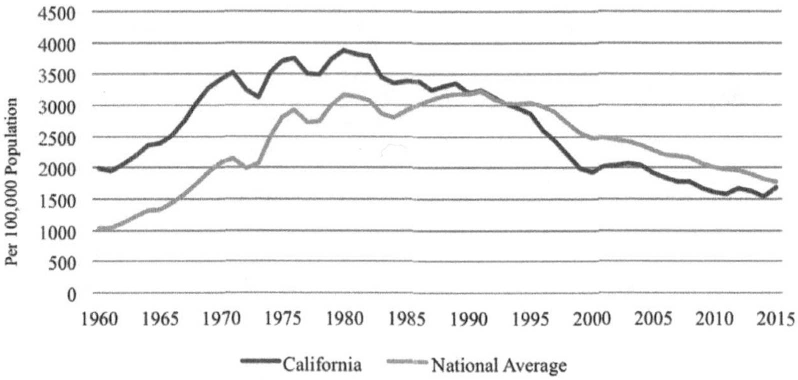

Source: Uniform Crime Report

Table 1.9 provides a closer look at the dollar amount lost and the location for larceny-thefts in California in 2015. Most larceny-thefts involved the loss of less than $50 ($n$ = 204,858; 31%) or more than $400 ($n$ = 238,456; 36%). The largest proportion of property was stolen from motor vehicles (n = 235,419; 36%) or involved "other" methods of larceny-thefts such as pick-pocketing and purse-snatching (n = 144,655; 22%). Shoplifting (n = 108,659; 17%) and thefts from buildings (n = 77,023; 12%) were also common types of larceny-thefts in California in 2015.

Motor Vehicle Theft

Motor vehicle theft (MVT) is the theft or attempted theft of a motor vehicle (FBI, 2004). Examples of motor vehicles are automobiles, buses, motorcycles/motor scooters, and snowmobiles. The trends in motor vehicle thefts over the years in California and the nation over the last 55 years reveal several important points (see Figure 1.12). First, the trend lines for motor vehicle thefts in California is most unlike the trend lines for the other index crimes. It looks "wavy" in comparison to the other crimes. Taking these large changes into account, the overall trends of crime is relatively similar to other crimes in California. With patches of plateaus, motor vehicle thefts generally increased in California and the nation from 1960 to 1992 and then decreased to the present. Unlike for the nation, California had a marked spike in motor

Table 1. 9. Number, Percentage and Rate of Larceny-Thefts According to Dollar Amount and Location in California in 2015

Larceny-Theft Characteristics	n	%
Total	655,851	100.0
Dollar Amount		
Under $50	204,858	31.2
$50–$199	120,590	18.4
$200–$400	91,947	14.0
$Over $400	238,456	36.4
Location		
Shoplifting	108,659	16.6
From motor vehicles	235,419	35.9
Motor vehicle accessories	53,541	8.2
Bicycles	36,554	5.6
From Buildings	77,023	11.7
All Other[a]	144,655	22.1

Note: Data taken from Crime in California, 2015, Tables 10-11.
Percentages may not add up to 100 due to rounding.
[a] The other category included pocket-picking, purse-snatching, theft from coin machines and other

vehicle thefts from 1998 to 2005 that decreased to its present rate. A second important point about the trends in MVT is that the yearly crime rates were consistently higher in California compared to the national average since 1960. Currently the incidence of MVT in California (437 per 100,000 population size) is almost twice that of the nation (220 per 100,000 population size).

In summary, California had higher than average crime rates for many of these Part I index crimes for much of the period between 1960 to, depending upon the crime, 1990–2005. However, crime dropped in California to the point where in the past 10 or so years California has had similar to lower crime rates than national averages (save robbery and motor vehicle theft). It is important to note that despite these absolute changes in crime, the patterns or trends in crime in California are similar to the nation. For both, crime rates

Figure 1.12. Rates of Motor Vehicle Theft in California Compared to the National Average, 1960–2015

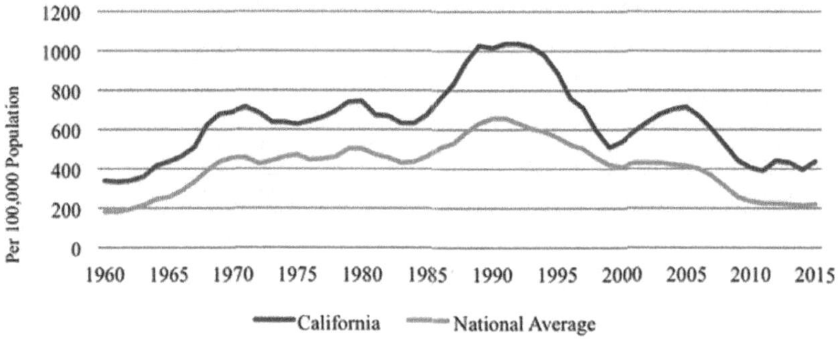

Source: Uniform Crime Report

rose in the 1960s to their peak near 1980 or in the early 1990s (or both) and then roughly fell to current levels not seen since the 1960s.

Two Crime Trends

The yearly crime rates in California and the nation since 1960 suggest that crime follows two general trends. The first crime trend is a general trend upward starting in the 1960s that lasts at least a decade. The second crime trend is a decline in crime that starts in the 1980s or 1990s that also lasts at least a decade. The peak year, or the year that the crime trends decrease, differs based on whether violent or property crime is examined.

Figures 1.13 and 1.14 show aggregated violent and property crime rates for California and the nation from 1960 to 2015. While the absolute rate of crime between California and the nation is different, a visual inspection of these figures depicts these two general crime trends. In Figure 1.13, violent crime in California and the nation increased in the 1960s to their peak in 1992 and then decreased to their present rate. In Figure 1.14, property crime also increased in California and the nation in the 1960s but, unlike with violent crime, it peaked for both in 1980 and then decreased to the present level.

Using those two crime trends, similar percentage change figures for crime in California and the nation are apparent for violent crime, and to a lesser

Figure 1.13. Rates of Violent Crime in California Compared to the National Average, 1960–2015

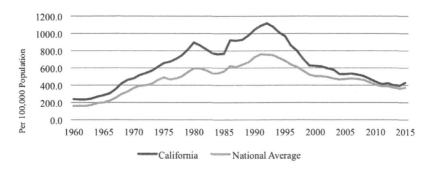

Source: Uniform Crime Report

extent property crime as seen in Figures 1.15 and 1.16. From 1960 to 1992, the violent crime rate increased fairly equally in California (369%) compared to the nation (371%). Violent crime then similarly decreased from 1992 to 2015 in California (−62%) and the nation (−51%). Like violent crime, property crime also increased in California and the nation from 1960 to 1980 and then decreased to the present. However, property crime did not increase and decrease at similar rates. Figure 1.15 shows that while property crime increased by 210% across the nation, it only increased by 115% in California. After the peak in 1980, crime declined a little more in California

Figure 1.14. Rates of Property Crime in California Compared to the National Average, 1960–2015

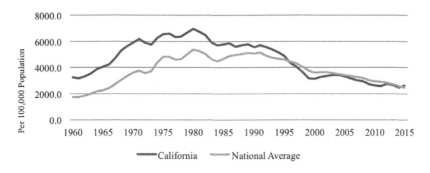

Source: Uniform Crime Report

Figure 1.15. Percentage Change in Violent Crime in California Compared to the National Average as Two Trends

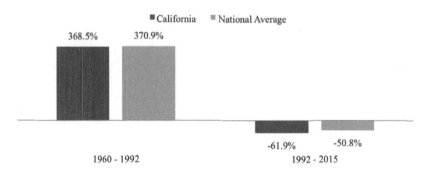

Source: Uniform Crime Report

(−62%) than the nation (−54%). Still, violent crime is 78% higher in California and 132% higher for the nation today than it was in 1960 and property crime is currently 19% lower in California but 44% higher in the nation today than it was in 1960.[21]

Figure 1.16. Percentage Change in Property Crime in California Compared to the National Average as Two Trends

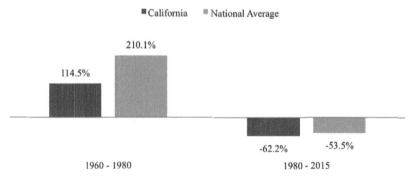

Source: Uniform Crime Report

---

21. These percentage change analyses were not shown.

Conclusions

This chapter draws two major conclusions. First, crime increased in California in 2015 (from 2014 to 2015) after years of decline. However, a one-year increase is not a *crime trend*. Supplemental analyses into whether Realignment or Proposition 47 could have caused this past year's increase showed mixed results. Despite this recent increase in crime, the crime rate is still as low as it was in the late 1960s. Second, a review of over 50 years of crime rate data for California, and comparing them to yearly national averages, shows that California's crime rate was historically higher than the national average but has evened out over the past 10–15 years. Still, California's crime rates have trended upwards and downwards in conjunction with the rest of the nation for the past 55 years and is at levels not seen since the 1960s.

Key Terms and Definitions

Aggravated Assault—The unlawful attack against another person using a weapon or other means to induce great bodily harm.

Burglary—The illegal entry into a structure with the intent to commit theft.

California Realignment—A 2011 state policy (AB109) that requires counties to retain jurisdiction over their adjudicated N3s (non-serious, non-sexual, non-chronic offenders) rather than refer them to the state.

Crime Rate—A standardized measure of crime calculated by dividing a crime count by a population size.

Crime Trend—A series of crime rates that show an increase, decrease stability of crime for a period of at least 3 years.

Crimes—Behaviors or lack of behaviors that are in violation of laws.

Larceny-Theft—The taking of property from the possession of another.

Laws—Codified rules that pronounce to a population the behaviors that are permissible, required and prohibited by their government.

Motor Vehicle Theft—The theft or attempted theft of a motor vehicle.

Murder/Non-negligent Manslaughter—The purposeful or intentional killing of another person.

Part I Index Crimes—A group of crimes collected by the Uniform Crime Report that include murder/non-negligent manslaughter, forcible rape, robbery, aggravated assault, burglary, larceny-theft, motor vehicle theft and arson.

Property Crimes—Crimes that involve property which include burglary, larceny-theft and motor vehicle theft.

Proposition 47—A California law that requires reclassification of certain non-violent felony crimes to misdemeanors for eligible offenders.

Rape—Penetration, no matter how slight, of the vagina or anus with ant body part or object, or oral penetration by a sex organ of another person, without the consent of the victim.

Robbery—The taking or attempting to take anything of value from the care, custody or control of a person or persons by force or threat of force or violence and/or by putting the victim in fear.

Uniform Crime Report (UCR)—A nationwide data-gathering program established in 1929 to count the number of crimes reported to the police in the United States.

Violent Crimes—Crimes that violate persons which include murder, forcible rape, robbery and aggravated assault.

Internet Websites

Criminal Justice Statistics Center: http://oag.ca.gov/crime
Demographic Research Institute, Department of Finance, California: http://www.dof.ca.gov/Forecasting/Demographics/
Uniform Crime Report: http://ucrdatatool.gov/
Gallup: http://www.gallup.com/topic/crime.aspx
U.S. Census Bureau: https://www.census.gov/popclock/?intcmp=home_pop

Review Test Questions

1. Describe the Uniform Crime Report Program. Make sure to include when the program began, the crimes it collects, and where it is housed.
2. Describe the change in crime rates from 2014 to 2015. What happened to crime and why?
3. Provide evidence from this chapter to support the following statement: "a review of over 50 years of crime rate data for California, and comparing them to yearly national averages, shows that California crime rate was historically higher than the national average but has evened out over the past 10-15 years. Furthermore, California's violent and property crimes trends followed the same pattern as national trends for the past 55 years."

Critical Thinking Questions

1. The chapter concludes with the following statement: "California crime rate was historically higher than the national average but has evened out over the past 10–15 years. Furthermore, California's violent and property crimes trends follow the same pattern as national trends for the past 55 years." First, explain the difference between yearly crime levels and crime trends over time? Second, provide evidence to support the points in the above statement? Third, discuss what this finding suggests in the context of California's "get tough" correctional policies of the last several decades?
2. The individual trends for California's Part I Index Crimes demonstrate peaks in crime over the past 55 years. First, note the time period(s) that the crime peaked for crimes. Second, provide possible reasons why crime trends changed during those peak years?
3. Use the data in this chapter to describe a typical crime for each Part I Index crime in California in 2015. Make sure to include important given characteristics for each crime. For example, when describing the typical murder in California, make sure to note the gender, race and age of the victim, the use of weapon in the crime, the victim-offender relationship, and the county in which it is located. Taking this task further, how do the facts about these crimes, particularly murder, differ from the portrayal of these crimes on TV shows and other media?

References

Chang, C., Gerber, M., & Poston, B. (2015, November 5). Unintended consequences of Prop. 47 pose challenge for criminal justice system. *Los Angeles Times*. Retrieved from http://www.latimes.com/local/crime/la-me-prop47-anniversary-20151106-story.html

Criminal Justice Statistics Center. (2010). *Crime in California, 2009*. Sacramento, CA: California Department of Justice. Retrieved from http://oag.ca.gov/cjsc/pubs

Criminal Justice Statistics Center. (2016). *Crime in California, 2015*. Sacramento, CA: California Department of Justice. Retrieved from http://oag.ca.gov/cjsc/pubs

Gallup. (2016a). *In U.S., concern about crime climbs to 15-year high*. Retrieved from http://www.gallup.com/poll/190475/americansconcerncrimeclimbs yearhigh.aspx

Gallup. (2016b, March 2–6). *Crime*. Retrieved from http://www.gallup
.com/poll/1603/crime.aspx

Federal Bureau of Investigation. (1960–2015). *Uniform crime report* [Data file].
Retrieved from https://ucr.fbi.gov/ucr

Federal Bureau of Investigation. (2004). *Uniform crime reporting handbook*. U.S.
Department of Justice. Retrieved from http://www2.fbi.gov/ucr/
handbook/ucrhandbook04.pdf

Krisberg, B., & Taylor-Nicholson, E. (2011). *Criminal justice: Realignment:
A bold new era in California Corrections*. Berkeley Law Center for Research
and Administration. Retrieved from https://www.law.berkeley
.edu/files/REALIGNMENT_FINAL9.28.11.pdf

Lofstrom, M., Bird, M., & Martin, B. (2016, September). *California's historic
corrections reforms*. Sacramento, CA: Public Policy Research Institute. Retrieved from http://www.ppic.org/main/publication.asp?i=1208

Politico. (2016). Full text: Donald Trump 2016 RNC draft speech transcript.
Retrieved from http://www.politico.com/story/2016/07/full-transcript-
donald-trump-nomination-acceptance-speech-at-rnc-225974

Rothfield, M. (2009). Judges indicate that they may order prison population
reduced by 58,000. *Los Angeles Times*. Retrieved from http://www.latimes
.com/news/local/la-me-prisons10-2009feb10,0,815133.story

Tjaden, P., & Thoennes, N. (2000). *Full report of the prevalence, incidence, and
consequences of violence against women*. (NCJ 183781). Retrieved from
https://www.ncjrs.gov/pdffiles1/nij/183781.pdf

U.S. Census Bureau. (2017). *National totals, 2017: Unites States*. Retrieved from
https://www.census.gov/population/projections/data/national/2014/sum-
marytables.html

Warr, M. (1994). Public perceptions and reactions to violent offending and
victimization. In A. J. Reiss & J. A. Roth (Eds.), *Understanding and
preventing violence* (Vol. 4, pp. 1–66). Washington, DC: National Academy
Press. Retrieved from http://www.nap.edu/catalog/4422.html

Warr, M. (2000). Fear of crime in the United States: Avenues for research and
policy. *Criminal Justice*, 4, 451–489. Retrieved from https://www.ncjrs
.gov/criminal_justice2000/vol_4/04i.pdf

The White House, Office of the Press Secretary. (2012). Attorney General Eric
Holder announced revisions to the Uniform Crime Report's definition of
rape: Data reported on rape will better reflect state criminal codes, victim
experiences [Press Release]. Retrieved from http://www.justice.gov
/opa/pr/2012/January/12-ag-018.html

Chapter 2

Demographics of Crime in California

Veronica M. Herrera, Gregory Brown, and Robert Castro[1]

Learning Objectives

After reading the chapter, students should be able to:

- Explain how victimization differs by race and gender.
- Describe how the perpetration of crime differs by race, gender, and immigration status.
- Demonstrate an understanding of how racial minorities and women are represented in the criminal justice system.
- Explain how various legislation (both state and federal) affects immigration enforcement in California.

Introduction

Understanding California's criminal justice system requires an understanding of Californians and those who become involved in the system in the first place. Social science tells us a great deal about the relationship between race, ethnicity, gender, and immigration status and the criminal justice system. Sheer numbers of detentions, arrests, and incarcerations belie deeper biases and prejudices within society that affect the criminal justice system. Moreover, socio-economic status is correlated with the above characteristics, which deserves our attention as well. As students of criminal justice, we must recognize that while data can be collected on demographics, deeper meaning cannot be attributed to sheer numbers without

---

1. The racial and ethnic minorities section is authored by Gregory Brown, the immigrants section is authored by Robert Castro, and the gender section is authored by Veronica Herrera.

also recognizing that each of us is influenced by social norms and expectations perpetuated by images in the media. The following chapter reviews demographics in terms of victimization, perpetration, and treatment of offenders.

Racial/Ethnic Minorities in the California Criminal Justice System

This section focuses on minorities in the California criminal justice system. It examines minorities as victims and perpetrators of crime, comparing violent crime with property offenses. It also reviews the racial/ethnic composition in the state's penal institutions, community correctional centers, and parole populations. The vast majority of available data on racial and/or ethnic groups in the California criminal justice system focus on whites, African Americans/blacks, Hispanics/Latinos, and "others." There is a dearth of information on Asians/Pacific Islanders and Native Americans. Women are also a minority in the California criminal justice system and are underrepresented. Since women in the California criminal justice system are discussed in another part of this chapter, we will not discuss them here.

Minority, Race, and Ethnicity Defined

African Americans/blacks, Hispanics/Latinos, Asians/Pacific Islanders, and Native Americans/Alaska Natives are considered to be minorities by the U.S. Centers for Disease Control and Prevention (Centers for Disease Control and Prevention, 2014). The United Nations defines a minority as:

> A group numerically inferior to the rest of the population of a State, in a non-dominant position, whose members—being nationals of the State—possess ethnic, religious or linguistic characteristics differing from those of the rest of the population and show, if only implicitly, a sense of solidarity, directed towards preserving their culture, traditions, religion or language (United Nations Human Rights, 2014).

Minority is considered a pejorative term, suggesting some groups are "less" than others (Walker, Spohn, & Delone, 2016). It often refers to African Americans/blacks and Hispanics/Latinos. Even though Asians fall under the category of minority, they are often considered the "model minority," and thus are not commonly associated with the term minority or with crime.

The term "ethnicity" is derived from the Greek "ethnos" or "nation," and refers to groups of people that share a common language, culture, or religion

(Gabbidon & Green, 2013). Generally, ethnic groups are also defined by visibly identifiable traits within the group (Walker et al., 2016). The only major ethnic group for which data is available in California is Hispanic/Latino.

Historically, race has been used as a biological descriptor, referring to a person's appearance such as color of skin, hair, and eyes. There are three major racial groups: Mongoloid, Negroid, and Caucasian (Walker et al., 2016). According to the Human Genome Project, humans share 99.9% of their genetic make-up (Soo-Jin Lee, 2005). Use of the term race is not fixed or based on biology. Rather, it is attached to groups based on historical context, and influenced by racial dynamics and politics. Race is a social construct (Zatz & Mann, 2006; Gabbidon, 2010). Much of the crime reported by the media and politicians in California, and across the U.S., is associated with racial minorities, also referred to as "people of color." Rodriguez (2006) aptly states, "the color of the skin is the color of crime" (p. 38).

The major racial and ethnic groups reported in the California criminal justice system are whites, Hispanics/Latinos, and African Americans. According to the U.S. Census Bureau, as of 2015 there were approximately 39 million people in California, and the population was 38% white, 6% black/African American, 14% Asian, 39% Hispanic/Latino, 1% Native American/Pacific Islander/Other, and 3% of the population claimed two or more races (United States Census Bureau, 2015).

Minorities as Victims of Crime in California

Violent crimes are crimes in which the offender or the perpetrator uses or threatens to use force on the victim.[2] They include homicides, robbery, forcible rape, assault, and kidnapping. As you learned in Chapter 1, 43% of California murder victims in 2015 were Hispanic, 28% were black, 21% were white, and 7% were classified as "other." These numbers do not tell the whole story though, as some races are over-represented as homicide victims and others are under-represented. Blacks, in particular, are continuously the most over-represented category of homicide victims in California (and usually the nation); in 2015, they were 28% of homicide victims but only 6% of the population (Harris, 2016a; VPC, 2017). In comparison, Hispanics were 39% of the population in California but 43% of homicide victims, whites were 38.5% of the population but only 21.2% of homicide victims, and "other" races were 16.8% of the population but only 7.0% of homicide victims (Harris, 2016a).

---

2. We focus on violent crime victimization because the Bureau of Justice Statistics only provides victimization data by race and ethnic group for violent crimes, not for property crimes.

Figure 2.1. Homicide Victimization by Relation to Perpetrator and Race 2015

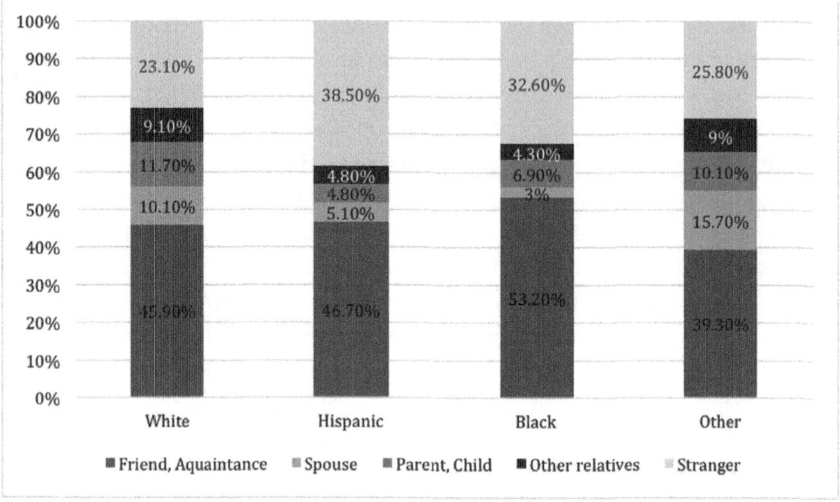

Source: (Harris, 2016, Table 12)

Between 2006 and 2015, the homicide rate decreased 29.2% for blacks, 39.1% for Hispanics, 37.5% for others, and 7.1% for whites in California (Harris, 2016a). All races were most likely to be killed by a friend or acquaintance, but Hispanics and blacks were significantly more likely to be killed by a stranger than an immediate family member, and whites and "others" were equally likely to be killed by a stranger as an immediate family member (see Figure 2.1).

As Figure 2.2 illustrates, Hispanics and blacks were most likely to be killed on the street (43.1% and 55.1% respectively) while whites and other races were most likely to be killed in their residence (40.1% and 31.5% respectively) (Harris, 2016a). Eighty-three percent of blacks were killed with a firearm as compared to 73.0% of Hispanics, 66.1% of other races, and 47.9% of whites (Harris, 2016a). Homicides of blacks and Hispanics were most often gang-related (40.3% and 36.4% respectively) in comparison to whites and other races, which were most often the result of an argument (51.6% and 40.4% respectively) (Harris, 2016a). Remarkably, drug-related homicides only accounted for 1.3% of homicides involving black victims and 1.8% of Hispanic victims but 3.4% of victims of other races and 4.5% of homicides involving white victims (see Figure 2.3). Also interestingly, homicide victimization peaked for blacks and Hispanics during ages 18–29 (44.0% and 46.7% respectively) but not until 40+ for whites (56.7%) (Harris, 2016a). This coincides with national

Figure 2.2. Homicide Victimization by Place and Race 2015

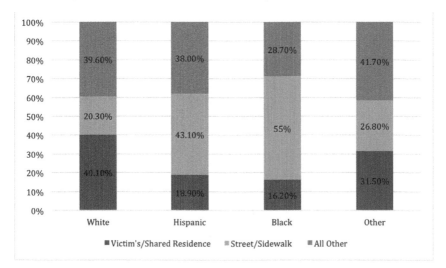

Source: (Harris, 2016, Table 19)

data that show black and Hispanic juveniles are much more likely to be a victim of homicide rather than suicide and white juveniles are much more likely to be a victim of suicide rather than homicide (Sickmund & Puzzanchera, 2014).

Minorities as Perpetrators of Crime in California

In 2015, there were 1,158,812 felony and misdemeanor arrests in California (Harris, 2016b). Of those, 719,638 (62.6%) were arrests of minorities. While that may seem like a lot, keep in mind that an estimated 62% of Californians belong to an ethnic minority group (U.S. Census, 2015). Felony arrests represented 27.2% (314,748) of all arrests in 2015 and minorities were responsible for 213,982 (68%) of them; including 71% of violent crime arrests, 67.2% of property crime arrests, 63.8% of drug crime arrests, and 70.9% of sex offense arrests (Harris, 2016b). In 2015, Hispanics had the highest number of total felony arrests as well as the highest number of felony arrests for each felony type (except for arson) compared to blacks, whites, and others (including those of Asian descent and American Indians) (Harris, 2016b; see Table 2.1).

In terms of misdemeanors, minorities accounted for 61.5% of all misdemeanor arrests, 66.9% of assault and battery arrests, 64.6% of burglary arrests, 62.5% of petty theft arrests, 54% of drug arrests (excluding marijuana), 68.4% of vandalism arrests, 82% of prostitution arrests, and 92% of gambling

Figure 2.3. Homicide Victimization by Precipitating Factor and Race 2015

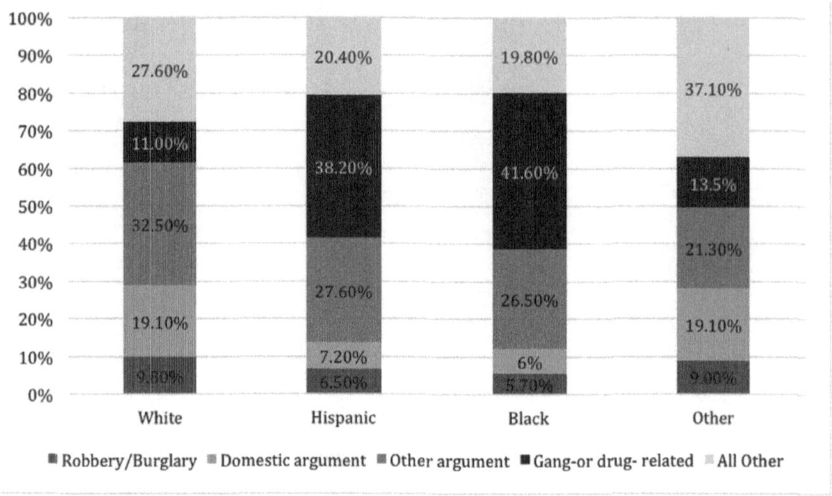

Source: (Harris, 2016, Table 25)

arrests (Harris, 2016b). While it is natural to assume that arrests are representative of perpetrators, we caution against that strategy as arrests are as much about detection and enforcement practices as they are about the actual perpetration of crime. As with felonies, more Hispanics are arrested for almost every misdemeanor crime category than any other race; this makes sense because the largest percentage of Californians identify as Hispanic (U.S. Census, 2015).

Minorities in the Criminal Justice System (CJS) in California

This section describes the number and representation of minorities in the state of California's criminal justice system. Figure 2.4 compares the racial/ethnic composition of the state's total population to the racial/ethnic composition of its institutional populations, community corrections populations in 2013, and parole populations in 2010 (latest available data). The data show that blacks are dramatically overrepresented in the state's institutions and in the parole population, and somewhat overrepresented in community corrections centers. Hispanics are slightly overrepresented in the state's institutions and more noticeably overrepresented in community corrections. Whites and other groups (including Asians) are underrepresented in institutions, community corrections, and the parole system.

Table 2.1. Arrests for Felony Violent, Property, and Drug
Offenses by Race, 2015

	White	Hispanic	Black	Other
California Population	38.0%	38.8%	6.5%	16.7%
Violent Crime (Total)	31,831 (29%)	46,433 (42.3%)	24,386 (22.2%)	7,106 (6.5%)
Homicide	300 (20.8%)	684 (47.5%)	375 (26.1%)	80 (5.6%)
Rape	594 (24.1%)	1,249 (50.6%)	442 (17.9%)	182 (7.4%)
Robbery	3,248 (20.4%)	6,267 (39.4%)	5,718 (36.0%)	670 (4.2%)
Assault	27,339 (30.9%)	37,474 (42.4%)	17,483 (19.8%)	6,052 (6.9%)
Kidnapping	350 (21.9%)	759 (47.5%)	368 (23.0%)	122 (5.2%)
Property Crime (Total)	24,246 (32.8%)	30,647 (41.4%)	14,667 (19.8%)	4,410 (6.0%)
Burglary	7,669 (31.8%)	9,145 (37.9%)	6,040 (25.1%)	1,247 (5.2%)
Theft	9,436 (35.6%)	10,756 (40.5%)	4,610 (17.4%)	1,731 (6.5%)
Motor Vehicle Theft	5,045 (29.3%)	8,397 (48.7%)	2,895 (16.8%)	897 (5.2%)
Forgery, checks, access cards	1,660 (32.8%)	1,982 (39.1%)	976 (19.3%)	450 (8.9%)
Arson	436 (42.2%)	367 (35.5%)	146 (14.1%)	85 (8.2%)
Drug Offenses (Total)	16,136 (36.2%)	17,878 (40.1%)	7,564 (16.9%)	3,051 (6.8%)

Sources: Crime in California 2015, Table 31

Figure 2.5 shows the trend in the felon institutional population by racial/ethnic group from 1991 to 2010. As you may already be aware, black males are notoriously overrepresented in the criminal justice system. For example, although the percentage of black males in the state's institutions declined 16% between 1991 and 2010 (from 34.6% to 29.0%), blacks were only 7.4% of the state's

Figure 2.4. Racial/Ethnic Composition of California's Total, Institutional, Community Correction Center and Parole Populations, 2010

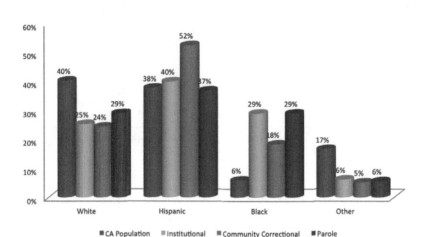

Source: California Department of Corrections and Rehabilitation, 2010, Tables 11, 12, 42(A); U.S. Census, 2010.

population in 1991 and 6.6% in 2010. Thus, the overrepresentation of black males in California's correctional institutions was relatively consistent between 1991 and 2010. In contrast, the percentage of Hispanic inmates increased from 32.1% to 40.4% over this time, an increase of 26% but their percentage of the general population grew more (from 25.8% to 38.2%). Thus, their overrepresentation in the institutional population shrank slightly over this time period. The percentage of other ethnic groups in the state's total population increased from 7.6% in 1990 to 15.6% in 2010, while their representation in institutions only increased from 4.9% to 6.2%. Other races, like whites, are underrepresented in our state's correctional institutions (CDCR, 2011).

The trend lines in Figure 2.6 indicate a dramatic increase in the percentage of Hispanics in the state's community correctional centers between 1991 and 2010, from 35.1% to 52.3%, outstripping their growth in the overall population (data is for males only). The percentage of blacks in community correctional centers declined sharply over this period, from 34.3% to 18.2%. The percentage of whites increased and then declined, while the percentage in "other" ethnic groups increased slightly.

Figure 2.7 displays the trends in the racial/ethnic composition of the male parole population in California between 1991 and 2010. The percentage of

Figure 2.5. Racial/Ethnic Composition of Male Felon Institution
Population, 1991 to 2010

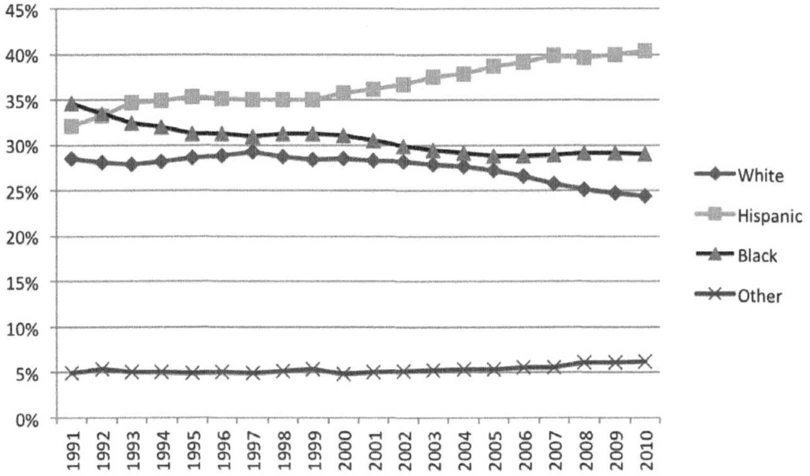

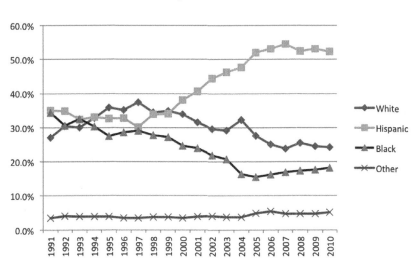

Source: California Department of Corrections and Rehabilitation, 2010, Table 11.

Figure 2.6. Racial/Ethnic Composition of Male Community Correctional
Center Population, 1991 to 2010

Source: California Department of Corrections and Rehabilitation, 2010, Table 21.

**Figure 2.7. Racial/Ethnic Composition of Male Parole
Population, 1991 to 2010**

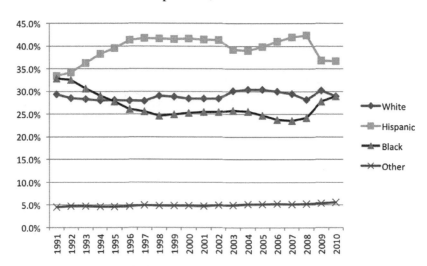

Source: California Department of Corrections and Rehabilitation, 2010, Table 42(A).

Hispanics under parole supervision increased during the early 1990s, peaking in 2008 and declining sharply in 2009 and 2010. The percentage of blacks declined during the early 1990s, remained fairly stable through the mid-2000s and then spiked in 2009 and 2010. The percentage of whites remained fairly stable over this time period, while the percentage in other racial groups increased only marginally.

Women in the California Criminal Justice System

Historically, women were left out of any serious discussions of crime and the criminal justice system. This is the result of both presumptions about the nature of women and because of the way official crime statistics have been collected, disseminated, and understood. Moreover, traditional discussions of women and crime involved women as victims, particularly vulnerable to abuse by men, both physical and sexual.

Sex and Gender Defined

In this section we will refer to both sex and gender. Sex refers to the biological assignments of men and women due to chromosomal, reproductive, and biological composition, while gender refers to the sociological attributes of masculine and feminine. Therefore, while a person may be a "woman" (sex) she may behave in a way that is masculine (gender) by society's standpoint. This gendered lens of men and women has made understanding women's criminal behavior quite complicated. Historically, theory and research on crime has focused on men. This is the result of deeply rooted cultural and societal beliefs about the proper roles and behaviors of men and women. This has also been true for criminology until more recently. Even today women are expected to behave in a feminine manner, which involves passive behaviors and nurturing traits. There are repercussions for not conforming to socially prescribed roles. For example, women who physically abuse their children have violated not just the penal code, but society's expectations of how a woman behaves. This hurdle is higher for women than men in that respect. However, in other ways, the bias may favor women since society expects that men are more likely to engage in criminal activities than women.

Early theoretical assumptions about women's nature led to the belief that crime was a masculine behavior because crime often involved violence, a behavioral trait associated with masculinity and therefore, men. It was believed that women were responsible for only a small amount of official criminal behavior and that women's crimes were predominately sexual in nature. As this section discusses, today while women's involvement in criminal activity remains lower than that of men, women are increasingly facing arrest and incarceration for criminal activity. The irony of women's increasing rights and participation in the economy is their concomitant rise in representations in the criminal justice system. For many years, females were responsible for somewhere between 10 and 15 percent of all arrests. While there is still much debate about the criminal behavior of women and girls, it is clear that women should not be ignored if we are to address the needs of victims, offenders, and the justice system.

Women and Men as Victims of Crime in California

In order to determine how crime affects women as victims, researchers must rely on official reports from the UCR and other crime databases such as the National Crime Victimization Survey (NCVS). According to the NCVS, it is estimated that in 2015, over 1.4 million U.S. women experienced a violent victimization (Truman & Morgan, 2016). However, research suggests that less than half of all women who have been the victim of violence report their victimization to police (Mallicoat & Ireland, 2014). Therefore, the numbers presented by any organization are likely to be severely under-representative of the population in California. The violent crimes that women and girls are most likely to experience, sexual violence and battering, are not only the most underreported, but also are abusive, fear inducing, humiliating, and often forceful (Belknap, 2007). The explanations for women's failure to report crimes against them are complex and intertwined with gender, class, race, ethnicity, and culture. As Mallicoat and Ireland (2014) explain, in some cases, women fear retaliation from their attackers particularly where the violence was perpetrated by an intimate partner. In other cases, women feel ashamed, believing they share responsibility for their victimization. Society cautions women about their behavior, their dress, the time of day they are in public, and their drinking habits. Those who fail to follow society's unwritten rules are then blamed if they are victimized. Internalizing any and all of these factors, women may be reluctant to report violence against them for fear they "caused" or "attracted" part of the violence. Victim blaming places the responsibility of not being victimized onto the victims rather than placing responsibility on offenders not to victimize others. For example, girls and young women are trained on how to avoid being raped rather than training men and women on how to behave properly and *not* rape (Broderick et al., 2014).

Homicide

In terms of homicide, men are still more likely to be victims, as the California Attorney General's Office indicates: 82.8% of homicide victims were men, and 17.2% women (Harris, 2016a). Figure 2.8 offers a glimpse into the racial and ethnic dimensions of victimization by gender. The demographics between men and women victims differ, as noted above in the discussion of race and ethnicity. Among white homicide victims in 2015, 33.2% were female; this is the largest proportion of female victims of any race. Among Hispanic victims, 12.7% were female, and among black victims 9.7% were female (Harris, 2016a).

A closer examination of the data provides interesting insight into gender differences in the context of homicides. For example, the location of these types of crimes differs by sex: 51.7% of women were killed in their homes, while the largest percentage of men (46.5%) were killed on the street or sidewalk. The perpetrators of homicide differ as well by sex. Figure 2.9 illustrates these differences between men and women. For male victims, 37.8% were strangers to their attackers, while just 12.3% of women were unknown to their attackers. While both male and female victims were about as likely to be killed by a friend or acquaintance (49.3% for men, 41.5% for women) significant differences emerge for family members. Less than 1% of men were killed by a spouse while 25% of women were; 6% of male victims were killed by a parent or child but 13.5% of female victims were killed by this group (Harris, 2016a). Therefore,

Figure 2.8. Homicide Victims by Race/Ethnicity and Gender 2015

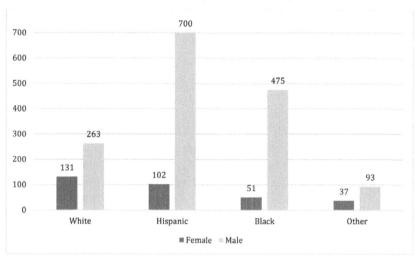

Source: Harris, 2016

consistent with findings at the national level, women are more likely to be victimized by a spouse or family member than men and more likely to be killed in their home (Mallicoat & Ireland, 2014).

Figure 2.9. Victimization by Relation to Perpetrator and Sex 2015

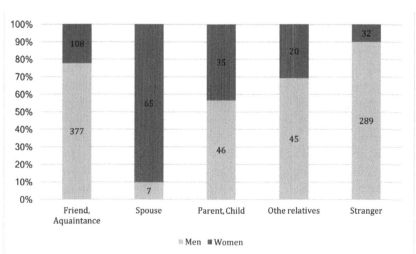

Source: Harris, 2016b, Table 12

Sex Trafficking

As will be discussed in detail in Chapter 11, sex trafficking is a crime where prostitution is present but the perpetrator holds a victim hostage using force, fraud, or coercion to engage in acts of prostitution. The number of victims of human trafficking is unclear as the crime occurs far below the radar of law enforcement. The Human Trafficking Work Group, created by Attorney General Kamala Harris in 2012, examined the nature and scope of human trafficking in California. The Work Group found that from mid-2010 to mid-2012, California's nine regional human trafficking task forces identified 1,277 victims, initiated 2,552 investigations, and arrested 1,798 individuals (Harris, 2012). Fifty-sex percent of victims who received services through California's task forces were sex trafficking victims. The Orange County Human Trafficking Task Force (2016) identified 225 victims in Orange County alone in 2015; almost all of whom were female and most (75%) of whom were trafficked for sex. Transnational criminal organizations and affiliated domestic gangs have expanded from drug and firearm trafficking to the trafficking of human beings. Criminal organizations and street gangs have set aside traditional rivalries to set up commercial sex rings that profit from the sale of human beings, in particular young women and girls (Harris, 2012). "In California, traffickers take advantage of the state's borders, major international airports and ports and major interstate (and intrastate) highways to move victims to where they can be exploited for the highest prices" (Harris, 2012, p. 20).

Domestic Violence

It is estimated that 1 in 3 U.S. women (32.9%) has experienced physical violence by an intimate partner in her lifetime (Black et al., 2011). According to the NCVS, there was an average of 1.3 million nonfatal domestic violence victimizations that occurred annually in the United States during the 10-year period from 2006 to 2015 (Reeves, 2017). Women made up 82% of the victims reporting intimate partner violence specifically. Despite the high prevalence of domestic violence, it is a crime that is often not reported to the police. Forty-four percent of the victims did not report their victimization to the police (Reaves, 2017). Reasons victims did not report a victimization to police included believing the issue was a personal private matter (32%), protecting the offender (21%), considering the crime was minor (20%), and fear of reprisal (19%). Female victims (24%) were four times as likely as male victims (6%) to not report due to fear of reprisal (Reaves, 2017). Other studies have found that women do not report their victimization due to fear for their children or a belief she was complicit in her victimization (Mallicoat & Ireland, 2014).

California laws dating back as far as 1945 criminalized "trauma causing" violence by a husband on his wife. As discussed in Chapter 4, those laws have been updated and now include abuse of a spouse. This also includes domestic violence against same-sex partners. According to the California Governor's Office of Emergency Services (CalOES), in the 2014–2015 fiscal year, 133,827 twenty-four-hour crisis line calls were received, 16,793 domestic violence victims and children were provided emergency shelter, and 22,948 were provided emergency food/clothing (CalOES, 2016). Law enforcement responded to 15,235 emergency calls and referred 17,406 new domestic violence victims to services. Despite the high numbers of domestic violence victims, a study examining domestic violence shelters and services in California showed that only one-third (33%) of domestic violence victims seek assistance, shelter, or involve law enforcement (Bugarin, 2002).

Rape and Sexual Violence

The National Intimate Partner and Sexual Violence Survey estimated that nearly 1 in 5 women in the United States have been raped in her lifetime (18.3%), translating into 22 million women (Black et al., 2011). More than one half (51%) of female victims reported having been raped by a current or former intimate partner and 41% reported having been raped by an acquaintance. Rape, like domestic violence, often goes unreported to the police. Victims often experience fear, humiliation, self-blame, and shame. In addition, the credibility of rape survivors is examined more closely than that of any other crime victims. Unlike other victims, they must prove non-consent. When faced with unsupportive warning signs and doubt, survivors are less likely to report. Prior to 2013, the Uniform Crime Reports defined rape as "The carnal knowledge of a female forcibly and against her will." It has since been expanded to include both female and male victims and reflect the various forms of sexual penetration understood to be rape.

While there are specific legal definitions of rape and sexual assault in the California Penal Code (including but not limited to PC 261, 243.4, 220, 269, 285, 286, 288, 289, 311.3), sexual violence is best understood as a broader continuum of unwanted, non-mutual sexual activities that range from subtle to extremely violent. Sexual assault can include, but is not limited to, rape, sexual threats and intimidation, incest, sexual assault by intimate partners, child sexual abuse, human sexual trafficking, sexual harassment, street harassment, and other forms of unwelcome, coerced, or non-consensual activity. In California, it is estimated that there are 2 million female victims of rape and 5.6 million female victims of sexual violence other than rape (Smith et al., 2017). Rape crisis centers in California served 31,778 survivors of sexual assault during the fiscal year 2014–2015. In addition, 16,832 received follow-ups services, 8,999 received in-person counseling, 10,791 received accompaniment services, and 7,389 were accompanied to sexual assault forensic medical examinations (CalOES, 2016). Like domestic violence, rape is underreported to the police. According to 2015 California crime statistics, there were 12,793 rapes reported, 5,304 clearances, and 2,467 arrests for felony rape were made (Harris, 2016b).

Women as Perpetrators of Crime in California

In 2015, there were 1,158,812 felony and misdemeanor arrests in California (Harris, 2016b). Of those, 271,498 (23.6%) were arrests of women. Felony arrests represented 27.2% (314,748) of all arrests. Women were responsible for 63,428 (20%) of all felony arrests.

Felonies

Less than one quarter (23.4%) of all female arrests were for felonies as compared to males (28.6%) who were responsible for 271,498 felony arrests. There were 109,756 arrests for violent crime, of those 21.3% (23,404) arrests were of women. Among this figure, 89.2% of homicide arrestees were male, and 10.8% were female (Harris, 2016b). Of the 73,970 arrests for property crimes, 23.9% (17,750) were women. Felony drug offenses are the third highest category of felony offense for women — 17.2% (7,694) of all felony drug arrests in California were of women. (See Chapter 11 for further discussion of drug offenses by sex.)

These data indicate that the distribution of arrests of women mirror arrests of males; however, at a lower frequency. Furthermore, the age distribution of arrests for males and females look quite similar, with the vast majority of arrests of both males and females between the ages of 20 and 39; however, males are more likely to be arrested into their 40s (Harris, 2016b).

Misdemeanors

Of the 835,370 misdemeanor arrests, 24.9% (208,070) of those arrested were women. Women accounted for 25.9% of misdemeanor assault and battery, 44.9% petty theft, and 22.9% of drug offenses. Though, historically, it was assumed that female offending was predominately sexual, examination of current data indicates that arrests for prostitution account for only 2.6% (5,491) of all misdemeanor arrests of women. When both felony and misdemeanor arrests for women are combined, arrests for prostitution accounted for only 2% of all female arrests in California in 2015 (Harris, 2016b).

Juveniles

Felony arrest data for juveniles in California indicate that females made up 16.3% (3,502) of all those arrested who were under 18. Examination of felony arrests of juveniles for various types of crime reveal that females were responsible for 19.3% (1,423) of all arrests for violent crimes of those under 18, 15.7% (1,024) of property offenses, and 12.9% (199) of drug arrests (Harris, 2016b). Of the misdemeanor arrests, females represented 32% of them. Examination of misdemeanor arrests data indicate that females represent 35.6% of assault and battery arrests, 47% of petty theft arrests, and 25% of drug offense arrests. With regards to prostitution, of the 16,930 arrests of juvenile females, only 135 were for prostitution.

Women in the Criminal Justice System (CJS) in California

Data from the California Department of Corrections and Rehabilitation (CDCR) give us information about those individuals committed to state prisons in California. While the prison population rose at an alarming rate in the 1980s through the 2000s due to various legislation (see Chapter 7), we are now seeing a decrease in the number of both male and female prisoners throughout the state. For instance, in 2010 there were 153,047 males and 9,774 females incarcerated in California state prisons. However, as of April 30, 2017, those numbers have decreased to 120,178 and 5,874 respectively (CDCR, 2017). Women currently make up 4.6% of the prison population, whereas in 2009, women made up 11% of the total California prison population. Only 19 juvenile females were sentenced to a state facility in 2016; eight years ago (2009) that number was 79 (CDCR, 2016; CDCR, 2011). This represents a dramatic change in policy from earlier years.

Of the adult women incarcerated in California prisons in 2013 (the latest data available), 32.3% were white, 32.8% Hispanic, 27.3% African American, and 7.6% other (including Asian, American Indian, and Hawaiian/Pacific Islander) (CDCR, 2014). The latest data available show that 62.5% of the adult female prison population was incarcerated for crimes against persons, 21.2% for property offenses, and 8.9% for drug offenses (CDCR, 2014). As you can see, the female prison commitment offenses do not match female arrest data (which indicate women commit more drug and property offenses than persons crimes); this is because state prison since Realignment is reserved for offenders who commit the most serious crimes and the rest (non-violent, non-serious, non-sexual offenders) are sentenced to county jail or probation.

The statistics gathered from California's Attorney General's office and Department of Corrections and Rehabilitation tell us a story about the crimes and victims of men and women, but they do not explain why and under what dynamics. This is a far more complex question, involving interconnected webs of socialization, economics, power, education, culture, race, and ethnicity.

Immigrants and the California Criminal Justice System

Like women and other ethnic minority Americans, immigrants have a complex relationship with police and the criminal justice system in California. While most immigrants face false stereotypes about their potential criminality, many also face focused scrutiny regarding their immigration status. Tragically, this has also led to situations whereby law enforcement have detained and deported U.S. citizens of Latino ancestry (Stevens, 2011). These issues, combined with past experiences with police in their home country and current policies and practices, often complicate immigrants' relationship with law enforcement and our criminal justice system.

On October 5, 2013, Governor Jerry Brown signed into law the California Trust Act (CTA) (Brown, 2013). CTA limits the authority of local police to hold individual arrestees for Immigration & Customs Enforcement (ICE) authorities beyond the time these arrestees would typically be eligible for release (Ca Gov't Code §7282). CTA is a major piece of legislation that speaks to the relationship between local police and Latino communities in the realm of immigration enforcement.[3,4] Four years later, on October 5th, 2017, Governor Brown signed a more expansive piece of legislation known as the California Values Act (SB 54), that dramatically broadened the symbolic underpinnings of the CTA. Under SB 54, police throughout California are prohibited from arresting individuals solely based on an outstanding civil immigration warrant; proscribed from inquiring as to the political status of individuals; and barred from participating in joint task forces with federal federal officials for the exclusive purpose of enforcing federal immigration laws.[5]

---

3. Although immigrants come to California from all corners of the world, for the purposes of this chapter we focus our attention on immigrants from Latin countries specifically.

4. We include in our definition of legislation the role that agency-led policy like ICE's 287(g) plays in immigration enforcement.

5. https://leginfo.legislature.ca.gov/faces/billNavClient.xhtml?bill_id=201720180SB54

Expansion in Immigration Enforcement

All states that border other nations like Mexico have active border patrol units working in them and the federal government has purview over immigration enforcement. In California, there are several border area ports-of-entry (i.e., international crossings) in places like San Ysidro, Otay Mesa, Tecate, and Calexico, CA.[6] The U.S. border patrol, an arm of U.S. Customs and Border Protection (CBP) is part of the Department of Homeland Security (DHS).[7] The border patrol has both permanent and strategic checkpoints along the major highways leading up from the international border inland.[8] As of 2016, there were approximately 2,325 border patrol agents staffing the San Diego sector and 927 agents working in the El Centro sector for a combined total of 3,252 agents working in California's southern sectors alone (USBP, 2016). In San Diego, CBP apprehended 31,891 persons, and they apprehended 19,448 persons in the El Centro region for a combined total of 51,339 apprehensions in southern California in 2016 (USBP, 2016).

Since the early 2000s, immigration enforcement has become much more intense as high rates of deportation have continued to increase and enforcement agencies like the border patrol have dramatically expanded through the infusion of additional manpower, technology, and resources (Pew Research Center, 2013; USBP, 2012; WOLA, 2013).

However, along with this build-up have come serious questions regarding the ability of enforcement agencies like the border patrol to responsibly manage this growth. Recent internal reports have identified and documented troubling issues having to do with the misapplication of force and rampant alcohol use amongst armed border patrol personnel (Blacher, 2013; USOIG, 2013). In fact, a 2013 DHS Inspector General's Report documented 1,187 use-of-force allegations against border patrol agents over the previous five years, with the report ultimately concluding that "many agents and officers do not understand the use of force policy and extent to which they may or may not use force" (*Los Angeles Times*, 2013a). Use-of-force deaths involving the border patrol include a 16-year-old Mexican youth that was killed when a U.S. border agent poked his gun through the border fence and shot him seven times after, it was alleged, the Mexican youth had thrown rocks at the border patrolmen (*Los Angeles*

---

6. State-by-state port-of-entry list is located at: https://www.cbp.gov/contact/ports/ca.

7. Border Patrol homepage located at: https://www.cbp.gov/border-security.

8. A list of San Diego area checkpoints is located at: http://en.wikipedia.org/wiki/United _States_Border_Patrol_interior_checkpoints.

Times, 2013a). In another incident, a Mexican national died of a heart attack after repeatedly being tasered by San Diego-area border patrol agents (*Los Angeles Times*, 2013a).

More recently, the U.S. Supreme Court considered a 2010 cross-border shooting case involving CBP agent Jesus Mesa Jr. and Mexican teenager Sergio Hernandez Guereca, wherein Agent Mesa, while standing in U.S. territory, fired across the international boundary and into Mexico, killing Guereca (Liptak, 2017; *Hernandez v. Mesa*). Agent Mesa claimed self-defense subsequent to a rock-throwing incident, but cell phone video at the scene does not support Agent Mesa's account and instead shows Mesa firing on the Mexican teen who was attempting to hide behind a concrete pillar on the Mexican side (Liptak, 2017). These situations are particularly alarming because the border patrol is one of the chief instruments in the aforementioned expansion of immigration enforcement and such incidents undermine their credibility and perceived legitimacy among immigrant communities and the public-at-large.

Bottom-Up Immigration Enforcement (State-Sponsored Legislation)

Recently, President Trump signed Executive Order 13768, "Enhancing Public Safety in the Interior of the United States," that called for strengthening operational ties between federal immigration enforcement and local police agencies by revitalizing two dormant programs: Secure Communities (S-COMM) and 287 (g) (EO 13768). Prior to President Trump's election, some states had already begun work on passing legislation to regulate immigration enforcement with varying levels of success.

Perhaps the most far-reaching attempt by states to regulate immigration began with Arizona's Support Our Law Enforcement and Safe Neighborhoods Act (hereinafter SB 1070).[9] Generally speaking, SB 1070 authorized local police in Arizona to act in the capacity of federal immigration agents. SB 1070 had five key components: (1) a provision requiring police to ascertain the immigration status of individuals when the police have a *reasonable suspicion* that the individual is in the nation without proper legal documentation; (2) a provision establishing that the willful failure of individuals to carry an alien registration card is a state misdemeanor offense; (3) a provision establishing a state misdemeanor for individuals that knowingly

---

9. SB 1070, 2010 Ariz. Sess. Laws 0113, amended by 2010 Ariz. Sess. Laws 0211 (H.B. 2162, 49th Leg., 2d Sess. (Ariz. 2010)).

or recklessly transport, conceal, or harbor illegal aliens; (4) a provision establishing a law that prohibits public gestures (e.g., nods, waives, hails, etc.) for the purpose of soliciting work; and (5) a provision expanding the warrantless arrest authority of police to include individuals that have committed offenses that would render them removable from the United States. Popular within politically conservative circles, other states quickly followed suit in developing "copycat laws" similar to SB 1070 (National Council of La Raza, 2011).

Concerns were immediately raised that SB 1070 would foster unconstitutional forms of policing rooted in racial profiling and spark the unlawful detention of legal populations like Mexican Americans and American Indians (Castro, 2011; Nill, 2011). On July 6, 2010, the U.S. Justice Department filed suit in the U.S. District Court seeking a preliminary and permanent injunction against the enforcement of SB 1070 on the grounds that SB 1070 was both unconstitutional and preempted by federal law (1, *United States v. Arizona*, 2010). On July 28, 2010, U.S. District Judge Susan Bolton issued a preliminary injunction against the enforcement of much of SB 1070. On April 11, 2011, the Ninth Circuit Federal Court of Appeals affirmed Judge Bolton's ruling and upheld the preliminary injunction that she issued (*United States v. Arizona*). Arizona subsequently filed a petition to the U.S. Supreme Court to overturn these lower court decisions and the U.S. Supreme Court agreed to review the case.

On June 25, 2012, the U.S. Supreme Court issued an opinion on the merits of SB 1070 in *Arizona v. United States*. In a 5–3 majority opinion, with Justice Elena Kagan recusing herself, the Justices ruled that much of SB 1070 was preempted by federal law. Federal preemption is a mechanism—developed through federal case law—that prohibits states and/or localities from acting in certain areas of law or policy if their action would compromise an area that has already been "occupied" by federal action. Federal preemption in the immigration law field played a key role in *Arizona v. United States* (2012). With respect to Arizona's SB 1070—the justices found that the following provisions were preempted by previous federal action: Section 3, the state alien registration requirements; Section 5(c), state sanctions against aliens who solicit or obtain employment; and Section 6, the warrantless arrest of aliens for criminal activity that makes them eligible for removal. However, the justices upheld the most controversial component of SB 1070 that authorizes local police to investigate the immigration status of persons suspected of being unlawfully present in the United States. In permitting Section 2(b) to survive, Justice Kennedy emphasized that an enforcement action that detained individuals—solely to verify their immigration status—would raise "constitutional concerns" and might be the subject of future legal challenges. Yet, despite the Supreme Court ruling that prohibited much of SB 1070, fear still lingers amongst the Latino community in Arizona (Costantini & Ross, 2012). Petra Falcon, a fourth-generation Mexican American living in Arizona, openly worried that her children, grandchildren, or "anybody of color" would nonetheless still be subject to police scrutiny or harassment under the surviving Section 2(b) (Costantini & Ross, 2012). Follow-up litigation targeting Section 2(b) is currently underway in federal court (ACLU, 2012). The California Legislature has never voted to enact laws similar to Arizona's SB 1070.

Top-Down Immigration Enforcement (Federal Initiatives to Incorporate State Assistance)

As mentioned previously, Executive Order 13768 has resurrected two programs aimed at strengthening state-level cooperation in the enforcement of federal immigration law, known respectively as S-COMM and 287(g). A number of California agencies like the Orange County Sheriff's Department have participated in 287(g) in its initial iteration, particularly when it was fully funded.[10]

A corollary to both S-COMM and 287(g) is the Criminal Alien Program (CAP). As originally conceived, CAP was intended to identify, process, and remove dangerous aliens incarcerated in local, state, and federal institutions (ICE, 2011). CAP has been successfully used to deport alien gang members across the nation (ICE, 2013). However, it has also raised alarming concerns regarding its operational proclivity to foster unconstitutional forms of policing rooted in racial profiling. Two reports, one by the Immigration Policy Center (IPC) and a second by UC Berkeley's Warren Institute, strongly suggest that police agencies in Texas exceeded CAP's congressional mandate to focus its resources on "dangerous alien offenders" and instead used CAP policies to target Latino citizens generally or low-level immigrant offenders (Gardner II & Kohli, 2009; Guttin, 2010). In effect, researchers found that police agencies were casting an overly broad net by increasing their petty offense arrests to scrutinize as large a number of Latinos as they could for the purposes of ascertaining their immigration status (Gardner II & Kohli, 2009; Guttin, 2010).

---

10. The Orange County Sheriff's Department's signed Immigration Enforcement MOU can be found at: http://www.ice.gov/doclib/foia/memorandumsofAgreementUnderstand ing/r_287-proactive-orange_county_sheriffs_dept-moa-signed.pdf

287(g)

ICE's 287(g) program established a formal partnership between local police agencies and ICE authorities on the basis of a Memorandum of Agreement (MOA). 287(g) delegated to local police the authority to enforce federal immigration laws as well as provided immigration enforcement training to rank-in-file police officers (ICE, n.d.a). During 2012, ICE claimed success in working with the Las Vegas Metropolitan Police Department to remove dangerous aliens suspected of sexual assault and firearms violations under 287(g) (ICE, n.d.b). However, the Obama administration, citing controversies associated with its implementation in places like Arizona, defunded most of 287(g) in favor of programs like Secure Communities (Duda, 2012; Howerton, 2012; *New York Times*, 2011).

ICE's Secure Communities Program (S-COMM)

ICE's Secure Communities (S-COMM) program is in effect in several states including California and technically counties and localities cannot "opt-out" of it (ICE, n.d.c). The S-COMM program utilizes pre-existing information-sharing networks to facilitate the removal of criminal aliens that pose a threat to public safety or that are habitual criminal offenders (ICE, n.d.d). The S-COMM process works in the following way: once local police make an arrest, that person's fingerprints are taken, digitized, and sent to the FBI database for analysis and storage. Once these scanned prints have been cross-checked against FBI records, they are automatically sent to ICE authorities who compare them against their own organizational databases to determine if the arrestee is also eligible for removal from the United States based on their immigration status (e.g., previous deportations, outstanding removal orders from an immigration judge) (ICE, n.d.d). If, after evaluating the fingerprint scans, it appears to ICE agents that an arrestee is eligible for removal, ICE authorities issue a detainer or "ICE hold," requesting that the local police or jail facility hold an individual for up to 48 hours after they would typically be eligible for release. During this detention period, ICE agents are supposed to interview the arrestee to determine whether or not to ultimately remove them. ICE authorities claim that more than 166,000 immigrants convicted of crimes were removed from the United States, including 61,000 immigrants convicted of Level 1 aggravated felonies (e.g., murder, rape, and the sexual abuse of children) (ICE, n.d.d). However, independent academic analysis indicates that few ICE detainers actually target serious offenders (TRAC, 2013b).

Take, for example, Blanca Perez who had been arrested by the LAPD for selling ice cream on the street without an ID (Taxin, 2011; Tokumatsu, 2011). After Blanca's arrest, she was summarily turned over to ICE authorities under the S-COMM program and faced deportation despite the fact that she had a one-year-old U.S. citizen child (Taxin, 2011; Tokumatsu, 2011). Juana Reyes-Hernandez, a single mother, also found herself entangled within S-COMM on a two-week ICE hold after she had been arrested for selling tamales in front of a Sacramento Wal-Mart store (Ammiano, 2012). Upon hearing about the circumstances surrounding her arrest, a federal immigration judge terminated her detention (Ammiano, 2012).

Recent research strongly suggests that on a nationwide basis, immigrants are five times less likely to be in prison than native-born citizens (Ammiano, 2012). Further, crime rates have actually fallen in states where the size of the immigrant population (inclusive of undocumented persons) has increased (IPC, 2013). In fact, The UC Berkeley Center for Criminal Justice estimates that between 1991–2008 California's two border jurisdictions—San Diego and Imperial Counties—crimes rates dropped substantially despite a dramatic increase in immigrant populations, both legal and undocumented (Krisberg, 2010). For example, in San Diego County, while the county received more than a quarter million new immigrants, violent crime (e.g., homicide, rape, robbery) dropped by 58% and serious property crime (e.g., theft, grand larceny, arson) declined 35% (Krisberg, 2010). In Imperial County during the same period, close to 50,000 immigrants arrived and violent crime dropped 53% while serious property crime declined by 13% (Krisberg, 2010). Researchers concluded that attempts to show causal links between immigration and crime are both "misleading and unproductive" (Krisberg, 2010, p. 10).

U.S. citizens have been swept up in S-COMM as well. Antonio Montejano, a 40-year-old U.S. citizen residing in Los Angeles, was incorrectly placed on an ICE hold after being arrested on minor shoplifting charges—without his knowledge, his small child had slipped candy and a small bottle of perfume into his shopping cart (Preston, 2011). He spent four days in police custody and continued to remain in custody on an ICE hold even after a criminal court judge had ordered his release (Preston, 2011).

Antonio Montejano's case is not an anomaly. According to Syracuse University's Transaction Records Access Clearinghouse (TRAC) website, from 2008–2012 ICE authorities, working through S-COMM, issued 834 ICE holds on U.S. citizens, with 77 of those incidents occurring in California (TRAC, 2013a). A report from the Warren Institute at UC Berkeley places the actual numbers of U.S. citizens detained under the S-COMM much higher (Kohli, Markowitz, & Chavez, 2011). The report indicates that from 2008–2011, approximately 3,600 U.S. citizens have been apprehended by ICE authorities (Kohli, Markowitz, & Chavez, 2011). Further, the report concluded that Latinos are disproportionately impacted by S-COMM detention practices (Kohli, Markowitz, & Chavez, 2011).

It is unlawful to place immigration holds on U.S. citizens because U.S. citizens are not immigrants and thus, not subject to U.S. immigration laws. The TRAC report also indicates that there were a total of 28,489 ICE detentions issued against permanent legal residents with 4,965 of those taking place in California (TRAC, 2013a). Permanent residents are legal immigrants that have qualified for the right to settle indefinitely within the United States and can only be removed under specific circumstances (TRAC, 2013a). In Los Angeles County, individuals subject to ICE holds spend an average of 20.6 extra days in custody (Greene, 2012).

S-COMM's proclivity to entangle U.S. citizens has become the subject of federal lawsuits (*Gonzalez & Chinivizyan v. ICE*; *Guzman v. Chertoff*; Esquival, 2011; James, 2000; Stevens, 2011). In one such federal complaint, lawyers argued that ICE holds are procedurally defective because they are structured in such a way so as to detain individuals without first establishing probable cause to believe that the person is actually subject to removal, without any judicial probable cause determination, and routinely issued in excess of ICE's statutory authority—triggering violations of Fourth Amendment rights (probable cause requirements) and Fifth Amendment rights (unconstitutional liberty deprivations) (*Gonzalez v. Chinivizyan*, 2011).

A growing body of evidence suggests that operationally, S-COMM has routinely exceeded its congressional mandate to focus its resources principally on dangerous alien offenders and this has borne serious financial and efficacious costs (*Gonzalez v. Chinivizyan*, 2011). For instance, in Los Angeles County, S-COMM has proven exceedingly expensive to operate, costing local taxpayers $26 million dollars a year to detain immigrants for ICE (Foley, 2012; Greene, 2012). In fact, California taxpayers spend an average estimated $65 million dollars annually for ICE holds (Foley, 2012; Greene, 2012). This doesn't include the untold negative impact it has on immigrants' willingness to call upon and cooperate with local police to prevent and solve crime.

With respect to S-COMM's efficacy, crime victims have also been affected, directly or indirectly, by the S-COMM program. For example, 36-year-old Elena Cabrera was assaulted in a domestic violence incident but arrested by Escondido PD anyway and placed on an ICE hold despite the fact that she had children as young as three years old left to care for themselves (SiFuentes, 2011). After evaluating her case, the San Diego District Attorney's Office refused to press charges against her (SiFuentes, 2011). Undocumented UC Berkeley student, Jirayut Latthivongskor, was robbed at gunpoint but never reported the incident to police because he was fearful of becoming entangled in the S-COMM process and summarily deported (Sabate, 2013).

Several of the aforementioned cases also underscore the aggregate effect of S-COMM's aggressive removal practices on the 4.5 million U.S.-born children living in mixed-status families (Passel & Cohn, 2011). A DHS Inspector General's Report estimates that between 1997 and 2007, approximately 108,000 parents of U.S. citizen children were removed from the United States (USOIG, 2009). When parents are removed, U.S.-born children are sometimes left with relatives or more often put into a state's foster care system. One of these parents, Felipe Montes, has been fighting to reunite with his three young children who were channeled into North Carolina's foster care system following his removal from the United States by ICE authorities in 2010 (IPC, 2012; see also Nazario, 2013).

The Chill Cast by ICE's Secure Communities Program on Latino Communities

Historically, the relationship between police agencies and Latino communities has been uncertain at best. However, the involvement of local police in programs like S-COMM has cast a chill over the willingness of Latino communities to cooperate with local police as either crime victims or witnesses.[11] Researchers at the University of Illinois, Chicago reached just these same conclusions in their four-county survey of Latino populations. In a 2013 report titled *Insecure Communities*, researchers conducted a statistical analysis of Latino attitudes in Cook, Harris, Los Angeles, and Maricopa counties regarding their willingness to voluntarily contact police if they knew police were also involved in immigration enforcement (Theodore, 2013). Based on their investigation, researchers concluded that a substantial portion of Latino populations in the aforementioned counties were much less likely to contact police because they feared police would ask them or people they knew about their immigration status (Theodore, 2013). As a consequence, police involvement in immigration enforcement also made Latino residents in these areas feel less safe, because these residents also knew that crime would go unreported by crime victims and witnesses, and criminal activity would flourish as a result (Theodore, 2013; see also Kohli, Markowitz, & Chavez, 2011; Strunk & Leitner, 2013; Pleich, 2013).[12]

Latino communities living in fear in localities where S-COMM is enacted seems to be a common theme in even cursory reviews of news and organizational accounts. In Vermont, hundreds of farm workers employed in the state's dairy industries feel imprisoned because they fear police will deport them under the

---

11. The reluctance to cooperate with police is not unique to the Latino community; other immigrant origin groups like the Vietnamese community also have the same proclivity, see Do & Christopher, 2014.

12. For a concise yet detailed discussion of how S-COMM impacts minority women in particular, see Pleich, 2013.

S-COMM program should they venture off the dairy farms in which they work (Rathke, 2011). Fear of local police agencies in S-COMM jurisdictions is palpable in places like Alameda County, CA. "People here, we stay quiet about crimes in our community. We're afraid that there will be reprisals by police," states Daniela from Oakland, CA (Romulo, 2013). Marisela from Hayward stated, "the police are supposed to be there to protect us but no, they aren't doing that" (Romulo, 2013). Maria from Oakland stated, "they [police] don't stop you because you actually did something. They stop you because you look Latino and then they make up an excuse like you were driving too slowly or your license plate light is too dim" (Romulo, 2013). To be sure, S-COMM's proclivity to entangle Latinos has generated widespread angst amongst both legal and undocumented Latino communities nationwide.

California's Transparency and Responsibility Using State Tools Act (CTA)

On Saturday, October 5, 2013, California Governor Jerry Brown dramatically changed the direction and tone of state-sponsored immigration law from restrictive models to a more cosmopolitan (e.g., free thinking) prototype by signing the California Trust Act (CTA) into law (Brown, 2013). Simply put, the CTA limits the authority of local police to hold arrestees for ICE authorities beyond the time these arrestees would typically be eligible for release (e.g., bail, recognizance, sentence completion, dismissal of charges, etc.) (Cal. Gov't Code § 7282). While some law enforcement organizations like the California Sherriff's Association oppose the CTA and have objected to the CTA (Barnes, 2012), the new legislation merely puts into law what police departments in Oakland, San Diego, and Los Angeles support as common sense reform (Florido, 2013; *Los Angeles Times*, 2013b; Lewis & LaFleur Vetter, 2013).

The CTA applies only to individuals arrested for minor or low-level offenses (Cal Gov't Code § 7282). Police are still empowered to detain individuals for ICE authorities based on the severity of their crime(s). For instance, police can still enact ICE holds if an individual has been convicted of a serious or violent felony; if there has been a judicial probable cause determination made after an individual has been charged with a serious or violent felony; if an individual has been convicted of a felony punishable by imprisonment within a state prison; if an individual has been convicted within the past five years of a "wobbler crime" (e.g., an offense punishable as either a misdemeanor or a felony) or convicted at any time of an enumerated felony (e.g., assault, battery, sexual abuse, burglary, firearms possession, etc.); if an individual is currently listed on the California sex and/or arson registry; and if an individual committed a crime that meets the definition of an aggravated felony of the INA (8 U.S.C. 1101) or is the subject of an outstanding ICE felony arrest warrant.

Federal Preemption and the CTA

While federal preemption[13] blocked much of Arizona's SB 1070, federal preemption does not create obstacles to the successful implementation of the CTA. Federal preemption speaks only to situations where states pass laws that are inconsistent with or try to replace federal law (e.g., immigration law). With respect to the CTA, California is not directly trying to replace or compromise the enforcement of federal immigration laws—only "opting out" of a voluntary component within the S-COMM program (e.g., honoring ICE hold requests). In fact, the Supreme Court, in *Printz v. United States* (1997), expressly ruled that the Constitution forbids the federal government from requiring municipalities to assist in the enforcement of federal law (*Printz v. United States*, 1997; see also *New York v. United States*, 1992). Perhaps most importantly, the CTA is an attempt to foster bonds of trust and safety between local police agencies and the communities they serve by thawing out the frosty relations that restrictive and unforgiving policies like SB 1070 and S-COMM have created.

Now that the Trump administration has signaled its intent to take a more aggressive and expansive approach towards immigration enforcement, a "collision course" of sorts has been set into motion with municipal entities that have operationalized "sanctuary policies." So-called "sanctuary cities" are local governments like cities and counties that—to varying degrees—follow policies that limit or curb their participation in the enforcement of federal immigration laws. Sanctuary policies can take several forms but generally fall into the following categories: (1) local governments that refuse to honor ICE hold requests by DHS; (2) local governments that instruct their local police agencies not to inquire about immigration status when officers interface with the communities that they serve; (3) states that issue driver's license or identification cards to undocumented immigrants; and (4) local governments that have established legal defense funds for undocumented immigrants to provide legal counsel on both civil and criminal matters (Davis, 2017).

---

13. "The rule of law that if the federal government through Congress has enacted legislation on a subject matter it shall be controlling over state laws and/or preclude the state from enacting laws on the same subject if Congress has specifically stated it has 'occupied the field.'" See http://dictionary.law.com/Default.aspx?selected=1575

Prevailing federal law prohibits local governments from enacting laws that restrict information between local governments and DHS regarding an individual's immigration or citizenship status (8 U.S.C. § 1373). From the Trump administration's perspective, strict compliance with § 1373 is necessary to identify and remove criminal aliens and undocumented law-breakers that are plaguing American cities and counties. However, the most recent empirical research suggests that overall crime is actually lower in sanctuary jurisdictions than in non-sanctuary areas (Cornelius et al., 2017). Conversely, in those areas where local police agencies are seen as working too closely with immigration authorities, criminal activity seems to go unreported because immigrant victims and witnesses fear deportation should they contact local police agencies to report crimes (Queally, 2017; Medina, 2017). Further, evidence also suggests that median incomes tend to be higher, poverty and unemployment are lower, and reliance on public assistance is also lower in sanctuary jurisdictions (AIC, 2017).

The impending legal dispute is over whether or not local governments— where sanctuary policies are in force—are in compliance with § 1373. The Trump administration and justice department believe not and have threatened to withhold federal funding to sanctuary cities as a punitive measure for non-compliance (Cohen, 2017). The problem, however, is that standing federal case law strongly limits the type of funding that the Trump administration can withhold—amounting to only the power to withhold that funding from sanctuary cities that is specifically related to the federal policy in question (*South Dakota v. Dole*, 1987). Thus, the Trump administration would be hard pressed to legally withhold general funding (e.g., Medicare, education, transportation, etc.) to sanctuary cities on the basis of non-compliance with immigration enforcement (Cameron, 2017). Complicating matters for the Trump administration, recently U.S. District Judge William Orrick issued a temporary injunction freezing (e.g., enjoining) President Trump's executive order on the grounds that only Congress had the authority to limit funding and that President Trump had acted outside the scope of his presidential powers in issuing the executive edict threatening federal funding to local sanctuary jurisdictions (Order Granting Motion to Enjoin, 2017). Further, the enumerated language in the Constitution's Tenth Amendment specifically states that the federal government "may neither issue directives requiring the States to address particular problems, nor command the States' officers, or those of their political subdivisions, to administer or enforce a federal regulatory program" (Amen. X; AIC, 2017). The end of this current stalemate has yet to be written but does underscore the complicated nature of how the quixotic realities of immigration and its enforcement sometimes grate coarsely against the administration of justice.

Conclusion

Demographics play a part in understanding crime in California but do not tell a complete story. As discussed in the several sections above, both crime and victimization are the result of a complex web. Socioeconomic status, which can be correlated with race, ethnicity, immigration status, and gender, plays a role in both. Different parts of the state are likely to see different demographics in their arrest population, also a result of migration and population and habitation patterns. Finally, not addressed here are questions about perpetration and victimization of crime by sexual orientation. The Bureau of Justice statistics indicate that hate crimes with bias towards sexual orientation were the second most common hate crimes in California for the decade 2006–2015 (about a quarter of all hate crimes). Given the current level of heated debate regarding same-sex marriage, time will reveal how sexual orientation manifests in both crime and victimization.

Key Terms and Definitions

Customs & Border Protection (CBP)—This agency is responsible for policing Ports-of-Entry (POE's) and the international border in between ports of entry.

Ethnicity—Relates to the shared cultural factors such as nationality, language, ancestry, and culture.

Gender—The sociological attributes of masculinity and femininity.

Immigration & Customs Enforcement (ICE)—This is the agency that is responsible for the deportation of individuals who did not immigrate to the United States legally.

Minority—A group that is numerically less than the dominant group, that is in a non-dominant position, and whose members share religious, ethnic, cultural and/or linguistic characteristics.

Race—As a biological term, race refers to a person's physical appearance such as skin color, eye color. More accurately race is a social construct, attached to groups based on historical context, and influenced by racial dynamics and politics.

Sanctuary Cities—Local governments that limit or prohibit cooperation with immigration authorities to enforce federal immigration laws within their jurisdictions.

Sex—The biological assignments of men and women due to chromosomal, reproductive, and biological compositions.

Sex Trafficking—A crime where prostitution is present but the perpetrator holds a victim hostage to engage in acts of prostitution.

Internet Websites

American Civil Liberties Union (ACLU). Immigrant Rights: https://www.aclu.org/immigrants-rights

American Immigration Council (AIC). https://www.americanimmigration council.org

California Crime Statistics: http://oag.ca.gov/crime

California Department of Corrections and Rehabilitation, Offender Information Reports: http://www.cdcr.ca.gov/Reports_Research/Offender_Information_ Services_Branch/Offender_Information_Reports.html

Immigration Policy Center (IPC) http://www.immigrationpolicy.org/

National Council of La Raza http://www.nclr.org

United Nations Human Rights Watch www.hrw.org/topic/united-nations

Review Questions

1. What are the three major racial and ethnic groups that are reported in the California criminal justice system?
2. What are some of the main reasons why more minorities end up in the California criminal justice system than whites?
3. What is the percentage of women who report that they were a victim of a violent crime and why is it that they are less likely to report it to the authorities?
4. List 5 reasons why domestic violence victims are less likely to report their victimization to the police.
5. How many people were victims of sex trafficking in 2012?
6. What is the name of the Department that handles the U.S. border patrol, U.S. customs and Border Protection (CBP)?
7. What do the acronyms ICE and CAT stand for?
8. What is federal preemption and how does it impact the ability of local governments to regulate federal immigration enforcement?
9. What are sanctuary policies and are these policies legal?
10. What does it mean when a U.S. district court judge issues an order "enjoining" a federal policy or order?

Critical Thinking Questions

1. The research presented in this chapter demonstrates that minorities are overrepresented in California's criminal justice system. Why is this? What are some possible solutions to alleviate the problem?
2. What contributes to the pattern of women's victimization discussed in the chapter? What are the limits of the criminal justice system's abilities to reverse these trends? What can the system do to improve the conditions for women?
3. Why are immigrant groups reluctant to involve the police and the criminal justice system as a whole when they are in need of help? How does this exacerbate some of the problems already experienced by immigrant communities?
4. Should CBP agents be liable for killing Mexican nationals in cross-border shootings?
5. Do Mexican nationals have actionable rights under the U.S. constitution even if not on U.S. soil?
6. How do we prevent U.S. citizens of Latino ancestry from being deported?

References

American Civil Liberties Union (ACLU). (2012, July 17). Civil rights groups ask federal court to block remaining section of Arizona's racial profiling law. Retrieved from https://www.aclu.org/immigrants-rights/civil-rights-groups-ask-federal-court-block-remaining-section-arizonas-racial

American Immigration Council Fact Sheet. (2017, February 23). Sanctuary policies: An overview. Retrieved from https://www.americanimmigrationcouncil.org/research/sanctuary-policies-overview

Ammiano, T. (2012, August 16). Assembly member Ammiano salutes immigration's release of single mother tamale vendor. Retrieved from http://www.asmdc.org/members/a17/press-releases/assemblymember-ammiano-salutes-immigration-s-release-of-single-mother-tamale-vendor

Barnes, B. (2012, August 28). California sheriffs oppose bill on illegal immigrants. *New York Times*. Retrieved from http://www.nytimes.com/2012/08/29/us/california-sheriffs-oppose-bill-on-illegal-immigrants.html?_r=0

Belknap, J. (2007). *The invisible woman: Gender, crime, and justice* (3rd ed.). Belmont, CA: Thomson Wadsworth Publishing.

Blacher, M. (2013, November 14). *US Border Patrol has 'alarming' alcohol problem, says internal memo and inside source*. ABC 10 News. Retrieved from http://www.10news.com/news/investigations/us-border-patrol-has-alarming-alcohol-problem-says-internal-memo-and-inside-source11142013

Black, M. C., Basile, K. C., Breiding, M. J., Smith, S. G., Walters, M. L., Merrick, M. T., Chen, J., & Stevens, M. R. (2011). *The National Intimate Partner and Sexual Violence Survey (NISVS): 2010 summary report.* Atlanta, GA: National Center for Injury Prevention and Control, Centers for Disease Control and Prevention. Retrieved from https://www.cdc.gov/violenceprevention/pdf/nisvs_report2010-a.pdf

Broderick, R., Nigatu, H., & Testa, J. (2014, February 4). What is rape culture? *Buzz Feed.* http://www.buzzfeed.com/ryanhatesthis/what-is-rape-culture

Brown, E. G. (2013, October 5). *Governor Brown signs immigration legislation.* California Office of the Governor Press Release. Retrieved from http://gov.ca.gov/news.php?id=18253

Bugarin, A. (2002). *The prevalence of domestic violence in California.* California Research Bureau. Retrieved from http://www.library.ca.gov/crb/02/16/02-016.pdf

California Department of Corrections and Rehabilitation. (2011). *2010 Annual Report: California prisoners and parolees.* Offender Information Services Branch, Estimates and Statistical Analysis Section, Data Analysis Unit.

California Department of Corrections and Rehabilitation. (2014). *2013 Annual Report: California prisoners and parolees.* Offender Information Services Branch, Estimates and Statistical Analysis Section, Data Analysis Unit.

California Department of Corrections and Rehabilitation. (2016, December 31). *DJJ population overview as of December 31, 2016.* Offender Information Services Branch, Estimates and Statistical Analysis Section, Data Analysis Unit. Retrieved from http://www.cdcr.ca.gov/Juvenile_Justice/Research_and_Statistics/index.html

California Department of Corrections and Rehabilitation. (2017, May 1). *Monthly population report as of April 30, 2017.* Offender Information Services Branch, Estimates and Statistical Analysis Section, Data Analysis Unit. Retrieved from http://www.cdcr.ca.gov/Reports_Research/Offender_Information_Services_Branch/Population_Reports.html

Cal OES. (2016, February). *Joint legislative committee report.* Criminal Justice and Victims Service Division. Retrieved from http://www.caloes.ca.gov/GrantsManagementSite/Documents/2016%20JLBC%20Report.pdf

Cameron, D. (2017, January 18). How sanctuary cities work, and how Trump's executive order might affect them. *Washington Post.* Retrieved from https://www.washingtonpost.com/graphics/national/sanctuary-cities/

Castro, R. F. (2011). XENOMORPH!! Indians, Latinos, and the alien morphology of Arizona Senate Bill 1070. *Harvard Civil Rights–Civil Liberties Law Review, 46,* 1–12.

Centers for Disease Control and Prevention. (2012). *Gang homicides—Five U.S. cities, 2003–2008*. Retrieved from http://www.cdc.gov/mmwr/preview /mmwrhtml/mm6103a2.htm#tab2

Centers for Disease Control and Prevention. (2014). *Definitions*. Retrieved from http://www.cdc.gov/

Cohen, K. (2017, May 22). Jeff Sessions stuck in sanctuary city quandary. *Washington Examiner*. Retrieved from http://www.washingtonexaminer.com/jeff-sessions-stuck-in-sanctuary-city-quandary/article/2621661

Cornelius, W. A., Garcia, A. S., & Varsanyi, M. W. (2017, February 2). Giving sanctuary to undocumented immigrants doesn't threaten public safety— It increases it. *Los Angeles Times*. Retrieved from http://www.latimes.com/ opinion/op-ed/la-oe-sanctuary-cities-trump-20170202-story.html

Costantini, C., & Ross, J. (2012, June 25). Despite Supreme Court SB 1070 ruling, climate of fear persists in Arizona. *Huffington Post*. Retrieved from http://www.huffingtonpost.com/2012/06/25/supreme-court-sb-1070-ruling-arizona_n_1624708.html

Davis, A. C., Jamison, P., & Nirappil, F. (2017, January 25). D.C., other 'sanctuary cities' defiant in the face of Trump's threats. *Washington Post*. Retrieved from https://www.washingtonpost.com/local/dc-politics/ 2017/01/25/65f15428-e315-11e6-a547-5fb9411d332c_story.html?utm_term=. d6b81864957b

Duda, J. (2012, June 25). Homeland Security revokes 287(g) agreements in Arizona. *Arizona Capitol Times*. Retrieved from http://azcapitol times.com/news/2012/06/25/homeland-security-revokes-287g-immigra-tion-check-agreements-in-arizona/

Florido, A. (2013, August 16). San Diego police chief endorses Trust Act. *KPBS*. Retrieved from http://www.kpbs.org/news/2013/aug/16/san-diego-police-chief-endorses-trust-act/

Foley, E. (2012, August 23). Secure Communities costs Los Angeles County more than $26 million a year: A report. *Huffington Post*. Retrieved from http://www.huffingtonpost.com/2012/08/23/secure-communities-los-an-geles_n_1824740.html

Gabbidon, S. L. (2010). *Race, ethnicity, crime and justice: An international dilemma*. Thousand Oaks, CA: Sage Publications.

Gabbidon, S., & Greene, H. (2013). *Race and crime*. Thousand Oaks, CA: Sage Publications.

Gardner II, T., & Kohli, A. (2009, September). *The C.A.P. effect: Racial profiling in the ICE Criminal Alien Program* [Policy Brief]. The Chief Justice Earl Warren Institute on Race, Ethnicity & Diversity at University of California, Berkeley Law School.

Greene, J. (2012, August 22). *The cost of responding to immigration detainers in California.* Justice Strategies. Retrieved from http://big.assets. huffingtonpost.com/Justicestrategies.pdf

Guttin, A. (2010, February 17). The Criminal Alien Program: Immigration enforcement in Travis County, Texas. *Immigration Policy Center.* Retrieved from http://www.immigrationpolicy.org/special-reports/criminal-alien-program-immigration-enforcement-travis-county-texas

Harris, K. D. (2012). *The state of human trafficking in California 2012.* California Department of Justice. Retrieved from https://oag.ca. gov/sites/all/files/agweb/pdfs/ht/human-trafficking-2012.pdf

Harris, K. D. (2016a). *Homicide in California 2015.* California Department of Justice. Retrieved from https://oag.ca.gov/sites/all/files/agweb/pdfs/cjsc/publications/homicide/hm15/hm15.pdf

Harris, K. D. (2016b). *Crime in California 2015.* California Department of Justice. Retrieved from https://oag.ca.gov/sites/all/files/agweb/pdfs/cjsc/publications/candd/cd15/cd15.pdf

Howerton, J. (2012, June 25). Obama admin. ends immigration enforcement program following high court ruling. *The Blaze.* Retrieved from http://www.theblaze.com/stories/2012/06/25/obama-admin-ends-immigration-enforcement-program-following-high-court-ruling/

Immigration and Customs Enforcement (ICE). (n.d.a). *Fact Sheet: Delegation of immigration authority section 287(g) Immigration and Nationality Act.* Retrieved from http://www.ice.gov/news/library/factsheets/287g.htm

Immigration and Customs Enforcement (ICE). (n.d.b). *287(g) success stories.* Retrieved from http://www.ice.gov/287g/success-stories.htm

Immigration and Customs Enforcement (ICE). (n.d.c). *Secure communities: Get the facts.* Retrieved from http://www.ice.gov/secure_communities/get-the-facts.htm

Immigration and Customs Enforcement (ICE). (n.d.d). *Secure communities.* Retrieved from http://www.ice.gov/secure_communities/

Immigration and Customs Enforcement (ICE). (2011, March 29). *Fact sheet: Criminal Alien Program (CAP).* Retrieved from http://www.ice.gov/news/library/factsheets/cap.htm

Immigration and Customs Enforcement (ICE). (2013, July 2). *ICE deports MS-13 gang member wanted for 4 murders in El Salvador.* Retrieved from https://www.ice.gov/news/releases/1307/130702houston.htm

Immigration Policy Center (IPC). (2008, September 10). *From anecdotes to evidence: Setting the record straight on immigrants and crime.* American Immigration Council. Retrieved from http://www.immigrationpolicy.org/just-facts/anecdotes-evidence-setting-record-straight-immigrants-and-crime-0

Immigration Policy Center (IPC). (2012, December). *Falling through the cracks: The impact of immigration enforcement on children caught up in the child welfare system.* Retrieved from http://www.immigrationpolicy.org/just-facts/falling-through-cracks

James, I. (2000, September 3). Wrongly deported, American citizen sues INS for $8 million. *Los Angeles Times.* Retrieved from http://articles.latimes.com/2000/sep/03/news/mn-14714

Kohli, A., Markowitz, P., & Chavez, L. (2011, October). *Secure communities by the numbers: An analysis of demographics and due process.* The Chief Justice Earl Warren Institute on Race, Ethnicity & Diversity at University of California, Berkeley Law School. Retrieved from https://www.law.berkeley.edu/files/Secure_Communities_by_the_Numbers.pdf

Krisberg, B. (2010, October 1). *Where is the fire? Immigrants and crime in California.* Berkeley Center for Criminal Justice. Retrieved from http://www.law.berkeley.edu/files/Where_is_the_fire.pdf

Lewis, S., & LaFleur Vetter, S. (2013, November 24). Trust Act builds trust between law enforcement and the immigrant community. *Richmond Confidential.* Retrieved from http://richmondconfidential.org/2013/11/24/trust-act-builds-trust-between-law-enforcement-and-immigrant-community/

Liptak, A. (2017, February 21). Justices weight agents' cross-border shooting of Mexican teenager. *New York Times.* Retrieved from https://www.nytimes.com/2017/02/21/us/politics/justices-weigh-agents-cross-border-shooting-of-mexican-teenager.html?_r=0

Los Angeles Homicide Report. (2016). *Los Angeles Times.* Retrieved from http://homicide.latimes.com

Los Angeles Times Editorial Staff. (2013a, November 12). Too much force at the border. *Los Angeles Times.* Retrieved from http://articles.latimes.com/2013/nov/12/opinion/la-ed-border-use-of-force-20131112

Los Angeles Times Editorial Staff. (2013b, November 25). Faith in the Trust Act. *Los Angeles Times.* Retrieved from http://www.latimes.com/opinion/editorials/la-ed-trust-act-california-20130827,0,6823924.story#axzz2mLLT19oj

Mallicoat, S., & Ireland, C. (2014). *Women and crime.* Thousand Oaks, CA: Sage.

Medina, J. (2017, April 30). Too scared to report sexual abuse. The fear: Deportation. *New York Times.* Retrieved from https://www.nytimes.com/2017/04/30/us/immigrants-deportation-sexual-abuse.html?_r=0

National Council of La Raza (NCLR). (2011, April 18.). *One year later: A look at SB 1070 and copycat legislation.* Retrieved from http://issuu.com/nclr/docs/alookatsb1070v3/5?e=1871004/2284794

Nazario, S. (2013, October 15). Heartache of an immigrant family. *New York Times.* Retrieved from http://www.nytimes.com/2013/10/15/opinion/the-heartache-of-an-immigrant-family.html?_r=0

New York Times Editorial Staff. (2011, December 16). The case against Sheriff Arpaio. *New York Times.* Retrieved from http://www.nytimes.com/2011/12/17/opinion/the-case-against-sheriff-arpaio.html

Nill, A. C. (2011). Latinos and S.B. 1070: Demonization, dehumanization, and disenfranchisement, *Harvard Latino Law Review, 35,* 14.

Orange County Human Trafficking Task Force. (2016). *Human trafficking victim report 2016.* Retrieved from https://www.egovlink.com/public_documents300/ochumantrafficking/published_documents/OCHTTF%20Victim%20Report%202016/2016%20OCHTTF%20Victim%20Report.pdf

Passel, J., & Cohn, D. (2011, February 1). *Unauthorized immigrant population: National and state trends, 2010.* Washington, DC: Pew Hispanic Center.

Pew Research Center. (2013, September 19). *High rate of deportations continue under Obama despite Latino disapproval.* Retrieved from http://www.pewresearch.org/fact-tank/2013/09/19/high-rate-of-deportations-continue-under-obama-despite-latino-disapproval/

Pleich, S. (2013, October 26). Secure Communities program makes minority women live in fear. *Santa Cruz Sentinel.* Retrieved from http://www.santacruzsentinel.com/opinion/ci_24394167/steve-pleich-secure-communities-program-makes-minority-women

Preston, J. (2011, December 14). Immigration crackdown also snares Americans. *New York Times.* Retrieved from http://www.nytimes.com/2011/12/14/us/measures-to-capture-illegal-aliens-nab-citizens.html?pagewanted=all&_r=0

Queally, J. (2017, March 21). Latinos are reporting fewer sexual assaults amid a climate of fear in immigrant communities, LAPD says. *Los Angeles Times.* Retrieved from http://www.latimes.com/local/lanow/la-me-ln-immigrant-crime-reporting-drops-20170321-story.html

Rathke, L. (2011, September 4). Mexican farm workers in Vt. fear federal program. *Deseret News.* Retrieved from http://www.deseretnews.com/article/700176272/Mexican-farm-workers-in-Vt-fear-federal-program.html?pg=all

Reaves, B. A. (2017, May). *Police response to domestic violence, 2006–2015.* Bureau of Justice Statistics Bulletin Special Report. Washington, DC: U.S. Department of Justice. Retrieved from https://www.bjs.gov/content/pub/pdf/prdv0615.pdf?ed2f26df2d9c416fbddddd2330a778c6=fvadfdjdfr-fvgadgrqm

Rodriguez, N. (2006). Latinos and Latinas. In C. R. Mann, M. S. Zatz, & N. Rodriguez (Eds.), *Images of color, images of crime* (pp. 36–41). New York: Oxford University Press.

Romulo, I. (2013, July). *From the base: The human impact of 'Secure Communities' in Alameda County.* Congressional Hunger Center Report. Retrieved from http://hungercenter.wpengine.netdna-cdn.com/wp-content/uploads/2013/07/From-the-Base-Romulo.pdf

Sabate, A. (2013, April 10). *TRUST Act moves forward and could 'force' Fed's hand on immigration.* Retrieved from http://fusion.net/abc_univision/news/story/trust-act-moves-forward-california-copied-connecticut-florida-18293

Sickmund, M., & Puzzanchera, C. (2014, December). *Juvenile offenders and victims: 2014 national report.* Washington, DC: National Center for Juvenile Justice, Office of Juvenile Justice and Delinquency Prevention.

SiFuentes, E. (2011, October 24). ESCONDIDO: ACLU probes case of woman turned over to immigration. *UT San Diego.* Retrieved from http://www.utsandiego.com/news/2011/Oct/24/escondido-aclu-probes-case-of-woman-turned-over/

Smith, S. G., Chen, J., Basile, K. C., Gilbert, L. K., Merrick, M. T., Patel, N., Walling, M., & Jain, A. (2017). *The National Intimate Partner and Sexual Violence Survey (NISVS): 2010–2012 state report.* Atlanta, GA: National Center for Injury Prevention and Control, Centers for Disease Control and Prevention. Retrieved from https://www.cdc.gov/violenceprevention/pdf/NISVS-StateReportBook.pdf

Soo-Jin Lee, S. (2005). Racializing drug design: Implications of pharmacogenomics for health disparities. *American Journal of Public Health, 95*(12), 2133–2138.

Stevens, J. (2011). U.S. government unlawfully detaining and deporting U.S. citizens as aliens. *Virginia Journal of Social Policy & the Law, 18,* 606.

Strunk, C., & Leitner, H. (2013, December 8). Redefining Secure Communities. *The Nation.* Retrieved from http://www.thenation.com/article/165295/redefining-secure-communities#

Taxin, A. (2011, August 16). Immigrants plead for an end to fingerprint sharing. *Huffington Post.* Retrieved from http://www.huffingtonpost.com/2011/08/16/immigrants-plead-for-end-_n_927965.html

Theodore, N. (2013, May). *Insecure communities: Latino perceptions of police involvement in immigration enforcement.* University of Illinois at Chicago, Department of Urban Planning and Policy. Retrieved from http://www.uic.edu/cuppa/gci/documents/1213/Insecure_Communities_Report_FINAL.pdf

Tokumatsu, G. (2011, February 18). New front in the immigration fight: Ice cream carts. *NBC News Los Angeles.* Retrieved from http://www.nbclosangeles.com/news/local/New-Front-in-the-Immigration-Fight-Ice-Cream-Carts-116436884.html

Transactional Records Access Clearinghouse (TRAC). (2013a, February 20). *Few ICE detainers target serious criminals.* Syracuse University. Retrieved from http://trac.syr.edu/immigration/reports/311/

Transactional Records Access Clearinghouse (TRAC). (2013b, September 17). *Few ICE detainers target serious criminals.* Syracuse University. Retrieved from http://trac.syr.edu/immigration/reports/330/

Truman, J., Langton, L., & Planty, M. (2013). *Criminal victimization, 2012.* Bureau of Justice Statistics Bulletin. Washington, DC: Bureau of Justice Statistics.

Truman, J., & Morgan, R. (2016). *Criminal victimization, 2015.* Bureau of Justice Statistics Bulletin. Washington, DC: Bureau of Justice Statistics.

United Nations Human Rights. (2014). *Minorities under international law.* Retrieved from http://www.ohchr.org/EN/Issues/Minorities/Pages/internationallaw.aspx

United States Border Patrol (USBP). (2016). *Scaled staffing numbers for border patrol agents broken up by sector.* Retrieved from http://www.cbp.gov/linkhandler/cgov/border_security/border_patrol/usbp_statistics/usbp_fy16_stats/usbp_sector_profile.ctt/usbp_sector_profile.pdf

United States Census Bureau. (2015). Retrieved from http://quickfacts.census.gov/qfd/states/06000.html

United States Customs and Border Protection (USBP). (n.d.). *2012–2016 Border Strategic Plan, The mission: Protect America.* Retrieved from http://nemo.cbp.gov/obp/bp_strategic_plan.pdf

United States Office of the Inspector General (USOIG). (2009, January). *Removals involving illegal alien parents of United States citizen children.* Washington, DC: Department of Homeland Security.

United States Office of the Inspector General (USOIG). (2013, September). *CBP use of force training and actions to address use of force incidents [redacted].* Retrieved from http://www.oig.dhs.gov/assets/Mgmt/2013/OIG_13-114_Sep13.pdf

Violence Policy Center. (2013). *San Joaquin County ranks #1 for youth homicide victimization in California, new study reveals.* Retrieved from http://www.vpc.org/press/1303ca.htm

Walker, S., Spohn, C., & Delone, M. (2016). *The color of justice: Race, ethnicity and crime in America* (6th ed.). Belmont, CA: Wadsworth.

Washington Office on Latin America (WOLA). (2013, June 26). *Seven bad things that will happen after a "border surge."* Retrieved from http://www.wola.org/commentary/seven_bad_things_that_will_happen_after_a_border_surge

Zatz, M. S., & Mann, C. R. (2006). The power of images. In C. R. Mann, M. S. Zatz, & N. Rodriguez (Eds.), *Images of color, images of crime* (pp. 1–30). New York: Oxford University Press.

Cases Cited

Arizona v. United States, 132 S. Ct. 2492 (2012)

Gonzalez & Chinivizyan v. ICE, No. 13-CV-4416 (C.D. Cal. Filed Sept. 9, 2013)

Guzman v. Chertoff, No. 08-013227 (C.D. Cal. Filed Feb. 27, 2008)

Hernandez v. Mesa, Oyez, http://www.oyez.org/cases/2016/15-118 (last visited May 5, 2017)

New York v. United States, 505 U.S. 144, 166 (1992)

Printz v. United States, 521 U.S. 898, 935 (1997)

South Dakota v. Dole, 483 U.S. 203, 208 (1987)

United States v. Arizona, 703 F. Supp. 2d 980 (D. Ariz. 2010) (No. CV-10-1413-PHX-SRB)

United States v. Arizona, 641 F.3d 339, 366 (9th Cir. 2011), cert. granted, 132 S. Ct. 845 (2011) (No. 11-182)

Constitution

U.S. CONST. AMEN. X

Court Orders

Order Granting the County of Santa Clara's and County of San Francisco's Motion to Enjoin Section 9(a) of Executive Order 13768 [ECF #98] (N.D. Cal.). Retrieved from https://www.cand.uscourts.gov/who/sanctuary-litigation

Federal Statutes

8 U.S.C. § 1373

Presidential Papers, Proclamations, and Executive Orders

Exec. Order No. 13768 (2017)

Chapter 3

California's Constitution, Direct Democracy, and the California Criminal Justice System

Phillip L. Gianos and Stephen J. Stambough

Learning Objectives

After reading the chapter, students should be able to:

- Define and describe in detail the notion of direct democracy.
- Summarize and discuss the intersection of direct democracy and criminal justice policy in California.

Constitutions establish governments. In a basic sense, constitutions govern governments. In this chapter, we examine how California's political process is governed by its constitution with an eye towards a relatively unique feature of our constitutional structure, direct democracy. Our ability to pass both statutory laws and constitutional amendments by direct vote of the citizens has impacted many areas of California policy and governance, including criminal justice policy. After discussing the foundations of this governance technique, we explore some of the areas of crime policy that have been most effected by our system of direct democracy.

State Constitutions in the Federal System

Constitutions establish the basic institutions of government and allocate power among those institutions in two ways: by granting certain powers to one or more institutions, and also by denying certain powers to one or more institutions. Frequently, constitutions also deny specific powers to any governmental institution by granting (or "reserving") them solely to the people. Constitutions also provide for their own change through their mechanisms for amendment.

California's Constitutional History

One of the more interesting features of California's political history is that the state has had two constitutions (Louisiana leads all the states in this respect with eleven). The first was adopted in 1849, just before California became a state in 1850. Hastily drafted, much of the language was taken from other state constitutions without taking into account the essentially frontier nature of the territory that became California. While the document served reasonably well for thirty years, by 1879 its deficiencies became so severe that a constitutional convention was called to draft a new document.

Delegates to the convention fashioned an extremely long and detailed document, with particular emphasis on expanding and strengthening the bill of rights and placing severe limits on the power of the state legislature. This period was also the dawn of the progressive movement in California, a movement whose profound effects we still see in the present-day state constitution and state laws, including laws involving the criminal justice system. Progressivism *was essentially a middle-class movement created in response to the political consequences of great economic power. It is this movement that created the process for citizens to approve policies directly while circumventing the legislature and the governor, including several issues of criminal justice policy.*

"Direct Democracy" in California

We know that California is unique. It has been the home of innovative leaders and ideas in our technological age. It is the origin of many cultural trends that sweep the nation. It is also a place of great policy innovations. Many national policy trends either get their start in California or gain needed legitimacy and momentum by succeeding in California. One reason for the power of California as a leader in setting the policy agenda is our system of direct democracy. Political battles have been waged over taxes (Proposition 13), legislative term limits (Proposition 140), gay marriage (Proposition 8), and many other prominent issues in high-profile and well-funded campaigns that captured the attention of the public and the media. Crime policy is another area often impacted by the high-profile campaigns associated with direct democracy in California.

To understand the impact of direct democracy on crime policy, we need to understand the forms, procedures, and underlying values present in California's system of direct democracy. Direct democracy comes in three primary forms: *initiative, referendum,* and *recall.* Although there are slight variations of each across the states, some basic definitions of each are possible. *Initiatives* are proposals for new laws or amendments to a state's constitution that are placed on the ballot by citizens or groups for direct approval/rejection by the voters. Both the state legislature and the governor are bypassed in this process. A *referendum* is a proposal for the voters to directly ratify or overturn a law passed by the legislature and signed by the governor. *Recalls* are when voters decide to remove an elected official before their normal term expires.

At the heart of each of these is an underlying value of citizen power over entrenched political interests. As with many of the direct democracy states, California's system dates to the early 1900s and finds its roots in two related yet distinct intellectual traditions: *populism* and *progressivism.* Bruce Cain and Kenneth Miller (2001) do a thorough job explaining the differences between these two movements and their importance for understanding uses of direct democracy. They correctly trace the roots of populism to an agrarian revolt in the Midwest and West against monopolistic banking and industrial forces from the East. Adding mechanisms of direct democracy to state governmental structures was one of the highest priorities for populist reformers and they were successful in pushing this reform in most of the states west of the Mississippi River, including California.

For populists, the ability for citizens to pass laws without interference from the state legislature or the governor was critical to their overall agenda because they believed elected politicians were necessarily corrupt and beholden to the very special interest groups they were fighting against. As Cain and Miller (2001) document, both early populism such as this movement and later-day incarnations such as tax revolts and term limits are perfect examples of the populist legacy. For many in the movement, the goal of direct democracy was to establish a parallel legislature that would circumvent the state legislature and have all but the most routine issues handled directly by the people instead of through their elected representatives.

The progressive movement was similar to its populist predecessor, however the focus was a little different. Instead of finding its roots in rural America, progressivism was mostly an urban, working-class reaction to the political and economic situations of the Industrial Revolution. One of the political consequences of the creation and concentration of great wealth during the Industrial Revolution was the corruption of political power. Progressive reformers proposed several ideas to reduce this and open the process up for greater participation. Some of the more famous progressive reforms in this area include using secret ballots, expanding voting rights to women, and removing the power to choose U.S. senators from state governments and giving it to the people through direct elections.

In the area of direct democracy, progressives were just as supportive of the practice as the populists. However, their belief about its role and its usage were significantly different. While populists wanted to strive towards replacing the elected legislature with a parallel legislature of direct democracy, progressives wanted direct democracy to serve as a check on abuses by the legislature. Their view of direct democracy is referred to as "the gun behind the door" (Cronin, 1989, p. 155). It is a potential threat that alters behavior but is not used unless absolutely necessary.

This "gun behind the door" model is one that envisions direct democracy being used as a last resort. When popular programs or reforms are being stalled or completely rejected by either the legislature or the governor, citizens could use the initiative option in direct democracy to pass the law over the objection or inaction of elected officials. When the legislature and governor enacted a law the public did not want, citizens could use the referral option to prevent the implementation of the law and overturn it. When elected officials became too removed from the will of the people, citizens could use the recall option in direct democracy to remove that officeholder before the end of the normal term. Progressives believed that after several successful examples of direct democracy in action, elected officials would feel constrained by it and would refrain from either abusing their power or straying too far from the will of the people in determining policies.

The traditions of the populist and progressive models produce different expectations about how direct democracy will be used. Under the populist model one would expect a high number of ballot propositions every election cycle. If it was to truly be used as a parallel legislature, both the number of total measures and the diversity of issues brought before the voters should be significantly large for the voters to govern. Under the progressive model, we should see short periods of active use against a discredited political system followed by long periods of inaction after the system had been corrected. Even a brief period of successful and active use of direct democracy would remind politicians that the citizens could override their decisions and, thus, the need for active use of direct democracy would subside.

The data presented in Table 3.1 show that the history of direct democracy in California is one of significant variation in the frequency of direct democracy

Table 3.1: Number of Qualified Ballot Measures by Decade in California

Decade	Total Number of Ballot Measures
1912–1920	40
1922–1930	29
1932–1940	31
1942–1950	21
1952–1960	10
1962–1970	9
1972–1980	24
1982–1990	55
1992–2000	54
2002–2010	99
2012–2016	39

Sources: 1912–2000 data (Initiative and Referendum Institute, n.d.); 2002-2016 (California Secretary of State, n.d.b.)

usage. It is clearly evident that California began with a period of active use followed by a decline. Over the last three decades, however, California has seen a tremendous growth in the number of qualified ballot measures. There were more ballot measures in the last 30 years of California history than in the previous 70 years combined. The last decade in particular was witness to a tremendous increase in direct democracy usage.

The typical explanation for the increase in the last two decades was the reaction of the political actors in California to the successful passage of Proposition 13 in the late 1970s (McCuan & Stambough, 2005). The success of such a groundbreaking and sweeping reform showed that this process was a legitimate path to policy reform by outside groups. Therefore, the passage of Proposition 13 was almost like opening the floodgates. Once groups and political leaders realized the power of direct democracy, they were much more likely to use it. Therefore, the last few decades of California's direct democracy usage approximates the populist model of active usage—a replacement for the elected legislative bodies—instead of the progressive model of using it only to check legislative abuse or inaction.

Direct Democracy and Crime Policy in California

The history of direct democracy in California is filled with several issues related to crime policy. In 1912, the very first year of direct democracy in California, there was an attempt to abolish the death penalty. That attempt failed to qualify for the ballot. This failure is instructive because the very first hurdle propositions face is to obtain enough signatures to qualify for the ballot. Between 1912 and 2010, only 348 of the 1,657 measures that were officially circulated for signature gathering obtained enough valid signatures to qualify for the ballot (California Secretary of State, n.d.a).

Throughout the years, however, crime policy has been a popular topic for direct democracy measures in California. The chief criminal justice-related beneficiary of the direct democracy provisions of the California Constitution has been get-tough-on-crime related measures — specifically, initiatives toughening sentences, and bond measures earmarked for prison and jail construction. Getting tough on crime is a very popular political issue; it's hardly a controversial stand to be opposed to crime and so it should not be surprising that statewide initiative measures often deal with crime, especially since the constituency for tough-on-crime measures is so wide. That constituency is not just comprised of citizens who feel threatened by crime but also and very importantly (since they command financial resources) the interest groups that benefit from such measures: prosecutors, police departments, sheriff's departments, prison guards, and other correctional personnel, not to mention the contractors and labor unions who build prisons and other correctional facilities, including large urban jail facilities; all benefit from tough-on-crime measures. Historically, getting tough on crime is an almost-sure political winner.

So it's not surprising that in recent decades Californians have used the initiative process to advance anti-crime policies. Some examples:

In 1982: Two bond measures to build prisons and county jails; a constitutional amendment to limit releasing prisoners on bail, and another dealing with sentencing and release for the accused and convicted.

In 1984: Two more bond measures expanding and remodeling state correctional facilities and county jails.

In 1986: Two more bond measures to expand state prisons and to expand youth and adult correctional facilities.

In 1988: Two more bond measures for more prison and correctional facility construction; a constitutional amendment that stays for thirty days any parole authority decision until it has been reviewed by the governor of the state; an initiative proposed by the legislature that increases the penalty for second-degree murder for anyone convicted of knowingly killing a peace officer.

In 1990: Another bond for new prison construction; a constitutional amendment permitting state and county prison officials to contract with public and private organizations for inmate labor.

In 1994: The famous "three strikes" initiative, which required, among other things, a minimum sentence of 25 years to life for three-time repeat offenders with multiple prior serious or violent offenses; another measure that increased the penalty for second-degree murder when a firearm is used from a vehicle.

In 1996: Two initiatives covering increased punishment for drive-by shootings, carjacking, and murder of a juror.

In 2000: Five initiatives covering increased punishment by redefining special circumstances, the murder of Bay Area Rapid Transit District officers, or California State University officers; increasing punishment for gang-related offenses and lowering the age that juveniles can be transferred to adult court (Proposition 21); and one measure allowing some drug offenders to undergo treatment rather than imprisonment (Proposition 36).

Two things stand out from this brief list: criminal penalties were increased and, even more dramatically, the period of the 1980s and 1990s was characterized by a substantial and rapid expansion of prisons and jail facilities and increases in corrections personnel. The public was worried about crime, decided that tougher penalties, more stringent sentencing guidelines, and more prisons were the answer, and voted for both repeatedly when given the opportunity.

But the consensus of the 1980s and 90s on crime ran headlong into two hard realities. The first was the state budget crisis of the late 1990s and 2000s, in which the state budget deficit soared and pressure was put on all government programs, including but not limited to criminal justice system-related programs (including prisons), to reduce budgets.

But even the new prisons built by bond measures approved by voters could not keep up with new prisoners incarcerated under tougher definitions of serious crime—which were also approved by voters.

Legal challenges based on prison overcrowding began in 1990, and by 2011 the U.S. Supreme Court ruled in the case of *Brown v. Plata* (2011) that California's prisons were so overcrowded that serious constitutional violations had occurred under the Eighth Amendment to the U.S. Constitution's prohibition of "cruel and unusual" punishment, essentially invoking the Supremacy Clause of the federal Constitution. The court majority concluded that prisoners' mental and physical health had been compromised. The U.S. Supreme Court's decision was close and controversial; state officials opposed it, and the court majority was the bare minimum five of nine votes required. The initial effects of the decision indicated that it could lead to the release or transfer—to county facilities from state prisons—of up to 30,000 inmates, a matter with which state, county, and local officials are presently dealing at a time of severe state budget limitations. The history of this judicial decision and its effects on California's correctional system is discussed in detail in Chapter 7.

In 2012 California voters passed a reform to the three-strikes law. This was one of the first successful efforts to weaken a "tough-on-crime" law. Voters overwhelmingly approved changing the law so that the third strike had to be a serious offense, including violent offenses. One of the main reasons that seem to resonate with voters to change a previously popular law was the financial question. By easing the third strike sentence for lesser offenses, the state would save significant money by reducing the prison population. In a time of economic crisis, this was an appealing message that led to a change in policy. The public, in other words, had changed its mind and was unwilling to support higher taxes or to support cuts in other programs to provide for more prison space.

In addition to standard issues of crime policy, direct democracy has been used to forward political agendas concerning decriminalization policies as well. An instructive comparison in the attempt at decriminalization at the ballot box was Proposition 19 in 2010 compared with more recent attempts in the 2016 elections. To develop this picture, we begin with a discussion of Proposition 19 and how it was instructive for future attempts at marijuana decriminalization.

Proposition 19 in 2010 would have legalized marijuana usage in California and developed a system for future taxation of marijuana. The measure failed by a vote total of 53.5% opposed to decriminalization to 46.5% in favor of de-criminalization. What is interesting about this particular case is that unlike the normal public campaign about crime issues, from the beginning this issue was presented as a multi-dimensional issue. Instead of the debate being dominated with arguments centered around "making our streets safer" or "being tough on crime" such as is often the case when the public decides crime issues, with this issue the proponents of reform immediately tried to pivot from marijuana itself to the financial aspect of it. In the official ballot statement (California Secretary of State, 2010), proponents made the argument that current marijuana policy is failed but then quickly focused on how it could be a source of taxation. The strategy was clear. In times of a massive economic recession and state voters faced with tough budget cuts, the proponents were offering a way to ease the budget crunch—even slightly—by focusing on the tax revenue.

Opponents did not wish to engage in the same type of debate. In the same voter guides, the opponents to this reform clearly tried to frame the campaign around the harmful effects of drugs, the impact on children, and dangers due to behavior such as driving while under the influence of marijuana. One side was focused on the impact of the—currently—criminal behavior on society while the other side focused mostly on the economic impact of taxation policy.

Proposition 19, therefore, offers us a chance to see how voters react to a traditional issue of crime when the campaign surrounding it is not a typical one we see for issues of crime. In other words, how successful were the campaigns in convincing people to vote on the proposition based upon the framework they presented?

While most public opinion polls on the issue focused on the simple questions of who supported it and who did not, the Center for Public Policy at California State University Fullerton conducted a more in-depth survey of residents in Orange County, California, about voter perceptions of numerous dimensions of Proposition 19 (Sonenshein, Gardiner, & Spiropoulos, 2010). The results suggest some interesting findings. While Orange County residents were similar in their opposition to the measure, the authors of this study were able to disaggregate the data to determine a more in-depth explanation as to why. Proponents of reform seem to have been successful in their attempt to convince people that raising money by taxing marijuana was a good idea. Approximately 61.5% of the survey respondents stated that they believed raising money through taxing marijuana was a good idea. It is impossible to say whether the campaign convinced people of this position or if the campaign tapped into a pre-existing belief. According to the survey, Orange County residents also agreed with proponents in the belief that legalizing marijuana would not increase the crime rate. 58.1% of the respondents disagreed with the statement that legalizing marijuana would increase the crime rate. Only 39.5% of those surveyed agreed that it would increase the crime rate.

Therefore, Orange County voters seemed primed for a vote to decriminalize marijuana. They believed that legalizing it would have no real effect on crime and that it would be a good way to raise money. This combination seemed like a great campaign success except for the fact that the proposition lost. The data suggest that although people thought the crime rate would not increase and that it was a good way to raise money, they still did not want the activity near them and could not bring themselves to actually make this change when they thought about actually seeing it being bought, sold, and used. Voters were against the idea of corporations selling it and they were even more opposed to the idea of neighbors growing it in their yards. They also disagreed that it should be sold in easy-to-find locations such as convenience stores. Therefore, although they did not believe it would increase crime and they liked the idea of making money off of it, they do not want it sold by corporations or at stores such as convenience stores; nor do they want their neighbors growing it.

This case study is an interesting one because of the complex way voters perceived the issue but also because it can be instructive in the future. As a result of the 2016 elections, that future is now. Supporters of decriminalization returned to the system of direct democracy to propose, campaign for, and pass Proposition 64. Proposition 64 decriminalized marijuana use for persons over 21 and levied taxes on the cultivation and retail sale of the product (California Secretary of State (n.d.b)). Unlike the previous failed attempts, this measure passed with 57% of the vote. Supporters simplified the issue and found success after learning from previous attempts.

Decriminalization ballot measures in 2016 did not stop at supporters finding success at the state level. Even more instructive is the case of local direct democracy in the Orange County city of Costa Mesa. Voters in Costa Mesa were faced with making decisions on three separate ballot measures about marijuana that all appeared on the same ballot in the fall election. Measures W, V, and X all dealt with the issue of marijuana dispensaries and businesses in the City of Costa Mesa (Orange County Registrar of Voters (n.d.)). The first two measures were placed on the ballot by citizen petitions. Measure W would support the licensing of up to eight marijuana businesses in the city of Costa Mesa. Measure V would support a smaller number of marijuana businesses in the city by limiting the number to no more than four.

After these measures qualified for the ballot, city leaders worked with the activist groups supporting these measures to promote a compromise measure, Measure X. Measure X proposed allowing marijuana related businesses in a specially zoned area of the city and limiting it to businesses that research, test, and manufacture products. The reaction by the elected city government to the threat of popular initiative is similar to the concept of "gun behind the door" discussed earlier in this chapter. Without the threat of the popular measures being passed while circumventing the city council, it is doubtful that the city council and proponents of the marijuana measures would have formed a coalition to support Measure X. In fact, as stated on the official materials from the Orange County Registrar of Voters, the people who pushed Measure W and Measure V withdrew their support for those measures and encouraged people to vote only for Measure X.

On election day, voters agreed with the coalition and passed the compromise Measure X while rejecting the more lenient Measures W and V. Measure X passed with 54% of the vote while the most lenient (8 facilities), Measure V, was only supported by 37% of the voters and the slightly less lenient (4 facilities), Measure W, received slightly more supported but still failed with only 42% of the vote in favor of the measure. Costa Mesa voters were tasked with differentiating between three competing measures on marijuana legalization and showed the sophistication to distinguish measures and support the one that was designed to appeal to a broader coalition by taking into consideration the public's well-known concern about zoning marijuana businesses away from areas such as schools.

Conclusion

The presence of direct democracy holds many implications for crime policy in California. Whether it is more traditional reform like the three-strikes reforms or issues that help determine the legality of certain behaviors such as marijuana decriminalization, direct democracy permits interest groups and voters to push the agenda faster and further than what is often possible through the normal legislative process filled with compromise. Initiatives are inherently uncompromising. People either vote yes or no. They cannot vote "yes but only with some reforms" or "no but I do kind of like some of this." The dichotomy of the choice often makes issues seem simple for voters, but as we discovered with the voter beliefs on marijuana decriminalization, even seemingly simple initiatives have several dimensions to them and voters have positions on these dimensions.

Since California has entered a seemingly unending era of hyper-initiative usage, we should expect to see more issues that capture the public's attention placed before the voters for their approval. Groups frustrated with legislative inaction will rightly see this method as an alternative. Entrepreneurial politicians may see championing a popular measure as a way to raise their profiles. Regardless of the motive one prediction seems safe. We will see crime policy of all types debated and sometimes approved directly by the voters, whether the politicians like it or not.

Key Terms and Definitions

Direct democracy—The ability that Californians have to pass both statutory laws and constitutional amendments by direct vote of the citizens.

"Gun behind the door"—The argument that direct democracy serves as a deterrent to bad behavior by elected officials.

Initiative—Proposals for new laws or amendments to a state's constitution that are placed on the ballot by citizens or groups for direct approval/ rejection by the voters.

Parallel Legislature—The active and frequent use of direct democracy to push issue agendas without consultation from the elected legislature or governor.

Populism—A political movement rooted in an agrarian revolt against monopolistic banking and industrial forces that was the origin of direct democracy movement in the United States.

Progressivism—Political movement rooted in the industrial sector union movement that pushed direct democracy as a way to check abuses among political officials.

Proposition 19 (2010)—Failed ballot measure that would have legalized and taxed marijuana in California.

Recall—Elections in which voters decide to remove an elected official before their normal term expires.

Referendum—A proposal for the voters to directly ratify or overturn a law passed by the legislature and signed by the governor.

Supremacy clause—A clause in the U.S. federal (national) constitution that establishes that the U.S. Constitution, U.S. Treaties, and laws made pursuant to the U.S. Constitution, shall be "the supreme law of the land", that these are the highest form of law in the U.S. legal system, and that requires that all state judges must follow federal law and the federal constitution when a conflict arises between federal law and either a state constitution or the law of any state.

Internet Websites

Initiative and Referendum Institute: www.iandrinstitute.org
California Secretary of State Initiative Information: http://www.sos.ca.gov/elections/
California Constitution: http://www.leginfo.ca.gov/const-toc.html

Review Questions

1. Which decades had the greatest initiative usage in CA? In these comparisons, explain the recent era.
2. What are the different policy dimensions of the marijuana policy discussed in the chapter?
3. Distinguish between initiative, referendum, and recall.
4. How do state constitutions relate to the national (federal) constitution?
5. How have the voters of California, through the initiative process, affected criminal justice-related policies?
6. How has the U.S. Supreme Court affected significant actions taken by California voters through the initiative process?

Critical Thinking Questions

1. Using the information from the Center for Public Policy poll about Orange County views on the marijuana initiative, design a "winning message" about Proposition 19. Is there any way to make the popular portions of the argument more compelling than the reservations they had about its passage?
2. Describe the difference between the Populist and Progressive approaches to the system of direct democracy. How does the use of direct democracy for the passage of crime policy fit into each of these perspectives?
3. When state laws—including those state laws that involve the criminal justice system and criminal justice policy, including penalties for serious crimes— are believed to come into conflict with federal law, what institutions and in terms of what principles is that possible conflict resolved?
4. Criminal justice policy in California has been strongly affected in recent decades by the "direct democracy" provisions of the California state constitution. In what ways have those policies been affected? With what consequences for the state as a whole?
5. What makes "getting tough on crime" such a durable political issue? What elements of the California political community have been involved in supporting get-tough-on-crime proposals?

References

Cain, B., & Miller, K. (2001). The populist legacy: Initiatives and the undermining of representative government. In L. Sabato, H. Ernst, & B. Larson (Eds.), *Dangerous democracy? The battle over ballot initiatives in America.* Lanham, MD: Rowman and Littlefield.

California Secretary of State. (n.d.a.). *History of California initiatives.* http://www.sos.ca.gov/elections/ballot-measures/resources-and-historical-information/history-california-initiatives/

California Secretary of State. (n.d.b.). *Elections.* Retrieved from http://www.sos.ca.gov/elections/

California Secretary of State. (2010). *2010 voter guide.* Retrieved from http://cdn.sos.ca.gov/vig2010/general/pdf/english/19-arg-rebuttals.pdf

Cronin, T. E. (1989). *Direct democracy: The politics of referendum, initiative, and recall.* Massachusetts: Harvard University Press.

McCuan, D. S., & Stambough, S. J. (2005). Initiative-centered politics: The new politics of direct democracy. Durham, NC: Carolina Academic Press.

Orange County Register of Voters (n.d.) Voting. Retrieved from https://www.ocvote.com/voting/current-election-info/2016-presidential-general-election-info/measures-gen2016/
Sonenshein, R., Gardiner, C., & Spiropoulos, G. (2010). Orange County poll probes county residents' views about legalizing marijuana. Center for Public Policy, CSU Fullerton. Retrieved from http://webcert.fullerton.edu/advocacy/OCPolls/TopicsAreas.html#Marijuana

Cases Cited

Brown v. Plata, 563 U.S. _____ (131 S. Ct. 1910) (2011)

Chapter 4

California Criminal Law

Gary LoGalbo

Learning Objectives

After reading the chapter, students should be able to:

- Demonstrate an understanding of how law is enacted.
- Explain the differences between criminal and civil law, parties to crime, and procedural versus substantive law.
- Describe the types of crimes found in each of the major statutory criminal codes.

California statutes are spread among 29 separate statutory codes.[1] The statutes, or laws, are enacted by the state legislature and approved by the governor. Laws can also be enacted in California through the proposition or initiative process. The majority of the laws in the 29 codes are regulatory in nature. This means they are enacted to control things such as smog equipment performance requirements for vehicles sold in California, requirements and tests for different types of contractor's licenses, and rules governing the sale of car and homeowners insurance. Some laws are procedural and define rules for the flow of cases through the judicial system. The remaining statutes are criminal, which define specific crimes and punishments, or civil, which define wrongs and remedies for legal disputes between two or more people or entities.

First, this chapter will discuss how laws are enacted. Second, the chapter will address the differences between criminal and civil law, parties to crime, and procedural versus substantive law. Third, the chapter will focus on the major criminal statutory codes and describe the types of crimes to be found in each, detail their punishments, and provide examples to put the crimes discussed into context. Finally, the chapter will touch on criminal laws found in other legal codes.

---

1. See Appendix A for a list of all the California Statutory Code titles. The entire set of codes can be found at http://leginfo.legislature.ca.gov/

How Laws Are Made

Laws enacted through the legislative process are the most common form of law in California. When a state assemblyperson or senator proposes a law, it goes through several reviews, committees, and revisions and is then often debated on the assembly and senate floors. The legislature may also take testimony from experts in the appropriate field to help guide their lawmaking. Through this process, things are added to and deleted from the proposed law or laws. Wording is also changed and bargaining occurs between the elected representatives. Concessions are made to get the necessary votes in the assembly and senate. Funding must be approved if necessary. Although the enactment of all laws may not require funding, many do for the laws to be carried out. Often, laws enacted through the proposition process lack adequate funding because the legislature does not participate in the process. This can create a major issue during difficult fiscal times. If the law is ultimately passed by a majority vote of the assembly and senate, it is then forwarded to the governor for approval. The governor can sign the law, thereby enacting it, or veto it by refusing to sign it. If enacted, it is placed in the designated statutory code.

Laws enacted through the proposition process in California follow a different path. The proposition or initiative process allows for the direct enactment of laws by the voters. This direct enactment or vote is known as a plebiscite. The initiative process can also amend the California Constitution. Whether amending the state constitution or enacting a law directly, the process requires filing fees, procuring the required number of registered voter signatures, getting the proposition placed on the next ballot, and securing a majority vote during the election period. This is a costly endeavor, and as such, is used only on rare occasion when compared to the legislative process. We have seen the proposition process recently used in the Background Checks for Ammunition Purchases and Large-Capacity Ammunition Magazine Ban Initiative (Proposition 63, 2016),[2] the California Marijuana Legalization Initiative (Proposition 64, 2016),[3] the Reduced Penalties for Some Crimes Initiative (Proposition 47, 2014),[4] California's Three-Strikes law (Proposition 36, 2012),[5] the Compassionate Use Act (Proposition 215, 1996),[6]

---

2. See California Penal Code section 30370, et seq.
3. See California Health and Safety Code section 11357, et seq.
4. See California Penal Code and Health and Safety Code.
5. See California Penal Code section 1170.12.
6. See California Health and Safety Code section 11362.5.

Substance Abuse and Crime Prevention Act (Proposition 36, 2000),[7] and Jessica's Law (Proposition 83, 2006), among others.

The Compassionate Use Act was originally enacted by voters via Proposition 215 in 1996. It was developed by Dennis Peron in memory of his partner who used marijuana to treat symptoms caused by AIDS. Its stated purpose was to allow marijuana to be prescribed by doctors to patients who would benefit from its effects to treat their underlying medical condition. Health and Safety Code section 11362.5(b)(1)(A) states a physician may issue a medical marijuana card to anyone whose health would benefit from such use. It goes on to cite eight different medical conditions that can be treated legally with marijuana use. It also has an all-encompassing phrase that allows marijuana to be used for "any other illness for which marijuana provides relief." Such language gives doctors wide latitude for prescribing marijuana.

However, many law enforcement agencies and organizations were opposed Proposition 215. The main argument in opposition was that the law was too vague and virtually legalized marijuana. Further, opponents argued unlimited quantities could be grown by anyone and anywhere without any regulation or restrictions. Unlike other prescribed pharmaceutical drugs, this law allows people to grow and harvest their own prescribed drug. The passing of proposition 64 in 2016 makes marijuana possession legal for persons 21 years or older. And in 2018, it will be legal to sell if certain requirements are complied with as well. However, since it is still illegal to cultivate, possess, transport, distribute, or sell marijuana under federal law, the California statutes offer no protection against federal prosecution.

Another example of the direct democracy process is Jessica's Law. Jessica Lunsford was a nine-year-old Florida girl who was raped and murdered in 2005 by John Couey. Couey had previous convictions for sex crimes and was required to register with the police as a term of his conviction. Registration required that he give police his home and work addresses and vehicle information and that he check in at regularly scheduled times. Couey failed to do so and his whereabouts became unknown. When he raped and murdered Jessica Lunsford there was public outrage. As a result, Florida and many other states began the process of enacting harsher punishments and release requirements for sex offenders. In 2006, California's movement became known as "Jessica's Law" or Proposition 83. Proposition 83 was a series of laws to punish sex offenders who target children and adults more severely, including life sentences under some circumstances. The enacted statutes mandate that sex offenders

---

7. See California Penal Code section 1210.

cannot live within 2,000 feet of parks and schools and must wear GPS tracking devices, and extends parole periods when they are released from prison, among other things.

Types of Laws: Federal, State, and Local

Federal criminal laws are enacted by the United States Congress and Senate. These laws are contained in the United States Codes. Laws enacted by the federal government often flow from the interstate compact clause in Article I, section 10 of the United States Constitution. This section has been broadly interpreted by the United States Supreme Court to permit Congress discretion in enacting laws that affect interstate commerce, or commerce between the states. Under this provision, Congress has regulated firearms, prostitution, drugs, money laundering, fraud, and a variety of other criminal actions. Of course, the president of the United States has the power to sign the law, thereby enacting it, or veto the law.

States have the power to enact laws under the Tenth Amendment of the United States Constitution. The Tenth Amendment provides that all powers not granted to the federal government or prohibited to the states by the Constitution are reserved to the states. Based on this, states have legislatures where persons elected by the people of each state enact laws on their behalf. State laws must be signed into law, or vetoed by the governor. States enact a variety of laws concerning public health and welfare that fall into the criminal realm. As long as the area the law pertains to has not been *preempted* by Congress, it will be valid, provided it is constitutional.

Counties and cities also have the power to enact laws by vote of the County Board of Supervisors or City Council. Laws enacted by counties and cities usually pertain to the general health, welfare, and beautification of the respective counties and cities. County laws are usually called ordinances and city laws are usually referred to as municipal codes. These laws are only valid and binding on the county and/or city in which they are enacted. For instance, the county of Orange has an ordinance that makes it illegal to walk a dog without a leash (Orange County Code Ordinance section 4-1-46). Another example is a municipal code enacted by the City of Fullerton making it a crime to park on residential streets between 2:00 a.m. and 5:00 a.m. unless the street has been exempted from the rule (Fullerton Municipal Code section 8.44.080).

As you can see, criminal laws are enacted at many different levels within our government. The legislative bodies at each level are elected by the people of that jurisdiction to represent them. Hence, Congress is composed of elected representatives from the states. State legislatures are composed of elected representatives from the different districts within the state. County supervisors are elected by the people of the different districts within the county and city council persons are elected by persons who reside in each particular city.

Criminal vs. Civil Law

All criminal laws have some core requirements. One set of those requirements is listed in California Penal Code (PC) section 15, which states, "A crime or public offense is an act committed or omitted in violation of a law forbidding or commanding it, and to which is annexed, upon conviction, either of the following punishments: 1) Death; 2) Imprisonment; 3) Fine; 4) Removal from office; or, 5) Disqualification to hold and enjoy any office of honor, trust or profit in this state." As you can see from this definition, all criminal laws require some punishment. Further, criminal laws are enforced by the government. Criminal charges are filed on behalf of the people of a state by the government. The government prosecutes the crimes, imposes punishments, and enforces the crimes and punishments with its power to mete out the above listed punishments upon conviction of an individual.

Felonies are the most serious crimes in the codes. They are crimes punishable by imprisonment in the state prison as well as fines. With the enactment of Assembly Bill 109, non-serious and non-violent felonies may now be punished by incarceration in the county jail for a period not exceeding the maximum confinement proscribed by law for the particular violation. This bill was enacted to reduce overcrowding in the state prison system and save money at the state level. Misdemeanors are less serious crimes and are punishable by incarceration in the county jail and fines. Wobblers are crimes that may be punished as felonies or misdemeanors. This discretion is vested in the prosecuting agency in the first instance. They can file the criminal charges as a felony or a misdemeanor and look at many factors in making that decision. Some of the factors include the prior criminal history of the defendant, the seriousness of any injury, the amount of loss, etc. The court may also reduce a felony to a misdemeanor using its discretion if the crime is a wobbler. The court looks at the same factors in making its decision. Infractions are rule violations punishable by a fine only.

Civil laws are spread throughout the 29 statutory codes in California. However, there are a few codes dedicated primarily to civil law. They include the Civil Code and Code of Civil Procedure. The Code of Civil Procedure establishes the procedural rules for civil cases, including filing deadlines, discovery rules, settlement requirements, trial procedures, and so forth.

Civil laws were developed to enforce a legal right one person or entity may have with respect to another. Actions are brought by one party against another and the government sits as the mediator via the judicial branch. The damages sought are usually monetary, although injunctive relief is also available in some circumstances. The O. J. Simpson case is a good example. In the criminal prosecution for the murder of Nicole Brown Simpson and Ronald Goldman, he was found not guilty. The burden of proof in a criminal case is proof beyond a reasonable doubt. There was also a civil wrongful death case filed by the heirs of both victims. They were suing for money damages to compensate them for the loss of a loved one. In the civil case, the heirs (plaintiffs) won and the jury awarded $33.5 million in total damages to the families. In the civil case, the burden of proof was by a preponderance of the evidence, which is a lower standard than beyond a reasonable doubt.

Parties to Crime

State and federal criminal law recognizes several types of participants to crime who can be held criminally liable. They are commonly referred to as principals, which include aiders and abettors, and accessories. Co-conspirators are often placed in the principal category as well.

Every person who directly participates in a crime; aids and abets a crime whether present at the scene of the crime or not; or encourages, advises, or counsels another to commit a crime is liable for the crime committed by the other party (PC 31). Accessories are defined as "Every person who, after a felony has been committed, harbors, conceals or aids a principal in such felony, with the intent that said principal may avoid or escape from arrest, trial, conviction, or punishment, having knowledge that said principal has committed such felony or has been charged with such felony or convicted thereof, is an accessory to such felony" (PC32). Accessories are charged with the distinct crime of being an accessory and can be punished by up to three years in state prison (or now, county jail). Principals are charged with the crime they participated in and are punished as if they were the direct participant or actor involved in the criminal conduct regardless of their role.

Let's look at an example to illustrate this concept. Four people, Adam, Bob, Chris, and Dave, participate in a jewelry store robbery. Adam works at the jewelry store and provides Bob and Chris with all the store policies to be followed if a robbery occurs, where the alarms are, where the video cameras are, where the keys to the jewelry cabinets and safe are kept, etc. Adam does not go to the jewelry store on the day of the robbery. Bob and Chris go to the jewelry store, and Bob goes into the store while Chris waits in the getaway car outside. Bob accomplishes the robbery, comes running out to the car, and Chris drives them both away to Dave's house where they change clothes and hide for a couple days. Adam, Bob, and Chris are equally liable for and may be convicted of robbery. Adam's conduct amounts to advising and counseling others to commit robbery; Chris's conduct amounts to participation by working as the getaway driver; and Bob's conduct was the actual robbery inside the jewelry store. Hence, all three are liable for the same crime and can be punished equally for the crime even though Adam and Chris did not go into the jewelry store and commit the actual robbery. Dave would be punished under a separate crime as an accessory because he aided and concealed the above principals with the intent that they avoid arrest and prosecution.

Procedural vs. Substantive Criminal Laws

Procedural laws dictate how the criminal justice system must operate. For example, procedural laws detail such things as when after an arrest a criminal charge must be filed or the person released; when a person must be brought to trial or the case dismissed; how much notice is required for a hearing to modify bail; timelines for a sentencing hearing if the person is convicted; etc. Substantive laws define actual crimes such as murder, rape, arson, robbery, burglary, kidnapping, etc. and their associated punishments.

Procedural Laws

Criminal procedural laws are contained throughout the California Penal Code, as well as some of the other codes. The majority of the procedural laws for criminal cases are in the Penal Code. Within the Penal Code, most of the procedural laws are in Part 2. For instance, Title 2 of Part 2 dictates how a felony complaint or indictment is filed, what is required in it, when it must be filed if the person charged is being held on bail, and so on. It also addresses the rules for misdemeanor complaints including the timeline for filing a complaint, when bail is required, when the person must be released without bail being posted, when the trial must commence, etc. Other statutes relating to procedural rules for both felony and misdemeanor crimes are scattered throughout the remainder of the Penal Code. They include things such as rules for pre-trial motions, when sentence must be pronounced if there is a conviction, the time to file a notice of appeal, and the rules governing motions for new trials.

Substantive Laws

Substantive laws are contained in many different California statutory codes. These include the Penal Code, Health and Safety Code, Business and Professions Code, Fish and Game Code, Vehicle Code, Welfare and Institutions Code, etc.

Each substantive law requires the concurrence of a volitional act, or failure to act, and a criminal mental state. The act must be voluntary and of the person's own free will. Hitting someone during an epileptic seizure is likely not a voluntary act under the criminal law. Nor would hitting someone at the demand of another who was holding a gun to the head of the would-be attacker and threatening his life if he doesn't strike the other individual. As you can see, the elements of voluntariness and free will are missing in the above examples.

The most common criminal mental states include specific intent, general intent, knowledge, recklessness, negligence, and strict liability. Specific intent requires the intent cause a particular result. An example of a specific intent crime would be first-degree murder. The specific intent to kill is required when the act that results in the death is committed. General intent only requires that the criminal act be done willfully. When a person gets into a car and drives while under the influence of alcohol that person acts with general criminal intent. It does not require any intent to violate the law (*People v. McKinnon*, 2011; West, 2011). If the mental state is knowledge, it must be shown that the actor had the actual knowledge of a particular fact, or in some states, reasonably should have known a particular fact. Knowingly possessing a controlled substance such as methamphetamine (speed) requires the actor to have knowledge the substance is methamphetamine, an illegal drug. A person acts recklessly with respect to a material element of an offense when he consciously disregards a substantial and unjustifiable risk that the material element exists or will result from his conduct (Samaha, 2011). Drag racing on a residential street and causing an accident where someone dies would be an example of this. Criminal negligence is present when a person acts without reasonable care and caution, thereby creating a risk of harm and a reasonable person would have known that acting that way would create such a risk (West, 2011). Accidentally shooting and killing someone while playing with a gun that was thought to be unloaded would be an example of involuntary manslaughter, which requires the mental state of criminal negligence. Strict liability is liability without fault. There is no mental state in the generic sense, but the law imposes liability regardless. For instance, having sex with someone who by all accounts seemed to be 18 years old or more but was not will result in criminal liability in some states. This is true even though any reasonable person would have believed the person was 18 years old or more.

California's Penal Code

The California Penal Code (PC) contains the vast majority of the criminal laws. It is organized into six "Parts" and each "Part" has several "Titles." Each "Title" contains the actual statutory sections with the individual laws. Preceding these are the "Preliminary Provisions" of the code. The actual substantive laws are generally grouped by type. These groups are the Titles and each Title has a name.

Offenses against the Sovereignty of the State

Here you will find the crime of treason in section 37 of the Penal Code. "Treason against this state consists only in levying war against it, adhering to its enemies, or giving them aid and comfort, and can be committed only by persons owing allegiance to the state. The punishment of treason shall be death or life imprisonment without possibility of parole" (PC 37). Although rarely used in modern times, you can see that this crime was very serious in the early years of our state. The punishment is the most severe available under our state law.

Crimes by and against the Executive Power of the State

This section includes crimes such as the offering or acceptance of bribes by public officers and officials, resisting and threatening public officers including law enforcement officers, and threatening or bribing school officials. Many of these crimes are felonies due to the position of trust held by public officials. An example is Penal Code section 69, which states:

> Every person who attempts, by means of any threat or violence, to deter or prevent an executive officer from performing any duty imposed upon such officer by law, or who knowingly resists, by the use of force or violence, such officer, in the performance of his duty, is punishable by a fine not exceeding ten thousand dollars ($10,000), or by imprisonment pursuant to subdivision (h) of Section 1170, or in a county jail not exceeding one year, or by both such fine and imprisonment.

This section is often used when a person threatens harm to a law enforcement officer to attempt to prevent him or her from performing a law enforcement duty. It is most commonly seen in cases involving gangs and organized crime where threats are made to harm the officer or a family member if the investigation or activity continues.

Crimes against Public Justice

Crimes such as escaping from prison, perjury, falsifying evidence, conspiracy, money laundering, and gang crimes are contained in Title 7, crimes against public justice. The crime of perjury is defined in section 118 of the Penal Code. A person can be guilty of perjury for testifying under oath to a material fact he or she knows to be false or by signing a document under oath where the person attests that its contents are true as to all material facts and they know they are not. Anyone who applies for a California driver's license must fill out an application. That application asks several questions about citizenship, age, medical issues, and so on. When the applicant signs the document, he is signing it under penalty of perjury and stating that all statements made therein are true. If it is later determined that he lied, he can be prosecuted for perjury, a felony crime punishable by imprisonment in the state prison for 2, 3, or 4 years. Perjury charges can also arise from giving false testimony under oath. Barry Bonds, former baseball great, was convicted of perjury for giving false testimony during a grand jury investigation into his use of performance-enhancing drugs. Barry Bonds was sentenced to two years of probation and 30 days house arrest, fined $4,000, and ordered to do 250 hours of community service (Brooks, 2011).

Conspiracy to commit a crime (PC 182) is another statute that falls within the scope of crimes against public justice. To be guilty of conspiracy two or more people must agree to commit a crime and must have the specific intent that the crime be committed. Many states also require that at least one member of the conspiracy commit an overt act in furtherance of the conspiracy. This overt act can be a legal act. For instance, if two people agree to rob a bank and they have the specific intent to commit the bank robbery, they may be liable for conspiracy to commit robbery. If one buys ski masks or writes a note demanding money that they intend to pass to a bank teller, either of those acts could satisfy the overt act requirement. This requirement is in place in some states to ensure the participants are serious about committing the crime they've agreed to commit. The crime is complete once the agreement, with the necessary specific intent, is reached unless the additional requirement of an overt act in furtherance of the conspiracy is necessary. The criminal act is the agreement and the mental state is the specific intent that the crime be committed. Conspiracy is punishable as if the crime the participants conspired to commit was actually completed. Hence, conspiracy to commit robbery is punished the same as a completed robbery is even though the crime of conspiracy may be compete long before the actual robbery would ever take place. Conspiracy is a very powerful criminal law for a prosecutor when two or more people put their heads together for a criminal endeavor.

Crimes against the Person

The crimes against the person section comes next in the penal code's structure. The section begins with homicide and includes crimes such as mayhem, robbery, kidnapping, aggravated assault, and battery. Murder is contained in Penal Code section 187(a), which states: "Murder is the unlawful killing of a human being, or a fetus, with malice aforethought." Murder is divided into first- and second-degree murder. Almost all first-degree murders may be punishable by the death penalty in California (PC 190.2). Examples of first-degree murders include murders that are willful, deliberate, and premeditated, or committed by poisoning, lying in wait, killing multiple people, and using a bomb or other destructive device. Murdering police officers, firefighters, and other classes of people may also fit into the statutory definition of first-degree murder. All murders that do not meet the statutory definition of first-degree murder are considered second-degree murder (PC 189).

In 2002, Laci Peterson, who was eight months pregnant, went missing from her Modesto, California, home. The stories given by her husband, Scott Peterson, during his interviews with the police and media conflicted. On April 14, 2003, the remains of a fetus washed ashore in the San Francisco Bay near where Scott had been boating on the day of Laci's disappearance. A partial female body washed ashore in the same area the next day. The remains were identified as those of Laci Peterson and her unborn fetus. Scott Peterson was charged with the murder of Laci Peterson and the fetus. The trial began in June 2004 and lasted seven months. At the conclusion, the jury convicted Scott Peterson of first-degree murder with special circumstances because he killed both Laci and the fetus. On December 13, 2004, the same jury recommended the sentence of death for Scott Peterson. Many pieces of circumstantial evidence pointed to Scott's guilt and the culmination of all the evidence was enough to convince 12 jurors beyond a reasonable doubt that Scott Peterson was guilty of murder.

In 2012, California voters enacted Proposition 35, known as the Californians Against Sexual Exploitation (CASE) Act. This act prescribed long prison sentences, including life sentences, for forced labor, including sex. "Pimps," who force prostitutes to work for them and sell their bodies for money that is then given to the "pimp," are frequently prosecuted under these new statutes and receive anywhere from five years to life in state prison. This body of law can be found in section 236.1 of the Penal Code.

Crimes against the Person Involving Sexual Assault and Crimes against Public Decency and Good Morals

The statutes in this Title include rape, oral copulation, sodomy, sexual crimes against children, child pornography, spousal abuse, elder abuse, and indecent exposure. Rape is an act of sexual intercourse with a person not the spouse of the perpetrator and without the consent of the person (PC 261(a)). There are many ways to accomplish the crime of rape. One is to use force or threat of force against the victim. Another is when the person is unable to resist because she's/he's been drugged in some way. Also, sexual intercourse with a person who does not have the capacity to consent due to mental illness or infirmity would constitute rape (PC 261(a)(1)—(a)(7)). These same circumstances would satisfy other sexual assault statutes such as oral copulation and sodomy as well.

Where the victim is under 18 years of age, he or she is incapable of giving legal consent as a matter of law. This means sexual acts with persons under 18 years of age are criminal, even if they agreed to them and initiated them. The factors listed above for accomplishing sexual crimes become aggravating factors when minors are involved and result in longer prison sentences.

Domestic violence has become more prevalent in the law in the last three decades. Statutes have been enacted for crimes of violence committed against a spouse, cohabitant, mother or father of the perpetrator's child, or persons who have or have had a dating relationship (PC 13700). There are now statutes that make it a felony to commit a domestic battery and cause a visible injury or traumatic condition (PC 273.5(a)). Further, domestic batteries with no visible injuries are punished more severely when a legally recognized domestic relationship exists. In addition, convicted offenders are required to attend a year-long domestic violence batter's treatment program as a condition of his or her sentence (PC 1203.097).

Crimes against Property

Crimes against property is the next large area of criminal laws in the Penal Code. This section includes crimes such as burglary, forgery, theft, and vandalism among many others. Crimes against property account for the largest percentage of crimes seen in the criminal justice system. Further, with the enactment of Proposition 47 in 2014, many former felony or wobbler theft crimes are now misdemeanors and the value to determine a potential felony has risen to $950.

This value determination effects crimes such a forgery and credit card/identity theft in addition to general larceny.

Burglary is defined in general terms as the entry of a building or locked motor vehicle with the specific intent to commit theft or any felony inside (PC 459). The crime of burglary is complete at the moment of entry with the requisite specific intent. Nothing need be taken nor any felony actually committed once inside. However, it can be difficult to prove the intent of the perpetrator if he or she has not moved toward completion of his or her objective once inside. In California there are two degrees of burglary. First-degree burglary is burglary of a residence, certain vessels, and certain inhabited buildings. All other burglaries are second-degree burglary (PC 460).

Forgery is defined as signing the name of another or a fictitious person to a long list of writings and legal instruments with the intent to defraud (PC 470). When a person signs his or her name to a legal instrument, he or she is taking on certain legal rights and duties. A breach of any of the duties can subject the person to civil or criminal liability. This crime has become much more prevalent as society has evolved into its current complex system of legal contracts and other instruments.

Identity theft has become a huge area of concern with the proliferation of electronic payments and the internet. It is the crime most often committed in the United States (Samaha, 2011). California has enacted laws making different forms of identity theft wobblers. The primary crime of identity theft is defined as obtaining personal identifying information of another person, and using that information for any unlawful purpose, including obtaining, or attempting to obtain, credit, goods, services, real property, or medical information without the consent of that person (PC 530.5). The damage to victims of identity theft can be devastating. There are more than 17 million annual identity theft victims across the nation, a third of whom reported experiencing moderate to severe emotional distress (Harrell, 2015).

Theft, or larceny, is an ancient crime that has had many names. The most common is stealing. As society became more complex, new types of theft crimes evolved. These include theft of intellectual property, embezzlement, theft by false pretenses, and so forth (Samaha, 2011). Theft is defined as the taking and carrying away of the personal property of another without their consent and with the specific intent to permanently deprive the person of their property (PC 484). Larceny is currently divided into two types—grand theft and petty theft. Grand theft is the taking of property over a certain value or the taking of specific items such as firearms, cars, certain animals, and livestock (PC 487). If the theft does not satisfy the definition of grand theft, it is petty theft (PC 488).

Maliciously damaging, destroying, or defacing another's property with graffiti is the crime of vandalism (PC 594). The amount of damage or loss determines whether the vandalism may be charged as a misdemeanor or felony. Any vandalism with damage or loss of $400 dollars is considered a felony. Also, vandalism of certain buildings such as churches or synagogues may be charged as felonies no matter the damage or loss (PC 594.3(a)). In addition, any conviction for the crime of vandalism can result in a one-year suspension of the perpetrator's driver's license. Also, if the vandalism is graffiti, a certain number of hours doing community service in the form of graffiti clean-up and removal may be imposed in addition to the jail and fines available to the sentencing judge.

Control of Deadly Weapons

This group of statutes makes criminal such things as manufacturing or possessing certain dangerous and deadly weapons, possessing firearms that are loaded or concealed in public, manufacturing or possessing explosive devices, and possession of firearms and ammunition by persons prohibited from doing so. These statutes also include *enhancements*, which increase the punishment when crimes are committed using a gun or other deadly weapon.

All persons convicted of a felony crime are prohibited from possessing any type of firearm (PC 29800(a)(1)). Convicted felons are also prohibited from possessing any ammunition for firearms (PC 30305(a)(1)). In addition, persons convicted of certain misdemeanor crimes such as battery, spousal abuse, and criminal threats are prohibited from possessing firearms (PC 29805). Further, persons on probation for any crime they were convicted of and persons who are the restrained party in any type of court issued restraining order, are prohibited from possessing any firearm during the time they are on probation or the court order is in effect.

People with no criminal history are also the subject of deadly weapons laws. All persons who possess a concealable firearm concealed on their person or in their vehicle in a public place are guilty of a crime (PC 25400(a)). All persons who possess any loaded firearm in a public place are guilty of a crime as well (PC 25850(a)). Concealable firearms are commonly pistols and other handguns, but rifles and shotguns with the stock and/or barrel made shorter such that the firearm is small enough to be capable of being concealed on the person would also qualify. There are also several exemptions to this set of statutes. Some of these are peace officers, persons with valid concealed weapons permits, and federal officers. Also, any person may carry a loaded and/or concealed firearm in his or her home or business, in certain geographical areas designated for hunting and shooting, and at shooting ranges.

The California Penal Code is full of substantive criminal laws. Those addressed here are but a small part of the sum total contained in the penal code. The penal code has a table of contents and an index to assist with finding statutes covering various conduct that has been made criminal.

Additional California Criminal Laws

Health and Safety Code

The Health and Safety Code is primarily a set of regulatory statutes that govern many things. Some areas covered by this statutory scheme are emergency medical services, pest abatement, sanitation, cemeteries and dead bodies, illegal drugs, explosives, and other areas that concern public health and safety.

The largest area of criminal statutes in this code addresses the manufacturing, sale, and possession of illegal drugs. The most common drugs included are cocaine, heroin, methamphetamine, ecstasy, phencyclidine (PCP), lysergic acid diethylamide (LSD), and marijuana. With limited exceptions, it is illegal to possess, possess with the intent to sell, sell, and manufacture or grow the above listed illegal drugs.

A major change in this set of laws occurred in 1996 and addressed the possession and cultivation of marijuana. The changes were brought about by the passing of Proposition 215, the Compassionate Use Act, by California voters in 1996. These changes in the law made it legal to possess and cultivate marijuana for medical purposes under California statute. There were several requirements to make the possession and cultivation of marijuana legal in California, but the proposition was still flawed. Federal law prohibited, and still prohibits, the possession and cultivation of marijuana. Since federal law preempts state law, persons who possess or cultivate marijuana may still be criminally prosecuted in the federal court system. In 2011, Governor Schwarzenegger signed legislation that reduced the crime of marijuana possession (less than one ounce) from a misdemeanor to an infraction, thereby decriminalizing this behavior in California.

In 2016, the possession of less than one ounce of marijuana by a person over age 21 became legal via Proposition 64, which was enacted by the voters. It also made the sale of marijuana legal when certain requirements were met. Marijuana smoking in public places has the same restrictions as cigarette smoking in public and driving under the influence of marijuana is still a crime.

In 2014, the voters passed Proposition 47, which reduced simple possession of controlled substances including heroin and cocaine to misdemeanors, among other things. The illegality of drugs such as those listed above remains a public controversy in this state. Advocates for both sides argue their respective positions for or against the legalization of such drugs. The future continues to move toward legalization of controlled substances. Only time will tell if this trend continues on its current path.

Business and Professions Code

The Business and Professions Code is also a highly regulatory body of statutes. However, it also contains some criminal statutes. For instance, there are several statutes that govern the illegal dispensing and possessing of certain prescription drugs. Also, it contains statutes that make criminal the unlawful possession of prescription tablets, forged and altered prescriptions, forgery of doctor signatures on prescriptions, etc. Further, there are statutes that control the sale and distribution of beverages containing alcohol and products containing tobacco. This code also governs the licensing of attorneys, doctors, real estate agents, and dentists, to name a few. The statutes make it unlawful to practice law, medicine, sell real estate, or cut hair without the appropriate license from the listed governing administrative agency.

Fish and Game Code

The Fish and Game Code is another set of statutes that are predominantly regulatory. This code covers such things as licensing for fishing and hunting, seasonal restrictions, limits on the number of fish or other animals that may be taken in a given time period by each person, the weapons that may be used for hunting, and when each type of weapon may be used. The code also proscribes what areas certain activities may occur in, as some areas are protected by state and federal laws. Also, state and federal laws protect some mammals, birds, and other wildlife as well.

Criminal violations of this code usually occur with respect to licensing and restrictions. For instance, it is illegal to hunt deer outside of the designated hunting season. Further, it is illegal to trap or catch lobster outside of lobster season. As for fishing, some fish require a special license before you can keep them. Some have a limit on how many of a particular type of fish can be caught and kept each day by an individual. There are also size limits for the keeping of some fish and other hunted creatures. Violations of any of these statutes can result in criminal liability, including fines and jail.

Although any law enforcement officer may enforce the Fish and Game Code, there are actual Fish and Game Officers employed by the Department of Fish and Game. They have police powers and patrol the hunting and fishing areas to enforce these laws. They have the power to issue citations, collect evidence, and arrest violators just like other law enforcement officers. Further, these crimes are prosecuted in the same criminal courts that prosecute other crimes such as theft, robbery, and murder.

Vehicle Code

The California Vehicle Code covers all things related to vehicles, including licensing and regulations for the equipment and maintenance of vehicles. Vehicles include cars, commercial trucks, motorcycles, off-road vehicles, boats, ships and other vessels, mobile homes, and planes. The California Vehicle Code is a mix of regulatory statutes and substantive criminal statutes. These statutes are designed to foster the safe operation of vehicles on the highways, roadways, and waterways of this state. Although enforced by all law enforcement officers, the agency most familiar with the enforcement of the Vehicle Code is the California Highway Patrol. This section will focus on the substantive criminal statutes.

As one might suspect, almost all traffic violations are contained in the vehicle code. Hence, driving without a license, driving on a suspended license, speeding, failing to stop at a stop sign or red light, failing to signal when turning, and having a light malfunctioning during darkness are some examples of statutory violations. Most crimes of this type are called infractions and are punishable only by a fine. Also, many violations relating to equipment malfunctions, often called "fix-it tickets," must simply be corrected and signed off by appropriate law enforcement personnel as fixed.

The California Vehicle Code (VC) also contains crimes classified as misdemeanors and felonies. Driving under the influence of alcohol or drugs and causing injury to someone as a result is an example of a felony violation (VC 23153(a)). Other examples of felony violations of this code include auto theft (VC 10851), evading police in a grossly negligent manner (VC 2800.2), falsifying vehicle registration documents (VC 4463(a)), and driving under the influence of alcohol or drugs with prior convictions within 10 years (VC 23550.5). Examples of misdemeanor violations of this code include driving while your license is suspended (VC 14601), failing to obey a traffic officer's directions (VC 2800(a)), engaging in a speed contest (also called drag racing) (VC 23109(a)), and reckless driving (VC 23103). Felony violations can be punished by imprisonment in the state prison and misdemeanor violations by imprisonment in the county jails as well as fines, license suspension or revocation, mandatory community service, and so on.

Welfare and Institutions Code

The California Welfare and Institutions Code primarily addresses mental health issues and juveniles.Although it has a large body of regulatory statutes, it also contains procedural and sentencing laws for juveniles who commit crimes (WIC Part I). These rules are specific to juvenile proceedings in juvenile court.

Welfare fraud crimes are also contained within the Welfare and Institutions Code. These crimes target those who fraudulently collect welfare supported by your tax dollars that they are not legally entitled to. They also punish those who perjure themselves on applications to receive welfare from the county or state (WIC 10980). The conduct and/or the amount of welfare money and services obtained by fraud determines whether the violation is a felony or a misdemeanor. There are special investigators who target these violators and many county prosecuting agencies have special units that handle the criminal prosecution in these cases. Sentencing for this crime always involves restitution. However, many violators will never have the means to repay the money they fraudulently obtained.

Other Statutory Codes

Many of the other statutory codes also have criminal statutes in them, although the number of such statutes is far less than the codes discussed above. Codes such as the Education Code, Tax and Revenue Code, Insurance Code, Corporations Code, and so on each have some criminal statutes specific to those subject matters. Often, there are special investigators assigned to the Department of Education, State Franchise Tax Board, Department of Insurance, and Department of Corporations who investigate those specific violations. Ultimately, those cases are brought to the prosecuting authority if appropriate and charges may be filed if there is sufficient evidence of a violation.

Conclusion

As you can see, there is a large amount of criminal legislation throughout the various statutory codes. The statutes reach a wide variety of conduct across many subject matters. The goal of the criminal law is to find a balance between individual liberties and social order. Without law, society would be survival of the fittest. Yet, in the United States, the Constitution provides people with certain rights in their relationship with the government. This balance is a constant target and it moves dynamically as societies change. The ultimate goal is to regulate conduct so that each person can live the life they want and yet not interfere with the lives others want to live. It is a goal constantly strived for, but yet to be achieved.

Key Terms and Definitions

Accessories—Persons who, with knowledge that a felony was committed, aid or assist a principle in avoiding arrest or prosecution, or who hide, conceal or destroy evidence.

Aiders and Abettors—Persons who are not the direct participants of a crime, but whoaid, encourage, facilitate, procure or assist in the commission of a crime before or during the crime.

Beyond a Reasonable Doubt—The standard of proof used in criminal cases for purposes of conviction. It requires the trier of fact to have an abiding conviction in the truth of the charge but does not require proof beyond all doubt because all things are subject to some possible or imaginary doubt.

Civil—That branch of law that pertains to suits outside of criminal practice, pertaining to the rights and duties of persons in contract, tort, real estate, etc.

Code of Civil Procedure—The body of statutory laws that defines all the rules for civil actions from the filing of such actions through the trial, award of judgment and appeal of the lawsuit.

Criminal—An act done with malicious intent, from an evil nature, or with a wrongful disposition to harm or injure other persons or property; also, laws, procedures and sanctions enforced, litigated and punished by the government.

Felonies—The more serious crimes where the punishment includes incarceration in a state prison or penitentiary for one year or more.

Misdemeanors—Less serious crimes punishable by fines or incarceration in a county jail not exceeding one year.

Penal Code—That body of statutory codes where criminal law, procedure and punishment are defined and proscribed.

Plebiscite—A vote by all eligible people in a given jurisdiction on a political issue or law.

Preponderance of the Evidence—The standard of proof commonly used for findings in civil cases. It requires the trier of fact to find the evidence on one side of an issue is more convincing than the evidence on the other.

Principles—Those participants, who directly participate, aid, encourage, facilitate, procure or assist in the commission of a crime before or during the crime. However, a principle need not be present at the scene of a crime.

Propositions—Changes to laws or enactment of new laws directly by the voters at an election in a state that allows for such.

Procedural Laws—The statutory laws that control how a lawsuit or criminal prosecution is adjudicated including pleading, process, evidence and practice.

Substantive Laws—The laws that create, define, and regulate the rights and duties of parties in a case or controversy and which may give rise to a cause of action or criminal proceeding.

Wobblers—Crimes that can be punished as felonies or misdemeanors depending on a variety of aggravating and mitigating factors.

Internet Websites

Find Law (Thomson Reuters): www.findlaw.com
California Laws and Legislative Information: http://leginfo.legislature.ca.gov/
California Courts: http://www.courts.ca.gov/
U.S. Supreme Court: www.supremecourt.gov/

Review Questions

1. What are the main differences between criminal and civil law?
2. What are the different classifications/levels of crimes in California?
3. How many statutory codes does California have?
4. What are the different parties to crime?
5. What is the difference between procedural law and substantive law?
6. What are three examples of crimes against property?
7. What statutory code contains the illegal controlled substances laws?

Critical Thinking Questions

1. Go to https://ballotpedia.org/California_Proposition_215,_the_Medical_ Marijuana_Initiative_(1996) and read the text of Proposition 215 (Compassionate Use Act). Then read the arguments for and against it. Can you re-write or modify the language of the act so it requires the same checks and balances as other prescription drugs? (i.e. doctor review at regular intervals, controlled amounts being dispensed by licensed pharmacy, etc.) Should it be that way?

2. Weapons laws limit or prohibit weapon possession by many classes of persons including convicted felons, certain convicted misdemeanants and others. Should all firearms be banned? Would such a ban violate the 2nd Amendment of the United States Constitution?

3. In some cases, does the "Three Strikes" law cause the administration of cruel and unusual punishment under the 8th Amendment of the United States Constitution? Should the law require a third serious or violent felony before the offender is subjected to sentence of 25 years to life in prison? What would you say to the victim of that third serious or violent felony? See also, http://www.oyez.org/cases/2000-2009/2002/2002_01_6978 and http://www.law.cornell.edu/supct/html/01-1127.ZO.html for a discussion of this issue.

References

Brooks, M. (2011, December 16). Barry Bonds obstruction of justice sentence: 30 days house arrest, 2 years of probation. *Washington Post*. Retrieved from http://www.washingtonpost.com/blogs/early-lead/post/barry-bonds-perjury-sentence-30-days-of-house-arrest-2-years-of-probation/2011/12/16/gIQAoFemyO_blog.html

Harrell, E. (2015, September). *Victims of identity theft, 2014*. Washington, DC: USDOJ, Bureau of Justice Statistics. Retrieved from https://www.bjs.gov/index.cfm?ty=pbdetail&iid=5408

Samaha, J. (2011). *Criminal law* (10th ed.). Belmont, CA: Wadsworth Publishing.

West. (2011). *California criminal jury instruction, section 580*. Thomson Reuters.

West. (2017). *California penal code*. Thomson Reuters.

Cases Cited

People v. McKinnon, 52 Cal.4th 610 (2011)

Appendix 4A

California Statutory Code

1. Business and Professions Code
2. Civil Code
3. Code of Civil Procedure
4. Commercial Code
5. Corporations Code
6. Education Code
7. Elections Code
8. Evidence Code
9. Family Code
10. Financial Code
11. Fish and Game Code
12. Food and Agricultural Code
13. Government Code
14. Harbors and Navigation Code
15. Health and Safety Code
16. Insurance Code
17. Labor Code
18. Military and Veterans Code
19. Penal Code
20. Probate Code
21. Public Contract Code
22. Public Resources Code
23. Public Utilities Code
24. Revenue and Taxation Code
25. Streets and Highways Code
26. Unemployment Insurance Code
27. Vehicle Code
28. Water Code
29. Welfare and Institutions Code

Chapter 5

Policing in California

Sigrid Williams and Christine L. Gardiner

Learning Objectives

After reading the chapter, students should be able to:

- Identify the historical changes in California law enforcement.
- Understand the different law enforcement agencies and organizations in California.
- Explain the professionalization and training required of California law enforcement personnel.
- Discuss current trends and other issues in law enforcement.

Policing is the most visible aspect of the criminal justice system and the one that most people will have some contact with during their lifetime, either as a victim or a law-breaker (or both). We are all basically familiar with the police function, but are often less clear on how agencies differ from one another. This chapter describes the history of policing in California from the earliest "official" law enforcement agencies to present day. Then it explains the responsibilities and jurisdiction of law enforcement agencies at the local (city and county), state, and federal levels. Next, professionalization and training are discussed. Finally, the chapter concludes with a conversation about other issues, such as use of force, ethics, and technology.

The Changing Scenery of California Law Enforcement

1847–1900s

James Marshall discovered gold at Sutter's Mill in Coloma on January 24, 1848. The resulting Gold Rush brought some 300,000 immigrants from around the U.S. and surrounding regions, as well as crime and disorder, to the territory known as California (Siskiyou County, n.d.). The rise of crime and disorder presented new challenges and several groups stepped up to keep peace in the region. In the mid-late 1800s, there were four groups that assumed responsibility for law enforcement in California: (1) U.S. Marshals, (2) private citizens, (3) businessmen, and (4) town police officers and/or county sheriff's deputies. Prior to the establishment of municipal, county, and state law enforcement agencies, U.S. Marshals enforced laws in many California towns and counties. However, they only had jurisdiction over federal crimes, such as mail theft, crimes against railroad property, and murder on federal lands. As a result, many crimes went unpunished by the authorities.

The first *statewide* agency with a legally mandated law enforcement purpose in California was the *California State Rangers*. This agency, which existed for a mere three months (from May 28, 1853, to August 28, 1853), was created by the state legislature to "capture the party or gang of robbers commanded by the five Juaquin" (Military Museum, n.d., paragraph 6). Twenty men were hired for the task. They were paid $150 per month and had to supply all of their own equipment, including horses, weapons, and ammunition. The men, led by Captain Harry S. Love, captured their targets after two months, were paid a handsome reward (on top of their salary), and then were disbanded (Military Museum, n.d.). For 34 years California operated without a state-level law enforcement agency. In 1887, however, the California State Rangers were resurrected (and were renamed the California State Police) when the state legislature appointed two rangers to protect the capitol (California Senate, n.d.; Statutes of California, 1887).[1]

The first *municipal* law enforcement agencies in California formed even before California was admitted as the 31st state. As the state's first municipal law enforcement agency, the San Francisco Police Department has roots that date to 1847, when local merchants hired men to protect their interests from outlaws in the seedy and crime-ridden Barbary Coast section of the city (San Francisco Patrol Special Police, n.d.). In August 1849, San Francisco's police department became "official" with one captain, one deputy chief, three sergeants, and 30 officers (Ackerson & Tully, n.d.). In the same year, Sacramento and San Jose also established police departments (Sacramento Police Department, n.d.; San Jose Police Department, n.d.a).

Once California was granted statehood in 1850, every county was required by law to elect a sheriff. That year, 20 (of the original 27) counties established

---

1. The California State Police eventually merged with the California Highway Patrol in 1995 (California Highway Patrol [CHP], n.d.a).

sheriff's departments.[2] The term "*sheriff*" refers to the person elected to enforce laws in a given county while the term "*chief*" or "*marshal*" refers to the person appointed (hired) to enforce laws in a given city or town. In the early days, sheriff's and chief's duties varied by charter and often included, (1) collecting taxes; (2) apprehending, jailing, and transporting criminals; and (3) providing specified community services. Some police chiefs (originally called marshals) and sheriffs were paid a salary while others were paid a percentage of the taxes/fees/rewards they collected (Ackerson & Tully, n.d.; Los Angeles Police Department [LAPD], n.d.a; Los Angeles Sheriff's Department [LASD], n.d.). This incentivized officers (and sheriffs paid on a tax basis) to spend considerably more time on income-generating activities than on other (non-income-generating) crime control or peacekeeping activities.

During this period, law enforcement agencies were very small (in comparison to today's West Coast standards). For example, Los Angeles County Sheriff's Department had one sheriff and two officers to patrol 383 square miles in 1850 (LASD, n.d.). For this reason, officers relied on support from citizens in the community to identify and apprehend perpetrators (Ackerson & Tully, n.d.; SJPD, n.d.a; San Luis Obispo Police Department [SLOPD], n.d.). The relationship between the police and the public, however, was not straightforward, nor always supportive. It was common practice for officers (and administrators) to take bribes and ignore crimes committed by certain individuals. Charges of corruption, and even criminal wrongdoing, were levied against officers in California and throughout the United States. In response, citizens in many California communities formed "vigilance committees" to administer law and order when the local government was believed to be unable or unwilling to do so[3] (Ackerson & Tully, n.d.; SLOPD, n.d.).

Officers at this time had neither training nor uniforms. They usually supplied their own equipment, often had no "office," and served at the whim of the executive (marshal, chief, or sheriff) (Ackerson & Tully, n.d.; LAPD, n.d.a). This last issue was especially problematic because sheriffs and chiefs/marshals were typically elected (or appointed) to one-year terms and when the chief was replaced, so too were his officers. The election cycle in most counties was extended to two years (and eventually four years) in the late 1800s–early 1900s

---

2. The 20 counties that established sheriff's departments in 1850 are: Butte, Calaveras, Contra Costa, El Dorado, Los Angeles, Mariposa, Monterey, Napa, Sacramento, San Diego, San Francisco, San Joaquin, San Luis Obispo, Santa Barbara, Santa Clara, Santa Cruz, Sonoma, Sutter, Tuolumne, and Yolo.

3. The first known vigilance committee in California was formed in "Pueblo de Los Angeles" in 1836 (California Department of Justice, n.d.).

but that offered only slightly more job stability (Ackerson & Tully, n.d.; LASD, n.d.). Not all officers, however, were subject to post-election replacement. Some agencies, such as San Francisco Police Department, stipulated that officers were to be removed for cause only (for example, breaking a rule) (Ackerson & Tully, n.d.).

1900s–1980s

As the industrial revolution gained momentum and cities throughout the state experienced massive population growth, departments grew in number and developed innovative ideas to improve and professionalize police services, especially as agencies began to perform more law enforcement functions. The Volstead Act of 1919 (Prohibition) was the first time that police officers were required to enforce a moral law that was actively resisted by members of the public. It also spawned citizen contempt of law enforcement and magnified corruption amongst rank-and-file officers. The 1930s brought civil uprisings, labor protests, and riots marked by violence, as well as a large number of transients, shanty towns (homeless encampments), and altercations at soup kitchens. Police officers were challenged to contain large, frequent, and often violent riots. At the same time, many police departments in California served as "reluctant relief agencies" (Starr, 1996, p. 227), providing food and shelter to unemployed residents (and migrants) during the Great Depression.

Starting in the Progressive Era, California led the police professionalization movement. Los Angeles Police Department (LAPD), for example, hired the first female special patrol officer in 1910 to patrol popular juvenile spots (penny arcades, skating rinks, dance halls, movie theaters, etc.) (LAPD, n.d.b); Alice Stebbins Wells gained national publicity and by 1916, 16 other cities across the country had hired policewomen for similar purposes. Also, *August Vollmer*, chief of Berkeley Police Department from 1909 to 1932[4] and considered the "father of modern policing," invented many devices and instituted policies that revolutionized policing. For example, he was the first in the country to introduce motor patrols in 1914, and he created the first scientific crime lab in 1916 (which included the first fingerprint repository and eventually the first lie detector) (Lasley, Hooper, & Dery, 2001). He developed a call box network (system of red lights hung on intersections) to alert officers to emergency situations, centralized police records, streamlined criminal investigations by

---

4. He took a one-year leave-of-absence from 1923–1924 to serve as police chief and reform the Los Angeles Police Department (Wilson, 1953).

classifying cases based on modus operandi, collected and used fingerprints to identify suspects, and established entrance exams for police recruits (Peak, 2009). He consulted with scores of police departments across the country to root out corruption, raise personnel standards, and improve operating practices (Wilson, 1953). He also served as police consultant to President Hoover's *Wickersham Commission* from 1929 to 1931. The commission, which spurred the movement to reform law enforcement, recommended that the selection, education, and training of officers be improved and that the management of personnel and resources be reoriented so as to be more efficient and effective at controlling crime; many of Vollmer's progressive ideas were represented throughout the report, which he helped author.

Schools specializing in law enforcement courses were integral to creating the educated and professional police force that leaders envisioned. Towards this end, August Vollmer founded a law enforcement training program at the University of California at Berkeley (UCB) in 1916. He also convinced T. W. MacQuarrie, president of State Teachers College at San Jose (now known as San Jose State University [SJSU]), of the need for a police training school. In 1930, SJSU became the first university in the nation to offer a two-year college police program that led to an associate's degree in police training[5] (San Jose State University, 2005).

Continuing Vollmer's tradition of excellence and influence, *O. W. Wilson*, police chief of Fullerton Police Department and dean of University of California at Berkeley's School of Criminology (among other esteemed positions), revolutionized police administration throughout the United States with the publication of his book, *Police Administration*, in 1943. Under his system, law enforcement agencies organized themselves along military lines with a distinct chain of command.

Another Californian who made a permanent mark on law enforcement in the United States was *William H. Parker*, chief of LAPD from 1950–1966. Parker, a controversial leader who coined the term "the thin blue line" to indicate the integral role police play in sustaining order over chaos, inherited a department filled with corruption. Determined to eliminate corruption and professionalize the LAPD, he reorganized and simplified the agency's organizational structure from the bottom up. He focused on administrative oversight (rather than political oversight), initiated a positive public relations campaign, increased the requirements for trainees, implemented a standardized

---

5. In 1936, the college added a four-year police science program that led to a B.A. (San Jose State University, 2005).

police academy, encouraged proactive law enforcement tactics, reduced foot patrols, and reassigned officers to motor patrol in accordance to Wilson's ideas (LAPD, n.d.a; Vila & Morris, 1999). As a result, he remade the image and job of a police officer to be that of a professional crime fighter and turned the LAPD into a model of reform.

Both society and policing changed dramatically in the 1960s. The U.S. Supreme Court ruled on several key cases that fundamentally and forever altered the methods used by police to investigate and control crime, and expanded and made clear the due process rights afforded to suspects. One of the repercussions of the professionalization movement and its reliance on motor patrol was that police officers became removed from the public. This distance made solving crimes more difficult and intensified tensions between police officers and community members. This hostility, which was most visible during the anti-war demonstrations, civil rights protests, and race riots in the 1960s, led to the assembly of two separate commissions to examine law enforcement practices throughout the United States. The *President's Commission on Law Enforcement* in 1967 offered 200 suggestions to improve the criminal justice system in the United States, including that police (the most "visible representatives of society") should communicate more openly with the public and that sweeping reforms were necessary as the situation was at a "critical level." The second commission, the Kerner Commission, issued a scathing report that concluded that the police were partly to blame for the urban race riots of the 1960s, including those in Watts, California (National Advisory Commission on Civil Disorders, 1968).

Based loosely on the recommendations of the President's Commission on Law Enforcement, the *Omnibus Crime Control and Safe Streets Act of 1968* (OCCSSA) created the Law Enforcement Assistance Administration (LEAA) to provide federal funds to municipal law enforcement agencies for criminal justice services, and made money available for criminal justice research, including weed and seed studies conducted in California cities. As a result of funding made available through the OCCSSA, we have learned much about what works and what doesn't work in policing. It is also a main reason criminal justice developed as an academic discipline. One of the advances made possible by this funding was the institution of a nationwide 911 emergency number system in the 1970s.

1980s–Present

Research funded by the OCCSSA revealed that rapid response to calls for service and random patrols, the hallmarks of professional policing, were not effective crime prevention strategies. This knowledge, combined with the discontent expressed by many communities toward law enforcement, caused departments to look for alternative models of policing in the 1980s and 1990s. Community-oriented policing (COP) and problem-oriented policing (POP) became the new paradigms embraced by innovative police agencies across the nation. Several California agencies were at the forefront of this movement. The Santa Ana Police Department, one of the first agencies in the nation to embrace team policing, has been recognized as a leader in COP since 1984 (Skolnick & Bayley, 1986; Boettcher, 1995). A recent study that found 93% of California law enforcement agencies ascribe to a community policing philosophy (Gardiner, 2012). Not surprisingly, California law enforcement agencies have received more POP (Herman Goldstein) Awards for inventive projects than any other state in the nation (Center for Problem-Oriented Policing [CPOP], n.d.).

In addition to a renewed focus on community–police relations, the later part of the twentieth century brought new technology that profoundly, and permanently, changed the job of police officers. Gone are the days when officers had to type their police reports manually on a typewriter (the 1980s!). Now many officers simply upload their reports from their patrol car, as most cars are equipped with laptops as well as encrypted radios that allow communication between different agencies, GPS devices, laser technology, license plate readers, and in-dash cameras. This is quite a change from the standard-issue map book and notepad carried by patrol officers prior to the 1990s. These powerful computers allow law enforcement agencies to digitize, map, and share police reports; identify criminals; and prevent and solve crimes.

Automated license plate readers affixed to patrol cars, for example, automatically read and run license plates for wanted and stolen vehicles (up to 4,000 per shift!). Officers in the field also have ready access to state and local databases on their smart phones using California's JusticeMobile app. Some agencies (such as Los Angeles Police Department) are using gunshot detectors that alert police when shots have been fired from a location. Following the Long Beach Police Department's lead, agencies are developing partnerships with local businesses that allow officers and dispatchers to view the business's surveillance cameras live over the Internet (this can be particularly helpful when responding to a serious in-progress call). Fingerprints and DNA requests are computerized and emergent requests through the Combined DNA Index System (CODIS) can be returned in as few as three to four weeks. Not only are agencies using technology to improve crime detection and clearance rates, they are using it to communicate and connect with residents (Facebook, Instagram, Twitter, Nextdoor, and Snapchat are the most common). These applications allow agencies to quickly broadcast events and incidents to heighten public awareness. They also can increase positive media attention and minimize negative publicity. These technological advances have improved law enforcement's ability to detect, analyze, predict, and solve crimes and have given birth to intelligence-led policing and the professional crime analyst (as well as other specialized support positions).

In addition to aiding law enforcement in detecting crimes and capturing criminals, technology has been used, both intentionally and unintentionally, to bring about change in law enforcement. For example, Californians have become accustomed to watching police events play out on live television since the early 1990s. A defining moment in law enforcement came when a bystander recorded Rodney King being beaten by several officers of the Los Angeles Police Department in 1991. While this may not have been the first time that someone recorded police officers acting badly, it was highly important and marked a new era in policing in which members of the public and media are increasingly armed with portable recording devices (mostly smart phones). These devices are so common now, twenty-five years later, that at least 20 California law enforcement agencies have responded by requiring officers to wear body-worn cameras on their person to capture the officer's perspective and to protect all stakeholders from false accounts of police encounters.

The volume of videos capturing questionable officer behavior during police–community member interactions over the past five years has sparked renewed interest in police accountability and a call for transparency, adherence to procedural justice principles, and an overall shift toward democratic policing (Gardiner & Hickman, 2017). Like elsewhere, California police chiefs have been expected to (1) hold officers accountable for their conduct, (2) report low crime rates (AB109/"Realignment" and Proposition 47 relieved some of this pressure), and (3) contain public safety costs (especially overtime, especially since the Great Recession) (Stone & Travis, 2011). In addition to using early warning systems and other mechanisms to identify potential problem officers and training needs, many departments in California have issued officers body-worn cameras to improve accountability and transparency. Other departments have made this optional wherein police officers can purchase their own body camera.

Another thing that profoundly changed policing in the twenty-first century is the 9/11 terrorist attacks on the World Trade Center. Specifically, there is now a greater emphasis on homeland security and intelligence gathering and sharing. It is now a priority for federal, state, and local agencies to share both intelligence and the responsibility for protecting critical infrastructure and information. To support this effort, there are six *regional intelligence centers* (a.k.a. *fusion centers*), in California; two in Sacramento and one each in San

Francisco, Norwalk, Santa Ana, and San Diego.[6] This is more than any other state except Texas and indicates just how many potential targets there are in the Golden State (DHS, 2017). California, like other states, has also witnessed increased police militarization over the past twenty years as agencies strive to have the most powerful tools (including acquisition of surplus military equipment and the proliferation of SWAT-like tactical teams).

California Law Enforcement Agencies and Organizations

Law enforcement agencies and organizations in California focus their attention on and engage in (1) maintaining order, (2) deterring crime, (3) investigating crimes which have occurred, (4) apprehending criminals, and/or (5) providing other miscellaneous services which have been incorporated into the police role. Police officers' specific duties and how they perform them depend on the size and type of their agency. In California, law enforcement is a local responsibility, meaning that all incorporated cities and counties are obligated to provide adequate public safety services for their constituents.[7] There are five types of law enforcement organizations in California: state police, county sheriff's departments, municipal law enforcement agencies, federal agencies (which work in collaboration with state and local agencies), and private police/security.

Law enforcement represents a sizeable portion of California's criminal justice system expenditures. In his 2017–2018 budget Governor Brown designated $11.3 billion for California's criminal justice programs (California Department of Finance, 2017). Within the $11 billion allocated for general criminal justice purposes, the governor's budget included $4.9 million for our juvenile justice system, $2.9 billion for inmate healthcare, another $2.9 billion for prison medical care, $114.9 million for community corrections, and $11 million for post release. The governor has also immersed our psychiatric programs into the California Corrections and Rehabilitation budget by designating $250.4 million of its funding from the general fund (California Department of Finance, 2017).

Today there 592[8] separate law enforcement agencies in California; 334 municipal police and public safety departments, 58 county sheriff departments,

---

6. The center in Norwalk (Los Angeles), which opened in July 2006 with 60+ staffers, has the distinction of being the first regional intelligence center in the nation (Surdin, 2006).

7. This responsibility is delegated to local governments by the state government.

8. Of these, 466 agencies report crime trends annually to the Uniform Crime Report (FBI, 2016).

Figure 5.1. Comparison of National and California Law
Enforcement Agency Sizes

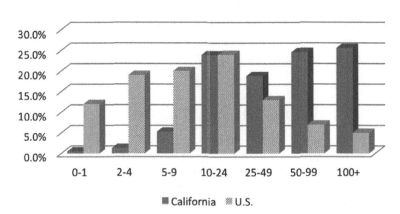

Source: Federal Bureau of Investigations, UCR (2011).

29 state agencies (e.g., Department of Insurance, Department of Fish and Game, California Highway Patrol), 68 higher education campus departments, and more than 100 "other" agencies that perform a variety of specialized services such as park rangers, housing authorities, school districts, transit districts, water districts, railroads, and district attorney's offices (California Commission on Peace Officer Standards and Training [CA-POST], 2017).

According to the Uniform Crime Report, there are currently 118,407 full-time law enforcement employees in California, more than any other state in the nation (FBI, 2016). Almost two-thirds (65.2%; 77,402) of these employees are sworn peace officers and a little more than one-third (34.6%; 41,005) are civilians.[9] In addition to the above paid employees, there are another 4,831 sworn reserve peace officers in the state (POST, 2017). California Penal Code Sections 830 through 831.7 list persons who are considered peace officers within the state of California (see Appendix A). California is unique because of the sheer size of most departments. Whereas only 20% of local law enforcement agencies in the nation employ at least 50 sworn officers, half of all agencies in California do (FBI, 2016). See Figure 5.1 above.

Moreover, our state is home to 5 of the 10 largest sheriff's departments and the third largest municipal agency in the country (United States Bureau of

---

9. Sworn peace officers in California have special training and enforce state laws, while civilian employees, such as dispatchers and other station staff, provide support.

Table 5.1. California's Ten Largest Law Enforcement Agencies

Agency	Full-Time Sworn Officers
Los Angeles Police Department	9,702
Los Angeles County Sheriff's Dept.	9,452
California Highway Patrol	7,205
San Diego County Sheriff's Dept.	2,669
San Francisco Police Dept.	2,222
Riverside County Sheriff's Dept.	2,007
San Bernardino County Sheriff's Dept.	1,903
San Diego Police Dept.	1,797
Orange County Sheriff's Dept.	1,796
Sacramento Police Department	1,286

Source: California Commission on Peace Officer Standards and Training (2017)

Labor Statistics [BLS], 2017). Table 5.1 identifies California's ten largest law enforcement agencies based on full-time employed sworn officers. Big or small, each law enforcement agency in the state of California has a significant role in providing services to those in our state.

State

There are two types of state police agencies in the United States—centralized and decentralized. State police functions in California are decentralized, which means that highway safety and criminal investigations functions are performed by separate agencies. The *California Highway Patrol* (CHP) was created through a legislative act on August 14, 1929, to enforce traffic laws on state and county highways. It is the largest state law enforcement agency in California (CHP, n.d.a). It has jurisdiction over 100,000 miles of roadways within the state, including county roads in unincorporated areas as well as state highways. The agency is under the direction of Commissioner Joseph A. Farrow (appointed by Governor Schwarzenegger in 2008), and is divided into eight geographical divisions—each with its own chain of command (CHP, n.d.a).

Today, CHP has four main responsibilities: (1) ensure safety and enforce traffic laws on California's state and county highways; (2) inspect commercial and other specialized vehicles; (3) investigate vehicular theft; and (4) provide protective services for state property and employees, including the governor and other dignitaries (CHP, n.d.b; LAO, 2005). This last responsibility was added in 1995, when the California State Police merged into the California Highway Patrol.

Whereas the CHP is responsible for highway safety in the state, the California *Attorney General's Office* (AGO), established in 1850, is responsible for criminal investigations and law enforcement (California Constitution). The Attorney General (currently Xavier Becerra[10]), is the chief law enforcement officer of the state. Unlike the head of CHP, who is appointed by the governor, the Attorney General (AG) is elected by the populace to a four-year term (he/she may serve up to two terms). The AGO, with the support and resources of the California Department of Justice, initiates its own criminal investigations and supports local law enforcement by coordinating state-wide crime prevention/suppression efforts, providing and disseminating research and other important information, operating a state-wide crime lab, and performing other functions. Beyond the AGO and CHP, there are 32 other independent state agencies with limited police powers in California. Examples of these agencies include the California Alcoholic Beverage Control, Department of Consumer Affairs, Department of Insurance Fraud, Department of Social Services, Horse Racing Board, State Lottery, and the Franchise Tax Board. Additionally, there are police departments on all California State University and University of California campuses.

County

Although the primary responsibility for maintaining law and order lies with the state of California, the state delegates these primary responsibilities to county governments and municipalities. The sheriff for each county presides over his/her county as the chief law enforcement officer. He/she derives his/her authority from the constitution of the state of California and state statutes, mainly found in the Penal Code and Government Code. The sheriff and deputy sheriffs of each county enforce the law at the county level, providing similar

---

10. Xavier Becerra, California's 33rd attorney general (AG) and first Hispanic AG, was sworn in on January 24, 2017. Governor Jerry Brown appointed him to fill the vacancy left by Kamala Harris when she won retiring Barbara Boxer's U.S. Senate seat in the November 2016 election. Kamala Harris was California's 32nd AG and the state's first female attorney general.

law enforcement services as municipal agencies. There are, however, some important differences between county and city law enforcement agencies.

A key distinction between sheriffs and police chiefs is that sheriffs are elected; chiefs are appointed or hired by city officials. This means that sheriffs can only be recalled by the voters in a county (not the politicians);[11] unlike chiefs who are either at-will or contract employees and can be terminated for various reasons. It also means that chiefs, unlike sheriffs, do not need to run for reelection every four years; they may serve for as long as city officials (or rules) allow them to serve.

Another major difference is that county sheriff's departments are required by law to provide services that municipal police departments are not mandated to provide. County sheriff's departments are the only criminal justice agencies in the state to perform vital functions at all three stages of the criminal justice system (law enforcement, courts, and corrections). First, sheriffs must own and operate a jail (to house defendants before, during, and after trial). Although a few municipal police departments have chosen to operate a jail, it is not required of them. Second, deputy sheriffs must also serve warrants, transport inmates, and provide security for county courthouses and judicial officers.[12] Third, deputy sheriffs must provide law enforcement services to unincorporated areas in the county. They do not, however, investigate traffic incidents in unincorporated areas. This is the jurisdiction and responsibility of the CHP. Many counties have consolidated the coroner's office into the sheriff's department; in these 41 counties, the county sheriff is also the county coroner and the sheriff's department performs coroner's operations, such as investigating deaths

---

11. California state law does allow an elected official to be removed from office if he/she vacates the office for 90 consecutive days (Pfeifer, 2008). In some counties, a sheriff can be removed from office by the County Board of Supervisors if she/he committed misconduct. For example, after San Francisco Sheriff Ross Mirkarimi was arrested on domestic violence charges in January 2012, the mayor appointed a temporary replacement, and the San Francisco Ethics Commission investigated the incident (Gordon, 2012). In the end, Mirkarimi pled guilty to false imprisonment, a misdemeanor, and the board of supervisors' vote to remove him did not pass, so he was reinstated as sheriff (Gordon, 2012; Knight, 2012). Another recent example is ex-Orange County Sheriff Michael Carona. Despite being indicted on federal corruption charges in October 2007, he could not be removed from office, because Orange County did not have any mechanism in place to do so. Had then-Sheriff Carona not resigned in January 2008, county voters would have needed to gather enough signatures to get a recall vote on the next ballot.

12. Prior to 1998, this function was provided by county marshal's departments. At this time, all but two counties have consolidated services by merging the marshal's department into the sheriff's department. In Shasta and Trinity counties, the marshal's department continues to perform this function (POST, n.d.; Shasta County Marshal, n.d.).

Table 5.2. California's Top Ten Counties for
Law Enforcement Employees, 2017

County	Total law enforcement employees	Total officers	Total dispatchers
Los Angeles	28,201	26,584	1,617
San Diego	6,577	6,075	502
Riverside	3,605	3,233	372
Orange	5,243	4,718	425
San Bernardino	3,820	3,452	368
Sacramento	13,881	12,745	1,136
Alameda	3,668	3,329	339
Santa Clara	3,688	3,317	371
San Francisco	3,461	3,222	239
Fresno	1,918	1,737	181

Source: Commission on Peace Officer Standards and Training, Current Employment (2017)

and serving as public administrator, along with their other duties (California Counties, 2010).

Sheriffs' departments in California range in size from 14 employees in Sierra County to 16,582 employees in Los Angeles County (UCR, 2016). Los Angeles County Sheriff's Department provides law enforcement services to more than 10 million people in an area of 4,084 square miles, including 40 contract cities, 90 unincorporated communities, 9 community colleges, and 216 facilities, hospitals, and clinics (LASD, 2017). It also protects 42 superior courts and manages the nation's largest local jail system (LASD, 2017).

Municipal

The majority of law enforcement agencies in California are municipal departments. Forty-eight percent of all sworn peace officers in the state are employed by city police departments (FBI, 2016). In most cases the police chief is appointed by the municipality's political system and confirmed by the city council. Duties at the local level include enforcing state laws, investigating crimes, arresting suspects, conducting searches of people and property, and enforcing a variety of municipal codes within their geographic jurisdiction. Each local law enforcement agency is independent of each other and has its own goals, purposes, and priorities. While each municipal agency is full service, many rely on other agencies for efficient and cost-effective resources. Uniformed police officers have general law enforcement duties including maintaining regular patrols and responding to calls for service.

By law, all incorporated cities must provide public safety services. Most cities fulfill this obligation by having their own police (or public safety) department. Some cities however, especially new and/or small cities, contract with another city or the county to provide public safety services. For example, the city of Santa Fe Springs contracts with the city of Whittier for police services and many cities in south Orange County (Aliso Viejo, Lake Forest, Mission Viejo, San Clemente, etc.) contract with the Orange County Sheriff's Department. This is a common practice, and usually a very cost-effective solution for cities. If a city contracts with the sheriff's department, then the sheriff's department will provide all law enforcement services expected of municipal agencies, including traffic and municipal code enforcement. Another option for municipalities is to enter into a Joint Powers Agreement (JPA) to share all public safety services. For example, the Central Marin Police Authority (a consolidated police organization representing the towns of Corte Madera and San Anselmo and the City of Larkspur) reduced public safety costs by more than 12 full-time employees by consolidating operations on January 1, 2013. Note, JPAs to share limited services (e.g., air support, regional task forces, etc.) are not unusual between agencies but this is only the second JPA for fully shared public safety services in California (the first was a JPA between Corte Madera and Larkspur in 1980).

Etna, Lake Shastina, Stallion Springs, and Tulelake police departments are the smallest departments in the state with only three full-time sworn officers each. The Los Angeles Police Department (LAPD), formed in 1869 with six officers, is California's largest local law enforcement agency today with about 10,000 full-time sworn officers (POST, 2017; LAPD, n.d.).

Federal

There are many federal agencies that enforce particular types of laws in California. For example, U.S. Drug Enforcement Administration (DEA) agents enforce laws and regulations relating to illegal drugs within our state, and the U.S. Marshal's Office provides security for the federal courts. The Bureau of Alcohol, Tobacco, Firearms and Explosives investigates violations of federal firearms and explosives laws, as well as alcohol and tobacco tax regulations (BLS, 2011). The Department of Homeland Security, which includes Customs and Border Protection, Immigration and Customs Enforcement, and the U.S. Coast Guard among other agencies, employs numerous law enforcement officers to protect our borders from people entering California illegally and from individuals illegally importing or exporting cargo (BLS, 2011).

Per Section 830.8 of the California Penal Code, agents employed by federal law enforcement agencies are not California peace officers but may exercise the powers of arrest in limited circumstances as specified in 836 WIC or 5150 WIC.[13] In order to exercise arrest powers, federal agents must have satisfied the training requirements stipulated in 832 PC. Furthermore, agents of some departments (Bureau of Land Management, Department of Agriculture-Forest Service) do not have any authority to enforce California statutes without the express, written permission of the sheriff or chief in the jurisdiction in which they are assigned (830.8[a] PC).

Interagency Collaboration

Collaboration between independent agencies within California and the federal government is critical to the success of the mission of law enforcement. However, interagency collaboration throughout California's history has been inconsistent and rare, except for cases involving mutual aid and special regional task forces devoted to specific crime problems such as drugs or auto theft. The situation has improved dramatically over the past fifteen years (since 9/11) and now there are many examples of agencies sharing information and resources. For example, there are three FBI-sponsored, but locally supported, Regional Computer Forensics Laboratories in California (Menlo Park, Orange, and San Diego) that examine digital evidence for any law enforcement agency within the center's service area (Regional Computer Forensics Laboratory, n.d.). Despite the progress, information sharing between agencies can be time-consuming and many times information is lost, misdirected, and/or late because of the bureaucratic maze it must go through to get from one department to another.

In southern California, Orange County has several agencies which make up "North County SWAT." They include La Palma PD, Brea PD, Fullerton PD, La Habra PD, Placentia PD, and California State University Fullerton PD. This is

---

13. These situations include when there is an immediate danger to persons or property, when enforcing federal law, or when requested to participate in a joint task force by a California law enforcement agency.

an example of consolidation, a cost-effective practice of sharing law enforcement services that is becoming more common as cities throughout the state seek to stretch their shrinking operating budgets.

Private Detectives, Investigators, and Security

In addition to the public law enforcement agencies mentioned above, California also has a thriving public safety sector, which includes private detectives, investigators, and security officers. According to the Bureau of Labor Statistics (2017) there are more private detectives, investigators, and security officers in California (146,740) than there are sworn public police (70,790). Private investigators provide a wide variety of security-related and investiga- tive-type services to individuals, businesses, schools, homeowners associations, attorneys, and even police departments.

The San Francisco Patrol Special Police, started in 1847, is the oldest private police force in the state of California and is unique because its existence is written into the city charter. Business improvement districts in downtown Los Angeles employ their own private security guards (known by the shirt color they wear) to keep the streets clean and safe so that businesses can flourish; "purple shirts" even assisted LAPD officers during Occupy LA protests in late 2011 (Romero, 2011). Santa Cruz Police Department also contracts with private security firms to provide extra eyes in places it cannot afford to place a sworn officer (Lyons, n.d.).

Professionalization and Training

Law enforcement agencies today require highly qualified and well-trained police officers. There are no federal regulations, however, regarding peace officer training. Each state is responsible for setting its own standards. In 1959, California pioneered statewide legislation that established minimum standards and qualifications for all entry-level law enforcement recruits and created the first *Commission on Peace Officer Standards and Training (POST)* in the nation (POST, 2011). The POST Commission is composed of 15 members appointed by the governor and the state's Attorney General. It meets three times per year to set training standards and regulations. Today POST (2011) focuses on three primary areas: (1) developing, implementing, and updating job-related standards to ensure consistency in the selection and retention of police officers in California; (2) guaranteeing all law enforcement officers access to sufficient training consistent with job requirements; and (3) providing professional growth and leadership development. Due to POST's strict training requirements, California peace officers are some of the best-trained officers in the world. Interestingly, California POST is not publicly funded; rather it is funded by penalty assessments that have been incorporated into criminal and traffic fines (POST, n.d.).

Basic Training

In order to become a peace officer in the state of California today, recruits must successfully complete the basic peace officer course (a.k.a. basic academy). Course content and testing is standardized across all 39 academies within the state. Recruits can expect, at a minimum, 560 instructional hours of material over 42 learning domains, as well as 104 hours of testing, for a total of 664 hours. Most basic training academies are much longer (up to 1,150 hours). In addition to demonstrating mastery of the 42 learning domains, recruits must also successfully complete a patrol field training component in order to satisfy California POST requirements to be a peace officer (POST, n.d.). Given these stringent training requirements, it is interesting to note that peace officers in California have only been legally mandated to complete training since 1975. Prior to that time, training requirements were voluntary and stipulated by each agency.[14]

The California Highway Patrol's academy is one of the most modern and innovative law enforcement training academies in the United States (CHP, n.d.c). Cadets spend 27 intense weeks living at the academy and learning all the material mandated by POST. In addition, cadets are certified as Emergency Medical Responders. Besides training its own cadets, the CHP opens its academy to other agencies to provide training in traffic accident reconstruction and commercial enforcement. Their emergency vehicle operations course is famous throughout the world as the finest law enforcement driving training program available (CHP, n.d.c).

While a field training component is standard practice today, the idea of providing additional training to new recruits was novel in the 1970s. San Jose Police Department was one of the first departments in the state to develop a Field Training and Evaluation Program in 1971 (commonly referred to as an F.T.O. Program, which stands for Field Training Officer) (SJPD, n.d.b). The

---

14. San Francisco Police Department's academy, which is probably the oldest police academy in the state, has been training new recruits since 1895 (Ackerson & Tully, n.d.). The California Highway Patrol, Los Angeles County Sheriff's Department, and Los Angeles Police Department each launched their own academy in the 1930s (1930, 1935, and 1936 respectively) (CHP, n.d.; LAPD, n.d.; LASD, n.d.). The CHP academy, which was two weeks long at inception, is now 1,100 hours (approximately six months) long (CHP, n.d.c).

14-week program paired a new recruit with a trained veteran officer to provide mentorship and assist the recruit in applying the book knowledge he/she learned in the academy to real-life situations on the street. Not only was the program nationally recognized by the International Association of Chiefs of Police in 1973, it was adopted by the California State Legislature in 1974 as the model for the state training standard. POST currently requires that agencies provide a minimum 10-week Field Training Program for new officers (POST, n.d.).

Continuing Education

Law enforcement agencies regularly provide their officers with training on the latest methods and technologies in law enforcement. Officers are required by law to complete 24 hours of continuing professional training every 2 years, including 12 hours of perishable skills training (POST, n.d.). They must also qualify in the use of firearms on a quarterly basis. Additionally, once promoted, officers must take and pass the appropriate course (investigators course or supervisory course). In addition to maintaining the training records for every peace officer (and dispatcher) in California, POST also operates Command College—a voluntary, competitive, and rigorous 18-month program for law enforcement agency leaders.

Formal Education

California POST requires entry-level officers to have at least a high school diploma or GED equivalent. Some agencies (approximately 18%), however, have set the bar higher. In fact, a recent study found that 14.6% of agencies in California require *some college*, 2.5% require a *two-year degree*, and a little less than 1% requires entry level officers to have a *four-year degree* (Gardiner, 2012). Despite these minimum requirements, most police officers have much more than the required minimum education. The above study revealed that more than half of all police officers in California have at least a two-year (associate's) degree, 34.7% have a four-year (bachelor's) degree, and 6.9% of police officers have a master's degree or more (Gardiner, 2012). In comparison, 91.7% of police chiefs/sheriffs in California have at least a four-year (bachelor's) degree, 54.5% have at least a master's degree and 3.2% have a doctoral degree (Gardiner, 2012).

Volunteers in Policing

Agencies have long relied on volunteers to supplement full-time staff in carrying out the law enforcement, order maintenance, and service functions they are expected to perform. A volunteer serves at the pleasure of the chief officer of a department and is non-vested, part-time, and uncompensated. Today's volunteers include reserve police officers, mounted posse units, chaplains, explorer scouts, citizen volunteers, aero squadron, and specialized rescue/recovery teams.

Depending on the department and the duties performed, volunteers may be required to participate in special training. For example, Level 1 reserve sworn officers perform the same duties, and must fulfill all the same training and education requirements, as full-time paid sworn officers. Moreover, some agencies (such as the Riverside County Sheriff's Department [RSD]) require volunteers to participate in a Citizen's Academy, which provides basic skills and knowledge in ethics, emergency management, radio operations and procedures, laws of arrest, courtroom testimony, traffic control, crime scene protection/preservation, crowd control, dealing with the public, press relations, and uniform wear.

Ethics

Although law enforcement agencies try to hire only the most ethical individuals, sometimes officers make very bad decisions that are misguided, abusive, or downright illegal. Due to the extensive background screening process and training that officers go through, very few officers are accused of improper behavior during their career. Those that do are protected by Government Code §3300-3313, better known as the California "Peace Officers' Bill of Rights" (it can be found at http://www.leginfo.ca.gov/). Typically, officers found to have committed an ethics violation are subject to disciplinary action by their agency. Rarely, though more frequently in recent years, officers may be criminally charged and prosecuted for their on-duty actions if they are considered to be illegal. For example, Fullerton Police Department officers Manuel Ramos and Jay Cicinelli were charged with beating to death Kelly Thomas, a homeless and mentally ill man, in 2011. The officers were acquitted of criminal charges in January 2014 but the city of Fullerton paid Thomas' family $4.9 million dollars as part of a civil lawsuit settlement in November 2015 (Ponsi et al., 2015). The federal Department of Justice also investigated the case but decided they were unable to prove that the officers "willfully disregarded [Thomas'] civil rights" and did not file criminal charges (Emery, 2017, para. 8).

On rare occasions, an entire unit or agency may be accused of unethical behavior, or a pattern or practice of violating citizens' civil rights. In this case, the California Attorney General or the U.S. Department of Justice may initiate an investigation. If allegations are substantiated, the judge may make suggestions to the agency to fix the problem/s, require steps be taken to fix the problem, appoint a court monitor to help fix the problem/s, or place the agency under receivership until the problems are fixed. The Los Angeles Police Department Rampart Division scandal is an example from the late-1990s of widespread corruption that resulted in numerous overturned criminal convictions, several officers going to prison, many more being disciplined or losing their jobs, and the entire department being placed under federal receivership for more than a decade. Oakland Police Department has been under court monitoring since 2003 but avoided a federal receivership in December 2012 by agreeing to relinquish certain powers to the court monitor (Collins, 2012).

Conclusion

Police and detective work requires shift work because protection must be provided around the clock, and it's work that can be very dangerous and stressful. Much of what is needed to survive is learned on the job. Police officers deal with social issues and crime on a daily basis. Personal characteristics such as honesty, sound judgment, integrity, and a sense of responsibility are especially important in law enforcement (BLS, 2011).

California's law enforcement agencies continue to lead the fight in the American law enforcement community. Besides being geographically and culturally diverse, California has demonstrated remarkable and agile success in its innovative response towards the challenges of crime and delinquency. Professionalism, standards, and exceptional training level demands continue to confront law enforcement agencies. As such California peace officers are required to continuously train and develop as law enforcement professionals to meet society's demands, keeping those residing in and/or traveling through the Golden State safe.

Key Terms and Definitions

California Attorney General—California's top law enforcement official. He/ she represents state residents in civil and criminal matters.
California Department of Justice—State law enforcement agency responsible for criminal investigations and law enforcement. The Attorney General runs it.

California Highway Patrol—State law enforcement agency responsible for highway safety in California.

California State Rangers—First statewide law enforcement agency in California.

Civilian Employee—An employee of a law enforcement not sworn to enforce state laws.

Community Oriented Policing—A policing philosophy that broadly defines an agency's mission as achieving the highest quality of life possible for an area. It proactively involves community members in partnerships and problem-solving efforts and requires organizational transformation to support the goals.

Deputy Sheriff—A sworn law enforcement officer employed by a county sheriff's department.

Fusion Center—Regional intelligence center that assists federal, state, and local law enforcement agencies within a specific region to gather, receive, analyze, and disseminate intelligence information.

Omnibus Crime Control & Safe Streets Act of 1968—Created the Law Enforcement Assistance Agency and provided federal grant money for law enforcement services and research.

William H. Parker—LAPD Chief from 1950-1996 who coined the term "the thin blue line" and created the image of police officers as professional crime fighters.

Peace Officer—A generic term used to describe an individual sworn to enforce local, state, and/or federal laws.

Penal Code—The body of statutory codes where criminal law, procedure and punishment are defined and proscribed.

Police Chief—The highest-ranking officer of a municipal police department.

Police Officer—A sworn law enforcement officer employed by a municipal police department.

Private Police—Non-sworn individuals hired by private entities to provide security-related and investigative-type services.

Problem Oriented Policing—A policing strategy that encourages officers to identify and address the root causes of crime problems using the SARA model.

Regional Intelligence Centers—Six centers in the state that assist federal, state, and local law enforcement agencies within a specific region to gather, receive, analyze, and disseminate intelligence information; also called fusion centers.

Reserve Peace Officer—A person sworn to enforce local and state laws that does not get paid but rather volunteers his/her time as a public service.

Sheriff—The highest-ranking law enforcement officer in a county.

Vigilance Committee—A group of private individuals formed to administer law and order when a local government was believed to be unable or unwilling to do so. Most were formed in the 1800s and early 1900s.

August Vollmer—Considered the "father of modern policing" due to his many innovations that revolutionized policing in the early 1900s.

Volstead Act—A law that existed from 1919 to 1933 that made alcoholic beverages illegal in the United States.

Wickersham Commission—Appointed by President Hoover between 1929 and 1931 to examine law enforcement practices throughout the nation. It began the movement to reform law enforcement practices.

O. W. Wilson—Police Chief of Fullerton Police Department and Dean of University of California, Berkeley's School of Criminology. He revolutionized police administration with the publication of his book, *Police Administration*, in 1943.

Internet Websites

California Attorney General's Office: https://oag.ca.gov/
California Laws and Legislative Information: http://leginfo.legislature.ca.gov/
California Highway Patrol: http://www.chp.ca.gov
California Peace Officers Standards and Training: http://www.post.ca.gov
Center for Problem Oriented Policing: http://www.popcenter.org/
Los Angeles Police Department: http://www.lapdonline.org/index.htm
Los Angeles Sheriff's Department: http://www.lasd.org/
Police Executive Research Forum: http://www.policeforum.org/
Police Foundation: https://www.policefoundation.org/

Review Questions

1. Identify the duties of sheriffs and chiefs in the early days of California statehood.
2. How do county sheriff's departments differ from municipal police departments?
3. Explain California's decentralized system of state-level law enforcement. Which agencies are considered our "main" state agencies and what are their responsibilities?
4. Which organization sets standards for California peace officers? What are the minimum training and education requirements for being a peace officer in California? What additional training do officers need to have each year/ every other year?

Critical Thinking Questions:

1. County sheriffs are elected by voters while city police chiefs are hired by city officials. How might this difference effect how each person does his/her job?
2. Compare how a rookie police officer experienced the job in the 1970s to how a rookie police officer experiences the job today. What tools are available to each rookie officer? How does that effect how he/she does his/her job? What types of skills does each rely on? How have the resources and required skills changed over the past 40 years?
3. How does policing in southern California, where large/very large departments are the norm, differ from policing in other regions of the county where very small departments are the norm? Consider things such as specialty assignment opportunities, available resources, patrol backup, and administration. How would you perform your job differently if you worked for a very small agency?

References

Ackerson, S., & Tully, D. (n.d.). *SFPD history: 150 years of history.* Retrieved from http://sf-police.org/index.aspx?page=1592

Boettcher, C. (1995). *Community policing: Is Santa Ana's acclaimed COP programme still a success?* (Unpublished master's thesis). University of Cambridge, England.

California Commission on Peace Officer Standards and Training (POST). (n.d.). *Training.* Retrieved from http://www.post.ca.gov

California Commission on Peace Officer Standards and Training (POST). (2017). *Employment.* Retrieved from http://www.post.ca.gov

California Counties. (2012). *County offices: Sheriff-marshal-coroner.* Retrieved from http://www.counties.org/default.asp?id=143

California Department of Finance. (2017). *Governor's proposed budget 2017-2018 revised.* Retrieved from http://www.ebudget.ca.gov/2017-18/pdf/BudgetSummary/PublicSafety.pdf

California Department of Justice. (n.d.). *California criminal justice timeline.* Retrieved from http://ag.ca.gov/cjsc/glance/timeline/tl4pg.pdf

California Highway Patrol (CHP). (n.d.a). *History of the CHP.* Retrieved from http://www.chp.ca.gov/html/history.html

California Highway Patrol (CHP). (n.d.b). *California Highway Patrol mission.* Retrieved from http://www.chp.ca.gov/html/mission.html

California Highway Patrol (CHP). (n.d.c). *California Highway Patrol academy.* Retrieved from http://www.chp.ca.gov/recruiting/academybrochure.html

California Legislative Analyst's Office. (n.d.) *Governor's proposed budget.* Retrieved from www.lao.ca.gov

California Office of the Attorney General. (n.d.). *History of the Office of the Attorney General.* Retrieved from https://oag.ca.gov/history

California Senate. (n.d.). *History of the sergeant-at-arms.* Retrieved from http://www2.senate.ca.gov/portal/site/SENSergeant/SENSergeantNavHistory

California State Constitution, Article 11, Section 5b.

Center for Problem-Oriented Policing. (n.d.). *Goldstein award information.* Retrieved from http://www.popcenter.org/library/awards/goldstein

Collins, T. (2012, December 6). Oakland Police reach deal, avoid federal takeover. *Huffington Post.* Retrieved from http://www.huffingtonpost.com/2012/12/06/oakland-police_n_2252963.html

Community Oriented Policing Services (COPS). (2011). *The impact of the economic downturn on American police agencies.* Retrieved from http://www.cops.usdoj.gov/Default.asp?Item=2602

Employment Development Department (EDD). (2017).*Labor market information.* Retrieved from https://www.labormarketinfo.edd.ca.gov/

Emri, S. (2017, January 24). Kelly Thomas case: 5 years later, feds say no criminal charges against Fullerton police officers. *Orange County Register.* Retrieved from http://www.ocregister.com/2017/01/24/kelly-thomas-case-5-years-later-feds-say-no-criminal-charges-against-fullerton-police-officers/

Federal Bureau of Investigation (FBI). (2016). *Uniform crime report, 2015.* Retrieved from http://www.fbi.gov/about-us/cjis/ucr/ucr

Gardiner, C. (2012). *College cops: A study of police education in California.* Paper presented at the American Society of Criminology annual meeting in Chicago, IL.

Gordon, R. (2012, March 20). Mayor says he'll suspend Mirkarimi as sheriff. *San Francisco Chronicle.* Retrieved from http://www.sfgate.com/crime/article/Mayor-says-he-ll-suspend-Mirkarimi-as-sheriff-3421327.php

International Association of Crime Analysts. *Membership.* Retrieved from http://www.iaca.net/faq_membership.asp

Knight, H. (2012, October 9). Mirkarimi apparently has enough votes to keep his job. *San Francisco Chronicle.* Retrieved from http://blog.sfgate.com/cityinsider/2012/10/09/supervisors-hearing-on-mirkarimis-fate-gets-underway/

Lasley, J. R., Hooper, M., & Dery III, G. M. (2001). *The California criminal justice system* (2nd ed.). Upper Saddle River, NJ: Prentice Hall.

Legislative Analyst's Office. (2005). *California Highway Patrol: Enhancing road patrol service through efficiencies.* Retrieved from http://www.lao.ca.gov/2005/chp/chp_013105.htm

Los Angeles County Sheriff's Department (LASD). (n.d.a). *About the Los Angeles County Sheriff's Department.* Retrieved from http://www.la-sheriff.org/s2/page_render.aspx?pagename=org_about

Los Angeles Police Department (LAPD). (n.d.a). *History of the LAPD.* Retrieved from http://www.lapdonline.org/history_of_the_lapd

Los Angeles Police Department (LAPD). (n.d.b). *Women in the LAPD.* http://www.lapdonline.org/join_the_team/content_basic_view/833

Lyons, J. (n.d.). *Privatization of police services.* Retrieved from http://www.fdle.state.fl.us/Content/getdoc/cbe81692-8662-46ed-a59b-b3861986f301/Lyons.aspx

Military Museum. (n.d.). *California State Militia and National Guard unit histories: California State Rangers.* Retrieved from http://www.militarymuseum.org/CaliforniaStateRangers.html

National Advisory Commission on Civil Disorders. (1968). *Report of the National Advisory Commission on Civil Disorders.* New York, NY: Bantam Books. Retrieved from http://www.eisenhowerfoundation.org/docs/kerner.pdf

Peak, K. (2009). *Policing America* (6th ed.). New York, NY: Pearson-Prentice Hall.

Pfeifer, S. (2008, January 4). Indicted O.C. sheriff set to return to work. *Los Angeles Times.* Retrieved from http://www.latimes.com/news/local/la-me-carona4jan04,0,7357299.story#axzz2sZ85BtKT

Ponsi, L., Emery, S., & Walker, T. (2015, November 24). $4.9 million settlement reached in Kelly Thomas wrongful-death case. *Orange County Register.* Retrieved from http://www.ocregister.com/2015/11/24/49-million-settlement-reached-in-kelly-thomas-wrongful-death-case/

Regional Computer Forensics Laboratory. (n.d.) Retrieved from http://rcfl.gov/

Riverside County Sheriff's Department (RSD). (2011). *Riverside County Sheriff's Department county statistics.*

Riverside County Sheriff's Department (RSD). (2011, October). *Riverside County Sheriff's Department general operations manual.*

Romero, D. (2011, December 8). Occupy L.A. demonstrators policed with help of private security known downtown as "The Shirts": LAPD says "that's not typical." *LA Weekly.* Retrieved from http://blogs.laweekly.com/informer/2011/12/occupy_la_lapd_assisted_private_security.php

Sacramento Police Department (SPD). (n.d.). *Department history.* Retrieved from http://www.sacpd.org/inside/history/

San Francisco Patrol Special Police. (n.d.). *History of San Francisco Patrol Special Police.* Retrieved from http://sfpatrolspecpolice.com/history.html

San Jose Police Department (SJPD). (n.d.a). *San Jose Police Department history.* Retrieved from http://www.sjpd.org/InsideSJPD/SJPD_History/SJPDHistory.pdf

San Jose Police Department (SJPD). (n.d.b). *Field Training Officer Program.* Retrieved from http://www.sjpd.org/bfo/FieldTraining/home.html

San Jose State University, Justice Studies Department. (2005). *1930-2005: 75 Years of educating and inspiring those who protect our property, our homes, our lives, and our rights.* http://www.sjsu.edu/justicestudies/docs/JS_75_Years_of_Excellence.pdf

San Luis Obispo Police Department (SLOPD). (n.d.). *San Luis Obispo Police Department history.* http://www/slocity.org/police/historicpdf%20old/180s.pdf

Shasta County Marshal. (n.d.). *Shasta County Marshal's Office: History and functions.* Retrieved from http://www.shastacourts.com/marshal/marhist.php

Siskiyou County. (n.d.). *California gold rush.* Retrieved from http://www.siskiyou-county-online.com/California_Gold_Rush.html

Skolnick, J., & Bayley, D. (1986). *New blue line: Police innovation in six American cities.* New York, NY: Free Press.

Starr, K. (1996). *Endangered dreams: The Great Depression in California.* New York, NY: Oxford University Press.

The Statutes of California and Amendments to the Codes Passed at the Twenty Seventh Session of the Legislature. (1887). Sacramento, CA: P L Shoaff, Supt. State Printing (Digitized by Google Books).

Surdin, A. (2006, July 28). FBI, state, local officers join under one roof. *Los Angeles Times.* Retrieved from http://articles.latimes.com/2006/jul/28/local/me-homeland28

Thompson II, R. (2012, September). *Drones in domestic surveillance operations: Fourth Amendment implications and legislative responses.* Washington, DC: Congressional Research Service. Retrieved from http://www.fas.org/sgp/crs/natsec/R42701.pdf

U.S. Bureau of Labor Statistics (BLS). (2013, May). *Occupational employment and wages.* Retrieved from http://data.bls.gov/cgi-bin/print.pl/oes/current/oes333051.htm

U.S. Bureau of Labor Statistics (BLS). (2013). *Occupational outlook handbook.* Retrieved from http://www.bls.gov

U.S. Department of Homeland Security. (2017). *Fusion center locations and contact information.* Retrieved from https://www.dhs.gov/fusion-center-locations-and-contact-information

Wilson, O. W. (1953). August Vollmer. *Journal of Criminal Law and Criminology, 44*(1): 91–103. Retrieved from http://scholarlycommons.law.northwestern.edu/jclc/vol44/iss1/10/

Appendix 5A

Penal Code Classifications of Law Enforcement

Penal Code §	Classifications of Law Enforcement
830.1[a]	Police, sheriffs, undersheriffs, and their deputies
830.1[b]	The California attorney general and special agents and investigators of the California Department of Justice
830.2[a]	Members of the California Highway Patrol
830.2 [b]&[c]	University of California Police Department or the California State University Police Department
830.2[d]	Special agents of the California Department of Corrections and Rehabilitation
830.2[f]	California State Park Rangers
830.3[c]	Certain employees of the California Department of Motor Vehicles
830.3[e]	State Fire Marshal and assistant or deputy state fire marshals
830.3[i]	Fraud investigators of the California Department of Insurance
830.3[q]	Criminal investigators of the Employment Development Department
830.33 [a]	Members of the San Francisco Bay Area Rapid Transit District Police Department
830.35[a]	Welfare fraud investigators employed by the California Department of Social Services and all county welfare departments
830.35[c]	County coroners and deputy coroners
830.5 [a]&[b]	Parole officers and correctional officers of the California Department of Corrections and Rehabilitation
830.37	Firefighter/security officers of the California Military Department
830.8	Federal criminal investigators and law enforcement officers

Source: California Penal Code, Part 2, Title 3, Chapter 4.5, Peace Officers.

Chapter 6

Courts in California

Pamela Fiber-Ostrow

Learning Objectives

After reading the chapter, students should be able to:

- Explain the court system, including its structure and the advent of specialty courts.
- Present the main actors in the court system and their primary duties.
- Describe the primary purposes of the appellate and supreme courts. Describe these courts with particular note to California.

Introduction

Every state in the union has a justice system, as does the federal government, but the operation of each is unique, as are the rules and laws that govern its establishment and practices. This separation of authorities, known as *judicial federalism*, allows states to determine various aspects of their justice system, but also makes discussions of states' court systems more difficult; while they may share a lot in common, they will also have many differences. The majority of trials that occur in the United States occur in state courts with the remaining belonging to the federal government in federal courts. As the largest court system in the nation, California's courts employ over 2,000 judicial officers and 19,000 court employees, heard over 8 million cases in 2016, and serve over 39 million people (California Judicial Branch Fact Sheet, 2016). It is with the courts that most Californians will have contact with their government either through the adjudication of some civil matter, or for some, criminal law. The primary function of the courts is to resolve disputes among parties. In criminal law, this requires determining whether someone is guilty of a crime (violating a section of one of California's legal codes), and in civil law may require determining responsibility in a question about damages to property or person, settling the estates of deceased persons, or protecting citizens' rights from state or local government (California Legislature, n.d.).

In both civil and criminal cases, the law as contained in California's codes guides the court process. Moreover, increasingly costs and state budgets have had a major effect on how the courts and the judicial system operate. Each of these are explored below.

Structure of the Courts

Most students have seen a television show or a movie where a court and its players are depicted. While some of these depictions capture parts of our justice system, like all good movies and TV they suspend reality and glamorize what can be a mundane and/or complex system. For example, TV depicts a trial as having a judge, a lawyer on each side, a jury, bailiff, and witnesses, while costume and sets call for a black robe for the judge, jury boxes, and evidence. However, as we will discuss, different types of trials require different types of actors and sets. Further, many cases do not even go to trial, while others face a judge without a jury; moreover, appellate hearings require an entirely different set of actors and sets. Like the federal government, California's courts are considered adversarial common law courts where judges serve as referees to ensure both sides are given equal opportunities to present their cases and the law is faithfully followed. Lawyers present their most persuasive arguments to the finders of fact (either jury or judge) and may present the weaknesses of the other side. The role of the lawyer is to best represent the needs of the client (the state or the defendant in a criminal trial) in order to convince the triers of fact. When judges make rulings, they have the force of law. California's courts were modeled after the federal system and are divided among trial and appellate jurisdictions.

The *trial courts* are the fact-finding courts, so-called because their job is to determine the facts of a case. In criminal cases, this involves determining whether a crime occurred and making decisions based on the facts presented to the courts (or the absence thereof) while in civil cases deciding if the facts are strong enough to support the claim that a person is responsible for damaging another's property. The standard for finding a defendant guilty in a criminal trial is guilt beyond a reasonable doubt. In a civil case, the plaintiff enjoys a lower standard and must merely show that they deserve the judgment based on the preponderance of the evidence.

Trial courts are the first courts to hear a case and therefore have original jurisdiction in most cases. The *courts of appeal*, which include the California

Figure 6.1. California Court System

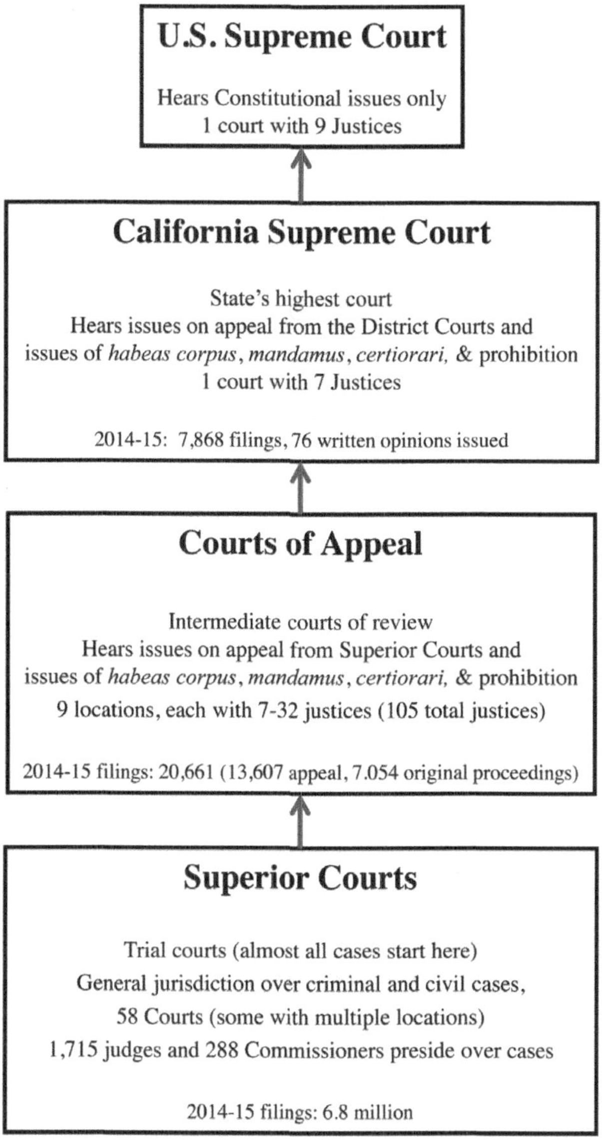

U.S. Supreme Court

Hears Constitutional issues only
1 court with 9 Justices

California Supreme Court

State's highest court
Hears issues on appeal from the District Courts and
issues of *habeas corpus*, *mandamus*, *certiorari*, & prohibition
1 court with 7 Justices

2014-15: 7,868 filings, 76 written opinions issued

Courts of Appeal

Intermediate courts of review
Hears issues on appeal from Superior Courts and
issues of *habeas corpus*, *mandamus*, *certiorari*, & prohibition
9 locations, each with 7-32 justices (105 total justices)

2014-15 filings: 20,661 (13,607 appeal, 7.054 original proceedings)

Superior Courts

Trial courts (almost all cases start here)
General jurisdiction over criminal and civil cases,
58 Courts (some with multiple locations)
1,715 judges and 288 Commissioners preside over cases

2014-15 filings: 6.8 million

Source: Judicial Council of California (2016). Court statistics report: Statewide caseload trends 2004-2005 through 2014-2015. Retrieved from http://www.courts.ca.gov/documents/2016-Court-Statistics-Report.pdf

Supreme Court, review questions of law and due process and have appellate jurisdiction, hearing cases on appeal, and in certain limited cases may have original jurisdiction. *Jurisdiction* here refers to the authority of a court to interpret and apply the law.

Superior Courts

California's trials take place in superior court. Superior courts cover nearly all of the work of the courts and most cases begin and end at trial. They are established in each of the 58 counties in more than 450 locations to deal with both civil and criminal matters (California Courts, n.d.a). Civil disputes occur when citizens or legal entities sue each other, either for damages (usually money) or to prevent harm or irreparable damage; criminal cases involve violation of criminal laws, ranging from minor infractions, such as jaywalking, to serious felonies, such as murder. Juries are commonly used in superior court. California's courts have not always been organized in this way. In 1998 Californians approved Proposition 220, an initiative which granted judges the option of unifying their municipal and superior structures into a single superior court in each county. By 2001, all 58 counties had approved unification. Despite this, many differences exist among the 58 counties' court operations. Each has a unique budget; budgets depend on caseloads, voters, population, and the economy both in the counties and in the state and the nation as a whole. This makes the operation of each court system unique despite all residing in the same state.

Not all cases that go to court are seen by a jury. Depending on the desires of the litigants (in criminal cases the defendant chooses) superior court cases can be heard by juries or by the judge in a *bench trial*. The number of judges assigned to each jurisdiction varies according to population and caseload.

Since the consolidation of municipal and superior courts, specialized subdivisions of superior courts have been created to ease the burden on the superior court. *Traffic court* deals with all traffic violations except those committed by juveniles. Private citizens may use *small claims court* to sue each other over damage to property, landlord/tenant disputes, collection of money owed, and many other types of claims if the amount involved is $10,000 or less; however, these courts do not employ lawyers or juries. According to the California Courts official website, the $10,000 limit applies to a "natural person (an individual)"; government and corporations may only ask for $5,000 in small claims courts. Further, the limit is $7,500 in a suit over a car accident with an insured motorist (California Courts, n.d.b). *Probate court* involves the administration of wills and estates. *Family law courts* settle domestic disputes; they are concerned with divorce and child custody. Finally, as Chapter 9 will discuss, juvenile courts deal with matters affecting accused persons under the age of 18 years. However, prosecutors may try minors accused of particularly heinous crimes as adults.

In criminal cases, defendants are guaranteed certain rights under both the United States Constitution and California's constitution. The rights of the accused are listed in Article I, the Declaration of Rights of California's constitution. Like the federal rights guaranteed under the United States Constitution's Fourteenth Amendment, Section 7 of California's constitution guarantees due process and equal protection of the laws, and like the Fifth through Eighth Amendments of the United States' Constitution, Sections 14–17 of California's constitution include guarantees of rights to a speedy trial, a preliminary hearing before a magistrate, counsel, be advised of the charge against the accused, trial by jury, confront witnesses, and summon witnesses on his or her own behalf. California's justice system must, at minimum, adhere to the federal Constitution's provisions but may provide greater protections for the accused.

There are several distinctions among the types of criminal cases that get processed through California's courts, reflecting three types of crime that are codified in California's penal code, which include infractions, misdemeanors, and felonies (see Chapter 4 for further distinctions in California's penal code).

Felonies are the most serious crimes and include crimes such as murder, possession of dangerous drugs for sale, rape, and armed robbery.[1] In a felony the judge may impose a sentence of one year or more in state prison or a heavy fine or both. Lesser crimes called *misdemeanors* carry less severe penalties of up to, but not more than, one year in county jail or a fine of not more than $1,000 or both. Misdemeanors include petty theft, prostitution, and vandalism.

The Players at Trial

Judges

The players in a criminal trial include the judges, prosecution, defense, and juries. Judges have a variety of different duties in the court process. Generally speaking, the judge listens to the evidence presented and makes a determination of the law based on the application of these facts to the legal code. In cases involving a jury, judges make decisions about what types of evidence will be presented to the jury. In a criminal case, if a defendant is found guilty, the judge determines the sentence for the offender. Most importantly, they preside over

---

1. As of October 1, 2011, AB109/AB117 requires that offenders convicted of non-sexual, non-serious, non-violent crimes serve their sentence in county jail rather than state prison.

the legal process as an independent representative of the system, meaning that they do not have a bias towards the prosecution or the defense.

The process for selecting judges is straightforward. *Superior court judges* are elected countywide on a nonpartisan ballot for six-year terms. Candidates must be attorneys who have been members of the California bar for 10 years. If the incumbent is unopposed then his or her name will not appear on the ballot. If a vacancy occurs between elections, the governor may appoint a qualified replacement to be voted on by the electorate at the next general election. Often, as the workload of a court exceeds the capacity of the existing staff, the judges appoint attorneys to serve as temporary judges, called *commissioners*.

Typically, these elections are low-key affairs. Unlike in other states, California judges do not run in partisan races and therefore there are few cues for voters when they approach the ballot box. These elections are rarely high profile. In order to remove a superior court judge, voters have two options: vote "no" at the next election, or recall the judge during the six-year period. Voters do have some tools at their disposal for deciding whether or not to approve a judicial candidate. The California Commission on Judicial Performance (CCJP) evaluates the fitness of judges and in the case of Scott Steiner, a judge in Orange County, censured him for conducting sexual activities in his chambers and for not disqualifying himself in a case involving a friend. Steiner had been on the bench since 2010 when he was approved to fill a vacancy due to a retirement. In addition to the CCJP, the Orange County Bar Association (OCBA) circulated a press release after a review of the nine candidates running for superior court judge in the June 7, 2016, election. Of the 9, only Judge Steiner received a "Not Qualified" by the OCBA (Orange County Bar Association, 2016). Despite this, Steiner won reelection even after a challenger emerged to unseat him, beating Orange County senior district attorney Karen Schatzle (Rocha, 2016a). Voters are so focused on the elections up-ballot, most would not have been aware of the censure and the OCBA rating.

In order to remove a judge from the bench after the election, voters must mount a campaign for a recall. This precise type of recall campaign began against Judge Aaron Persky after his March 30, 2016, sentencing for then-20-year-old Brock Turner who was found guilty of sexually assaulting an unconscious woman behind a dumpster at a party at Stanford University. The judge ignored Santa Clara County Deputy District Attorney Alaleh Kianerci's request for six years (two years for each count against him) as punishment and instead sentenced Turner to six months in county jail and three years' probation; Turner served just three months of this as a result of California's felony sentencing Realignment (Rocha, 2016b). According to the legal record, Judge Persky took into consideration, "among other factors, that Turner was remorseful, was not previously convicted of any crimes, was young, was not armed during the crime, that he would comply with the terms of probation, and he would not be a danger to others if not imprisoned" (Koren, 2016). He further said that while alcohol played a role in the assault, it was "not an excuse" yet was "a factor that, when trying to assess moral culpability in this situation, is mitigating" (Koren, 2016). He said a prison sentence would have "a severe impact" and "adverse collateral consequences" on Turner (Koren, 2016). Judge Persky ran unopposed and was reelected in the June 2016 primary as well. This may be explained by the short time frame between the sentencing and the election, but Persky had supporters in the judicial community. However, the public outcry from across the country as a result of the sizable news coverage this received was sufficient to move Persky from the criminal division to the civil division: "Judge Persky believes the change will aid the public and the court by reducing the distractions that threaten to interfere with his ability to effectively discharge the duties of his current criminal assignment" (Grinberg & Simon, 2016).

Outrage over the leniency of the sentence led to a recall campaign that began to raise money in June 2016 while an investigation by California's Judicial Council began. The Judicial Council ultimately cleared Judge Persky, indicating he had acted within the legal guidelines and had the authority to exercise his discretion. This only fueled the recall campaign. However, in late March 2017 the campaign announced a decision to postpone their efforts until the 2018 election cycle as there were no elections scheduled for 2017 and the special election could cost taxpayers about $6.9 million compared to $576,075 (Kadvany, 2017).

Attorneys: Prosecution and Defense

In a criminal case, the prosecution represents the people of the state of California and it is the authority of the *district attorneys* to prosecute cases in superior courts. They are elected in each county on a countywide, nonpartisan ballot. Their offices include numerous deputy district attorneys who prosecute the cases. In some cases, defendants will hire private defense attorneys to represent them in court; however, indigent defendants will be assigned an attorney. *Public defenders* are appointed by the county boards of supervisors to represent defendants who cannot afford a private attorney. Many counties have public defender offices, although in some cases the court appoints a private attorney to provide legal services.

Juries

Trial by jury is a right protected in the federal Bill of Rights in both criminal (Sixth Amendment) and civil (Seventh Amendment) trials and in California's constitution. It is the job of a jury to review facts and make decisions in legal proceedings. There are two types of juries, a grand jury and a trial jury.

Every county in the state has a *grand jury* of voluntary members who serve two functions. The first and primary responsibility is to investigate and examine ways to improve county governance. The second and less frequently used responsibility is to issue criminal indictments based on the grand jury's determination if a crime has been committed and there is enough evidence to charge. Under California law, grand juries in counties with a population of over 4 million have 23 members; other counties have 19 (Jameson, 2004). In order for a criminal grand jury to issue an indictment or an accusation, it needs at least 12 of the 19 grand jurors, or 15 of the 23-member jury to approve. When grand juries are convened for the purpose of criminal indictment, they meet in secret, hearing testimony of witnesses and accounts from the district attorney. The transcripts of the proceedings are released to the defendant and may be released to the public unless they pose a risk to the integrity or due process of the criminal proceedings, in which case they are sealed. For example, in mid-2004, a 19-member grand jury in Santa Barbara County issued an indictment against mega pop star Michael Jackson in molestation charges. The grand jury convened March 29, 2004, for 13 days to determine whether there was enough evidence to indict the singer. The proceedings were closed to the public, which replaced a preliminary hearing which would be open to the public. The transcripts are now available to the public and have been published in various places online (Madigan, 2004).

Most of us are more familiar with *trial juries* whose responsibility it is to review the facts of a case and determine whether there is reasonable doubt that a defendant committed a particular crime. The jury pool is drawn from both Department of Motor Vehicles registration and voter registration lists. Once selected for a case, the judge and lawyers conduct *voir dire*, to determine whether a prospective juror is able to objectively hear a case. Both the judge and the lawyer may excuse individual jurors from service in a particular case for various reasons. Lawyers use a "challenge" to excuse a juror; challenges can be for cause or peremptory. A lawyer has an unlimited number of challenges for cause, but a limited number of peremptory challenges, which require no reason to exercise (Hannaford-Agor & Walters, 2004). Lawyers for both sides are entitled 10 peremptory challenges in criminal cases, 20 in death penalty cases, and six in civil cases (California Code of Civil Procedure, sec. 231). Once seated at trial, jurors must listen to both sides of the case, during which time they cannot discuss the case with anyone until deliberations begin, and then only with fellow jurors. During deliberations, jurors must consider only information and evidence presented in the courtroom. If the jury is not able to agree on a verdict, the judge may dismiss the jury as a "hung jury," and call for a mistrial. This also may mean the case will go to trial again with a new jury.

There is certainly controversy surrounding the United States' requirements for trial by jury, including the ability of a jury to come to an impartial decision. Bias that pervades our understanding of society is likely to creep its way into the court room; lawyers may exploit those biases in their presentations of witnesses and evidence. For example, in attempting to make a female defendant more sympathetic the defense team may appeal to the juries' understanding of women as mothers or society's belief that women are typically more nurturing. Conversely, a prosecutor may reverse that by exploiting our understanding of women as more caring and nurturing by showing how much a woman has violated that norm.

Another controversy that surrounds juries is their potential for *jury nullification*. This refers to the refusal of a juror or an entire jury to convict a defendant despite evidence to the contrary because of objections to the law under which the defendant has been charged or sympathies with the defendant. For example, if a jury believes they are about to strike out a defendant on a non-serious, non-violent felony under California's three-strikes law and one or more of the jurors objects to the law, they may vote not guilty. Similarly, some scholars have argued that racial pride may lead to jury nullification, whereby a juror of a particular race will not support a guilty conviction out of racial sympathy (Butler, 1995).

Increasingly, counties were seeing thinner ranks of prospective jurors showing up for jury duty. In response, California adopted "a one-day-or-one-trial" system in which a juror reporting for service is either assigned to a trial on the first day he or she reports or is dismissed from service for at least 12 months. Failure to report for jury service in California may result in a fine up to $1,500, and although unlikely, it is possible to face jail time in addition to the fine. It is against the law for an employer to prevent an employee from serving on a jury by threatening to fire or terminating employment on that basis. California pays jurors $15 a day, and reimburses them at least 34 cents per mile starting on the second day of service. However, a person who is over the age of 70 and has a serious health problem may be excused from jury service; in addition, a person who is sick or disabled may postpone jury service or request to be excused.

To serve on a jury in the state of California, prospective jurors must be U.S. citizens and at least 18 years old. In addition, jurors must be able to understand English enough to understand and discuss the case; be a resident of the county in which the summons was delivered; have completed jury service more than 12 months prior; and not be serving currently on a grand jury or on another trial jury. A person who is in prison or on parole is ineligible for jury service. Just a glance at the numbers helps contextualize the process. Over 8.6 million

Californians who were summoned to jury service completed their service in 2011, but this does not mean they all served as jurors. Completing service could mean that they phoned in each day and were never asked to appear at a court. The better representation is the number of Californians sworn to serve as jurors: 164,512 (California Courts, n.d.a).[2] The court procedure in a criminal case begins long before a jury is seated.

High-Profile Cases in California

Arguably, one of the most well-known cases to emerge from California's criminal justice system is the O. J. Simpson murder trial and wrongful death civil suit. A former football star turned actor, Simpson was accused of murdering his ex-wife and her friend Ronald Goldman in 1994. While the legal process began in early summer 1994, the trial did not actually begin until January 1995 and concluded ten months later with a not-guilty verdict after only four hours of deliberation. In response, a civil case was brought against Simpson one year later in October 1996 for wrongful death. On February 4, 1997, the civil jury found Simpson liable and awarded the families 8.5 million dollars in compensatory damages and 25 million dollars in punitive damages (Linder, n.d.).

Other notable celebrity trials include the Michael Jackson molestation case as discussed above. In 2005 Michael Jackson was acquitted of four charges of child molesting, one charge of attempted child molesting, one conspiracy charge, and eight possible counts of providing alcohol to minors (Broder & Madigan, 2005). In this case, the jury took nearly seven days to deliberate before finding him not guilty of all charges.

A manslaughter case followed against Dr. Conrad Murray, Michael Jackson's physician, who supplied him with the drugs that led to his death. It was a high-profile case centered on criminal negligence. The prosecution brought nearly 50 witnesses over 22 days of testimony. It took the jury two days of deliberation to find Dr. Murray had "abdicated his duty or of acting with reckless criminal negligence, directly causing his patient's death" (Medina, 2011). In a state like California, home to Hollywood and the nouveau rich, the courts' profile is high. With celebrities behaving badly, or at least with the appearance thereof (see for example Winona Ryder's shoplifting scandal [Lyman, 2002]; Lindsay

---

2. Numbers based on 52 of the 58 (90%) superior courts reporting (as of Dec. 31, 2012).

Lohan's accusation of jewelry theft [Winton, 2011]) California's criminal courts have been busy and in the news.

More recently, the Orange County courts received local attention for the trial of two Fullerton police officers in the brutal beating and subsequent death of Kelly Thomas, a long-time Fullerton resident who was both mentally ill and homeless. Video captured by mobile phones in the 2011 beating immediately went viral on social media and the internet with graphic images of the beating and a plea for help from the victim. This video, coupled with audio from recorders worn by the officers, was the heart of the county's evidence against the police officers. Charges were initially brought against three Fullerton police officers, but after the January 2014 trial, which ended in the acquittal of Manuel Ramos and Jay Cicinelli, the involuntary manslaughter charges against Joseph Wolfe were dropped. The two officers that were brought to trial were charged with second-degree murder and involuntary manslaughter, and involuntary manslaughter and use of excessive force, respectively. The district attorney himself, Tony Rackauckas, prosecuted the case. Following the criminal trial, Thomas' parents sued the city for damages in two separate civil suits. In November 2015, the city of Fullerton agreed to settle the civil case raised by the father of Kelly Thomas for $4.9 million. As part of the agreement the city would not have to admit any liability or fault. Thomas' mother had already accepted a $1 million settlement from the city in May 2012 (Goldenstein, 2015).

The Judicial Process

The court procedure in criminal cases may take multiple paths, but to sum it up briefly, the court's involvement begins at *arraignment*.[3] Here defendants are informed of the charges against them after the district attorney's office (prosecutor) decides whether to file charges and whether it should be filed as a misdemeanor or a felony. During arraignment defendants are advised of their constitutional rights and the court determines if defendants can afford an attorney and appoints one if needed. Defendants then enter a plea of not guilty, guilty, or no contest.[4] The court then sets the bail and defendants are returned to custody or released on their own recognizance. During this time,

---

3. See more generally www.courts.ca.gov
4. In a no contest plea, as in a guilty plea, defendants admit they committed the crime, except that the subsequent conviction cannot be used against defendants as evidence of liability in a civil suit.

defendants may change their pleas to guilty or no contest or agreements may be reached between the prosecution and the defense or the judge and the lawyers about resolution without a trial. If no change in plea occurs, misdemeanor cases proceed to discovery. In felony cases, a *preliminary hearing* is held next, and the judge determines if sufficient evidence exists to proceed with a trial. If the judge determines sufficient evidence exists, the district attorney files an *information* on which the defendant will be arraigned for a second time, or the county's grand jury votes for an indictment. In either case of misdemeanor or felony, following a not guilty plea the lawyers for both the prosecution and defense conduct *discovery*, which involves an exchange of information. In addition, motions may be filed ranging from requests to exclude evidence to even dismiss the case. In the case of a guilty plea, the judge sentences the defendant. If a defendant waives a jury trial the judge determines guilt or innocence; if not then a panel of potential jury members is summoned and jury selection for trial begins. Finally, after the trial in which both the prosecution and defense provide evidence and witness testimony to use as facts, the jury must decide if the evidence supports the guilty charge beyond a reasonable doubt. If the jury finds the defendant is guilty a sentence is handed down.

Infractions are the least serious offenses and are comprised mostly of vehicle code violations and include illegal parking and operating an automobile without proper equipment. The punishment for an infraction is a fine. The court involvement for an infraction is very limited. Typically, a person who has received a citation will pay the ticket to the clerk of a nearby justice or court. The ticket is actually posting bail and pleading guilty, which forfeits the bail. If a trial is requested it will occur as a bench trial and no free counsel is guaranteed. Special commissioners rather than judges typically hear traffic violation cases, which comprise a large portion of infractions.

To put things in better perspective, there were 6.8 million criminal filings in the 2014–2015 year, with 5.6 million criminal dispositions. Felony cases totaled 223,339 cases with 218,285 (97.8%) felony cases disposed of before trial and 5,045 (2.2%) after trial. Misdemeanors accounted for 922,730 filings: 750,264 misdemeanor cases were disposed of before trial and 7,039 after trial. Finally, during that period there were 4,424,870 infraction filings with 3,761,011 infraction cases disposed of before trial and 377,876 after trial (Judicial Council of California, 2016). Figure 6.2 illustrates the number of cases that are completed after trial.

The numbers do not capture the number of judicial officers needed to process these cases, and during California's lean budget years California's justice system has been suffering as new judges are needed, but not enough budget is provided to support new judges and officers.

Figure 6.2. Disposition of Criminal Court Cases 2014–2015

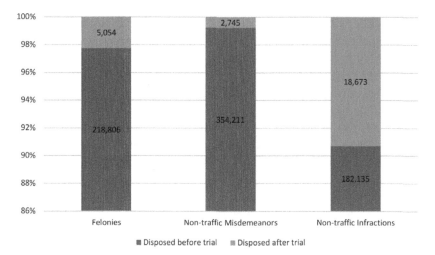

58 Counties and 58 Court Systems

To get a better perspective on what the system looks like, it is important to keep in mind some of the decentralized nature of California's courts. California has 58 counties and each county has its own judicial system with its own prosecutor, public defense team and court rooms, and employees. As previously discussed, district attorneys are elected locally so the person serving in the office will reflect the county voting preferences. This may be reflected in how crimes are treated in the criminal justice system. So even though the penal code is state level, the administration of justice occurs at a much more decentralized level.

Specialty Courts

In addition to the courts discussed above, California has established several additional specialty courts to address specific needs of its citizens. These include domestic violence courts, DUI/drug courts, mental health courts, and community and homeless courts covered below. In addition, California has created specialized DUI/drug courts as well as juvenile drug courts to address the needs of both offenders and scarce judicial and prison resources. In all specialized courts, the mission includes public safety and efficiency of both time and resources of the courts and judicial officers, as well as best practices for addressing the needs of the offenders and any victims.

Domestic Violence Courts

Family Code section 6390 as mandated by the legislature requires California's courts to make efforts to establish special practices for cases involving domestic violence. These cases occur in both civil and criminal courts. According to section 6390, "domestic violence courts" are courts that have judicial officers to hear a special domestic violence calendar; they may be exclusively assigned to domestic violence cases or as part another assignment. According to the California Court website, "the common features in domestic violence cases include "attention paid to how cases are assigned, the need to screen for related cases, who performs intake-unit functions, what types of services are provided to victims and perpetrators, and the importance of monitoring respondents or defendants" (California Courts, n.d.c). As McLeod and Weber (2000) describe in a report released in May 2000, California had 39 court locations in 31 of the 58 counties that met the definition of a domestic violence court (see also Labriola, Bradley, O'Sullivan, Rempel, & Moore, 2010).[5] Given the differences in size and resources of California's counties as well as the flexibility in section 6390, there is no single model or definition of domestic violence courts. According to the Judicial Council report, the common feature unifying these courts is efforts to enhance victim and child safety and ensure batterer accountability.

Mental Health Courts

California began implementing mental health courts in 1999 and are only assigned in criminal courts. Like domestic violence courts, they have a dedicated calendar and judge to address mental illness. The goal of these courts is to provide court supervision with treatment services for offenders in place of in-carceration. All potential offenders are carefully screened for inclusion in mental health courts and given the option to participate. According to the May 2011 Fact Sheet on the issue, there are over 40 mental health courts in 30 counties, including both juvenile and adult mental health courts. According to California's courts' website, the goals are to make efficient use of limited resources in the criminal justice and mental health systems so that both offenders and society have their needs met as well as addressing jail overcrowding (California Courts, n.d.d; *see also* Judicial Council of California, 2011a).

---

5. For an excellent discussion on Domestic Violence Courts, see Julia Weber, J.D., M.S.W. Center for Families, Children & the Courts "Domestic Violence Courts: Components and Considerations" available at http://www.courts.ca.gov/5978.htm

Homeless Courts

As is the case with other specialty courts, homeless courts have been established to meet the needs of California's homeless population. According to California's courts' website, court sessions are held in a local shelter or other community site. During homeless court, citizens are given the opportunity to resolve outstanding misdemeanor criminal warrants. The courts acknowledge that these crimes consist of "quality-of-life" infractions, including unauthorized removal of a shopping cart, disorderly conduct, public drunkenness, and sleeping on a sidewalk or on the beach (California Courts, n.d.e). San Diego's pilot program in 1999 helped establish homeless courts across the state. In San Diego the majority of the homeless are veterans, allowing homeless courts to meet several needs of the community.

Veterans' Courts

Also known as Veteran's Treatment Courts, Veterans' courts are equipped to handle issues common to veterans, including drug treatment and mental illness. In some ways these courts resemble drug courts and homeless courts but specifically address the needs of veterans. These courts work with the federal Department of Veterans Affairs healthcare networks, the Veterans' Benefits Administration, and, in some programs, volunteer veteran mentors and veterans' family support organizations. California currently has nine veterans' courts programs throughout the state (California Courts, n.d.f).[6]

Alternate Dispute Resolution

Plea bargains occur before and in lieu of a trial by entering an agreement with the prosecutor to reduce the charge. Commonly under the terms of a plea bargain the prosecutor under the leadership of the district attorney's office will accuse the defendant of a less serious crime in return for a guilty plea to the lesser offense. The practice of plea-bargaining serves several purposes and those in favor tend to cite the ability of courts to save money and time. Since trials are costly to the county by using the resources of judges and juries, plea bargains are helpful to county budgets. In addition, where the evidence may produce an unfavorable outcome for the prosecution, a plea bargain ensures them of a "win" with a guilty plea over a "loss" at trial or dismissal. Moreover, they clear

---

6. Alameda County, Los Angeles County, Orange County (national mentor court), Riverside County, San Bernardino County, San Diego County, San Mateo County, Santa Barbara County, Santa Clara County (national mentor court), Tulare County, and Ventura County.

the docket for another case and lessen the load on the superior court. In terms of defendants' rights, under the terms of a plea bargain defendants are granted a lesser charge than they would have received had they gone to trial and been found guilty. Under certain circumstances felonies may be reduced to misdemeanors or serious felonies reduced to felonies, which carry lesser penalties.

However, there are opponents of plea bargains, many coming from the perspective of victims' rights, who argue that criminals get a lesser sentence than they should have gotten. In addition, defendants' rights advocates argue that a trial may produce fairer outcomes with a chance for a jury's finding of not guilty. In these cases, advocates for defendants' rights argue prosecutors lure the accused in with a lesser charge but the accused may not fully understand the options or may not have the opportunity to fully understand the possibility of being found not guilty in a trial. This has had some profound implications under the three-strikes law as more fully discussed in Chapter 7.

Reforms to the Trial System

As was discussed in Chapter 3, direct democracy empowers Californians to reform their state through the initiative and referendum. California voters may be well intentioned in attempts to "fix" problems they see with the system and have done so a number of times; they often pass initiatives that are later found to violate the federal or California's constitution. In 1982, victims' rights advocates who opposed over-reliance on plea bargains helped to pass Proposition 8, also known as the Victims' Bill of Rights.[7] Among the many provisions of the law, it strengthened the rights of victims, allowing them to seek restitution from criminal assailants, secured the right of the victims' family to appear and testify at parole hearings, limited plea bargaining in serious felony and drunk driving cases, and lengthened some sentences. The law also required judges to weigh considerations of public safety in making bail, abolished the exclusionary rule regarding illegally collected evidence, cut back on insanity defense, and allowed use of defendants' prior criminal record in considerations before the court. Some of these provisions violated the United States Constitution and were struck down, but the law made an impact on California's courts nonetheless.

Other influential reforms affecting California's courts include Proposition 115, passed in 1990. Among the provisions in the law, it expanded the list of special circumstances allowing imposition of the death penalty to include killing a witness; a provision allowing minors as young as 16 to be tried as adults, and if convicted of first-degree murder with special circumstances, to be

---

7. See Chapter 12 for a comprehensive discussion of California's Victims' Bill of Rights.

punished by life in prison without parole; and introduction of hearsay evidence at preliminary hearings if given by trained and experienced officers among other sentencing and criminal conduct reforms. In March 2000, voters again supported a tough on crime initiative, passing Proposition 21, which included lowering the age at which juveniles can be tried in adult court to 14 years of age. Most recently, in November 2008 Californians passed Proposition 9, "Victims' Bill of Rights of 2008," which strengthened victims' rights and inserting them into the Constitution rather than just the code as they had done in 1982's Proposition 8 Victims' Bill of Rights. Under Proposition 9, victims have a constitutional right "to reasonable notice of all public proceedings ... at which the defendant and the prosecutor are entitled to be present" and "to be heard ... at any proceeding ... involving a post-arrest release decision, plea, sentencing, post-conviction release decision, or any proceeding in which a right of the victim is at issue" (California Secretary of State, 2008). While all of the measures have public safety and rights of victims in mind, they do not necessarily take into account the burdens the laws impose on the courts. They all demand increases in financial resources as well as judicial officers but do not provide funding sources for the changes.

Courts of Appeal and the Supreme Court

Trial courts decide questions of fact: does the evidence support the charge that the defendant murdered the victim in cold blood? Appellate courts decide questions of procedure or law: were the rights of the accused violated by the police for failure to produce a warrant to search his or her home? Does California's law violate an individual's guarantee of free speech or equal protection of the laws? Here the focus of the court is not the facts but the law. There are no juries, and lawyers do not produce evidence and witnesses. Instead, lawyers submit written briefs and may also appear before the appellate court in oral argument. The process is adversarial like the trial courts, but in the appellate courts, the attorneys are questioned by the judges during their oral arguments, whose goal is to persuade the court that their interpretation of the law is the most accurate. California has two levels of appellate courts: the courts of appeal and the state supreme court.

California Courts of Appeal

California has six district courts of appeal, with 105 justices serving in the courts. Judges sit in a panel of three to hear appeals from superior courts or

Figure 6.3. California Judicial Officers and Court Employees

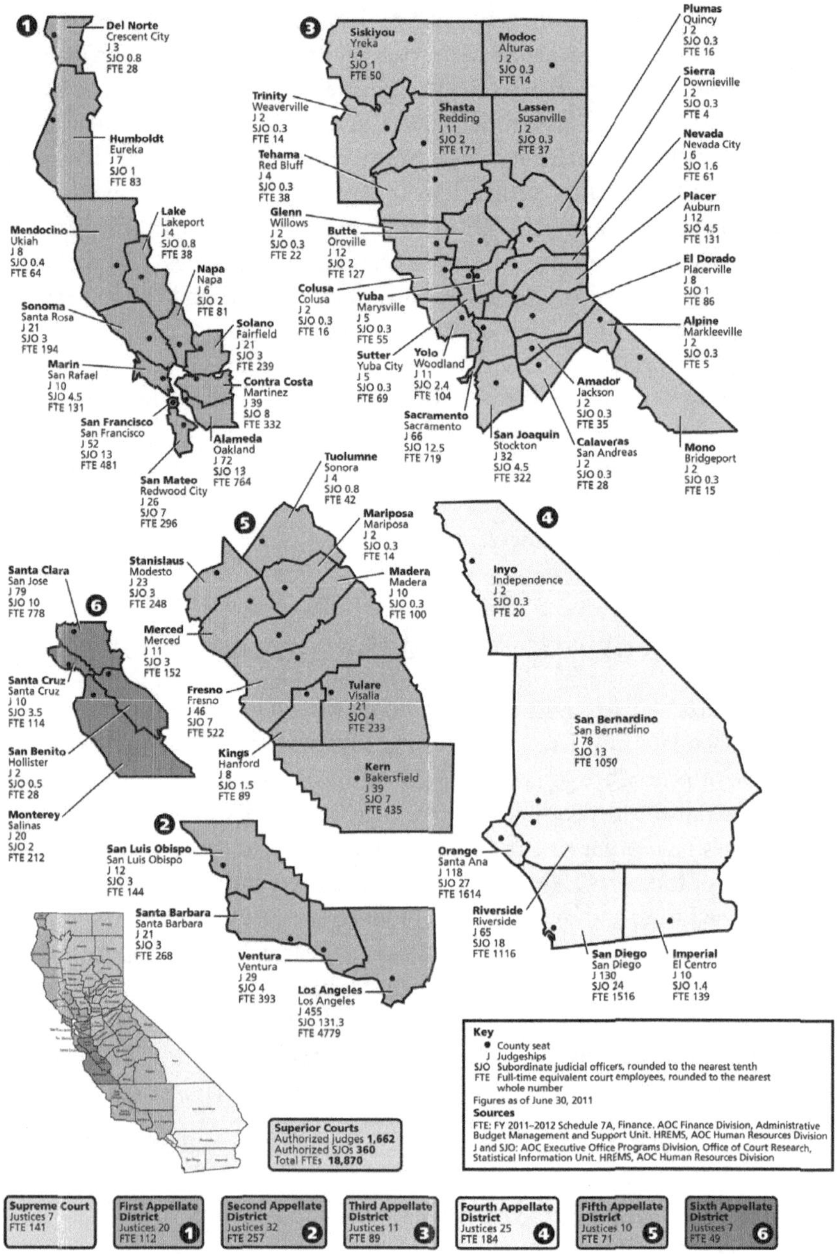

1

Del Norte
Crescent City
J 3
SJO 0.8
FTE 28

Humboldt
Eureka
J 7
SJO 1
FTE 83

Mendocino
Ukiah
J 8
SJO 0.4
FTE 64

Sonoma
Santa Rosa
J 21
SJO 3
FTE 194

Marin
San Rafael
J 10
SJO 4.5
FTE 131

San Francisco
San Francisco
J 52
SJO 13
FTE 481

San Mateo
Redwood City
J 26
SJO 7
FTE 296

Lake
Lakeport
J 4
SJO 0.8
FTE 38

Napa
Napa
J 6
SJO 2
FTE 81

Solano
Fairfield
J 21
SJO 3
FTE 239

Contra Costa
Martinez
J 39
SJO 8
FTE 332

Alameda
Oakland
J 72
SJO 13
FTE 764

3

Siskiyou
Yreka
J 4
SJO 1
FTE 50

Trinity
Weaverville
J 2
SJO 0.3
FTE 14

Tehama
Red Bluff
J 4
SJO 0.3
FTE 38

Glenn
Willows
J 2
SJO 0.3
FTE 22

Colusa
Colusa
J 2
SJO 0.3
FTE 16

Sutter
Yuba City
J 5
SJO 0.3
FTE 69

Shasta
Redding
J 11
SJO 2
FTE 171

Butte
Oroville
J 12
SJO 2
FTE 127

Yuba
Marysville
J 5
SJO 0.3
FTE 55

Yolo
Woodland
J 11
SJO 2.4
FTE 104

Sacramento
Sacramento
J 66
SJO 12.5
FTE 719

Modoc
Alturas
J 2
SJO 0.3
FTE 14

Lassen
Susanville
J 2
SJO 0.3
FTE 37

San Joaquin
Stockton
J 32
SJO 4.5
FTE 322

Amador
Jackson
J 2
SJO 0.3
FTE 35

Calaveras
San Andreas
J 2
SJO 0.3
FTE 28

Plumas
Quincy
J 2
SJO 0.3
FTE 16

Sierra
Downieville
J 2
SJO 0.3
FTE 4

Nevada
Nevada City
J 6
SJO 1.6
FTE 61

Placer
Auburn
J 12
SJO 4.5
FTE 131

El Dorado
Placerville
J 8
SJO 1
FTE 86

Alpine
Markleeville
J 2
SJO 0.3
FTE 5

Mono
Bridgeport
J 2
SJO 0.3
FTE 15

5

Stanislaus
Modesto
J 23
SJO 3
FTE 248

Merced
Merced
J 11
SJO 3
FTE 152

Tuolumne
Sonora
J 2
SJO 0.8
FTE 42

Mariposa
Mariposa
J 2
SJO 0.3
FTE 14

Madera
Madera
J 10
SJO 0.3
FTE 100

Fresno
Fresno
J 46
SJO 7
FTE 522

Tulare
Visalia
J 21
SJO 4
FTE 233

Kings
Hanford
J 8
SJO 1.5
FTE 89

4

Inyo
Independence
J 2
SJO 0.3
FTE 20

San Bernardino
San Bernardino
J 78
SJO 13
FTE 1050

Santa Clara
San Jose
J 79
SJO 10
FTE 778

6

Santa Cruz
Santa Cruz
J 10
SJO 3.5
FTE 114

San Benito
Hollister
J 2
SJO 0.5
FTE 28

Monterey
Salinas
J 20
SJO 2
FTE 212

2

San Luis Obispo
San Luis Obispo
J 12
SJO 3
FTE 144

Santa Barbara
Santa Barbara
J 21
SJO 3
FTE 268

Ventura
Ventura
J 29
SJO 4
FTE 393

Los Angeles
Los Angeles
J 455
SJO 131.3
FTE 4779

Kern
Bakersfield
J 39
SJO 7
FTE 435

Orange
Santa Ana
J 118
SJO 27
FTE 1614

Riverside
Riverside
J 65
SJO 18
FTE 1116

San Diego
San Diego
J 130
SJO 24
FTE 1516

Imperial
El Centro
J 10
SJO 1.4
FTE 139

Key
● County seat
J Judgeships
SJO Subordinate judicial officers, rounded to the nearest tenth
FTE Full-time equivalent court employees, rounded to the nearest whole number

Figures as of June 30, 2011

Sources
FTE: FY 2011–2012 Schedule 7A, Finance. AOC Finance Division, Administrative Budget Management and Support Unit. HREMS, AOC Human Resources Division
J and SJO: AOC Executive Office Programs Division, Office of Court Research, Statistical Information Unit. HREMS, AOC Human Resources Division

Superior Courts
Authorized judges **1,662**
Authorized SJOs **360**
Total FTEs **18,870**

Supreme Court	First Appellate District	Second Appellate District	Third Appellate District	Fourth Appellate District	Fifth Appellate District	Sixth Appellate District
Justices 7 FTE 141	Justices 20 FTE 112 ❶	Justices 32 FTE 257 ❷	Justices 11 FTE 89 ❸	Justices 25 FTE 184 ❹	Justices 10 FTE 71 ❺	Justices 7 FTE 49 ❻

certain state agencies. Cases are appealed from the superior court to review the decision of that court by a party who is challenging that decision. Decisions of the panels (opinions) are published in the California Appellate Reports. Opinions will be published if they establish a new rule of law, involve a legal issue of continuing public interest, criticize existing law, or make a significant contribution to legal literature (Judicial Council of California, 2011b). Each of the six courts selects one of its members to be the presiding justice, who is the administrative head of the court. The six courts are located in San Diego (with divisions in Riverside and Santa Ana), Los Angeles (with a division in Ventura), Fresno, San Jose, San Francisco, and Sacramento.

Courts of appeal have both appellate jurisdiction (hearing appeals) and original jurisdiction (first court to hear a case). Like the Supreme Court, the courts of appeal have original jurisdiction in habeas corpus, mandamus, certiorari, and prohibition proceedings (California Constitution, Article VI, Section 10). Habeas corpus proceedings are used when a person believes he or she has been unlawfully denied freedom to appear before a court or a judge. A writ of certiorari is the term used when the court grants a case on appeal from a lower court. A writ of mandamus and a writ of prohibition are prerogative writs available in civil proceedings to appellate courts in California. A writ of mandamus is issued by a court to order a government agency to perform an act as required by law. A writ of prohibition is issued to stop a lower court from proceeding in a specific case.

Generally, a criminal or civil defendant who loses in superior court has the right to appeal to the court of appeals for a reversal of the decision. In civil cases, however, if a party appeals a monetary award and loses, interest will be added to the amount to cover the extra time consumed on appeal. The six appellate courts had 20,661 filings of records of appeal; of those, 13,607 were criminal cases. In addition, there were 7,054 criminal case filings of original proceedings (Judicial Council of California, 2016).

California Supreme Court

The Supreme Court of California is the state's highest court. Its decisions are binding on all other California courts. The court conducts regular sessions in San Francisco, Los Angeles, and Sacramento; it also occasionally holds special sessions elsewhere.

Most of California's Supreme Court caseload is appellate, usually decided in superior court, and then reviewed by one of the courts of appeals. The court has discretionary power to hear cases, so in most cases, the Supreme Court may decide which cases it chooses to hear. In cases where the death penalty has been imposed, however, the Supreme Court must hear the case on appeal.

In these cases, the Supreme Court hears the case directly from the superior court. In all cases, the decision by the court is final unless the U.S. Supreme Court finds a constitutional issue in the case.

The state constitution gives the Supreme Court the authority to review decisions of the state courts of appeal. This reviewing power enables the Supreme Court to decide important legal questions and to maintain uniformity in the law. The court selects specific issues for review, or it may decide all the issues in a case. In 2014–2015, the Supreme Court issued 76 written opinions. There were 4,038 petitions seeking review from a court of appeal decision and 3,874 of these were from appeals in criminal matters. There were 18 automatic appeals filed from Superior Court following a sentence of the death penalty; in addition to these, the Supreme Court disposed of 19 automatic appeals by written opinion. The court's opinions are made accessible in various ways, including publication in the *Official California Reports*.

Membership and Qualifications

The California Supreme Court is composed of seven justices: a chief justice, who is appointed specifically to that position, and six associate justices. While all justices and appellate judges are eventually voted on by the public during regular elections, their appointments begin earlier than that. The governor forwards the names of potential justices to the Commission on Judicial Nominee Evaluation (JNE). This 25-member commission includes 19 members elected by the bar, which is the association of attorneys admitted to the practice of law in California. The other six are public members appointed by the governor. This commission considers the qualifications, including the character, of each proposed nominee, and rates him or her exceptionally well qualified, well qualified, qualified, or unqualified. Following the JNE ratings, the governor chooses whom to nominate to the Supreme Court or courts of appeal. This nomination is forwarded to the Commission on Judicial Appointments, which is composed of the chief justice of the state supreme court (or an associate justice if the vacancy is the office of chief justice), the senior (longest serving) presiding justice of the court of appeals, and the attorney general. The commission holds public hearings and receives testimony about the nominee in both oral and written form from anyone who wishes to submit it. The three then vote. If two vote to confirm the appointment, the nominee becomes a justice and takes his or her place on the bench. The new justice is either confirmed or rejected by the electorate at the next election, running unopposed. If a majority of the voters affirm the selection, the justice serves the rest of the 12-year term. Subsequently the justice must run for another 12-year term. If a majority of California voters do not support the justice, the office becomes vacant and the process begins again. Judges are removable through recall as well.

Jobs of Appellate Courts

As described above, the appellate courts generally review issues of law. This is called judicial review, which involves judgment as to whether a law or action by government is constitutional. A complex society generates complex laws that require judicial untangling. As new technologies emerge, laws and their implementation do not always keep pace. For example, while law enforcement must obtain a warrant before using a wiretap on a telephone,[8] must they also obtain a warrant to track a cellphone through the International Mobile Subscriber Identity (IMSI) that a mobile phone emits to connect with a cellphone tower in order to receive service, even though the individual took precise measures to ensure their privacy? Moreover, many statutes tend to be written ambiguously, leaving them open to question and judicial interpretation. As discussed above, Californians' use of the popular initiative often results in enactment of law that is constitutionally suspect or just poorly drafted. This means California's courts must reconcile the meaning of the statute with California's constitution and the federal Constitution.

State Bar of California

Many students wishing to practice law hear stories about the "Bar" exam. According to the Fact Sheet issued by the Judicial Council of California, the State Bar of California is a public corporation, established within Article VI of the California Constitution. The bar is the "administrative arm of the Supreme Court in matters of attorney admission and discipline." It is most well-known for the Committee of Bar Examiners, who administers the bar examination and other requirements for admission to the practice of law and certifies qualified applicants to the Supreme Court for admission.

Conclusion

As the largest court system in the United States, the California courts system represents a major component of our criminal justice system. As you have

---

8. See *Katz v. United States*, 389 U.S. 347 (1967).

learned, there are a variety of different actors and components that all have to work together in the pursuit of justice. Whether it is the trial of a Hollywood celebrity or the depiction of the courtroom in a television series, the realities of the courts extend far beyond these limited portrayals. However, California's court system faces significant challenges in light of the economic demands of maintaining such a large entity. Given the tough on crime stance of California's legislature and voters over recent years, it seems that the courts will continue to be a busy place in the future.

Key Terms and Definitions

Arraignment—Defendants are informed of the charges against them after the District Attorney's office (Prosecutor) decides whether to file charges and whether it should be filed as a misdemeanor or a felony.

Bench trial—A trial without a jury.

Commissioners—Judge-appointed, to ease the workload of a court as it exceeds the capacity of the existing staff, attorneys to serve as temporary judges.

Courts of appeal—Review questions of law and due process and have appellate jurisdiction, hearing cases on appeal, and in certain limited cases may have original jurisdiction.

District Attorneys—Attorneys who represent the people of the state of California in a criminal trial.

Family law courts—Settle domestic disputes; they are concerned with divorce and child custody.

Felonies—Crimes punishable by one year or more in state prison (or county jail in some cases) or a heavy fine or both.

Grand jury—Voluntary members who investigate and examine ways to improve county governance and issue criminal indictments based on the determination if a crime has been committed and there is enough evidence to charge.

Judicial federalism—Every state in the union has a justice system as does the Federal government, but the operation of each is unique as are the rules and laws that govern its establishment and practices.

Jurisdiction—Authority of a court to interpret and apply the law.

Misdemeanors—Lesser crimes, less severe penalties of up to, but not more than, one year in county jail or a fine of not more than $1000 or both.

Plea bargains—Occur before and in lieu of a trial by entering an agreement with the prosecutor to reduce the charge.

Preliminary hearing—In felony cases, following arraignment, the judge determines if sufficient evidence exists to proceed with a trial.

Probate court—Administration of wills and estates.

Public Defender—Attorney appointed by the county boards of supervisors to represent defendants who cannot afford a private attorney.

Small claims court—Court available for private citizens to sue each other over damage to property, landlord/tenant disputes, collection of money owed and many other types of claims if the amount involved is $10,000 or less.

Superior court judges—Elected countywide on a nonpartisan ballot for six-year terms.

Trial courts—The fact-finding courts, so-called because their job is to determine the facts of a case.

Traffic court—Deals with all traffic violations except those committed by juveniles.

Trial juries—Review the facts of a case and determine whether there is any reasonable doubt that a defendant committed a particular crime.

Internet Websites

California Courts Online Self-Help Center: http://www.courts.ca.gov/selfhelp.htm

Information on Jury Duty in California: http://www.courts.ca.gov/juryservice.htm

California Courts Programs Homepage: http://www.courts.ca.gov/programs.htm

California Rules of Court: http://www.courts.ca.gov/rules.htm

The State Bar of California: http://www.calbar.ca.gov/

Review Questions

1. What are the levels of courts in California and how do their functions differ?
2. What are the three types of crime prosecuted in California?
3. What changes have been passed by California voters to improve the operation of the judicial system? How have the changes impacted the Judiciary and its functioning?
4. What are the ways of removing a sitting judge? How likely is this to happen?

Critical Thinking Questions

1. The plea bargain evolved as a way to save time and money and incidentally offered the accused an opportunity for a reduced sentence. However, much

controversy surrounds the use of the plea bargain. What are benefits of plea bargaining both to the system and to the defendant? What are the costs?

2. Most Californians dread jury service and yet it is a Constitutional guarantee for every person accused of a crime to have a trial by jury. Why do Californians dread jury service so much? How has California attempted to respond to these complaints? Have they helped?

3. There is an inherent tension between the rights of the accused and the perceived rights of the public. How have California and its voters tried to balance these rights? What are the results?

References

Broder, J. M., & Madigan N. (2005, June 14). Michael Jackson cleared after 14-week child molesting trial. *New York Times*. Retrieved from http://www.nytimes.com/2005/06/14/national/14jackson.html?pagewanted=all

Butler, P. (1995). Racially based jury nullification: Black power in the criminal justice system. *Yale Law Journal, 105*, 677.

California Courts. (n.d.a). *About California courts*. Retrieved from http://www.courts.ca.gov/2113.htm

California Courts. (n.d.b). *Resolving small claims cases*. Retrieved from http://www.courts.ca.gov/20129.htm

California Courts. (n.d.c) *Domestic violence courts*. Retrieved from http://www.courts.ca.gov/5978.htm

California Courts. (n.d.d) *Mental health courts*. Retrieved from http://www.courts.ca.gov/5982.htm

California Courts. (n.d.e) *Community/homeless courts*. Retrieved from http://www.courts.ca.gov/5976.htm

California Courts. (n.d.f). *Veterans' courts*. Retrieved from http://www.courts.ca.gov/11181.htm

California Courts. (2013, September 13). *Court filings decrease for fiscal year 2011–2012*. Retrieved from http://www.courts.ca.gov/23492.htm

California Legislature. (n.d.). *California's legislature, Chapter V: Judicial department*. Official California Legislative Information. Retrieved from http://www.leginfo.ca.gov/pdf/caleg5.pdf

California Secretary of State. (2008). *Official voter information guide, text of proposed law, Proposition 9: Criminal justice system. Victims' rights. Parole. Initiative constitutional amendment and statute*. Retrieved from http://voterguide.sos.ca.gov/past/2008/general/text-proposed-laws/text-of-proposed-laws.pdf#prop9

Goldenstein, T. (2015, November 23). $4.9-million settlement in death of mentally ill homeless man Kelly Thomas. *Los Angeles Times*. Retrieved from http://www.latimes.com/local/lanow/la-me-ln-4-9-million-settlement-in-death-of-metally-ill-homeless-man-kelly-thomas-20151123-story.html

Grinberg, E., & Simon, D. (2016, August 25). Brock Turner judge to no longer hear criminal cases. *CNN*. Retrieved from http://www.cnn.com/2016/08/25/us/brock-turner-aaron-persky-judge-reassigned/

Hannaford-Agor, P. L., & Waters, N. L. (2004). *Examining voir dire in California*. Judicial Council of California. Retrieved from http://www.ncsconline.org/juries/CAVOIRREP.pdf

Jameson, M. (2004). *The grand jury: A brief historical overview*. California Grand Jurors Association. Retrieved from http://cgja.org/about-grand-juries

Judicial Council of California. (2011a, May). *Fact sheet: California mental health courts*. Retrieved from http://www.courts.ca.gov/documents/MHC_Eval_Fact_Sheet_5-11_FINAL.pdf

Judicial Council of California. (2011b). *Court statistics report: Statewide caseload trends 2000–2001 through 2009–2010*. Retrieved from www.courts.ca.gov/12941.htm#id7495

Judicial Council of California. (2013). *2013 court statistics report: Statewide caseload trends 2000–2001 through 2011–2012*. Retrieved from http://www.courts.ca.gov/12941.htm#id7495

Judicial Council of California. (2016, October). Fact sheet: California judicial branch. Retrieved from http://www.courts.ca.gov/documents/California_Judicial_Branch.pdf

Kadvany, E. (2017, March 21). Campaign postpones recall election of Brock Turner judge: Standalone November election could cost taxpayers $6.9 million. *Palo Alto Weekly*. Retrieved from https://paloaltoonline.com/news/2017/03/21/campaign-postpones-recall-election-of-brock-turner-judge

Koren, M. (2016, June 17). Why the Stanford judge gave Brock Turner six months: The California judge said the sexual-assault victim suffered "physical and devastating emotional injury," but a prison sentence for her offender was not appropriate. *The Atlantic*. Retrieved from https://www.theatlantic.com/news/archive/2016/06/stanford-rape-case-judge/487415/

Labriola, M., Bradley, S., O'Sullivan, C. S., Rempel, M., & Moore, S. (2010). *A national portrait of domestic violence court*. U.S. Department of Justice, National Institute of Justice Report. Document number 229659. Retrieved from https://www.ncjrs.gov/pdffiles1/nij/grants/229659.pdf

Linder, D. (n.d.). *Famous American trials: The O.J. Simpson trial 1995, a trial account*. Retrieved from http://law2.umkc.edu/faculty/projects/ftrials/simpson/simpson.htm

Lyman, R. (2002, November 7). Winona Ryder found guilty of 2 counts in shoplifting case. *New York Times*. Retrieved from http://www.nytimes.com/2002/11/07/national/07WINO.html

Macleod, D., & Weber, J. (2000). *Domestic violence courts: A descriptive study*. Judicial Council of California. Administrative Office of the Courts. Retrieved from http://www.courts.ca.gov/documents/dvreport.pdf

Madigan, N. (2004, April 22). Michael Jackson is indicted on child-molesting charges. *New York Times*. Retrieved from http://www.nytimes.com/2004/04/22/us/michael-jackson-is-indicted-on-child-molesting-charges.html

Medina, J. (2011, November 7). Doctor is guilty in Michael Jackson's death. *New York Times*. Retrieved from http://www.nytimes.com/2011/11/08/us/doctor-found-guilty-in-michael-jacksons-death.html?pagewanted=all

Orange County Bar Association. (2016, May 11). Press release: Orange County Bar Association releases ratings of candidates running for judicial office in the June 7 election. Retrieved from http://www.ocbar.org/About/PressReleases/May11,2016.aspx

Rocha, V. (2016a, June 8). O.C. judge who was censured for having sex in chambers wins reelection bid. *Los Angeles Times*. Retrieved from http://www.latimes.com/local/lanow/la-me-ln-judge-scott-steiner-reelection-win-20160608-snap-story.html

Rocha, V. (2016b, December 19). Judicial panel clears California judge who gave lenient sentence in Stanford sexual assault. *Los Angeles Times*. Retrieved from http://www.latimes.com/local/lanow/la-me-ln-judge-aaron-persky-no-judicial-misconduct-20161219-story.html

Winton, R. (2011, March 7). Lindsay Lohan surveillance video: Will sale hurt criminal case? *Los Angeles Times*. Retrieved from http://articles.latimes.com/2011/mar/07/news/la-lohan7-sl

Chapter 7

California Corrections

Jennifer Sumner and Kristy N. Matsuda

Learning Objectives

After reading the chapter, students should be able to:

- Describe the purpose and use of institutional and community corrections.
- Describe the organization and structure of the California corrections system historically and today.
- Explain California's growth in incarceration.
- Explain the role of politics and litigation in correctional reform efforts.
- Identify key changes in the use of jails, probation, prisons, and parole over time and the costs and benefits of these changes.

Introduction

For much of the past four decades, the California corrections system has been regularly used as an example for what *not* to do by policy and academic experts, even while it sustained "its reputation as a trendsetter for the nation" in crime and punishment policy (Kruttschnitt & Gartner, 2005, p. 9). The California corrections system has been the largest state corrections system in the United States in recent decades, reaching a prison population of over 173,000 in 2006 (CDCR, 2006). Just over a decade later, California no longer has the largest corrections system in the nation. The system has recently invited a new kind of attention for what has been referred to as a "drastic experiment in both decarceration and reallocation of carceral responsibility" (Schlanger, 2016, p. 65). The California corrections system is in the midst of historical reforms that have substantially reconfigured the system and significantly reduced the incarcerated population. A complete understanding of California corrections necessarily includes an examination of the system's numerous historical and contemporary changes: in sentencing models, use of correctional components, allocation of funding, and composition of the correctional populations. This chapter will demonstrate how a system that once consisted of clearly defined components with distinct roles has transformed into a system of interrelated parts that are no longer so clearly and easily distinguishable. Students of corrections will need to first understand each component of corrections to then make sense of how they have become so deeply intertwined.

The corrections system, the third subsystem of the criminal justice process, following arrest (through law enforcement) and conviction (through the courts) consists of both institutional and community components. Institutional corrections includes local and state correctional facilities (jails and prisons). Community corrections refers to correctional supervision in the community (probation and other community sanctions, and parole supervision). While the federal government also has a corrections system that spans the country, including California, this chapter focuses solely on state and local corrections operations. The juvenile corrections system is examined in Chapter 9; therefore, this chapter focuses solely on the system as it manages and treats adults.

This chapter is organized into three main sections. First, we introduce the basics of California corrections, including describing the various components and explaining the process. Second, we provide some context for understanding the current system and policies. Finally, we explain contemporary reform efforts and the rationale behind them.

Part I: The Basics

The corrections system is in place to implement a court-imposed sanction—a sentence—after an individual is found guilty of a crime. The purposes of these penalties are many: retribution, incapacitation, rehabilitation, deterrence, and restoration. For those convicted of misdemeanor crimes, sentences usually include fines, probation, and/or jail. For those convicted of felony crimes, the sentences include fines, probation, jail, prison, restitution, and/or the death penalty (see Chapter 8). Most often, those convicted of felonies are sentenced to probation and/or jail or prison.

Jails and Pre-Trial Services

Historically, jails were largely used for pre-trial detention for those accused of a criminal offense and waiting for trial or sentencing. Over time, jails increasingly began to serve the purpose of short-term incarceration for those convicted of misdemeanors and lower-level felonies. Operated at the local level, jails are commonly located in city centers near county courthouses. With their primary function to hold defendants prior to trial and sentencing, jails manage high daily populations and high rates of admission and release, making them most representative of the "churning" or "revolving door" characterization of the American criminal justice system.

In California, jails primarily fall under the jurisdiction of the state's 58 counties, and are operated by each county's sheriff's department. There are also many city jails that are operated by city police departments. The first formal county jail began operation in 1851 in San Francisco County, even before the first state prison was built. Like the rest of the United States, the majority of the individuals housed in California's jails are not serving a sentence but are "unsentenced," meaning they are defendants in the midst of their court process awaiting arraignment, trial, or sentencing.

Those booked into jail may remain there throughout the duration of their court processes. Others may post bail (a financial assurance that they will appear in court on the designated court date), be cited and released (particularly for those charged with misdemeanors), or even be released by the sheriff so that the jail may comply with court-ordered capacity requirements (Tafoya, Bird, Nguyen, & Grattet, 2017). Finally, others may be released on their "own recognizance"—with a "promise to appear" in court at the designated date and time—after an investigative process through pretrial services and with approval from a judge. Pre-trial release programs are designed to: relieve jail overcrowding, allow individuals to maintain their community ties throughout the court process, and address economic disparities inherent in the bail system.

Designed for temporary and shorter-term stays, jails are not suited to provide long-term care. High daily populations and high rates of turnover contribute to poor conditions of confinement and severely limit treatment and programming opportunities. Jails also regularly face strained budgets that can limit provision of basic hygiene and other necessities. These low-resourced jails are particularly problematic within the context of the populations they contain. Jail populations are disproportionately male, people of color, poor, homeless, undereducated, and unemployed; the population is also disproportionately mentally ill and in poor physical health, including with documented histories of substance abuse. Given these patterns, jails have commonly been described as "managing" society's "underclass" (Irwin, 1985) rather than a particularly "dangerous" population, although some argue this trend may be shifting (Rainville & Reeves, 2003).

Jails are frequently plagued by high rates of violence as well as disproportionately high suicide rates. In California jails, gangs also pose operational challenges. The Los Angeles County Sheriff's Department has estimated that possibly 80 percent of those incarcerated in the county jail are gang-affiliated and has attributed past widespread violence to "rival gang members or competing ethnic groups [vying] for power in the jail culture" (Bernstein & Garvey, 2006). Los Angeles County's jail, the nation's largest (Hare & Rose, 2016), has come under increased scrutiny due to legal challenges to its conditions of confinement, staff violence, and staff use of excessive force (Schlanger, 2016). Most recently, the jail gained notoriety for a massive corruption scandal in which former Los Angeles County Sheriff Lee Baca was convicted of three felonies for his effort "to obstruct attempts by the FBI to investigate allegations of corruption and abuse by deputies in his jails" (Rubin & Kim, 2017, para 10).

Pay-to-stay jails. One controversial approach to local incarceration that has emerged in California is pay-to-stay jails (also referred to as private jails). These facilities provide the option for convicted offenders to pay for higher quality conditions of confinement, including safety. The *Los Angeles Times* reports that between 2011 and 2015, 3,500 people served time in these facilities in southern California alone (Santo, Kim, & Flagg, 2017). The option of a pay-to-stay jail amplifies the economic inequities evident in the bail process and elsewhere in the system; those who can afford it may have a different experience of incarceration.

Probation

For those convicted of low-level offenses, sentences are often served in the community, under probation supervision. John Augustus is attributed with beginning the use of probation in the United States in 1841 in Massachusetts. Probation became a sentencing option in California in 1903 (Melnick, 1962). There are two broad categories of correctional community supervision: probation and parole. Probation is different from parole in two key ways. First, probation is a court sentence for those convicted of misdemeanors and some felonies. It can be imposed either independently or as part of a split sentence where the first part of the sentence is served in county jail and the second part is served on probation in the community. Parole is conditional release into the community *after* having served a prison sentence for one or more felony convictions. Second, in California, probation is under local jurisdiction, operated by counties, and parole is operated by the state. Each state operates parole and probation differently; many other states operate probation at the state level instead.

Probation has both surveillance and rehabilitative functions, achieved through supervision and treatment. Individuals are supervised while residing in the community, where they may stay close to home and maintain community ties (e.g., employment, familial bonds), and they are required to adhere to a specific set of conditions. In addition to its potentially rehabilitative functions, probation is also used to decrease jail overcrowding and correctional costs. In 2007, the average cost to supervise a convicted offender on probation was $3 a day versus $129 per day in state prison (LAO, 2009).

Probation conditions are based on one's determined risk level, which takes into account factors such as the severity and nature of the offense, past criminal history, and programmatic needs.[1] In California, probation officer caseloads are subsequently organized by these risk levels (LAO, 2009). "Banked" caseloads are used for the lowest risk offenders and require less frequent contact. Probationers on "regular" caseloads have more serious offense histories; therefore, face-to-face contact is more frequent (1–2 times monthly). "Specialized" caseloads are often used for those convicted of offenses requiring specialized supervision and treatment—for example, those convicted of sex, drug, or domestic violence offenses—and include increased reporting requirements tailored to the offense. In addition to varying frequencies of reporting to one's probation officer, probation conditions may also consist of drug testing, participation in programming, and maintaining employment.

A violation of conditions of probation may result in probation being revoked with the option to return the probationer to jail, increase time on probation and/or create more stringent conditions, or impose a prison sentence (LAO, 2009). "Failure to report to probation officers, unfulfilled participation in required treatment programs, leaving an assigned work area, or violations of other conditions imposed by the court are the most common reasons for probation revocations" (Nieto, 1996, p. 36). Much like patterns evident across parole, California's revocation rate for probationers has been found to be higher than the national average (LAO, 2009).

Risk Assessment. Risk assessments can be used in each part of the corrections system to help determine which offenders are at "high risk" for recidivism (i.e., reoffending), suicide, escape, violence, or any other behavior. Prior to the use of risk assessment instruments, risk was determined primarily by a correctional official and mental health professional. Toward the end of the twentieth century actuarial risk assessment instruments began to provide more systematic results.

---

1. Probation officers prepare pre-sentence investigation (PSI) reports for the courts. The report includes detailed information about an individual's criminal and personal history (e.g., past employment, education, familial relationships, substance use history, and mental health) and is ultimately submitted to the judge alongside a sentencing recommendation (in particular, whether or not probation should be granted). In addition, the PSI plays a significant role in correctional classification regardless of whether the sentence is served in the community or in a correctional facility.

An actuarial risk assessment instrument consists of a series of questions (or indicators) that can be used to determine, through review of an offender's file or an interview, the level of risk for a behavior. The indicators generate a "risk score." The higher the "risk," the more likely the individual will engage in the behavior the risk assessment is purported to measure. Research studies consistently show that actuarial risk assessment tools can far more accurately predict human behavior than professional judgment (even years of professional judgment) (Bonta & Andrews, 2007).

Actuarial risk assessment instruments come in two general types: static and dynamic. A static risk assessment instrument uses characteristics that do not change but are highly predictive of future behavior. In a correctional context, static factors include sex, age, offending history, and type of offense. Dynamic risk assessment instruments include static features and also factors that change over time (i.e., dynamic factors) such as social influences, familial relationships, employment, anger, or antisocial thoughts.

Dynamic risk assessments are used in "risk-need-responsivity" (RNR) program models. The three main principles of the RNR model are to: (1) assess an offender's likelihood of reoffending (i.e., risk); (2) assess an offender's criminogenic needs (i.e., those areas of need that may increase likelihood of reoffending); and (3) maximize the likelihood of success by not only providing effective treatment, but tailoring the treatment to the offender's needs, strengths, motivations, and learning styles (Bonta & Andrews, 2007). A dynamic risk assessment can be administered prior to incarceration, and reveal the actuarial risks and the criminogenic needs of an individual. Programs can then be assigned to the offender to address those risks and needs. Then, the risk assessment can be re-administered to see if the risks and needs of the offender have decreased or changed. If so, the correctional agency can adjust the plan according to that offender's responsivity (i.e., learning and motivation style). The use of actuarial risk assessments and the risk-need-responsivity framework has been shown to be an effective correctional strategy and is now being widely implemented as an "evidence-based" practice (Andrews, Bonta, & Wormith, 2006a; 2006b). Programs designed around these principles have demonstrated greater effects when targeting higher-risk offenders (Bonta & Andrews, 2007). Some correctional agencies in California are attempting to use this model. We discuss some of these efforts in greater detail later in the chapter.

Intermediate sanctions. In addition to a traditional probation sentence, community sanctions may include other requirements that make them more punitive than probation but less punitive than prison (Morris & Tonry, 1990; Petersilia, 1998). These intermediate sanctions are intended to divert offenders away from incarceration, often with increased supervision. Examples of intermediate sanctions include: intensive probation supervision, community service, day reporting centers, work release, home detention (also referred to as house arrest), electronic monitoring, residential drug treatment programs, or halfway houses.

Research suggests that some intermediate sanctions reduce reoffending and others do not. Those correctional programs that rely solely on services or surveillance, but not both, tend to be much less effective in reducing recidivism. Surveillance-oriented intensive supervision programs (e.g., reduced probation officer caseloads that allow for more intense supervision), adult boot camps, electronic monitoring, and restorative justice programs (when used on lower-risk adult offenders) have been shown to have no effect on recidivism rates (Aos et al., 2006). However, treatment-oriented intensive supervision programs, on average, have demonstrated almost a 22 percent reduction in recidivism (Aos et al., 2006). In their seminal work on intensive supervision probation and parole, Petersilia and Turner (1993) found that: "offenders who received counseling, held jobs, paid restitution, and did community service [in addition to the "intensive supervision"] were arrested 10–20% less often than were other offenders" (p. 321).

Prisons

In California, prisons are state-run institutions designed for long-term incarceration. San Quentin was established as California's first prison in 1852 (Bookspan, 1991). Folsom State Prison, the second oldest prison in California, began operation in 1880. Today, the state operates 35 prisons for adult offenders run by the California Department of Corrections and Rehabilitation's (CDCR) Division of Adult Institutions (DAI). Three prisons are designated for women only. The CDCR also operates smaller community correctional facilities, some of which are run by private contractors. The CDCR partners with the California Department of Forestry and Fire Protection (CalFire) as well as Los Angeles County Fire Department to operate 43 Conservation (fire) Camps for minimum-custody prisoners who have demonstrated "good behavior" while incarcerated.

Classification and housing. Prisoners enter the CDCR at a prison reception center. During the reception center period they undergo a review process in which life and social histories, criminal records, medical, psychological, and mental health histories are considered. Risk assessment instruments (discussed earlier in the section on probation) are administered in order to assign prisoners to a security level, which determines the type of long-term housing unit in which they will be placed. Housing designation is the centerpiece to the incarceration experience as it determines one's conditions of confinement, access to programming, and distance from home. Housing in California prisons is categorized according to four security levels (CDCR, 2017a). From Level I to Level IV there are increasing restrictions on freedom of movement both in terms of physical restrictions (i.e., walls, fences) and participation in programming and work. Level I, minimum security, is used for units or camps that are generally open dormitories with a low-security perimeter. Level II units have open dormitory living with a secure perimeter and may have armed officers. Level III units use cell living within a secure perimeter and include armed coverage. Level IV, or high security, uses celled living units with secure perimeters with armed coverage inside and outside of the institution. Each prison in California contains several housing units and usually serves multiple security levels. Prisoners who are sentenced to death are housed separately on "death row." San Quentin Prison holds death row for male prisoners, and Central California Women's Facility houses death row for female prisoners.

Beyond considerations of security level, prisoners can be placed in specific facilities or housing units depending on behavioral, programming, or other individualized needs. Sensitive Needs Yards (SNYs) are designated for those prisoners who may be able to participate in work and programming but who require separation from the rest of the population for their protection. Some prisoners with diagnosed medical and mental health needs may be housed in one of the two prisons with medical care as a central focus: California Medical Facility and the California Health Care Facility. "Administrative placements," which override these substantive considerations, can lead to housing prisoners according to prison characteristics like available bed space. These "administrative overrides" usually result in higher-level security placement than the individual's designation indicates (CDCR, 2011; Petersilia, 2006). Not only does housing prisoners at a higher security restrict access to resources such as programming, it also comes at a higher cost.

Restricted housing refers to housing units inside a prison or jail that "involve[] limited interaction with other inmates, limited programming opportunities, and reduced privileges" (Beck, 2015, p. 2) and it is usually used either as a punitive response to a disciplinary behavior or as a protective measure. Because of the restrictions imposed in these settings, its simultaneous use as both punitive (for those violating institutional rules) and also protective (for differentially vulnerable populations) has been criticized (Arkles, 2009; Sylvia Rivera Law Project, 2007). Such conditions are colloquially called "solitary confinement," but prison administrators may resist applying this term because of the controversial nature of the conditions. The CDCR refers to this sort of restricted housing as Segregated Program Housing Units (SPHU) and uses two types, Security Housing Units (SHUs) and Administrative-Segregation Units (ASUs), when removing prisoners from the general population. Administrative segregation is for prisoners in the general population who violate prison rules or are perceived to pose an immediate threat to the security of the institution. These prisoners can be taken out of the general population and temporarily placed in a restricted setting and then they are returned to the general population. The CDCR indicates that SHUs are designed to house offenders "whose conduct endangers the safety of others or the security of the prison" (2013). They are intended for much longer periods of housing. Generally, a prisoner would be housed in a SHU after being found guilty, in an internal administrative hearing, of committing a violent or serious offense while in prison. Until reforms in 2015, SHU beds were often filled with members of security threat groups (STGs) (i.e., prison gangs).

Pelican Bay State Prison's security housing unit, built in 1989, is the largest in the state and the second largest in the nation (Reiter, 2012). It is California's only archetypal supermax prison. Supermax prisons emerged in the 1980s as technologically advanced, concentrated confinement facilities, built specifically for the purpose of long-term solitary confinement (Reiter, 2016). Reiter (2012) reveals that the CDCR has been using the SHU housing units far beyond what was originally intended, both in terms of number of prisoners confined there as well as the duration of incarceration. The original guideline for a SHU sentence was set at a maximum of 18 months. Over time, the CDCR has converted multiple units at numerous facilities into SHUs, set the maximum determinate SHU term to five years, and used indefinite SHU terms that have resulted in people spending "up to 20 years or more" in these restrictive conditions (Reiter, 2012, p. 547).

The overuse and extended use of these housing units, their conditions, and the administrative decisions that result in a SHU term were some of the core complaints fueling three hunger strikes conducted by prisoners in California prisons between 2011 and 2013 (Reiter, 2015). These practices were subsequently challenged in a class-action suit, *Ashker v. Brown*, in which prisoners "allege[d] that CDCR's gang management regulations and practices [particularly the process for validating gang membership] violate the Due Process Clause of the Fourteenth Amendment and that the conditions of confinement in Pelican Bay's SHU constitute cruel and unusual punishment in violation of the Eighth Amendment" (*Ashker v. Brown*, 2015, p. 2). In 2015, this case was settled and the terms of the agreement included, among many other specifics, ending the practices of automatic isolation for validated gang members and indeterminate sentences to isolation (including both ASU and SHU terms) (Reiter, 2015). In response to court action, the CDCR reports that it reduced the segregated prisoner population by approximately 12 percent in 2014 (CDCR, 2015).

Programming. Prisoners' access to programming depends a great deal on their designated security level and housing assignment; SHU or ASU prisoners will not be eligible to participate in the same range of programs as prisoners in the general population. In the dozens of CDCR-operated fire camps, minimum-security prisoners are trained to actively fight forest fires or respond to other disasters in California. The Prison Industries Authority (PIA) is a state-run business in which goods and services made by prisoner workers are sold to government agencies. PIA positions are paid approximately 35 to 95 cents per hour (40% of which is designated for court and restitution fees) (CALPIA, 2011a). PIA is currently operating in 30 CDCR prisons and provides services including construction, laundry, license plate making, and dairy and egg production (CALPIA, 2011b). The CDCR also provides vocational training, educational programs, substance abuse treatment, anger management treatment, family reunification, religious programming, and prerelease planning. Despite the existence of these various programs, there are far fewer opportunities to participate in the programs than there are inmates who need them, especially in terms of drug treatment (Petersilia, 2006). Research shows that, upon release from prison, many prisoners who needed programming did not receive it (Petersilia, 2007), indicating that program expansion is always a need.

In 2005, the CDCR established an office of Female Offender Programs and Services. This is particularly notable within a historical context in which incarcerated women have been considerably overlooked (Kruttschnitt & Gartner, 2005). While the majority of California prisoners are male (women currently constitute less than 5% of the prison population), research on female offending has identified uniquely gendered "pathways" toward crime that warrant a different correctional response (Daly, 1992; DeHart, Lynch, Belknap, Dass-Brailsford, & Green, 2014; Salisbury & Van Voorhis, 2009). For example, female offenders have more extensive histories of abuse and trauma, substance abuse, and mental illness and are more commonly unemployed prior to incarceration. They are also more likely than men to have been the primary caregiver of children or others prior to incarceration. Gender-responsive programming is designed to address these different needs (Bloom, Owen, & Covington, 2003). The office of Female Offender Programs and Services oversees housing, program, and pre-release services for female offenders. It also runs fire camps for women and specialized community programs for female offenders. The Community Prisoner Mother Program, operated by private contractors, is designed to provide treatment for non-serious female prisoners with up to two small children under age six.

Prison Culture, Race, and Gangs. California's prisons for men have been both historically and contemporarily characterized as profoundly racialized spaces. This is evident both in the fabric of prison culture and in administrative practices. Scholars have examined the extent to which the prisoner subculture in California prisons is organized around a cohesive inmate "code of conduct" (i.e., shared informal prison rules) or instead fragmented into different groups divided by imported characteristics (e.g., gang affiliation, race category, gender identity) (e.g., Hunt et al., 1993; Trammell, 2009; Sexton & Jenness, 2016; Sumner, 2009). In her research conducted with men formerly incarcerated in California prisons, Trammell (2009) found prisoners follow an "inmate code" which includes "acting tough" and "keeping to yourself" in order to maintain their "convict identity." However, at times, the "code" conflicts with official prison policies. In these instances, Trammell (2009) found that prisoners choose to follow those rules established by their gang leaders. She argues that the inmate code has become reconfigured through the proliferation of organized gangs in California prisons.

"Prison gangs," otherwise known as security threat groups (STGs), present a significant operational challenge to prison management because of their notable contributions to violence and threats (Fleisher & Decker, 2001). "Prison gang" is the general term used for criminal entities that form inside of prison, recruit members, and then move out onto the streets.[2] While street gangs may be divided along geographic lines, prison gangs are very clearly divided along racial lines. For example, the members of the Mexican Mafia and Nuestra Familia are most often Mexican or Latino. The Black Guerrilla Family is usually comprised of black prisoners. And the Aryan Brotherhood and Nazi Low Riders are prison gangs generally made up of white prisoners. Thus, race becomes a proxy for security threat group membership, resulting in administrative practices that are organized around race, though ostensibly designed to control and separate gangs.

The CDCR's informal, yet routine reliance on severely limited racial categories to identify prisoners (i.e., "Black, White, Hispanic, and Other") in order to segregate by race in reception center housing assignments is one way in which the system is structured around race categories (Goodman, 2008; see also Goodman, 2014). This practice was the subject of legal challenge in *Johnson v. California* (2005) in which the U.S. Supreme Court found that the practice must be subject to the highest level of judicial scrutiny, returning the case to the lower court for review. Before the lower court reviewed the case under this standard, the CDCR entered into an agreement with Johnson, indicating it

---

2. This is in contrast to "criminal street gangs" that are formed out on the streets and whose members can be affiliated when they arrive in prison (e.g., Crips or Bloods). Criminal street gangs are often formed around geographic locations like neighborhoods.

would no longer use race as a determinative factor in housing assignments. Another race-based practice challenged through prisoner litigation consists of locking down (i.e., restricting the movement of) large groups of prisoners by race and ethnicity, in response to select incidents of violence, particularly those involving prisoners of different racial and ethnic groups (*Mitchell v. Cate* [2008]; Hunt et al., 1993; St. John, 2014). In the settlement of *Mitchell*, the CDCR agreed to, among other things, stop race-based modified programs or lockdowns and use individualized threat assessments to determine who would be on a modified program.

Research on women's prisons indicates they are not similarly organized around race in the way that men's prisons are, particularly in California. In her ethnographic research conducted at California Central Women's Facility, Owen (1998) found that "race and ethnicity, then, form one aspect of prison identity and social interaction, playing some role in the formation of prison culture" for women, but it is not "the primary basis for prison social order" (p. 152). Neither is the prisoner culture as attached to one particularly identifiable "inmate code." In prisons for women, prisoner culture is more defined by interpersonal relationships with children and family outside of prison, with staff, and with other prisoners (Owen, 1998). Perhaps one of the most notable distinctions between the subculture in prisons for women and that which is evident in prisons for men are the pseudo-families that women prisoners develop by taking on different familial roles.

Prison Violence

Sexual Assault and the Prison Rape Elimination Act (PREA). The Prison Rape Elimination Act, federal legislation signed into law in 2003, directed attention toward sexual victimization in correctional facilities. It mandated the development of new policies and practices to be put in place in pursuit of reducing the rate of sexual victimization, as well as national data collection efforts to document the extent and nature of sexual assault in prison. In one recent national study of sexual victimization in U.S. correctional facilities, researchers found that the rate of nonconsensual sexual acts in California prisons for men ranged from 0 to 4.5 percent (Beck, Berzofsky, Casper, & Krebs, 2013).[3] The rate in California women's prisons ranged from 1.4 to 6.1 percent. This national data collection effort also reveals that those who identify as gay, lesbian, bisexual, or another sexual identity (i.e., not heterosexual) reported particularly

---

3. This includes reports of unwanted sexual acts by other inmates and any sexual acts with staff (Beck et al., 2013).

high rates of sexual victimization by both prisoners and staff in jails and prisons in the U.S. (Beck et al., 2013).

A study of sexual victimization in California correctional facilities found wide disparity in rates of sexual victimization across samples of prisoners. Specifically, 4.4% of a random sample of prisoners interviewed in prisons for men reported sexual victimization in a California correctional facility, compared to 59% of a purposefully selected sample of transgender women (Jenness, Maxson, Matsuda, & Sumner, 2007). Increasing visibility of the unique vulnerability of transgender prisoners in correctional facilities, including as a result of numerous legal challenges brought against corrections systems for failing to provide adequate protection and care, have led corrections departments to begin to develop policies that specifically address the management and treatment of this group. The CDCR has enacted new policy that addresses staff treatment of transgender prisoners in searches, housing placement, and provision of gender-specific clothing items (CDCR, 2017b). In 2017, Shiloh Heavenly Quine, a transgender woman incarcerated in a California prison for men, became the first incarcerated prisoner to receive gender-affirming (known previously as sex-reassignment) surgery funded by a state department of corrections in the United States (Associated Press, 2017a). Quine was moved to one of California's women's prisons after the surgery was completed (Associated Press, 2017b).

Non-Sexual Prison Violence. The PREA legislation mandated the annual collection of data on the sexual assault of inmates in every state. There is not, however, a similar mandate for data collection on general prison violence information, either across the nation or by state. Therefore, an understanding of the level of violence in California prisons is limited. Prior to 2007, the CDCR released yearly reports on the number of inmate incidents in their institutions (CDCR, 2007a). These reports have since been discontinued, which means that since 2006 there are no statewide data on incidents in prison. A prison incident can include assault or battery, possession of a weapon, suicide, attempted suicide, or possession of a controlled substance. Research that examines California prison incidents between the 1970s through the last available data in 2006, suggests incidents in California prisons were increasing (CDCR, 2007a; Sumner & Matsuda, 2006). The California Legislative Analyst's Office (2005) reported that, according to their most recent data (in this case from 2000), California had an inmate assault rate that was higher than Texas and the federal system, both of which housed more prisoners than California's prison system at the time (LAO, 2005). These data might support the general conception that California prisons are dangerous places (e.g., Thompson, 2015); however, until new rates of prisoner violence are recorded and analyzed, we do not know the extent to which that is accurate in today's prisons.

Parole and Prisoner Reentry

Parole is a period of community supervision required of inmates released from prison. The parole term can vary depending on the commitment offense. In California, most parolees have a standard three-year parole term. But some offenders (i.e., sex offenders or lifers) can have between a five-year to ten-year parole supervision period. The conditions and general terms of parole vary from state to state and, as will become apparent in the rest of this chapter, California's parole history is somewhat unique. In general, once released from a California state prison, individuals are returned to the county in which they previously lived for parole supervision by California's Division of Adult Parole Operations (DAPO). Offenders are released with a small amount of "gate money" (approximately $200) and are required to check in with their parole office the next business day.

The court, the Board of Parole Hearings (BPH), or a parole agent may require special conditions for parolees related to their criminal offense or history. Conditions could also be statutorily required. For example, by statute all parolees are mandated to consent to a search with or without a warrant or cause. Another statutory requirement is for offenders convicted of some sex offenses to register with their local police department. California also requires registration for some drug offenders, arsonists, and gang members. Other special conditions of parole could include staying away from certain associates or victims, random urinalysis testing (i.e., drug testing), court ordered restitution, scheduled meetings with the parole officer, or participation in the CDCR required parole program.

In 2010, DAPO introduced a new parole model program called California Parole Supervision and Reintegration Model (CPSRM). CPSRM is a risk-need-responsivity (RNR) evidence-based model (introduced in the probation section) that has been widely implemented to assess and treat criminal offenders (Andrews, 2006; Bonta & Andrews, 2007). Before the implementation of CPSRM, parole in California was an offense-based, rather than offender-based, model. In the prior model, the length of time for a violation and the level of supervision (i.e., frequency of reporting to one's parole agent) were based on an individual's offense. The CPSRM model uses a risk assessment tool to determine the level of surveillance necessary. Parole officers use the needs of the offender to determine the programming or treatment plan for each offender. And parole officers use the responsivity component to determine the most suited set of incentives and rewards. In other words, parole plans can be tailored to the individual. If parolees perform well on parole and meet expectations, their supervision level can drop, which lowers the number of contacts they must have with their parole officer. If they perform very well on parole, the parole officer can recommend early discharge from parole supervision. Not all parolees are eligible for early discharge consideration, and there are minimum supervision times required before it would be considered.

DAPO caseloads vary depending on the type of offender. This is because parole is structured such that some types of offenders require more parole officer resources than others. A standard DAPO caseload is 52 parolees to 1 officer. Some DAPO officers have specialized caseloads in which they only supervise one "type" of parolee—and because of the increased demands this designation requires, their caseloads are smaller. For example, all sex offenders in California have longer parole periods, more special conditions, and are required to be monitored by GPS (Global Positioning System) technology. Because of the added workload, parole agents supervising sex offenders supervise 20 offenders at a time; gang caseloads are 20 to 1; and mental health caseloads are 40 to 1.

DAPO has also implemented gender-responsive training and programming for women on parole. One example of this effort is the Female Offender Treatment and Employment Program (FOTEP), a parole program designed to reduce female recidivism through substance abuse treatment, family reunification, vocational training, and employment services. It is designed only for women who have been identified as having related needs based on the risk assessment instrument.

When parolees violate the conditions of supervision and/or commit a new crime, they are returned to court and a county judge determines a resulting sanction such as a jail term, flash incarceration, community programming, or electronic or GPS monitoring. After completing the new sanction, they continue with parole supervision, though the parole agent may modify the conditions of parole to address the violation or a new requirement issued by the judge. Only parolees with an indeterminate life sentence are eligible to be returned to state prison for a parole violation. All other parolees will be sentenced to jail or another community alternative for the parole violation unless they are tried and convicted of a new crime. California's unique historical and contemporary approach to parole revocation is discussed in greater detail in the following section.

Part II: Historical Change

Changing Sentencing Models

One way in which California corrections may best be understood is through its changing sentencing structure and resulting use of parole. While the previous section describes what parole looks like now, the journey to this parole structure is decades in the making (and still changing) as this, and following sections, will demonstrate.

The concept of parole first began in 1840 when Alexander Maconochie developed a "mark system," in which prisoners would earn good marks toward their release for positive and productive activities (today's "good time credits"), at an English penal colony at Norfolk Island (Petersilia, 2003). Former prisoners tested these efforts upon release while being supervised in the community until they could demonstrate they could apply these successfully in the "real world" (Petersilia, 2003). Zebulon Brockway was the first to implement this "two-pronged strategy for managing prison populations and preparing inmates for release" in the United States at the Elmira Reformatory for youth in New York (Petersilia, 2003, p. 58). By 1942 all states were using an indeterminate sentencing structure, in which prisoners earned release through productive work and programming, followed by supervision on parole upon release, and including guidelines for when parole conditions were violated (Petersilia, 2003). This began in California in 1917 with the passage of the Indeterminate Sentencing Act (Dansky, 2008).

Indeterminate sentencing structures involve judicial discretion on the front end and high correctional discretion on the back end. Judges sentence individuals to a range of time to be served in prison (e.g., 2 to 10 years), yet the time actually served is at the discretion of a parole board. In California, the state's Board of Parole Hearings (BPH) uses the offender's case record and information regarding the individual's progress while incarcerated to determine whether or not the individual is safe to be released back into the community on parole. The factors considered include: the commitment offense and criminal history, the nature of the time spent in prison (e.g., participation in education, work, and programming and disciplinary issues), psychological evaluations, expressions of remorse and acceptance of responsibility, plans for release, and input from others (family members and/or those on the side of the victim).

Indeterminate sentencing structures coupled with discretionary parole remained the most common approach to sentencing in the United States through the 1960s. This approach to sentencing and punishment is consistent with positivist criminological theories that indicate the causes of crime can be identified and addressed to reduce someone's likelihood of reoffending. Within this context, a criminal sentence would target the underlying causes of crime. In addition to its rehabilitative goals, an indeterminate sentencing structure can help decrease levels of prison misconduct, as prisoners are incentivized to demonstrate "good behavior" in exchange for earlier release (Bales & Miller, 2012).

In the 1970s, however, a nationwide shift away from this model gained popularity for several reasons. First, after having reviewed studies that examined the effects of correctional rehabilitative programming, Robert Martinson and colleagues concluded that "With few and isolated exceptions, the rehabilitative efforts that have been reported so far have had no appreciable effect on recidivism" (Lipton, Martinson, & Wilks, 1975, p. 20; Martinson, 1974, p. 25). This caught on quickly as people embraced this broad claim that there was no scientific support for using rehabilitative efforts to reduce recidivism; thus, they concluded that there was also no longer a need for indeterminate sentencing and discretionary parole. Although this work was strongly criticized, and Martinson himself later withdrew his conclusion and argued for parole programming (Martinson, 1979), his initial statement was embraced by a populace ready for it. Second, the indeterminate sentencing model was perceived as both unduly harsh and unfair by the political left (Petersilia, 2003). The argument was that prisoners were being forced to participate in programs they did not want to participate in, and not knowing how much time they had to serve was particularly painful. Also, many argued that the high discretion by the parole board resulted in disparate and therefore, discriminatory, treatment across extralegal factors such as class and race. The political right was also in favor of abandoning the indeterminate sentencing structure, arguing that because of the wide term range, prisoners were being released too soon and not serving enough of their sentences. Within the context of these critiques the time was suited for a new approach to sentencing and punishment and Andrew Von Hirsch (1976) had one in his "just deserts" philosophy of punishment. Returning to classical theories of crime and punishment, he argued that those convicted of the same crime should be serving the same sentences; the punishment should be proportionate to the crime and not focused on offender characteristics.

California was one of the first states to move from an indeterminate to a determinate sentencing structure. Its Determinate Sentencing Law became effective in 1977. Included in this law was a clear statement "that the ultimate goal of imprisonment was 'punishment' and not 'rehabilitation'" (Petersilia, 2003, p. 65; see also Dansky, 2008). Under this structure, fixed sentences based on offense severity are imposed, rather than a range of years subject to the discretion of a parole board. A judge can select from three sentence ranges specified for each crime. The decision to choose the low, mid, or high sentence is determined by any mitigating or aggravating factors in the case.

Under the determinate sentencing structure, discretionary release by a parole board is eliminated. Instead, prisoners are automatically released once they have served their sentence, a process referred to as "maxing out." Depending on state law, prisoners may also be released earlier if they have earned "good time" credits through participation in work, education, or other programming and no disciplinary problems as long as they have served the required portion of their sentence. In 1994, California began "truth in sentencing," requiring violent offenders to serve 85 percent of their sentences, thereby qualifying for "federal incentive grants to build or expand correctional facilities" (Ditton & Wilson, 1999, p. 3).

In its shift to a determinate sentencing structure, California adopted an "unusual hybrid" approach, selecting pieces of both sentencing models (Petersilia, 2006). The state eliminated discretionary parole for convicted offenders except those serving indeterminate life sentences (either due to the severity of the crime or its designation as a third strike), and it also adopted mandatory parole for all of those released. Mandatory parole is automatic parole supervision upon release, in contrast to *discretionary* parole (at the discretion of a parole board) that is part of an indeterminate sentencing model. In California, all individuals released from prison were statutorily subjected to at least a three-year parole term, a term that was extended to up to five years for some offenders (e.g., sex offenders) in 2000. Petersilia (2006) argues that this approach leads to "the parole term functioning not as a reward for good behavior (as it would in an indeterminate system) but as a period of extended surveillance and scrutiny during which the parolee may be recalled to jail on fairly minimal grounds" (p. 64).

Since its enactment, California's sentencing model has come under attack from many sides. Even Governor Jerry Brown, who originally supported the law during his first run as governor of California, called it an "abysmal failure" (Warren, 2003). Well-renowned criminologist and leading expert on prisoner reentry, Joan Petersilia, argues that the "significance of the adoption of determinate sentencing cannot be overstated" (Petersilia, 2006, p. 61), as discretionary power shifted to the legislature, which continued to pass crime bills fueled by public anxiety around fear of crime even during a time in which crime rates had declined. In a report submitted to the Little Hoover Commission in 2007, researchers identified over 100 felony sentencing enhancements, including 80 "substantive increases in sentence lengths" as well as limitations to judicial discretion, since the Determinate Sentencing Act was passed (Little Hoover Commission, 2007). Furthermore, with vast power to make filing decisions, prosecutor discretion intentionally triggers these legislatively mandated sentence enhancements.

These changes have not only contributed to the dramatic growth in California's prison population, but have also "undercut" both rehabilitative and public safety goals (Petersilia, 2006). This is particularly evident in looking more closely at how mandatory parole operates in California specifically. Removing discretion entirely from the parole board means that prisoners are not required to participate in programs while incarcerated and must be automatically released whether or not they may pose a risk to public safety. Once released, they are subject to a set of parole conditions. Parole may be revoked because the individual has committed a new crime and/or a technical violation (violating a condition of parole that would not otherwise be considered a crime). In California, parole violations (for new crimes and technical violations) have significantly contributed to the prison population increase in past decades. In addition, the Bureau of Justice Statistics found that prisoners are actually more likely to successfully complete their parole period on discretionary, rather than mandatory, parole (Hughes, Wilson, & Beck, 2001).

Three-Strikes Law. Within this context, California's three-strikes habitual offender law found a welcome home in 1994. It was motivated first by Mike Reynolds, whose 18-year-old daughter Kimber Reynolds was murdered by two parolees (Auerhahn, 2003). His efforts gained momentum after national news covered the kidnapping and murder of a 12-year-old girl, Polly Klaas, in Petaluma, a suburb in the San Francisco Bay Area. Richard Allen Davis, a parolee with a previous history of violence and kidnapping, committed the crimes after he was released from prison after having maxed out on his sentence by way of determinate sentencing. He had previously been denied parole multiple times under the Indeterminate Sentencing Act (Petersilia, 2006). The original three-strikes law, AB 971, was passed by the legislature in March of 1994. Mike Reynolds' voter initiated Proposition 184 still remained on the ballot for the November election and subsequently passed as well. In its original form, this law designates certain felonies as "serious" or "violent," and thus, categorized as "strikes." A second "strike" brought forth double the amount of time it would have if it were the first strike. And a third "strike" which, in the original law only had to be a felony (not serious nor violent), resulted in either three times the term of the sentence for that crime or an indeterminate sentence of 25 years to life, whichever is longer (Auerhahn, 2003). This law, although more recently amended through voter-initiated Proposition 36 (discussed later in this chapter), has withstood challenges to its constitutionality regarding its proportionality to crimes committed (*Lockyer v. Andrade*, 2003).

Growing the Prison Population

Changes in sentencing laws have contributed to California's growth in prison population during what is regularly referred to as the state's prison "boom," "explosion," or "building spree." The state experienced dramatic prison growth across three decades, with its custody population at 21,088 in 1976, growing to 145,565 in 1996 (California Department of Corrections, 1997), and eventually surpassing 173,000 in 2006 (CDCR, 2006). "The largest population increase occurred between 1987 and 1997, when the institution population increased by 131.8 percent" (CDCR, 2007b). "The state's female prison population increased more than tenfold between the early 1970s ... and the late 1990s" (Kruttschnitt & Gartner, 2005, p. 32). Between 1964 and 1984, the racial and ethnic distribution also changed, increasing the proportion of African American and Latino/a prisoners as compared to whites (Petersilia, 2006).

Between 1984 and 1997, California also built and began operation of 21 new prisons. The first of these, California State Prison, Solano, built in 1984, was the first prison built since 1965. Since that "prison-building spree" in 1997, three more prisons have been built and only one has been deactivated. Finally, the prison budget has also increased exponentially since 1970 and is particularly telling when examined alongside state educational budgets, which have decreased over the same time period (LAO, 2009). Corrections constituted three percent of the state's general fund in 1970 (Martin & Grattet, 2015) and at its peak in 2011–2012 it constituted 11.4 percent (State of California, 2016).

In many ways, California is not particularly unique in its prison growth, as its incarceration rate during the mid-2000s was not markedly different from the national average (Petersilia, 2006). Contextual aspects of California corrections and the resulting effects are noteworthy. Crime and punishment legislation has been at the forefront of political campaigns that fuel public anxiety around fear of crime (even during its decline), essentially casting each individual as a potential victim (Simon, 2007). In California, the correctional officers' union (CCPOA) has played a unique—and substantial—role in this legislative trend toward increasingly punitive policies. The CCPOA, which represents correctional officers and parole agents in California, is one of the most powerful (and successful) labor unions in the country (Page, 2012). The CCPOA expanded alongside the prison buildup as the growing corrections system continued to hire more peace officers to staff its newly built prisons (Page, 2012). The political "tough on crime" climate supported the CCPOA's growing political infrastructure as it began to heavily influence increasingly punitive political agendas and related legislative change.

There are other aspects of the changes in use of incarceration that also must be highlighted. For example, while the prison population increased more than eightfold between 1976 and 2006, the percentage of parole violator returns increased by 40-fold; there were 2,233 parole violator returns to prison in 1976 (CDC, 1997) and 89,883 in 2006 (CDCR, 2007b). The nature of confinement changed during this time as well.

In a 2011 press release, Governor Brown pointed to some of the problems endemic to California's use of incarceration, stating:

For too long, the state's prison system has been a revolving door for lower-level offenders and parole violators who are released within months—often before they are even transferred out of a reception center.... Cycling these offenders through state prisons wastes money, aggravates crowded conditions, thwarts rehabilitation, and impedes local law enforcement supervision. (Office of the Governor, 2011)

In sharp contrast to the medical/treatment model that preceded it, the 1980s set the stage for a "warehouse" prison model, in which bunks began to fill "auditoriums," "hallways," and "storage rooms" (Kruttschnitt & Gartner, 2005, p. 32) and risk management of the group through systematic actuarial assessments became a central preoccupation of correctional managers (Feeley & Simon, 1992). With these changes in the size and nature of the California prison system came new legal challenges to the constitutionality of prisoners' conditions of confinement and a call for change, again.

Reorganizing the State Corrections System

By 2004, California operated 32 prisons and eight juvenile institutions and it had become clear that this enormous system was in crisis. Numerous allegations of correctional officer abuse of inmates were emerging, a lack of operational consistency across institutions was clear, and the inability of the system to provide adequate services to its inmates was becoming apparent. In short, California had been building and building and building, but still filling its prisons past their capacity. In doing so, the conditions inside the prisons were becoming noticeably worse.

In response, California Governor Arnold Schwarzenegger convened a Corrections Independent Review Panel to conduct an assessment of the California correctional system. The Corrections Independent Review Panel (2004) recommended that the California Youth and Adult Correctional Agency (YACA), as it was then known, be reorganized and that changes be made in training, recruitment, and other correctional policies in efforts to improve correctional culture, treatment of inmates, and public safety. The "reorganization," as it was regularly referred to, centralized each department branch beneath one hierarchical management structure. This meant that the previously independent departments of adult and juvenile corrections and parole would now be administrated under one system and under one Secretary of Corrections.[4] As part

---

4. The reorganization changed the administrative structure of the Department of Corrections, but it did not change the operational structure of the correctional institutions.

of the reorganization plan, the old agency also took on a new name, the California Department of Corrections and *Rehabilitation* (CDCR). The "R" was meant to espouse a visible commitment to rehabilitative, in addition to public safety, goals. In addition to a stated renewed focus on rehabilitation, the reconfiguration of the system, which included the first ever research office for adult corrections, also indicated a commitment to "evidence-based" policies and practices and a resulting increased use of actuarial risk measures.

Part III: Contemporary Reform Efforts

Brown v. Plata *(2011)*

An even more dramatic shift in the California correctional landscape surrounds the Supreme Court decision in *Brown v. Plata* (2011). Despite being decided as *Brown v. Plata*, in its review, the Supreme Court combined two court cases brought simultaneously in California: *Coleman v. Brown* (1990) and *Plata v. Brown* (2006). Coleman was a prisoner with serious mental illness being confined at Pelican Bay State Prison. At the time, Pelican Bay only employed one psychologist to treat all of the mental health needs of the 3,500 prisoners at the facility. The judge (and later the district court) in *Coleman* found that the CDCR was not providing adequate mental healthcare to its prisoners and that this deficiency constituted cruel and unusual punishment, violating the Eighth Amendment of the Constitution. The court appointed a Special Master to monitor the state's plan to improve the mental healthcare of prisoners.

Following *Coleman*, in 2001 *Plata* claimed that the medical care provided in California prisons was so inadequate it constituted cruel and unusual punishment and violated the Eighth Amendment. The case settled in 2002 with the CDCR promising to drastically improve healthcare. In 2005, and after very little progress, the judge in the case declared that the medical provision in prisons was so inadequate that it constituted "deliberate indifference" to California prisoners (*Plata v. Schwarzenegger*, 2005). In this context, "deliberate indifference" means that the CDCR was sufficiently aware of the subpar medical care, but did not sufficiently address the issue. The court appointed a receiver to oversee the remedial plan for medical care in California prisons. The appointment of a receiver was significant, because it removed the power to reform the state cor-

---

Juvenile facilities and juvenile parole were still operating separately from adult prison and adult parole although they remained under the management of the same Secretary.

rectional system from the state and put it in the hands of an outside entity. Control over the medical system would be not returned to the CDCR until the goal had been reached, in which case the receivership could end.

In the same year as *Plata* (2005), there were 164,179 prisoners housed in California prisons (CDCR, 2005). This was twice as many as the CDCR prisons were designed to hold. In 2006, Governor Schwarzenegger issued a state of emergency in California due to the size of the prison population. This allowed the CDCR to involuntarily transfer prisoners to contract beds out of the state to relieve the housing issue (Turner, Fain, & Hunt, 2015). That same year, both the Special Master for *Coleman* and the Federal Receiver for *Plata* reported that the size of the prison population in California was hindering the system's ability to comply with court orders to improve medical and mental healthcare for the state's prisoners; therefore, it was unconstitutional. The attorneys in *Plata* and *Coleman* claimed that a population limit should be required in order to remedy unconstitutional living conditions in California prisons. They brought the suit under the federal Prison Litigation Reform Act (PLRA) (Schlanger, 2013). In general, the PLRA had made it more difficult for prisoners to bring a lawsuit against prisons, because it requires that prisoners exhaust all internal grievance procedures. Indeed, the use of the internal grievance process in California state prisons is extensive, in spite of the rare instances in which they are granted (Calavita & Jenness, 2013). With the mandates in both *Plata* and *Coleman* and the state of emergency declared by the governor, it became an ideal moment for attorneys representing prisoners to move forward. A three-judge court was convened and settlement talks and negotiations were attempted for years (for a detailed discussion see Schlanger, 2013). Negotiations were ultimately unsuccessful, and the case went to trial in 2008. In 2009, the three-judge court found that the state must reduce the adult prison population to 137.5 percent of the prison designed capacity within two years. However, when the three-judge panel issued their ruling, they also temporarily suspended their own decision until the United States Supreme Court could review the case. This meant that the CDCR would not have to begin its population reduction efforts until the Supreme Court ruled on the case.

The Supreme Court could have changed the population goal or the timeframe to reach that goal as part of its ruling. Instead, in May 2011, the Supreme Court, with a five-to-four ruling, affirmed the three-judge panel's original ruling. But they noted that it should be in the three-judge court's power to modify the order at their discretion. The dissenting Supreme Court justices declared that the ruling was "perhaps the most radical injunction issued by a court in our Nation's history" (*Brown v. Plata*, 131 S. Ct. 1910, 1950 (2011) Scalia, J., dissenting). The court decision in *Brown v. Plata* gave the CDCR until the end of 2013 to reduce its prison population to 137.5 percent of the design capacity.

SB 678: Probation Revocations

California did not wait for the Supreme Court ruling to try to reduce its prison population. A report by the Legislative Analyst's Office had estimated that 40 percent of new prison admissions were due to probation revocations (LAO, 2009). With this identified as one potential avenue toward population reduction, the California Legislature passed SB 678, an incentive program for counties to reduce the number of offenders sent to prison for failing probation, in 2009. The legislation established a system of "performance-based funding" for probation departments (Administration Office of the Courts, 2013). If a county used evidence-based probation practices and reduced the number of probationers that were committed to state prison it could keep a portion of the money the state would save on the smaller prison population. This bill came with a caveat: The counties had to reinvest this money on more evidence-based probation programs or policies. Assessments of the bill have found that after the bill had passed, there was a notable increase in evidence-based programs run by probation departments and a reduction in the rate of probationers sent to state prison (Administration Office of the Courts, 2013). Forty-seven of the 58 counties reduced the number of probation failures they sent to prison in the first year. In 2010, the cost savings from this program alone was $179 million dollars (McCray, Newhall, & Snyder, 2012), of which counties could reinvest $87.5 million dollars on programs (PEW Center on the States, 2012). Despite the measurable success, SB 678 only reduced the prison population to about 180% percent of capacity (Lofstrom & Martin, 2015).

SB X3 18

Also in 2009, the California Legislature passed SB X3 18, which authorized eligible parolees to be placed on Non-Revocable Parole (NRP). Those under this parole program are removed from active parole supervision—thus, removing the requirement to meet regularly with parole officers and the option to be returned to jail or prison for parole violations (unless they were prosecuted and convicted of a new crime in criminal court). They are, however, still considered on "parole" and, therefore, subject to warrantless searches by law enforcement until their parole period is completed. The policy was designed to remove low-level offenders from parole. Parolees are not eligible for NRP if they are registered sex offenders, have prior or current serious or violent felonies, are validated prison gang members or associates, or are determined to be "high risk" based on a validated risk assessment tool used by the CDCR.

AB 109 & 117: Realignment (2011)

Even with the two Senate bills of 2009, the correctional population in California was still over the judge-mandated capacity. So, even before the Supreme Court published its ruling to uphold the three-judge panel, Governor Brown introduced AB 109 and AB 117 together known as *Public Safety Realignment*. Public Safety Realignment (hereafter referred to as "Realignment") went into effect in October 2011 and significantly changed the landscape of California corrections. In general, Realignment shifted much of the correctional and supervisory responsibility of felons away from the state, down to the 58 California counties. This was done both by diverting offenders to jail who would have otherwise gone to prison and by putting the responsibility for parole revocation in the hands of the county probation departments rather than those of state parole.

The belief behind Realignment was that local corrections agencies could re-habilitate lower-level offenders more effectively than the CDCR, and at a reduced cost. Local agencies may be better able to understand the needs of their offenders and provide them services while keeping them close to their homes, families, and employment or school. The major features of Realignment include:

1. *Barring those convicted of non-serious, non-violent, and non-sex crimes from being sentenced to prison.* The non-non-nons (or "triple nons") are those without serious, violent, or sex offenses on their current commitment and any prior commitments.

This move was intended to reserve prison space for only the most serious and violent felons. It is important to note that the "triple nons" can still be sentenced for the same length of time they would have been sentenced to before, but they will now serve that time in jail, not prison; sentencing requirements for this group can include any available county options (e.g., jail, split sentences, noncustodial community sanctions). Once the sentence has been served, the offender will be released without any post-release supervision (i.e., parole or probation).

2. *Changing post-release supervision.* Prior to Realignment almost all prisoners were supervised under state operated parole. Realignment brought about Post-Release Community Supervision (PRCS). PRCS is a mandatory community supervisory period under the county probation department. For prisoners other than those whose current commitment is for a violent or serious crime, some sex offenders, those serving an indeterminate life sentence, or those who have special mental health needs, their post-release supervision may now be served in the county under the jurisdiction of probation instead of under the

jurisdiction of the state through the Division of Adult Parole Operations (DAPO). DAPO continues to exist, but now only supervises those who do not qualify for PRCS.

3. *Returning parole and probation violators to county jail rather than state prison.*

Under PRCS, court officials, not the Board of Parole Hearings, determine what happens if a parole violation occurs. Regardless of whether the individual is on parole or on PRCS, those who commit a technical violation are incarcerated in county jails, not prison, unless they are tried and convicted of a new crime. Return to county jail for a violation can be subject to a "flash incarceration" or a jail period of one to ten days or up to 180 days. This does not apply to individuals serving indeterminate life sentences, who may be returned to prison for a parole violation.

Because Realignment quickly shifted much of the supervisory responsibility to the counties, the state also needed to provide counties with funds to supplement the cost. The California Legislature passed a series of bills to provide funding for Realignment. Counties were awarded block grants to use in any way that would support Realignment (e.g., increase jail and surveillance capacity, implement evidence-based programs). The legislature also provided one-time appropriations to cover costs of hiring, retention, training, and other structural resources to support counties in the implementation of their plan. The first two years of Realignment cost the state over two billion dollars (Petersilia & Snyder, 2013). In November 2012, California voters used Proposition 30 to create a constitutional amendment barring the legislature from reducing or removing county funding for Realignment.

County officials can use their discretion to determine what needs their county has and how to spend their Realignment funds, but the laws now state that California must reinvest its resources toward community-based programs and evidence-based practices. Therefore, a "punishment" could mean jail, home detention, or GPS monitoring, but it could also mean more rehabilitative community sanctions such as community service, restorative justice, work training, education, day reporting, substance abuse treatment, mother-infant care programs, or community-residential programs (McCray, Newhall, & Snyder, 2012). During their Realignment planning period, most probation agencies reported adopting actuarial risk assessment instruments (as detailed before) to help classify and identify the risks and needs of their new populations and almost all counties reported planning to use electronic or GPS monitoring as an alternative to incarceration (McCray, Newhall, & Snyder, 2012). Dozens of counties use day reporting centers, which provide those under community correctional supervision a wide range of services and programs to fit different needs such as education, counseling, and employment assistance (Petersilia, 2014).

Realignment was also intended to be a solution for state budgetary problems. Incarcerating offenders in the county is far less expensive than incarcerating them in prison. The Department of Finance plan around Realignment proposed under $30,000 per prisoner/per year for incarceration and additional treatment in county jail, a substantial savings from the $50,000 spent to house a prisoner in a state prison for a year during the same time period (Misczynski, 2011).

Unfortunately, "one of the great experiments in American incarceration policy" (*Economist*, 2013) did not come with any money or requirement for assessment of the policy. In other words, Realignment did not include any data collection requirement that would allow the state to determine its effects. Why would research on Realignment be important? Recall the organization of the first half of this chapter in which you were able to learn about each entity of corrections, somewhat independently. Realignment moved much of the supervisory role of offenders from one state agency to 58 local agencies with no requirement for how and what could and must be measured. In spite of this, the following section details what we do know about the effects of Realignment. Keep in mind that these findings may not apply across the entire state, nor do they answer all of the questions about Realignment we need to ask in order to thoroughly evaluate it.

The effects of Realignment. In the absence of a legislatively mandated assessment, most of the questions that have emerged since Realignment passed have not yet been thoroughly examined. Still, presented here are some of the most significant questions and the best-known answers to date.

1. Did Realignment reduce the entire correctional population of California or did it simply move offenders from prisons to jails? The CDCR prison population in June 2011, prior to Realignment taking effect (but after other population reduction measures), was over 162,000 inmates (see Table 7.1).[5] Realignment went into effect in October of that year, and in June 2012 the prison population was just over 135,000. This reduction was primarily due to the change in handling of parole technical violators, who are no longer returned to prison (Petersilia & Snyder, 2013). In addition, the exclusion of "triple nons" diverted an estimated 100,000 individuals who would have gone to prison into county jails (Petersilia & Snyder, 2013). Prior to Realignment, the CDCR parole population was over 105,000 parolees. After Realignment, changes to parole

---

5. Table 7.1 and Table 7.2 draw upon CDCR prison and parole data derived from CDCR Monthly Population Reports, Prison Census Data, and Parole Census Data. Table 7.1 also includes jail information derived from the Board of State Community Corrections Monthly Jail Profile Survey. Probation data have been retrieved from Open Justice by the California Department of Justice.

Table 7.1. Profile of California Corrections Before and After
Realignment and After Proposition 47

	Pre-Realignment June 2011	Post-Realignment June 2012	Post Prop 47 June 2015
Prison Population	162,368	135,238	128,900
In-State	152,749	126,022	121,467
Out-of-State	9,619	9,216	7,433
Parole Population	105,397	70,775	45,473
Jail Population	69,253	77,843	73,637
ADP Sentenced Jail	20,509	29,542	27,467
ADP Not Sentenced Jail	49,189	48,721	46,170
Probation Population	311,692	294,993	263,531

procedure reduced the parole population to 70,775. See Table 7.1 for a profile of California corrections before and after Realignment.

The county jail population increased around 12 percent in the 6 months post-Realignment (Turner et al., 2015) from 69,253 to 77,843 (see Table 7.1). By 2014, the jail population in California was almost 2,000 inmates over the capacity set by the California Board of State and Community Corrections (the capacity is 80,000 inmates). To relieve this surplus, counties released 14,321 inmates from their jails (both pre-sentenced and sentenced inmates) (Lofstrom & Martin, 2016).

Yet research on the correctional population before and after Realignment reveals an overall decrease in the number of offenders in the correctional population, because for every three offenders not going to prison, only one is going to jail (Lofstrom & Rafael, 2013a). Did Realignment reduce the incarcerated population in California? Yes. The total incarceration rate (both jail and prison together) was 619 per 100,000 residents pre-Realignment and 566 per 100,000 after Realignment (Lofstrom & Rafael, 2015). It should be noted that Martin and Grattet (2015) show that California's correctional population (i.e., probation, jail, prison, and parole) had been declining since 2008.

2. How have state-level correctional populations changed? The mandate to reduce crowding in CDCR affected both the institutional population and the

Table 7.2. CDCR Prisoner and Parolee Characteristics
Pre- and Post-Realignment

	CDCR Prison		CDCR Parole	
	Pre-Realignment June 30, 2007	Post-Realignment June 30, 2013	Pre-Realignment June 30, 2007	Post-Realignment June 30, 2013
Total Population	173,274	134,160	105,888	51,885
Sex				
Males	161,380 (93.1%)	128,178 (95.5%)	94,424 (89.2%)	48,290 (93.1%)
Females	11,894 (6.9%)	5,982 (4.5%)	11,454 (10.8%)	3,595 (6.9%)
Offense Categories				
Crimes Against Persons	87,804 (50.7%)	94,179 (70.2%)	31,667 (29.9%)	27,439 (52.9%)
Property Crimes	35,660 (20.6%)	18,343 (13.7%)	31,578 (29.8%)	10,842 (20.9%)
Drug Crimes	35,770 (20.6%)	11,656 (8.7%)	27,323 (25.8%)	5,615 (10.8%)
Other Crimes	14,040 (8.1%)	9,982 (7.4%)	15,320 (14.5%)	7,989 (15.4%)
Race/Ethnicity				
Other	10,088 (5.8%)	8,494 (6.3%)	5,837 (5.5%)	3,131 (6.0%)
Black	49,765 (28.7%)	39,451 (29.4%)	29,335 (27.7%)	14,934 (28.8%)
Hispanic	66,328 (38.3%)	55,421 (41.3%)	38,958 (36.8%)	18,964 (36.6%)
White	47,093 (27.2%)	30,794 (23.0%)	31,758 (30.0%)	14,856 (28.6%)
Age				
18–19	1,981 (1.1%)	1,415 (1.1%)	346 (.3%)	204 (.4%)
20–29	52,459 (30.3%)	35,714 (26.6%)	31,422 (29.7%)	16,093 (31.0%)
30–39	52,232 (30.1%)	38,737 (28.9%)	32,241 (30.4%)	15,529 (29.9%)
40–49	45,170 (26.0%)	30,714 (22.9%)	26,023 (24.6%)	11,045 (21.3%)
50–59	17,063 (9.8%)	20,389 (15.2%)	12,994 (12.3%)	6,839 (13.2%)
60+	4,369 (2.5%)	7,191 (5.4%)	2,862 (2.7)	2,175 (4.2%)

parole population. It is important to understand how the state correctional population changed (i.e., who was affected). Table 7.2 presents the offender characteristics of CDCR prisons and parolees prior to Realignment and Post-Realignment, with the most recent data available (i.e., 2013). After 2013, the CDCR stopped publishing demographic information. After Realignment, as expected, the number of offenders in prison and on parole for property and drug crimes declined, as the CDCR's role shifted to focus on more serious offenders. Table 7.2 shows that Realignment significantly reduced the female prisoner and parolee population. There were slight shifts in the racial/ethnic representation of prisoners. There was approximately a three percent increase in Hispanic prisoners and about a four percent decrease in white prisoners. There was virtually no change in the racial and ethnic distribution of parolees after Realignment. Interestingly, post-Realignment there was an increase in the proportion of older individuals in prison and on parole. This is most likely because "lifers" (those serving an indeterminate life sentence), who were to remain in prison and on parole under Realignment, would be older. Research on crime, however, shows that generally older individuals are far less likely to commit crime than younger people (e.g., Gottfredson & Hirschi, 1990; Sampson & Laub, 1993). It is more expensive to incarcerate older prisoners due to increased medical needs (Chiu, 2010). Post-Realignment changes (described in later sections) did target this group.

3. *What effects has Realignment had on jails and community sanctions?* Jails in California, like the prisons, are crowded. As stated earlier, jails were historically designed for short terms (generally, one year or less). Realignment did not necessarily reduce sentences; rather, it simply moved the location of the incarceration. Offenders can now be incarcerated in jail for many years to many decades (Rappaport, 2013). Thus, Realignment raises concerns about the impact of overcrowding on jail conditions. As suspected, Realignment increased the populations in jails—at least immediately. As jails began to reach their population capacity, the state released thousands of jail inmates early due to space constraints (Lofstrom & Martin, 2016; Petersilia & Snyder, 2013). California has also made a commitment to fund additional or replacement jails in most counties and to expand the resources within jails to assist with rehabilitation and reentry (Lofstrom & Martin, 2016).

It is important to keep in mind, however, that Realignment does not simply move the incarcerated population from prisons to jails; it is intended to move offenders into the community, providing increased access to rehabilitation. Research has shown that in the early stages of Realignment, approximately 23 percent of offenders were sentenced to a split sentence (CPOC, 2012). The use of split sentencing has increased in the years post-Realignment (Martin &

Grattet, 2015), though the use varies by county (Rappaport, 2013). The result is that it reduces the time incarcerated and increases the time in the community, potentially allowing the individual to participate in programming.

A review of adult offender programming in California found that despite the need for recidivism reducing programming, less than 10% of California prisoners and parolees participated in any (Petersilia, 2007). The report also found that half of all prisoners leaving prisons did not participate in any rehabilitation or work program during their prison term. One expectation of Realignment was that counties could better achieve rehabilitative goals than could the state. However, that requires counties to invest in, or have access to, effective rehabilitation programs (Petersilia & Snyder, 2013). It also requires counties to effectively implement or contract with agencies that can operate programs that have been shown to reduce recidivism. Initial research suggests that many counties are adopting the necessary rehabilitative strategies to work toward this goal (Turner et al., 2015).

4. If counties have discretion to design policy as they see fit, will this lead to "justice by geography"? "Justice by geography" is a term used to describe what can happen when individual actors or jurisdictions are given wide discretion in policy implementation. The result can be inconsistency in sentences or treatment for the same behavior in different jurisdictions even within the same state (Feld, 1999). Scholars question whether Realignment has the potential to result in "justice by geography" (Krisberg, 2011; Males & Buchen, 2013). The decision to send individuals convicted of a non-violent offense (*if* they have a violent history) to prison instead of using community supervision is a county decision and leads to wide discrepancy in prison versus jail placement. For example, in 2012, an individual arrested for a drug crime in King County was 19 times more likely to serve time in prison than a drug offender in San Francisco (Males & Buchen, 2013).

Another way that justice will differ by county involves the orientation of each county toward punishment versus rehabilitation. Counties can use Realignment block grant money for any purpose they see fit (Schlanger, 2013). In a study of 12 county probation departments after Realignment, researchers found that eight of the counties used the Realignment funds mostly to expand programming and alternatives to incarceration. Three counties used the money to increase jail space, surveillance, or probation resources; and one county used the funds about equally on rehabilitation and security (Turner et al., 2015). In practical terms, this may mean that offenders in some counties will have access to more (or better) rehabilitative programming than those in other counties that rely more heavily on incarceration in jails. A county's approach to rehabilitation or punishment can also signal how enforcement will be used.

Bird and Grattet (2014) found that counties that prioritized programming and reentry after Realignment had lower offender recidivism rates.

5. *Will Realignment make California safer?* There are different ways to examine changes in "safety" after Realignment. One way is to compare the crime rate of the state (or specific counties) before and after a policy is introduced. Another way is to examine the rate of recidivism, or reoffending, by offenders who were released before and after Realignment. Realignment legislation did not require a data collection component; what limited data are available had to be collected by counties and provided to researchers at their discretion. A study by Sundt, Salisbury, and Harmon (2016) found that the violent crime rate in California did not significantly change after Realignment compared to the trends observed in other states without Realignment. However, they did find an increase in motor vehicle theft the year after Realignment; but by 2014, the auto theft rate decreased back to the pre-Realignment level. In total, there is little evidence that Realignment significantly increased the rate of crime in California.[6]

Rate of recidivism. There are several ways to measure recidivism: arrest, conviction, return to prison, return to jail. However, the purpose of Realignment was to specifically decrease returns to prison thereby, potentially, increasing the jail population. Therefore, using the prison or jail admission rate could be misleading, because it would not reflect an offender's behavior but a change in policy regarding offender processing. For these reasons, scholars have been studying the effects of Realignment using rearrests and reconvictions. Research on the short-term effects has not shown much difference in the rearrest and reconviction rates of offenders before and after 2011 (CDCR, 2013; Byrd & Grattet, 2014). However, six months after Realignment, researchers found that the percentage point change in felony rearrests varied widely across the California counties. For example, Ventura County observed a 35-percentage-point increase in felony rearrest after Realignment, while Mendocino County measured almost a 15-percentage-point decrease in felony rearrest during the same period (Bird & Grattet, 2014). Bird and Grattet (2014) found that, on average, counties that prioritized enforcement had a 3.7 percentage point higher rearrest rate than those counties that prioritized reentry services. The same general pattern held for reconviction.

In the future, it will be change at the county level that will become the important measure because all counties are responsible for designing their own

---

6. Lofstrom and Rafael (2013b) found similar trends to those identified by Sundt et al. (2016). However, their study did not extend to 2014 and they did not conclude that the auto theft rate went back down.

correctional programs. While data collection must continue, preliminary findings reveal it can be done. San Francisco County for example, has reduced its reliance on incarceration (i.e., reduced the number of inmates in prisons and jails), increased the number of offenders in rehabilitative programming, and shown a reduction in recidivism (Still, 2016).

After Realignment: Still overcrowded. Realignment did reduce the state prison population by 27,400 in the first year, but it was not enough to meet the court mandate. Unfortunately, after initial declines there were no signs of further reductions around September 2012 (Males & Buchen, 2013). Despite the grand nature of the Realignment reform and the legislation before it, these efforts were not enough to get the population to the 137.5 percent level that was mandated by 2013. In 2013, the CDCR opened a new healthcare facility. The state legislature also quickly passed SB 105, which allowed prisoners to be sent out-of-state involuntarily, contract prison space, and the lease of California City Correctional Facility to increase bed space. Otherwise, the court would have required the immediate release of prisoners. By the end of 2013, the prisons were still 143 percent occupied. This did not take into account the 2,400 prisoners in contract beds and almost 9,000 housed in prisons outside of California (CDCR, 2013b). In February 2014, the three-judge panel extended the two-year deadline to meet the population capacity, which gave the state more time. The judges also ordered the state to implement more population reduction measures, including:

- Use prospective credit earnings for non-violent second-strike inmates and minimum custody inmates
- Allow non-violent second-strike inmates who have reached 50 percent of their total sentence to be referred to the BPH for parole consideration
- Release inmates on parole who have been granted release by Board of Parole Hearings but have future parole dates
- Expand medical parole
- Establish elderly parole
- Increase reentry services and alternative custody programs

Proposition 36 (2012)

In November 2012, California voters passed Proposition 36, a revision to the three-strikes law. The revision narrowed the scope of the law, indicating that a life sentence may only be imposed if the third strike was a serious or violent felony. There had been many attempts to alter California's three-strikes law since its passage in 1994, but this was the first time it was successful. Not only did it pass, but it passed with a very large margin: Over two-thirds of California voters supported the measure. It was also in 2012 that a repeal of the California death penalty nearly passed (52% opposed, 48% supported). Rappaport (2013) notes that legislative and voter support for this long list of changes to the state's punishment and corrections policies indicate a fundamental shift in California's public opinion from previous decades (Rappaport, 2013).

The passage of Proposition 36 also reduced the prison population, but still not enough. In 2014 the prison population was at 140.9 percent of capacity. The state still needed to reduce the prison population by about 2,850 inmates (Lofstrom & Martin, 2015).

Proposition 47 (2014)

It was not until California voters passed Proposition 47 in 2014 that the state correctional system finally moved below the level of crowding required by the *Plata* judge panel. Proposition 47 passed with almost 60 percent of the vote. Proposition 47 reduced the classification of many drug and property crimes from felonies to misdemeanors. This applies to certain drug possession felonies or petty theft, receiving stolen property, or forging/writing bad checks for $950 or less. Offenders with certain violent, serious, or sex offenses may not petition the court for resentencing regardless of the change in law. Individuals who do meet the Proposition 47 requirements can petition for a new sentencing hearing with the trial court, and a judge will decide what the new sentence befitting the misdemeanor, and not the felony, will be.

In one year after Proposition 47 the prison population dropped by 7,500 (see Table 7.1). It was only after Proposition 47 that the prison population dropped to levels mandated by the three-judge panel. It also reduced the jail population, which had increased after Realignment. The jail population fell by almost 10,000 by January 2015 and has remained stable since that time.

Naturally, people began to question whether Proposition 47 would increase or decrease public safety. This initiative released a number of inmates and reduced the prison and jail population as required, but would it also increase crime? If releasing offenders into the public from jail would increase crime, then counties that released more offenders after Proposition 47 should show a larger increase in crime than counties that released very few offenders (Males, 2016). Measured this way, Males (2016) found no apparent relationship between Proposition 47 and crime; instead, counties that released the largest numbers of jail inmates also had lower crime rates. However, not much time has passed since the passage of Proposition 47 and continued research is necessary to understand its lasting effects on crime and the criminal justice system. As noted in Chapter 1, the incidence of some Proposition 47 crimes increased in 2015 but we do not yet know if the levels of those crimes returned to normal in 2016.

Proposition 57 (2016)

Despite moving beyond the court mandate in *Plata v. Brown*, Californians were not finished reforming their correctional system. In November 2016, the voters passed Proposition 57,[7] The Public Safety and Rehabilitation Act (with 64% support), which provided credit-earning opportunities for good behavior and participation in rehabilitation in prison. The policy affords prisoners the ability to earn: (1) more Good Time Credits than allowed under previous policies; (2) Milestone Completion credits (for prisoners who demonstrate productive work and skill development); (3) Rehabilitative Achievement Credits for participation in self-help or volunteer public service activities; and (4) Education Merit Credits for earning a high school diploma or GED, higher education degree, or an offender mentor certification. All credits, except Education Merit Credits, can be lost for rule violations (CDCR, 2017c).

Proposition 57 also moved up parole consideration for non-violent offenders who served their full sentence for their primary offense but have remaining time for secondary offenses, if they demonstrate they are no longer a current threat to public safety (CDCR, 2017d). This does not necessarily mean that they would be granted parole; they will still be required to go before the Board of Parole Hearings, which determines whether they remain a "threat to public safety" (CDCR, 2017e). Most of the plan for Proposition 57 will be implemented in late 2017.

Corrections Today and Tomorrow

A recent review by the Public Policy Institute of California (2017) highlights where California corrections is now. While the CDCR has met the overcrowding requirement of 137.5 percent cap in *Plata*, it continues to house some prisoners out-of-state or in contract beds to keep the population within the requirement. The number of out-of-state and contract beds has decreased by about 3,800 prisoners and in-state contract beds have decreased by about 600 prisoners (see Table 7.1). The jail population first grew under Realignment and then declined after Proposition 47. Counties are also relying more on alternatives to incarceration and expanding treatment (PPIC, 2017). Unfortunately, the rate of recidivism (i.e., re-arrest and re-conviction) for parole violators is still

---

7. Proposition 57 also changed the requirements for juvenile waiver hearings. See Chapter 9 for a discussion of that provision.

as high as it was pre-Realignment. While California now relies less on imprisonment than other states, it still has one of the largest correctional budgets, even though one of the stated intentions of Realignment was to reduce it. There continue to be many unanswered questions regarding the long-term effects of the series of monumental changes in California corrections. As Zimring et al. (2001) pointed out, "any new wrinkle in criminal punishment will have a larger net effect in California than elsewhere because of the sheer size of the system" (p. 17). Learning from the state's previous history, it is critical that these changes are thoroughly and regularly scientifically evaluated in order to best understand how they can inform continued correctional reform in California and throughout the United States.

Key Terms and Definitions

Actuarial Risk Assessment Instrument—A series of questions (or indicators) that generates a "risk score." The higher the "risk" the more likely the individual will engage in the behavior the risk assessment is purported to measure.

Assembly Bill 109—Along with AB 117 is collectively known as "Realignment." *See Key Terms: Realignment.*

Assembly Bill 117—Along with AB 109 is collectively known as "Realignment." *See Key Terms: Realignment.*

Board of Parole Hearings (BPH)—Board that conducts parole consideration hearings for adult prisoners serving indeterminate sentences. The Board determines if a prisoner should be released from prison onto parole, and if not, determines the next possible consideration date.

Brown v. Plata (2011)—The United States Supreme Court decision that upheld the finding of the three-judge court that overcrowding in California's prisons led to violations of prisoners' Eighth Amendment rights to be free from cruel and unusual punishment. The case was decided on May 23, 2011 with a 5-4 split decision. *Brown v. Plata* (2011) was a decision incorporating both *Plata v. Brown* (2001) and *Coleman v. Brown* (1990). The case ultimately upheld the requirement for CDCR to lower their prison crowding to 137.5 percent by 2013.

California Correctional Peace Officers Association (CCPOA)—Correctional and parole officer union for employees in the California Department of Corrections and Rehabilitation (CDCR).

California Department of Corrections and Rehabilitation (CDCR)—Formerly known as the Youth and Adult Correctional Agency (YACA), this agency operates all adult and juvenile prison facilities and parole as well as a number of community corrections programs. The corrections system was renamed in 2005.

Coleman v. Brown (2009)—U.S. Federal Court decision finding that the CDCR violated the Eighth Amendment Constitutional rights of its prisoners by failing to provide appropriate mental health care. Has also been known as *Coleman v. Wilson,* and *Coleman v. Schwarzenegger.*

Corrections—The criminal justice subsystem that incorporates elements that occur both after arrest and sentencing. It includes jails, probation, prison, parole, and community-based programs such as halfway houses, day reporting centers, GPS monitoring, or specific treatment programs.

Determinate Sentencing—A fixed sentence that provides a specific number of years to be served.

Eighth Amendment—The Eighth Amendment of the United States Constitution states that: "Excessive bail shall not be required, nor excessive fines imposed, nor cruel and unusual punishments inflicted."

Indeterminate Sentencing—A sentence that provides a range of years to be served (e.g., 25 years to life). Prisoners serving indeterminate sentences in California go before the Board of Parole Hearings to determine when and if they will be released onto parole.

Jail—Local level facilities designed to hold pretrial detainees and sentenced inmates. Jails in California were previously used for short-term incarceration, but after Realignment they may now house lower level inmates serving longer sentences.

Lockyer v. Andrade (2003)—U.S. Supreme Court decision stating that a life sentence (i.e., an indeterminate sentence of 25 years to life in prison) does not violate the Eighth Amendment of the Constitution even if the Third Strike is not violent nor serious.

Non-Non-Nons ("Triple Nons")—Individuals convicted of non-serious, non-violent, non-sexual crimes who qualify to serve their sentence in county jail since Realignment.

Parole—Supervision of an offender in the community by the CDCR's Division of Adult Parole Operations (DAPO) after release from prison. Prior to 2011, virtually all individuals released from a California prison had at least a three-year parole supervision term. After 2011, most non-violent, non-serious, non-sexual offenders are supervised in the community by probation and not parole.

Plata v. Brown (2001)—U.S. Federal Court decision that the CDCR violated the Eighth Amendment Constitutional rights of its prisoners by failing to provide appropriate health care. Also known as *Plata v. Davis* and *Plata v. Schwarzenegger.*

Prison Litigation Reform Act (PLRA)—A Federal law that was enacted by Congress in 1996 in response to the number of lawsuits being filed by prisoners in the United States. This requires prisoners to go through all steps of an institution's grievance system before filing a lawsuit. This legislation allowed for a federal three-judge panel to be convened in cases of prisoner mistreatment in the states. Attorneys in *Plata* and *Coleman* sued the State under the PLRA over the effects of prison overcrowding on prisoner rights.

Prisons—State and Federal long-term correctional institutions. In California, the California Department of Corrections and Rehabilitation operates dozens of prisons, conservation (fire) camps, and community facilities to house convicted serious and violent felony offenders.

Probation—Correctional supervision in the community by county probation departments. Probation can be used as an alternative to incarceration or in conjunction with jail time (i.e., split sentence). Since Realignment, probation officers also may supervise parolees released from CDCR prisons on Post-Release Community Supervision (PRCS).

Proposition 36 (2012)—Voter initiative passed in 2012 that amended the California "Three Strikes" Law passed in 1994. Requires that the third strike be a serious or violent felony to invoke a 25-year to life sentence. Also may be used in the resentencing of offenders currently serving life sentences for a third strike that was not serious or violent.

Proposition 47 (2014)—Voter initiative passed in 2014 that reduced the penalties for nonviolent, nonserious crimes from felonies to misdemeanors unless the defendant has prior convictions for certain violent crimes. Also permitted resentencing offenders currently serving a prison sentence for a felony as a misdemeanor.

Proposition 57 (2016)—Voter initiative passed in 2016 that increased parole and good behavior opportunities and credits for felons convicted of nonviolent crimes. Also requires judges, not prosecutors to determine when a juvenile should be tried as an adult in court.

Realignment—Series of legislative bills (most notably, AB 117 and AB 109), which provide permanent revenue to counties to provide local public safety programs to retain offenders, previously committed to state prison, in county jails or other county level alternatives to incarceration. Realignment began in October 1, 2011 in response to the court finding in *Plata v. Brown* that required the CDCR to reduce its prison population to 137.5 percent crowding by 2013.

Recidivism—The likelihood that an individual convicted of a crime will reoffend after being released from their commitment. Recidivism can be measured in numerous ways: rearrest, reconviction, parole violation, return to prison, return to probation.

Reorganization—After the 2004 Corrections Independent Review Panel recommendation, the organizational structure and mission of the Youth and Adult Correctional Agency was reorganized. The new agency, the California Department of Corrections and Rehabilitation (CDCR), stated a new commitment to rehabilitation and changed the organizational structure under one Secretary of Corrections, who is appointed by the Governor.

Risk Assessment—A process of evaluating an individual for the likelihood of reoffending, engaging in violence, or escaping. Risk assessments may be conducted by professionals or experts on the basis of their experience, however, research shows that actuarial risk assessment instruments outperform professional judgement.

Security Housing Unit (SHU)—Housing units designed for long-term housing of offenders whose behavior endangers the safety of others or the prison. Individuals can be committed to a SHU if they have committed a serious or violent offense while in prison.

Senate Bill X3 18—This California Senate Bill authorizes eligible parolees to be placed on Non-Revocable Parole. Non-revocable Parole removes active supervision requirements, including regular meetings with parole officers and parole conditions. It allows law enforcement agents to conduct warrantless searches without cause until the individual is released from parole.

Senate Bill (SB) 678—Provides performance incentives to counties who use evidence-based probation practices and reduce the number of probationers committed to state prison for a probation violation. The compensation must be reinvested into more evidence-based programs or policies.

Internet Websites

Board of State and Community Corrections: http://bscc.ca.gov/
Bureau of Justice Statistics: http://bjs.ojp.usdoj.gov/
California Courts Realignment Resource Center: http:/www.courts.ca.gov/partners/realignment.htm
California Department of Corrections & Rehabilitation: http://www.cdcr.ca.gov/
California's Legislative Analyst's Office Reports: http://www.lao.ca. gov
California Secretary of State: http://www.sos.ca.gov/
California Sentencing Institute: http://casi.cjcj.org
Center for Evidence-Based Corrections: http://ucicorrections.seweb.uci.edu/

Chief Probation Officers of California: http://www.cpoc.org
Human Rights Watch: http://www.hrw.org/
Legislative Analyst's Office: http://www.lao.ca.gov/laoapp/main.aspx
National Institute of Corrections: http://nicic.gov/
Prison Law Office: http://prisonlaw.com/
Public Policy Institute of California: http://www.ppic.org/main/home.asp
The Sentencing Project: http://www.sentencingproject.org/template/index.cfm
The Urban Institute: http://www.urban.org/
The Vera Institute: http://www.vera.org/

Review Questions

1. What are the key organizing components and major elements of the corrections system?
2. Compare and contrast the use of probation and the use of parole.
3. Discuss the administrative and cultural organization and structure of state prisons in California.
4. What led to the change in sentencing structure used in California? How has sentencing in California changed over time and with what consequences?
5. Describe the motivations for and nature of California's "reorganization" of its corrections system.
6. Create a timeline that illustrates the key events led to California's Realignment. Include any relevant court decisions, agencies, and legislative actions involved in its implementation.
7. There have been several key pieces of legislation enacted by the California Government to implement realignment. List the key bills associated with realignment and describe their important functions and impacts.
8. Why is the Eighth Amendment to the United States Constitution important to California's prison reform efforts? Briefly describe the Eighth Amendment and why it is being used to mandate the transfer of responsibility for convicted felons from the state to the local level.
9. How did Realignment change the relationship between state and county corrections systems?

Critical Thinking Questions

1. How has the advent and growth of "evidence based practices" affected corrections practices over time?

2. What has been the effect of the general shift from discretionary to mandatory parole programs on prison populations and public safety?
3. How are factors of identity relevant to corrections policy and experience?
4. Realignment represents a shift in responsibility from California state government to local governments for monitoring and caring for convicted felons. Are local governments the best agencies to monitor convicted felons? Why/why not?
5. Should California voters be permitted to craft criminal laws through the voter initiative process (e.g., the three strikes law), or should elected officials retain this responsibility?
6. What role has prisoner litigation played in California correctional reform?
7. In addition to the policy changes mentioned in this chapter, what are some other strategies that California state and local governments could use to ensure they improve the conditions and treatment of those in their care as well as public safety?

References

Abarbanel, S., McCray, A., Newhall, K. M., & Snyder, J. G. (2012). *Realigning the revolving door? An analysis of California counties' AB 109 implementation plans.* Stanford Law School: Stanford Criminal Justice Center.

Administration Office of the Courts. (2013). *Report on the California Community Corrections Performance Incentives Act of 2009: Findings from the SB 678 Program.* Judicial and Court Operations Services Division.

Andrews, D. A. (2006). Enhancing adherence to risk-need-responsivity: Making quality a matter of policy. *Criminology & Public Policy, 5*, 595–602.

Andrews, D. A., Bonta, J., & Wormith, J. S. (2006a). The risk-need-responsivity (RNR) model: Does adding the good lives model contribute to effective crime prevention? *Criminal Justice and Behavior, 38*(7), 735–755.

Andrews, D. A., Bonta, J., & Wormith, J. S. (2006b). The recent past and near future of risk and/or need assessment. *Crime & Delinquency, 52*(1), 7–27.

Aos, S., Miller, M., & Drake, E. (2006). *Evidence-based adult corrections programs: What works and what does not.* Olympia: Washington State Institute for Public Policy.

Arkles, G. (2009). Safety and solidarity across gender lines: Rethinking segregation of transgender people in detention. *Temple Political and Civil Rights Law Review, 18*(2), 515–560.

Associated Press. (2017a, January 6). California murder convict becomes first inmate to receive state-funded sex reassignment surgery. *Los Angeles Times.*

Retrieved from http://www.latimes.com/local/lanow/la-me-ln-inmate-sex-reassignment20170106-story.html

Associated Press. (2017b, February 1). First U.S. inmate to get state-funded sex reassignment moves to a California prison for women. *Los Angeles Times.* Retrieved from http://www.latimes.com/local/lanow/la-me-ln-in-mate-sexchange-20170201story.html

Auerhahn, K. (2003). *Selective incapacitation and public policy.* Albany, NY: State University of New York Press.

Bales, W. D., & Miller, C. (2012). The impact of determinate sentencing on prisoner misconduct. *Journal of Criminal Justice, 40,* 394–403.

Beck, A. (2015). *Use of restrictive housing in U.S. prisons and jails, 2011–12.* (NCJ 249209). Washington, DC: Bureau of Justice Statistics.

Beck, A., & Berzofsky, M., Caspar, R., & Krebs, C. (2013). *Sexual victimization in prisons and jails reported by inmates 2011–2012.* (NCJ 241399). Washington, DC: Bureau of Justice Statistics.

Bernstein, S., & Garvey, M. (2006, February 12). Dorms fuel jail unrest. *Los Angeles Times.* Retrieved from articles.latimes.com/2006/feb/12/local/me-jails12/2

Bird, M., & Grattet, R. (2014, August). *Do local Realignment policies affect recidivism in California?* San Francisco, CA: Public Policy Institute of California.

Bloom, B., Owen, B., & Covington, S. (2003). *Gender-responsive strategies: Research, practice, and guiding principles for women offenders.* Washington, DC: National Institute of Corrections.

Bonta, J., & Andrews, D. A. (2007). *Risk-need-responsivity model for assessment and rehabilitation.* Public Safety Canada.

Bookspan, S. (1991). *A germ of goodness: The California state prison system 1851–1944.* Lincoln, NE: University of Nebraska Press.

Calavita, K., & Jenness, V. (2013). Inside the pyramid of disputes: Naming problems and filing grievances in California prisons. *Social Problems, 60*(1), 50–80.

California Department of Corrections. (1997). *Historical Trends (1976–1996).* Retrieved from http://www.cdcr.ca.gov/Reports_Research/Offender_In-formation_ServicesBranch/Annual/HIST2/HIST2d1996.pdf

California Department of Corrections and Rehabilitation. (2005). *Monthly report of population as of midnight June 30, 2005.* Sacramento, CA: Department of Corrections, Data Analysis Unit.

California Department of Corrections and Rehabilitation. (2006). *Midnight report of population, October 31, 2006.* Retrieved from http://www.cdcr.ca.gov/Reports_Research/Offender_Information_Services_Branh/Mothly/TPOP1A/TPOP1Ad0610.pdf

California Department of Corrections and Rehabilitation. (2007a). *Inmate incidents in institutions: Calendar year 2006.* Sacramento, CA: California Department of Corrections and Rehabilitation.

California Department of Corrections and Rehabilitation. (2007b). *Historical trends (1987–2007).* Retrieved from http://www.cdcr.ca.gov/Reports_ Research/Offender_Information_Services_Branh/Annual/HIST2/HIST2d2007.pdf

California Department of Corrections and Rehabilitation. (2007c, August). *Prison census data as of June 30, 2007.* Department of Corrections and Rehabilitation. Offender Information Services Branch.

California Department of Corrections and Rehabilitation. (2011). *Expert panel study of the inmate classification score system.* Sacramento, CA: Office of Research: Research and Evaluation Branch.

California Department of Corrections and Rehabilitation. (2013). *Realignment report: An examination of offenders released from state prison in the first year of Public Safety Realignment.* Sacramento, CA: CDCR.

California Department of Corrections and Rehabilitation. (2014, January 2). *Monthly report of population as of midnight December 31, 2013.* Sacramento, CA: Department of Corrections, Data Analysis Unit.

California Department of Corrections and Rehabilitation. (2015, June 19). *Notice of change to regulations: Section(s): 3000, 3044, 3269, 3269.1, 3335–3344.* Retrieved from http://www.cdcr.ca.gov/Regulations/Adult_Operations/docs/ NCDR/2015NCR/1-04/NCR_15-04_Notice_of_Proposed_Regulations_ Segregated_Housing.pdf

California Department of Corrections and Rehabilitation. (2017a). *Entering a California state prison: Reception and classification process.* Retrieved from http://www.cdcr.ca.gov/Ombuds/Entering_a_Prison_FAQs.html

California Department of Corrections and Rehabilitation. (2017b). *California Department of Corrections and Rehabilitation adult institutions, programs, and parole: Operations manual.* Sacramento, CA: California Department of Corrections and Rehabilitation. Retrieved from http://www.cdcr.ca.gov/ Regulations/Adult_Operations/docs/DOM/DOM%20207/2017_DOM.PDF

California Department of Corrections and Rehabilitation. (2017c, May 1). *Proposition 57– Credit earning for inmates. frequently asked questions.* California Department of Corrections and Rehabilitation. Retrieved from http://www.cdcr.ca.gov/proposition57/docs/faq-prop-57-credits.pdf

California Department of Corrections and Rehabilitation. (2017d, March 24). *Proposition 57—Public Safety and Rehabilitation Act of 2016.* California Department of Corrections and Rehabilitation Fact Sheet. Retrieved from http://www.cdcr.ca.gov/proposition57/docs/prop-57-fact-sheet.pdf

California Department of Corrections and Rehabilitation. (2017e). *Prop 57—Public Safety and Rehabilitation Act of 2016. Fact Sheet.* Retrieved from http://www.cdcr.ca.gov/proposition57/docs/prop-57-fact-sheet.pdf

California Department of Justice. (2014). *Crime in California 2014.* Retrieved from https://oag.ca.gov/sites/all/files/agweb/pdfs/cjsc/publications/candd/cd14/cd14.pf

California Prison Industry Authority. (2011a). *About CALPIA: Rehabilitating offenders through job training.* Retrieved from http://www.calpia.ca.gov/About_PIA/AboutPIA.aspx

California Prison Industry Authority. (2011b). *CALPIA enterprises and career technical education (CTE) locations.* Retrieved from http://www.calpia.ca.gov/About_PIA/InstitutionMap.aspx

California Probation Officers of California. (2012). Split sentencing in California under Realignment. *CPOC Issue Brief, 1*(2), 2.

Chiu, T. (2010). *It's about time: Aging prisoners, increasing costs, and geriatric release.* Vera Institute of Justice: Center on Sentencing and Corrections.

Corrections Independent Review Panel. (2004). *Reforming California's youth and adult correctional system.* Retrieved from https://www.dgsapps.dgs.ca.gov/DGS/CPR/Review_Panel/

Daly, K. (1992). Women's pathways to felony court: Feminist theories of law-breaking and problems of representation. *Southern California Review of Law and Women's Studies, 2,* 11–52.

Dansky, K. (2008). Understanding California sentencing. *University of San Francisco Law Review, 43*(1), 45–86.

DeHart, D., Lynch, S., Belknap, J., Dass-Brailsford, P., & Green, B. (2014). Life history models of female offending: The roles of serious mental illness and trauma in women's pathways to jail. *Psychology of Women Quarterly, 38*(1), 138–151.

Ditton, P., & Wilson, D. J. (1999). *Truth in sentencing in state prisons.* (NCJ 170032). Washington, DC: Bureau of Justice Statistics.

The Economist. (2013, May 11). Prison crowding: The magic number. *The Economist,* at 32.

Feeley, M., & Simon, J. (1992). The new penology: Notes on the emerging strategy of corrections and its implications. *Criminology, 30*(4), 449–474.

Feld, B. (1999). *Bad kids: Race and the transformation of the juvenile court.* Cary, NC: Oxford University Press.

Fleisher, M., & Decker, S. (2001). An overview of the challenge of prison gangs. *Corrections Management Quarterly, 5*(1), 1–9.

Goodman, P. (2008). "It's just Black, White, or Hispanic": An observational study of racializing moves in California's segregated prison reception centers. *Law & Society Review, 42*(4), 735–770.

Goodman, P. (2014). Race in California's prison fire camps for men: Prison politics, space, and the racialization of everyday life. *American Journal of Sociology, 120*(2), 352–94.

Gottfredson, M., & Hirschi, T. (1990). *A general theory of crime.* Stanford University Press: Palo Alto.

Hare, B., & Rose, L. (2016, September 26). Pop. 17,059: Welcome to America's largest jail. CNN. Retrieved from

Hughes, T., Wilson, D. J., & Beck, A. J. (2001). *Trends in state parole, 1990–2000.* (NCJ 184735). Washington, DC: Bureau of Justice Statistics.

Hunt, G., Riegel, S., Morales, T., & Waldorf, D. (1993, August). Changes in prison culture: Prison gangs and the case of the "Pepsi generation." *Social Problems, 40*(3), 398–409.

Irwin, J. (1985). *The jail: Managing the underclass in American society.* Berkeley, CA: University of California Press.

Jenness, V., Maxson, C., Matsuda, K. N., & Sumner, J. (2007). *Violence in California correctional facilities: An empirical examination of sexual assault.* Report submitted to the California Department of Corrections and Rehabilitation. Sacramento, CA.

Krisberg, B. (2011). Realigning the criminal justice system in California. *The Daily Californian.* Retrieved from dailycal.org.

Kruttschnitt, C., & Gartner, R. (2005). *Marking time in the Golden State: Women's imprisonment in California.* Cambridge: Cambridge University Press.

Legislative Analyst's Office. (2005). *Major issues: Judiciary & criminal justice.* Sacramento, CA: Legislative Analyst's Office. Retrieved from http://www.lao.ca.gov/Publications/Detail/1257

Legislative Analyst's Office. (2009). *Achieving better outcomes for adult probation.* Retrieved from www.lao.ca.gov/2009/crim/Probation/probation_052909.pdf.

Lipton, D., Martinson, R., & Wilks, J. (1975). *The effectiveness of correctional treatment and what works: A survey of treatment evaluation studies.* New York: Praeger.

Little Hoover Commission. (2007, January 25). *Solving California's corrections crisis: Time is running out.* Retrieved from www.lhc.ca.gov/lhc/185/Report185.pdf

Lofstrom, M., & Martin, B. (2015). *How California reduced its prison population.* San Francisco, CA: Public Policy Institute of California.

Lofstrom, M., & Martin, B. (2016). *California's county jails. Just the facts.* San Francisco, CA: Public Policy Institute of California.

Lofstrom, M., & Raphael, S. (2013a). *Impact of Realignment on county jail populations.* San Francisco, CA: Public Policy Institute of California.

Lofstrom, M., & Raphael, S. (2013b). *Public Safety Realignment and crime rates in California.* San Francisco, CA: Public Policy Institute of California.

Lofstrom, M., & Raphael, S. (2015). *Realignment, incarceration and crime trends in California.* San Francisco, CA: Public Policy Institute of California.

Males, M. (2016). *Is Proposition 47 to blame for California's 2015 increase in urban crime?* Center on Juvenile and Criminal Justice Research Report.

Males, M., & Buchen, L. (2013). *Beyond Realignment: Counties' large disparities in imprisonment underlie ongoing prison crisis.* Center on Juvenile and Criminal Justice Research Brief.

Martin, B., & Grattet, R. (2015). *Alternatives to incarceration in California.* San Francisco, CA: Public Policy Institute of California.

Martinson, R. (1974). What works? Questions and answers about prison reform. *Public Interest, 35*: 22–35.

Martinson, R. (1979). New findings, new views: A note of caution regarding sentencing reform. *Hofstra Law Review, 7*(2), 243–258.

Melnick, D. H. (1962). Probation in California: Penal Code Section 1203. *California Law Review, 50*(4), 651–671.

Misczynski, D. (2011). *Rethinking the state-local relationship: Corrections.* San Francisco, CA: Public Policy Institute of California.

Morris, N., & Tonry, M. (1990). *Between prison and probation: Intermediate punishments in a rational sentencing system.* New York: Oxford University Press.

Nieto, M. (1996). *The changing role of probation in California's criminal justice system.* Sacramento, CA: California Research Bureau, California State Library.

Office of the Governor. (2011). *Governor Brown signs legislation to improve public safety and empower local law enforcement.* Retrieved from https://www.gov.ca.gov/news.php?id=16964

Owen, B. (1998). *In the mix: Struggle and survival in a women's prison.* Albany, NY: State University of New York Press.

Page, J. (2012). Political realistic unionism: The California Prison Officers Association and the struggle over the "public good." *Labor & Society, 15,* 377–396.

Petersilia, J. (1998). A decade of experimenting with community sanctions: What have we learned? *Federal Probation, 62*(2), 3–10.

Petersilia, J. (2003). *When prisoners come home: Parole and prisoner reentry.* New York, NY: Oxford University Press.

Petersilia, J. (2006). *Understanding California corrections.* Berkeley, CA: California Policy Research Center.

Petersilia, J. (2007). *Review of the California expert panel on adult offender and recidivism reduction programming: Summary of findings from the program review subcommittee.* Retrieved from http://ucicorrections.seweb.uci.edu/files/2013/06/Petersilia-Machado-Testimony-with-Appendix-1.pdf.

Petersilia, J. (2014). California prison downsizing and its impact on local criminal justice systems. *Harvard Law & Policy Review, 8,* 328–357.

Petersilia, J., & Snyder, J. G. (2013). Looking past the hype: 10 questions everyone should ask about California's prison Realignment. *California Journal of Politics and Policy, 5*(2), 266–308.

Petersilia, J., & Turner, S. (1993). Intensive probation and parole. *Crime and Justice, 17,* 281–335.

PEW Center on the States. (2012). The impact of California's probation performance incentive funding program. *Public Safety Performance Project: Issue Brief.*

Public Policy Institute of California (PPIC). (2017). *California's future: Corrections.* Retrieved from http://www.ppic.org/content/pubs/report/R_117MLR.pdf

Rainville, G., & Reeves, B. A. (2003). *Felony defendants in large urban counties.* Washington, DC: U.S. Department of Justice.

Rappaport, A. J. (2013). Realigning California corrections. *Federal Sentencing Reporter, 25*(4), 207–216.

Reiter, K. (2012). Parole, snitch, or die: California's supermax prisons and prisoners, 1997–2007. *Punishment & Society, 14*(5), 530–563.

Reiter, K. (2015, September 28). (Un)settling solitary confinement in California's prisons. *Social Justice* blog. Retrieved from http://www.socialjusticejournal.org/unsettling-solitary-confinement-in-californias-prisons/

Reiter, K. (2016). *23/7: Pelican Bay Prison and the rise of long-term solitary confinement.* New Haven, CT: Yale University Press.

Rubin, J., & Kim, V. (2017, March 15). Former LA County Sheriff Lee Baca found guilty on obstruction of justice and other charges. *Los Angeles Times.* Retrieved from http://www.latimes.com/local/lanow/la-me-ln-baca-verdict-20170314story.html

Salisbury, E. J., & Van Voorhis, P. (2009). Gendered pathways: A quantitative investigation of women probationers' paths to incarceration. *Criminal Justice and Behavior, 36*(6), 541–566.

Sampson, R., & Laub, J. (1993). *Crime in the making: Pathways and turning points through life.* Cambridge, MA: Harvard University Press.

Santo, A., Kim, V., & and Flagg, A. (2017). Upgrade your jail cell—For a price. *Los Angeles Times.* Retrieved from http://www.latimes.com/projects/la-me-pay-tostay-jails/

Schlanger, M. (2013). *Plata v. Brown* and Realignment: Jails, prisons, courts, and politics. *Harv. C. R. C. L. L. Rev., 48*(1), 165–215.

Schlanger, M. (2017). The just-barely-sustainable California prisoners' rights ecosystem. *The Annals of the American Academy, 664,* 62–81.

Sexton, L., & Jenness, V. (2016). "We're like community": Collective identity and collective efficacy among transgender women in prisons for men. *Punishment & Society, 18*(5), 544–577.

Simon, J. (2007). *Governing through crime.* New York, NY: Oxford University Press.

St. John, P. (2014, October 22). California will end race-based punishment in state prisons. *Los Angeles Times.* Retrieved from http://www.latimes.com/local/crime/la-me-ff-pol-prison-settlement-20141023story.html

State of California. (2016). *Budget summary on public safety.* Retrieved from http://www.ebudget.ca.gov/201617/pdf/Revised/BudgetSummary/PublicSafety.pdf

Still, W. (2016). A practitioner's perspective on Realignment: A giant win in San Francisco. *ANNALS: American Academy of Political and Social Science, 664*(1), 221–235.

Sumner, J. M. (2009). *Keeping house: Understanding the transgender inmate code of conduct through prison policies, environments, and culture.* (Unpublished doctoral dissertation). University of California, Irvine, CA.

Sumner, J. M., & Matsuda, K. M. (2006). *Shining light in dark corners: An overview of prison rape legislation and an introduction to current research.* Bulletin for the Center for Evidence-Based Corrections, *1*(2), 1–8.

Sylvia Rivera Law Project. (2007). *"It's war in here": A report on the treatment of transgender and intersex people in New York State men's prisons.* Retrieved from http://archive.srlp.org/resources/pubs/warinhere

Tafoya, S., Bird, M., Nguyen, V., & Grattet, R. (2017). *Pretrial release in California.* San Francisco, CA: Public Policy Institute of California.

Thompson, D. (2015). "This is not safe": California prisons' high homicide rate makes them deadly for sex offenders. NBC. Retrieved from http://www.nbclosangeles.com/news/local/Homicide-Rate-for-California-Prisons-is-Double-the-National-Average-292094751.html

Trammell, R. (2009). Values, rules, and keeping the peace: How men describe order and the inmate code in California prisons. *Deviant Behavior, 30,* 746–771.

Turner, S., Fain, T., & Hunt, S. (2015). *Public Safety Realignment in twelve California counties.* Santa Monica, CA: RAND Corporation.

Turner, S., Hess, J., Bradstreet, C., Chapman, S., & Murphy, A. (2013). *Development of the California Static Risk Assessment (CSRA): Recidivism risk prediction in the California Department of Corrections and Rehabilitation.* Irvine, CA: Center for Evidence-Based Corrections.

Warren, J. (2003). Jerry Brown calls sentence law a failure. *Los Angeles Times.* Retrieved from http://articles.latimes.com/2003/feb/28/local/me-prisoners28

von Hirsch, A. (1976). *Doing justice: The choice of punishments.* New York: Hill and Wang.

Zimring, F. E., Hawkins, G., & Kamin, S. (2001). *Punishment and democracy.* New York, NY: Oxford University Press.

Cases Cited

Ashker v. Brown, Case No. 4:09-cv-5796-CW (N.D. Cal.)

Coleman v. Brown, Case No. 2:90-cv-00520-LKK-JFM (E.D. Cal.)

Johnson v. California, 545 U.S. 162 (2005)

Lockyer v. Andrade, 538 U.S. 63 (2003)

Mitchell v. Cate, Case No. 2:08-cv-01196-RAJ (E.D. Cal.)

Plata v. Brown, Case No. C01-1351 THE (N.D. Cal.)

Plata v. Schwarzenegger, 560 F.3d 976 (2009)

Chapter 8

California's Experience with the Death Penalty

Stacy L. Mallicoat and Brenda Vogel

Learning Objectives

After reading the chapter, students should be able to:

- Demonstrate an understanding of the history of capital punishment and how the practice has evolved in California since the nineteenth century.
- Explain the current state of the death penalty in California, including data on death row and executions.
- Describe life on death row in California.
- Discuss some of the challenges facing California's use of capital punishment.

While many states around the nation are famous for their use of the death penalty and carrying out executions, California holds a special distinction in regards to the practice of capital punishment. As of April 1, 2017, there were 749 people on California's death row (CDCR, 2017). Not only does the state have the largest death row in the United States, but there are more people awaiting execution in California than in any other region in the Western Hemisphere (Nichols, 2016). Despite the large number of people who have been sentenced to death, only 13 executions have been carried out in the state over the past four decades (CDCR, n.d.).

This chapter highlights the use of the ultimate punishment in California. The chapter begins with a discussion of the history of capital punishment and how the practice has evolved in California since the nineteenth century. Second, the chapter presents the current state of the death penalty and presents data on death row and executions in California. Third, the chapter highlights life on death row in California. The chapter concludes with a discussion on some of the challenges facing the state's use of capital punishment.

The History of California's Death Penalty

The death penalty in California was introduced in 1851 as part of the Criminal Practices Act and was incorporated into the State Penal Code in 1872. Under these rules, individual counties were responsible for carrying out executions. The law dictated that executions were to be carried out within the walls of the county jail where the crime was committed. In addition to the local sheriff, district attorney, and a physician, executions were observed by twelve local citizens who served as representatives of the community and the defendant was entitled to a maximum of two clergy members and five personal witnesses. Data indicate that 204 executions occurred in California between 1778 and 1890 under county jurisdiction (Espy File, n.d.). In 1891, the state legislature ordered the practice of carrying out executions to be moved to the jurisdiction of the state. Under these new regulations, executions were carried out at one of the two state prisons in operation at the time, San Quentin Prison and Folsom State Penitentiary. The first execution under these new rules occurred on March 3, 1893, by hanging (CDCR, n.d.).

Hanging was the most common method of execution in the United States during the late eighteenth and early nineteenth centuries. The practice of hanging involved a "long drop," whereby the fall created tension between the noose around the individual's neck that resulted in breaking the neck of the offender. The long drop was the preferred method by many states, as earlier methods resulted in the offender being strangled to death. Death by hanging did not come quickly and often tortured the offender. The long form of hanging also led to problems, as it could result in decapitation (Bohm, 2012). Between 1893 and 1937, California executed 303 men and 4 women by hanging. In 1937, the legislature mandated that the official method of execution be switched from hanging to lethal gas (CDCR, n.d.). With only one lethal gas chamber in the state, all executions were held at San Quentin State Prison. Here, a lethal dose of cyanide gas was deployed into an airtight chamber with the inmate restrained in a chair. Between 1930 and 1967, 292 people were executed by lethal gas in California, an average of eight executions a year (Culver & Boyens, 2002).

In 1972, the United States Supreme Court held that the death penalty was unconstitutional under the Eighth Amendment protections against cruel and unusual punishment. This holding in *Furman v. Georgia* echoed the themes of a case that had been decided earlier in *California v. Anderson* (1972), which held that the current administration of the death penalty in California was unconstitutional. In California, 107 inmates saw their death sentences converted to a prison sentence. Included in this group were some of the state's most noteworthy offenders, including Charles Manson and Sirhan Sirhan. Manson was originally sent to death row for his orchestration of the Tate-LaBianca murders in 1969. Sirhan Sirhan was convicted for the assassination of Robert F. Kennedy, a U.S. Senator from the state of New York (DPIC, n.d.). While both Manson's and Sirhan's death sentences were converted to a life sentence, they are considered eligible for parole. Under the decision in *California v. Anderson* (1972), prisoners who were previously under a sentence of death could apply for parole after being incarcerated for seven years. While both regularly apply for parole consideration, their applications have been continually denied. Given the high-profile nature of their crimes, it is unlikely that they will ever be released from prison.

Following the Supreme Court ruling in *Gregg v. Georgia* in 1976, California adopted a similarly structured law that created three new criteria for sentencing people to death. First, death penalty cases must allow for the admission of aggravating and mitigating evidence. The court argued that these factors should be used to direct the sentencing discretion of the court in order to protect against the arbitrary sentencing practices that had occurred throughout history. Aggravating factors involve circumstances about the crime that justify a harsh penalty. Section 190.2 of the California Penal Code provides 22 different aggravating factors for consideration. Table 8.1 lists these various aggravating factors that juries can consider in death penalty cases. While *Gregg* directs jurors to weigh out the aggravating and mitigating factors in handing down a sentence of death, research demonstrates that California jurors are often confused about this process as they receive very little guidance about what is considered a mitigating factor and often dismiss any information that might mitigate the crime (Haney, Sontag, & Costanzo, 1994).

Second, the decision in *Gregg* required states to restructure the death penalty process. Today, all death penalty proceedings throughout the United States involve a two-stage, or bifurcated process. Under this system of "super due-process," the state must hold two separate trial proceedings. In the first trial, the focus is on the guilt (or lack thereof) of the offender. If the offender is convicted of murder in the first degree with special circumstances, the case moves to a second trial. During this second trial, the same group of jurors from the first trial are presented with the aggravating and mitigating evidence to determine whether the offender should receive life without the possibility of parole or be sentenced to death. Finally, all death penalty sentences receive an automatic appeal of their case to the State Supreme Court. Here, the court reviews the case to determine whether any legal errors were made.

Table 8.1. List of Aggravating Factors in California's Death Penalty

1. The murder was intentional and carried out for financial gain.
2. Criminal history involves cases of 1st or 2nd degree murder.
3. Current case involves multiple convictions for 1st and 2nd degree murder.
4. The murder was committed by means of a destructive device (bomb or other explosive).
5. The murder was committed for the purpose of avoiding or preventing a lawful arrest, or perfecting or attempting to perfect, an escape from lawful custody.
6. The murder was committed by means of a destructive device, via the mail or delivery service.
7. The victim was a peace officer, and was intentionally killed in the line of duty or as a result of their professional identity.
8. The victim was a Federal law officer, and was intentionally killed in the line of duty or as a result of their professional identity.
9. The victim was a firefighter, and was intentionally killed in the line of duty.
10. The victim was a witness to a crime who was intentionally killed for the purpose of preventing his or her testimony in any criminal or juvenile proceeding.
11. The victim was a prosecutor or assistant prosecutor or a former prosecutor or assistant prosecutor of any local or state prosecutor's office in this or any other state, or of a federal prosecutor's office, and the murder was intentionally carried out in retaliation for, or to prevent the performance of, the victim's official duties.
12. The victim was a judge or former judge of any court of record in the local, state, or federal system in this or any other state, and the murder was intentionally carried out in retaliation for, or to prevent the performance of, the victim's official duties.
13. The victim was an elected or appointed official or former official of the Federal government, or of any local or state government of this or any other state, and the killing was intentionally carried out in retaliation for, or to prevent the performance of, the victim's official duties.
14. The murder was especially heinous, atrocious, or cruel, manifesting exceptional depravity.
15. The defendant intentionally killed the victim by means of lying in wait.
16. The victim was intentionally killed because of his or her race, color, religion, nationality, or country of origin.
17. The murder was committed while the defendant was engaged in, or was an accomplice in, the commission of, attempted commission of, or the immediate flight after committing, or attempting to commit, the following felonies:
    - Robbery
    - Kidnapping
    - Rape
    - Sodomy
    - The performance of a lewd or lascivious act upon the person of a child under the age of 14 years
    - Oral copulation
    - Burglary in the first or second degree

- Arson
- Train wrecking
- Mayhem
- Rape by instrument
- Carjacking

18. The murder was intentional and involved the infliction of torture.
19. The defendant intentionally killed the victim by the administration of poison.
20. The victim was a juror in any court of record in the local, state, or federal system in this or any other state, and the murder was intentionally carried out in retaliation for, or to prevent the performance of, the victim's official duties.
21. The murder was intentional and perpetrated by means of discharging a firearm from a motor vehicle, intentionally at another person or persons outside the vehicle with the intent to inflict death.
22. The defendant intentionally killed the victim while the defendant was an active participant in a criminal street gang, and the murder was carried out to further the activities of the criminal street gang.

Source: California Penal Code 190.2

Death Sentencing in California

While the rate of death sentences is decreasing nationwide, California remains active in sending offenders to death row. Table 8.2 displays information on the numbers of individuals sent to death row in California since 1978. Over the past 39 years, courts have handed down 792 death sentences. Not only has California been active in sentencing offenders to death, these sentences are often focused in specific geographic regions of the state. A review of sentencing patterns notes that three counties (Los Angeles, Orange, and Riverside) account for 52% of all death sentences in the state. Yet in other counties, prosecutors choose not to seek the death penalty for death-eligible defendants. This trend is not unique to California, as many states have shifted away from sentencing offenders to death. In 2010, there were 104 death sentences handed down across the U.S. and by 2016, there were only 30 (DPIC, 2017). These numbers represent a significant departure from sentencing trends in the 1990s, when 315 offenders were sent to death row nationwide in 1996 (DPIC, 2017; Snell, 2011).

Death Row in California

Men on death row are housed at San Quentin State Prison while the women reside at Central California Women's Facility, Chowchilla (NAACP, 2011). The racial makeup of death row is 36% white, 34% black, 24% Hispanic, and 6%

Table 8.2. Sentences to Death Row

Year	Total Number of Death Sentences	Year	Total Number of Death Sentences
1978	1	1998	31
1979	7	1999	40
1980	7	2000	32
1981	10	2001	22
1982	20	2002	16
1983	13	2003	20
1984	16	2004	10
1985	11	2005	22
1986	16	2006	16
1987	15	2007	16
1988	25	2008	20
1989	26	2009	29
1990	25	2010	28
1991	19	2011	10
1992	37	2012	12
1993	30	2013	24
1994	23	2014	14
1995	36	2015	14
1996	38	2016	9
1997	35	2017	3*

Source: http://www.cdcr.ca.gov/Capital_Punishment/docs/CondemnedInmateListSecure.pdf
* Data as of 3/31/17

other races (CDCR, 2017). They range in age from 24 to 86 years old (CDCR, 2017). Among the ranks of death row inmates include offenders such as Richard Allen Davis (kidnapping, rape, and murder of Polly Klaas), Rodney Alcala (the Dating Game killer), Charles Ng and Randy Kraft (serial killers), and Scott Peterson (murder of his wife and unborn child).

San Quentin Death Row

Condemned men are not housed on a single "row" or block in San Quentin but in one of five inmate housing units: north segregation, east block, the adjustment center, Donner housing unit, and the psychiatric inpatient hospital (St. John, 2016a). All condemned inmates at San Quentin are housed alone and are classified into one of two categories: grade A and grade B. Grade A inmates are those who follow the institution's rules and grade B inmates are those who do not.

North segregation, or "north seg," includes 68 cells and is located on the sixth floor of north block, which was built in 1934 and was San Quentin's original death row. The words "Condemned Row" are painted above the entrance in medieval script. North segregation, however, filled up shortly after the death penalty was restored in 1978, and prison officials then began using east block to house condemned inmates (St. John, 2016a).

Today, north segregation houses grade A inmates who have earned, through good behavior, special privileges. For example, inmates are released from their cells at 7am and are allowed access to a small common area until about 1:30pm (Mullane, 2012b). Natural light enters the unit through windows above the cell doors, which are made of thick bars overlaid with black, metal mesh. Additionally, inmates have access to a roof-top "yard" with views of the bay, Marin County, and Mount Tamalpais. While outside their cells, inmates have access to wall phones and showers. Conditions in north segregation are so far superior to those in the other four units for condemned inmates, that there is a waiting list to get in. Scott Peterson, who was convicted of killing his pregnant wife Laci, is housed in north segregation.

Most condemned men in San Quentin, all grade As, are housed in east block, which was built in 1930 as overflow for north block (St. John, 2016a). East block contains 520 cells configured in a long corridor with 57 cells on each side, stacked five tiers high. Each cell measures 4ft 6in wide, 10ft 8in long, and 7ft 7in tall; that's about 48 square feet (Mullane, 2013). Each cell door is made of black bars and perforated metal. At the top of the tiers, nearly 40 feet above the ground, are windows that allow fresh air and sunlight onto the tier. The walls are painted a pale yellow and the sound of clanging metal, yelling inmates, and banging reverberates throughout the block (St. John, 2016a). Wheelchairs line the hallway outside the bottom tier for those inmates who are unable to walk on their own. The bottom tier used to also house the most mentally ill inmates as well, until they were moved to the new psychiatric unit in 2014.

Condemned inmates on east block have access to television, yard time, phone calls (every other day), showers (every other day), and some programming, like educational and mental health programs (Mullane, 2013). East block has two group "yards," each the size of a basketball court, with heavy bags and basketball hoops (Mullane, 2012b). Both yards are asphalt and devoid of grass, and guards armed with rifles observe from a walkway above. Inmates receive a minimum of 10 hours of yard time a week. Conditions in east block have improved a great deal since the completion of a massive cleanup in 2009 sparked by an inmate lawsuit. Prior to the upgrades, rainwater would cascade off the tiers and cells were strewn with pigeon and rodent feces (Payne, 2016).

By the middle of 2015, east block and north segregation were reaching capacity for condemned inmates. The overcrowding is what results when there have been no executions since 2006, yet California continues to sentence people to death. Specifically, San Quentin nets roughly 13 death row inmates per year. This estimate is based on a six-year annual average of 20 new arrivals and offset by inmates who either die while incarcerated or have their sentences overturned (Gorman, 2015). Consequently, in 2015, Governor Jerry Brown asked the legislature for $3.2 million to open 97 more cells to accommodate more death row prisoners in the Donner housing unit (Gorman 2015; Halstead, 2015). The 97 cells were not new, but were converted from cells vacated by lower-level offenders who were released through Proposition 47. The new unit opened in early 2016 (Gogola, 2016).

In October 2014, as the result of a court order, San Quentin opened a 39-bed Psychiatric Inpatient Program (PIP) for condemned men who are severely mentally ill or in crisis (Barba, 2016; Segura, 2016). It is estimated to have cost the state $620,000 to convert existing facilities on the fourth floor of the prison's medical services building to house the new PIP. Inmates in the PIP receive group and individual therapy but must be confined to steel cages during their sessions. The irony of providing intensive psychiatric care to condemned men is not lost on Berkeley law professor Franklin Zimring. Since it is unconstitutional to execute people who are not aware of what is happening to them, Zimring quipped that "We are curing them to make them executable" (St. John, 2014, para. 11).

The fifth unit to house condemned men at San Quentin is the adjustment center. The 102-cell adjustment center is a prison within a prison (Stryker,

2016). About 80 percent of its residents are condemned inmates, all grade Bs, and the remaining are not condemned but are in administrative segregation (Mullane, 2012a). The cells doors are solid concrete with one small slat through which staff can cuff inmates prior to leaving their cell. The solid doors are designed to prevent inmates from throwing feces, urine, or other bodily fluids at staff (Ortiz, 2016). Inmates housed in the adjustment center take yard time three times a week in either one of two group yards or in one of 32 individual yards; they are cages the size of small living rooms (Mullane, 2012a). The individual cages are for inmates who either can't get along with others, or have been violent on the group yard. The adjustment center is the harshest of the five death row units at San Quentin. Inmates spend between 21 and 24 hours a day inside cells smaller than a parking space (Mullane, 2012a). "They remain there alone, with no exposure to natural light, no access to religious services, and devoid of recreational, vocational, and educational programming. They are denied contact visits or telephone calls" (*Lopez v. Brown*, Complaint, p. 3). The adjustment center is noisy; slamming cell doors and gates, yelling, and banging are constant and sleep deprivation is common. Access to healthcare, mental assessments, yard time, and visitations are severely limited or nonexistent. Because of the backlog of cases in California, inmates can spend *years* in the adjustment center.

Conditions are so dire that six death row inmates filed a class-action lawsuit in 2015, *Lopez v. Brown*, claiming that inmates were confined in inhumane conditions for extensive periods of time (up to 26 years) without meaningful review. Further, plaintiffs claimed that they were placed in the adjustment center based on allegations of gang membership without reliable evidence of such affiliation. As of May 2016, settlement negotiations were ongoing (Civil Rights Litigation Clearinghouse, 2017).

Central California Women's Facility Death Row

The original death row for women was located at the California Institution for Women near Chino in southern California. Today, however, condemned women in California are housed at the Central California Women's Facility (CCWF) near Chowchilla. Opened in 1990, CCWF is the largest women's prison in the U.S. with 2,905 inmates as of December 2016 (CDCR, 2017). Death row is located on the first floor in the 207 building, designed for maximum security inmates; death row originally included only 9 cells (Corwin, 1992).

Today, death row at CCWF has expanded to house all 21 condemned women. The 207 building is a large cell block, with double tiers along three of the four walls. Double-occupancy cells line both the top and bottom tiers, which house inmates convicted of various crimes. "Typically, inmates housed in this building have a history of disciplinary issues. Nonetheless, these women 'program' (eat, indoor recreation, receive commissary, have religious visits, use telephones, watch TV, etc.) almost entirely in the unit. In the middle of block on the first floor is a large common area with fixed tables and chairs, telephones, and TVs for inmate use when they are allowed out of their cells for programming" (C. E. Ireland, personal communication, January 25, 2017). A set of stairs leads to the common area from the second tier. The condemned women are housed in single-person, 6-by-11-foot cells along one wall on the first floor. The space immediately outside their cell doors is enclosed with chain-link fencing, creating a common space designated solely for death row females referred to as "the freeway" (Corwin, 1992). The freeway includes tables and chairs for death-row inmate use, as well as televisions, designated washers and dryers, telephones, and access to the law library. The chain link fence is the only thing separating the condemned women from the other women in the block (C. E. Ireland, personal communication, January 25, 2017).

CCWF does not have a death chamber. Although no women have been executed in California in the modern era, if a woman were to be executed, she would be transferred by bus to San Quentin, since it houses the only execution chamber in the state (Corwin, 1992).

Executions in California

While the historical practice of executing offenders was quite active with 709 executions, California's practice has slowed dramatically over the past four decades. Despite the reinstatement of capital punishment in 1978, it was another 14 years before the state carried out an execution. Table 8.3 lists the 13 individuals who have been put to death within the state since the reinstatement of the death penalty. However, there have been no executions for the past decade. Today, individuals on California's death row are more likely to die as a result of natural causes or by suicide rather than execution. The last execution in California was on January 12, 2006, when Clarence Ray Allen was executed by lethal injection after spending over 23 years on death row (Wagstaff, 2014). He was convicted of organizing the murders of three individuals who had testified against him in the 1977 trial where he was convicted of the murder of Mary Sue Kitts, his son's 17-year-old girlfriend (Finz, 2006). At the time of his execution, he was 76 years old and one of the oldest prisoners ever put to death in the U.S. (Doyle, 2006).

Table 8.3. Inmates Executed, 1978 to Present

Name	Date Executed	Time on Death Row
Robert Alton Harris	4/21/1992	13 years, 1 month
David Edwin Mason	8/24/1993	9 years, 7 months
William George Bonin	2/23/1996	13 years, 1 month
Keith Daniel Williams	5/3/1996	17 years
Thomas M. Thompson	7/14/1998	14 years, 1 month
Kelvin Malone	1/13/1999	15 years, 6 months
Jaturun Siripongs	2/9/1999	15 years, 9 months
Manuel Babbitt	5/4/1999	16 years, 10 months
Darrell Keith Rich	3/15/2000	19 years, 1 month
Robert Lee Massie	3/27/2001	21 years, 10 months
Stephen Wayne Anderson	1/29/2002	20 years, 6 months
Donald Beardslee	1/19/2005	20 years, 10 months
Stanley Williams	12/13/2005	24 years, 8 months
Clarence Ray Allen	1/17/2006	23 years, 1 month

Source: http://www.cdcr.ca.gov/Capital_Punishment/Inmates_Executed.html

With 747 offenders on death row, it would take over fourteen years just to carry out the punishments for those currently on death row if an execution were scheduled every week. Currently there are at least sixteen individuals who have all exhausted their appeals at the state and federal level and would be eligible for execution should the state resume executions. Collectively, these individuals have served more than 496 years on death row. They range in age from 50 to 79 years old (*Los Angeles Times*, 2015; CDCR, 2017). However, the current challenges to California's death penalty question if, when, and how these punishments will be carried out.

Current Challenges in California's Practice of Capital Punishment

Financial Facts about California's Ultimate Punishment

While theoretical debates on retribution and deterrence once provided the foundations for death penalty support and opposition, recent debates have focused on more practical issues. One of the biggest areas of concern regarding the use of the death penalty in California has been the cost. Since its reinstatement in 1978, California has spent over $4 billion on the death penalty. Given that only 13 executions have been carried out over the past 34 years, many have questioned whether these high costs are worth carrying out the ultimate punishment. Contrary to popular opinion, it is more expensive to carry out a death sentence than it is to incarcerate someone for the rest of their life. Research by the Commission on the Fair Administration of Justice (2008) indicates that the annual cost of incarcerating an inmate on death row is an additional $90,000 per inmate, compared to providing maximum-security housing for life without the possibility of parole inmates. Considering the current population of death row, this amounts to over sixty million dollars in costs. If these sentences were commuted to life without the possibility of parole, the annual cost would be $11.5 million per year, a savings of over $50 million dollars a year.

Housing is not the only excessively costly aspect of capital punishment. Research by the *Sacramento Bee* estimates that the additional trial costs of death penalty cases are approximately $78 million dollars each year outside of the traditional costs of the justice process (Magagnini, 1998). These costs are accumulated for all death penalty trials, including those that do not result in a verdict of death. Since 1978, California has conducted over 1,940 capital trials. Capital cases can cost upwards of $1 million dollars more than non-capital cases (Alarcon & Mitchell, 2011). Much of the costs of a death penalty case are incurred up front at the trial level. Death penalty cases generally involve greater levels of investigation, increased case preparation by the attorneys, and a longer time spent in the courtroom dealing with pretrial motions, the voir dire process (selection of a jury), and in the trial itself. Consider the case of Skyler Deleon, which represents a typical death penalty case in California. Deleon was arrested in November 2004 for the murders of Thomas and Jackie Hawkes, but his trial did not begin until September 22, 2008, almost four years later. It took almost a month for the case to be tried and for the jury to find Deleon guilty (October 20, 2008). The penalty trial in his case was completed on November 6, 2008, when the jury recommended that Deleon be sentenced to death for his crimes.

In addition to the increased costs at the trial level, death penalty cases involve a long and expensive appellate process. The mandatory appellate process is both time-consuming and expensive. On average, death row inmates can wait for years before the California Supreme Court reviews their convictions and sentences on direct appeal. To date, only 227 of the inmates on death row have had their death sentences affirmed by the California State Supreme Court. Nine sentences were reversed at this level and are currently awaiting retrial (CDCR, 2017). If the conviction and sentence are confirmed on direct appeal, the inmate can wait an additional three or more years before state habeas corpus counsel is appointed to them (Alarcon & Mitchell, 2011). Including the automatic appeal, there are 9 or 10 potential levels of review for a death penalty case, each of which increases the amount of time and financial support that is needed (Bohm, 2012). The delay for cases to be heard on automatic appeal impacts not only those offenders that will eventually be executed, but also cases of individuals whose cases are later overturned as a result of evidence of innocence or legal error.

Methods of Execution: The Use of Lethal Injection

As discussed earlier in this chapter, the history of executions in California includes the use of a number of different methods of execution, including hanging and the gas chamber. The first two executions following the reinstatement of the death penalty in 1978 (Robert Alton Harris and David Mason) were conducted using lethal gas. With the introduction of a "new" method of carrying out executions, California joined with other pro-death penalty states in adopting lethal injection as the method of carrying out modern-day executions. Initially, lethal gas remained an option that the condemned could choose. However, lethal gas was ruled unconstitutional by the state in 1994, a decision that was upheld by the Ninth Circuit Court of Appeals in 1996. As a result, lethal injection became the primary method of execution. Since 1996, 11 offenders have been executed by lethal injection (DPIC).

Today, challenges to the lethal injection process have resulted in a de facto moratorium in many states, including California. Death row inmates in various states have argued that the process of lethal injection amounts to cruel and unusual punishment. Here, a number of botched executions have been documented involving cases where it took several tries to get the tubes that administer the lethal drugs into a suitable vein, violent reactions to the lethal drugs, and concerns that the level of barbiturates were enough to cause paralysis but inadequate to effectively sedate the offender.

Since 2006, executions have been halted in the state of California as a result of several legal challenges. The case of *Morales v. Tilton* challenged the constitutionality of California's lethal injection protocol. Up until this point, the state of California had been using this protocol since the mid-1990s. The question before the court was whether or not California's lethal-injection protocol—as actually administered in practice—creates an undue and unnecessary risk that an inmate will suffer pain so extreme that it offends the Eighth Amendment. The three-drug injection process was designed to be painless and effective; however, the use of the first drug, sodium thiopental, concerned the courts. The intent of sodium thiopental is to induce unconsciousness so that the individual would not experience any pain associated with the administration of the other two drugs. The court agreed with Morales, noting that the possibility of an improper injection of sodium thiopental could lead to severe pain, which would be a violation of the Eighth Amendment.

While a federal district court judge found that the current practice of the three-drug protocol in California was unconstitutional, the court also noted that it could be fixed (*Morales v. Tilton*, 2006). In particular, the court was concerned about the lack of training of officers who were appointed to the execution teams, inconsistent record keeping, a poorly designed execution chamber, and the improper mixing and administration of execution drugs.

As a result of the court's decision, the California Department of Corrections and Rehabilitation (CDCR) was tasked with revising the state's lethal injection protocol. In their report to the court, the CDCR noted several changes to address the deficiencies raised in *Morales v. Tilton*. One of these recommendations included building a new lethal injection facility (Schwarzenegger & Tilton, 2007). The costs for this project were initially slated at $399,000, which fell just below the quota that required that legislative approval for the expense (Muhammad, 2007). However, rising construction costs led to the need for additional funding in order to finish the project. The new death chamber was completed in September 2010 and cost the state $853,000. Built with inmate labor, the new chamber has improved lighting, improved sightlines, and additional seating for witnesses. There are also separate viewing rooms for members of the victim's family and for friends and family members of the condemned (Fagan, 2010).

Meanwhile the courts continue to battle over the procedural aspects of the state's lethal injection process. In May 2013, the First District Court of Appeals unanimously held that the Department of Corrections failed to follow proper administrative regulations in determining a new protocol for carrying out executions. For example, officials did not explain their rationale behind keeping with a three-drug protocol for executions (Mintz, 2013). This has resulted in continued delays in reinstating executions. In November 2014, a lawsuit was filed to force the CDCR to develop a viable lethal injection protocol. The state reached a settlement of the case in June 2015, which required that these regulations be set within three months of the decision in *Glossip v. Gross*. *Glossip* was decided by the court on June 29, 2015, in a 5–4 decision and upheld the use of midazolam as the first drug of a three-drug lethal injection protocol. In late October 2015, the state announced its new regulations for carrying out executions. One of the more notable provisions of this plan was that it allowed executioners to choose from four different drugs. Two of these drugs, sodium thiopental and pentobarbital, had been used for executions in other states. However, both of these drugs were becoming increasingly difficult for states to obtain for use for executions. The other two drugs, amobarbital and secobarbital, have never been used in any execution. Public hearings on these proposed execution regulations were held in Sacramento in January 2016, and comments from the public concluded in April 2016. Throughout the remainder of 2016, CDCR was tasked with responding to these concerns, which could include changes to the proposed protocol. However, the process remains at a standstill with no new regulations confirmed and no executions scheduled as of early 2017 (Office of Administrative Law, 2016; Mallicoat, Vogel, & Crawford, 2017).

Issues of Wrongful Conviction

To date, 2,093 individuals across the U.S. have been exonerated for crimes that they did not commit. Their original convictions were overturned as a result of issues such as ineffective assistance of counsel, misconduct by the police or prosecutors, erroneous eyewitness testimony, and post-conviction DNA testing results. One hundred and eighty-eight of these cases involved individuals convicted in California (National Registry of Exonerations, 2017). Of these cases, three individuals had been sentenced to death (DPIC, n.d.). Ernest (Shujaa) Graham was convicted in 1976 for killing a correctional officer and spent five years on death row before he was exonerated. During his trial, the prosecutor used his peremptory challenges to exclude all black jurors from serving on the jury. His conviction was overturned, and he was acquitted during his retrial. Troy Lee Jones was convicted in 1982 for the murder of Carolyn Grayson. In his appeal, the court found that Jones's attorney was so deficient in his defense that it had a negative impact on the outcome of his case. After spending fourteen years on death row, his conviction was overturned and the state dismissed all charges against him (DPIC, 2017). Oscar Lee Morris was convicted in 1983, and his death sentence was vacated by the California Supreme Court in 1988 when the court held that there was no evidence that the murder was committed during the course of a felony, which was a requirement for a death sentence. After the main witness in the case recanted his testimony, his conviction was overturned, and prosecutors declined to retry the case. He was released from prison in 2000 (DPIC, 2017).

In addition to these exonerations, California has executed one individual who some suggest may have been innocent. Tommy Thompson was convicted of rape and murder in 1981. In addition to prosecutorial misconduct and ineffective assistance by his trial counsel, there was conflicting evidence in his case about whether he had consensual sex with Ginger Fleischli, the victim in this case. It was the conviction on the rape charge that made his case eligible for the death penalty. While the Ninth Circuit Court of Appeals voted to overturn his conviction, the U.S. Supreme Court overruled this decision as a result of a procedural error by the appellate court. His plea for clemency to Governor Pete Wilson was rejected. Thompson was executed on July 14, 1998 (Bailey, Schrader, & Hua, 1998).

Recommendations for Change: The Future of California's Death Penalty

Since the reinstatement of the death penalty in California, advocates for and against capital punishment have debated the merits of the practice. While supporters of the death penalty search for ways to expedite the process of carrying out executions, opponents of the death penalty fight to abolish the practice entirely.

The length of time between when a sentence of death is handed down and when the execution is carried out is extreme. As a result of the delays related to the automatic appeals process and limited resources to process cases, death row inmates in California are spending decades waiting to be executed. This is particularly ironic given that the state of California argued in *California v. Anderson* in 1972, that California's death penalty was unconstitutional and commented that the lengthy amounts of time that the condemned spent on death row amounted to cruel and unusual punishment under the Eighth Amendment. At the time of *California v. Anderson*, an inmate spent an average of eight years on death row awaiting execution. "The families of murder victims are cruelly deluded into believing that justice will be delivered with finality during their lifetimes" (CCFAJ, 116). While the national average of time from sentence to execution hovers around 12 years, in California it can take over 25 years to carry out an execution. For example, the last five executions in the state involved offenders who waited more than twenty years for "justice" to be served. Today, some of the state's most notorious offenders continue to wait for their punishment.

In 2004 the California Senate formed a committee to study issues related to wrongful conviction. The California Commission on the Fair Administration of Justice spent two years reviewing the state's criminal justice system. Their recommendations were compiled into an advisory report to the legislature and governor in August 2008. Within their discussions on the death penalty, the commission not only identified several flaws in the current system, but provided alternatives to the death penalty and recommendations for the administration of California's death penalty law.

The cost of the death penalty is exorbitant. If the state is concerned about the rising costs of maintaining the death penalty in California, changes must take place. Under the current system of capital punishment in California, it would be difficult to find a first-degree murder case that would be excluded from death penalty consideration under the current set of conditions. Research indicates that such a wide variety of conditions increases the risk of error and creates higher rates of racial and geographic discrimination (Liebman & Marshall, 2006). In their recommendation that the legislature reduce the number of death-eligible conditions, the California Commission on the Fair Administration of Justice highlighted five categories of crimes that should remain death eligible: (1) murder of a police officer; (2) murder of any person at a correctional facility; (3) murder of two or more people; (4) murder involving torture of the victim; and (5) murder to prevent prosecution (i.e., of witness, juror, judge, prosecutor, etc.). In addition, the commission specifically recommended the exclusion of general felony murder from the list of death eligible crimes. Assuming that future executions of those currently on death row were limited to these five factors, the current size of death row would be reduced by 45%. Commuting the remaining 55% of death sentences could save approximately $27 million dollars each year in housing costs alone. The number of death penalty trials (and their related costs) would decrease, and the appellate courts would be relieved of the current work demands that have virtually halted the use of the death penalty (CCFAJ, 2008).

Unlike states that have recently abolished the death penalty through legislative action, or in those where governors have declared a moratorium on executions, California requires that the state's death penalty law be amended through the ballot initiative process. In 2012, voters were asked to make this decision for the state of California. Proposition 34, also known as the SAFE (Savings, Accountability, Full Enforcement) California Act, called to replace the death penalty with life without the possibility of parole. In addition to converting the current death sentences to life without the possibility of parole, prisoners would have been required to make restitution to the victims' services fund and "be held accountable both to the families of their victims, and to society at large as the victim of every assault on the sanctity of human life" (Schulter, 2011). The measure failed with a narrow margin of 48% of voters in support of abolishing the death penalty and 52% of voters who wished to retain it.

In 2016, abolitionists made another attempt to abolish the state's death penalty via the voter initiative process. Similar to the efforts in 2012, Proposition 62 (Justice That Works) would have abolished capital punishment in California and replaced it with life in prison without the possibility of parole. The measure also required inmates to work and to direct 60% of their wages to any fines and restitution ordered by the court. If passed, it was projected that this change would save the state over $150 million dollars each year (Legislative Analyst's Office, 2016a). However, a competing measure to alter the way in which death penalty appeals are handled was also presented to voters on the same ballot. Proposition 66 proposed a number of changes to the existing law. One of these provisions would require the first appeal to be heard by the same judge who heard the original case and for all state appeals to be concluded within five years. Proponents of the measure argued that this would help ease the delay within the California Supreme Court and allow cases to be handled more quickly. The measure would also require any eligible attorney to serve as counsel for death penalty cases, which would expand the pool of eligible attorneys who could serve as counsel for death row inmates (Proposition 66). Currently, attorneys accept capital cases on a voluntary basis, and there are additional requirements in order to be approved as a capital attorney. Opponents to the measure have expressed concern that many attorneys would leave the appellate pool rather than accept a capital appointment (*Los Angeles Times*, 2016). Another concern is that the push to speed up the appellate process could increase the risk of executing an innocent individual.

With two competing measures on the ballot, it was possible that both propositions could receive a majority vote. Under California law, only the measure that received the greatest number of votes would ultimately be implemented, even if both measures received over 50% of the votes cast. Voters ultimately rejected Proposition 62 with 46% of voters in favor of the measure. Meanwhile, Proposition 66 passed with 51% of voters in favor of reforming the state's death penalty law (California Secretary of State, 2016). However, Proposition 66 has yet to be implemented as a result of legal challenges that question the constitutionality of the law (*Ron Briggs & John Van de Kamp v. Jerry Brown*, 2016).

Conclusion

It remains to be seen if and when executions will resume in California. While the voters supported an attempt to mend, not end, the death penalty, legal challenges to this process, as well as the current lethal injection protocol, have halted the resumption of executions. Until such a time that either of these issues are resolved, the state will remain in a de facto moratorium. In the meantime, the state's death row will continue to grow as district attorneys continue to pursue the death penalty and sentence offenders to death, resulting in a significant expense to California taxpayers for the trial, appellate, and housing costs associated with capital punishment.

Key Terms and Definitions

8th Amendment—Protects against cruel and unusual punishment.

Aggravating Factors—Characteristics of the crime that are particularly violent, heinous, or torturous. Used in sentencing offenders to death.

Bifurcated Process—Otherwise known as "super-due process", whereby the guilt phase of a trial is separated from the punishment phase of the trial.

California Commission on the Fair Administration of Justice—A committee appointed by the California State Senate to examine issues in criminal justice that may lead to wrongful convictions.

Central California Women's Facility, Chowchilla—Houses women who have been sentenced to death while they await their execution.

Death eligible—A murder that is considered eligible for the death penalty.

Deterrence—A punishment philosophy that specifies that the use of punishments will both inhibit an offenders likelihood to engage in future crime, but serves to inhibit the actions of society in general.

Execution—The deliberate cause of death by a government entity for the purposes of punishment.

First Degree Murder—An unlawful killing that is premeditated.

Hanging—A practice of execution whereby the offender dies via a broken neck or strangulation.

Just deserts—One explanation of retribution whereby an offender is punished for their crimes.

Lethal Injection—A practice of execution whereby the offender dies as a result of the use of intervenous drugs designed to stop the heart and central nervous system.

Lethal Gas—A practice of execution whereby the offender dies as a result of suffocation via a lethal dose of cyanide gas.

Life without the Possibility of Parole—Often used as an alternative to the death penalty as a maximum sentence for offenders.

Mitigating Factors—Characteristics of the crime or the offender that are used to minimize or explain the actions of an offender.

Proposition 34 (Savings, Accountability, Full Enforcement California Act)— California ballot initiative in 2012 that would replace the death penalty with life without the possibility of parole and require prisoners to make restititon to the victims' services fund. The measure failed with 48% of voters in support.

Proposition 62 (Justice That Works Act)—California ballot initiative in 2016 that would abolish the death penalty and replace it with LWOP. Measure would require inmates to work and pay 60% of wages to any fines and restitution. The measure failed with 46% of voters in support.

Proposition 66 (Death Penalty Reform and Savings Initiative)—California ballot intitiative in 2016 that would change the provisions on how death penalty appeals were handled and speed up the time to execution. The measure passed with 51% of voters in support.

Retribution—To punish an offender in an equal fashion proportionate to the crime or to give an offender a harsh punishment in response to their crime.

Revenge—Often seen in retributive statements, whereby individuals seek to cause harm to an offender in payback for their crimes.

San Quentin—Home to California's death row and execution chamber. Males who have been sentenced to death serve their time on death row while they await execution.

Sodium Thiopental—A general anesthetic that was historically used as the first drug in a three drug protocol in lethal injections.

Atkins v. Virginia—A 2002 US Supreme Court case that held that the execution of the mentally retarded is considered cruel and unusual punishment.

Baze v. Rees—A 2008 US Supreme Court case that held that the 3-drug protocol used by the State of Kentucky as part of its lethal injection process did not violate the 8th amendment.

California v. Anderson—A 1972 California Supreme Court case that held that the practice of the death penalty in the state of California was cruel and unusual.

Furman v. Georgia—1972 US Supreme Court ruling which held that the death penalty, as currently practiced throughout the United States, was arbitrary and discriminatory and therefore was deemed as a violation of the 8th Amendment protection against cruel and unusual punishment.

Gregg v. Georgia—A 1976 US Supreme Court case that reinstated the death penalty with four substantive areas of procedural reform: 1) bifurcated process, 2) guided jury discretion, 3) mandatory appeal; and 4) proportionality review.

Glossip v. Gross—U.S. Supreme Court decision that upheld the use of midazolam as the first drugs of a three drug lethal injection protocol.

Lopez v. Brown—A class action lawsuit filed in 2015 alleging that the conditions on death row in San Quentin constituted cruel and unusual punishment.

Morales v. Tilton—A 2006 California District Court case that held that the execution procedures used by the State of California violated the 8th amendment protection against cruel and unusual punishment.

Ron Briggs & John Van de Kamp v. Jerry Brown—A legal challenge to the bar the implementation of Proposition 66.

Roper v. Simmons—A 2005 US Supreme Court case that held that the execution of juvenile offenders (under the age of 18) is considered cruel and unusual punishment.

Woodson v. North Carolina—A 1976 US Supreme Court case that held that mandatory death sentences for the crime of murder are unconstitutional.

Internet Websites

Death Penalty Information Center: http://www.deathpenaltyinfo.org
Death Penalty Focus: http://www.deathpenalty.org
Bureau of Justice Statistics: https://www.bjs.gov/
California Department of Corrections: http://www.cdcr.ca.gov
California Commission on the Fair Administration of Justice: http://www.ccfaj.org
Legislative Analyst Office: http://www.lao.ca.gov

Review Questions

1. Discuss how the history of executions in California has evolved to our modern-day system of capital punishment.
2. What are the recent challenges that face the use of the death penalty here in California?
3. Why have so few executions been carried out in California over the past four decades?
4. In *Morales v. Tilton*, the court identified five major areas in California's lethal injection protocol that were at risk for causing cruel and unusual punishment towards the offender. Identify each of these areas and discuss why the court felt these issues violated the 8th amendment.
5. Discuss the changes that propositions 62 and 66 would have made to the state's death penalty law. Why do you think one measure passed? Why do you think the other measure failed?

Critical Thinking Questions

1. Recent research suggests that reasons such as retribution and deterrence no longer represent the primary justifications for supporting the death penalty. Do you agree? What issues do you think public opinion has shifted such that fewer people support the death penalty today?

2. In *Furman v. Georgia*, the U.S Supreme Court held that the present death penalty practice was unconstitutional due to discriminatory and arbitrary practices. Since this time, California has made a number of reforms to its system. Do you believe that our practice of capital punishment is constitutionally valid? Why or why not.

3. Given the current de-facto moratorium on executions in California, what does California need to do in order to resume executions? Do you think executions should resume?

References

Alarcon, A., & Mitchell, P. (2011). Executing the will of the voters?: A roadmap to mend or end the California Legislature's multi-billion dollar death penalty debacle. *Loyola of Los Angeles Law Review, 44*, 41–46.

Bailey, E., Schrader, E., & Hua, T. (1998, July 14). Killer put to death by injection at San Quentin. *Los Angeles Times*. Retrieved from http://articles. latimes.com/1998/jul/14/news/mn-3595

Barba, M. (2016, August 16). Behind the gates: The 'living hell' on San Quentin's death row. *San Francisco Examiner*. Retrieved from http://www. sfexaminer.com/behind-gates-living-hell-san-quentins-death-row/

Bohm, R. (2012). *Deathquest: An introduction to the theory and practice of capital punishment in the United States* (4th ed.). Waltham, MA: Anderson Publishing.

California Commission on the Fair Administration of Justice. (2008). *California Commission on the Fair Administration of Justice final report*. Northern California Innocence Project Publications. Retrieved from http://digitalcommons.law.scu.edu/ncippubs/1

California Department of Corrections and Rehabilitation (CDCR). (n.d.). *Capital punishment*. Retrieved from http://www.cdcr.ca.gov/Capital_Punishment

California Department of Corrections and Rehabilitation (CDCR). (2017, January 11). Retrieved from http://www.cdcr.ca.gov/Capital_Punishment/docs/Con-demnedInmateSummary.pdf?pdf=Condemned-Inmates

California Secretary of State. (2016). General election — Statement of vote, November 8, 2016. Retrieved from http://www.sos.ca.gov/elections/prior-elections/statewide-election-results/general-election-november-8-2016/statement-vote/

Civil Rights Litigation Clearinghouse. (2017, January 31). *Lopez v. Brown.* University of Michigan Law School. Retrieved from https://www.clearinghouse.net/detail.php?id=14816

Corwin, M. (1992, April 19). Death's door: State's only condemned woman awaits her fate. *Los Angeles Times.* Retrieved from http://articles.latimes.com/1992-04-19/news/mn-908_1_death-row

Culver, J. H., & Boyens, C. (2002). Political cycles of life and death: Capital punishment as public policy in California. *Albany Law Review, 65,* 991–1015.

Death Penalty Focus (DPF). (n.d.). *The history of California's death penalty.* Retrieved from http://www.deathpenalty.org/article.php?id=48

Death Penalty Focus (DPF). (n.d.). *SAFE California initiative spells swift justice.* Retrieved from at http://deathpenalty.org/blog/safe-california-initiative-spells-swift-justice/

Death Penalty Information Center (DPIC). (2017). Innocence cases. Retrieved from http://www.deathpenaltyinfo.org/node/4900#65

Doyle, J. (2006, January 12). Double life of a death row killer / Charismatic multiple murderer Clarence Ray Allen, 75, didn't turn really bad until his 40s. *SF Gate.* Retrieved from http://www.sfgate.com/news/article/Double-life-of-a-Death-Row-killer-Charismatic-2506688.php

Espy File. (n.d.). *Executions in the U.S. 1608-2002, Executions by state.* Retrieved from http://www.deathpenaltyinfo.org/documents/ESPYstate.pdf

Fagan, K. (2010, September 22). San Quentin gives glimpse of new injection space. *SF Gate.* Retrieved from http://www.sfgate.com/news/article/San-Quentin-gives-glimpse-of-new-injection-space-3173547.php

Finz, S. (2006, January 13). As execution draws near, families grieve for 3 killed at store in 1980. *SF Gate.* Retrieved from http://www.sfgate.com/news/article/As-execution-draws-near-families-grieve-for-3-2543499.php

Gogola, T. (2016, January 13). Inside San Quentin. *MetroActive.* Retrieved from http://www.metroactive.com/features/San-Quentin-Death-Row-Condemned-Men-Adjustment-Center.html

Gorman, S. (2015, March 30). Death row in California is just about booked up. *Business Insider.* Retrieved from http://www.businessinsider.com/r-californias-death-row-faces-no-vacancy-situation-2015-3

Halstead, R. (2015, May 24). Governor seeks $3.2 million for more death row cells at San Quentin. *Marin Independent Journal.* Retrieved from http://www.marinij.com/article/NO/20150524/NEWS/150529887

Haney, C., Sontag, L., & Costanzo, S. (1994). Deciding to take a life: Capital juries, sentencing instructions, and the jurisprudence of death. *Journal of Social Issues, 50*(2), 149–176.

Legislative Analyst's Office. (2016a). Proposition 62. Retrieved from http://www.lao.ca.gov/BallotAnalysis/Proposition?number=62&year=2016

Liebman, J. S., & Marshall, L. C. (2006). Less is better: Justice Stevens and the narrowed death penalty. *Fordham Law Review, 74*(4), 1607–1682.

Los Angeles Times. (2015, November 12). Next in line for execution. Retrieved from http://graphics.latimes.com/towergraphic-la-me-g-execution-proto-col-16-inmates/

Los Angeles Times. (2016, September 3). Editorial Props 62 and 66: California voters should end the death penalty, not speed it up. Retrieved from http://www.latimes.com/opinion/editorials/la-ed-prop-62-prop-66-20160826-snap-story.html

Magagnini, S. (1998, March 28). Closing death row would save state $90 million a year. *Sacramento Bee.* A1.

Mallicoat, S., Vogel, B., & Crawford, D. (2017). California's chaotic death penalty. In R. Bohm & G. Lee (Eds.), *Routledge Handbook on Capital Punishment.* New York, NY: Taylor & Francis.

Mintz, H. (2013, May 31). California's death penalty on hold again. *San Jose Mercury News.* Retrieved from http://www.mercurynews.com/ci_23355534/californias-death-penalty-hold-again

Muhammad, C. (2007, May 7). California's new secret death chamber. *The Final Call.* Retrieved from http://www.finalcall.com/artman/publish/National_News_2/California_s_new_secret_death_chamber_3463.shtml

Mullane, N. (2012a, October 22). The adjustment center: Where no one wants to go. Retrieved from http://kalw.org/post/adjustment-center-where-no-one-wants-go#stream/0

Mullane, N. (2012b, November 5). San Quentin's north segregation—The 'penthouse' of death row. Retrieved from http://kalw.org/post/san-quentins-north-segregation-penthouse-death-row#stream/0

Mullane, N. (2013, April 29). Walking death row at San Quentin State Prison. Retrieved from http://kalw.org/post/walking-death-row-san-quentin-state-prison#stream/0

Mullane, N. (2014, July 17). One reporter on California's death row. *Life of the Law.* Retrieved from http://www.lifeofthelaw.org/2014/07/reporter-on-death-row-2/

NAACP. (2011). *Death row USA.* Retrieved from http://naacpldf.org/files/publications/DRUSA_Winter_2011.pdf

National Registry of Exonerations. (2017). Retrieved from http://www. law.umich.edu/special/exoneration/Pages/about.aspx

Nichols, C. (2016, September 21). Did California spend $56 billion to execute 13 people? *Politifact California*. Retrieved from http://www.politifact.com/ california/statements/2016/sep/21/tom-steyer/did-california-spend-5-billion-execute-13-people/

Office of Administrative Law. (2016). Decision of disapproval of regulatory action. Retrieved from https://oal.blogs.ca.gov/files/2016/12/Decision-of_Disapproval_2016-1104-02S_CDCR.pdf

Payne, P. (2016, August 19). Inside San Quentin's death row with North Bay's condemned prisoners. *The Press Democrat*. Retrieved from http://www.press-democrat.com/news/5983392-181/inside-san-quentins-death-row?artslide=0

Schulter, M. (2011, November 3). Dear Governor Brown, We Are Turning the Tide! Retrieved from http://deathpenalty.org/blog/dear-governor-brown-turning-tide/

Schwarzenegger, A., & Tilton, J. E. (2007, May 15). *State of California lethal injection protocol review*. Retrieved from http://www.deathpenaltyinfo.org/ CALethInject.pdf

Segura, L. (2016, January 17). Ten years after last execution, California's death row continues to grow. *The Intercept*. Retrieved from https://theintercept.com/2016/01/17/ten-years-after-last-execution-cali-fornias-death-row-continues-to-grow/

Snell, T. (2011). *Capital punishment 2010—Statistical tables*. Washington, DC: U.S. Department of Justice, Office of Justice Programs, Bureau of Justice Statistics.

St. John, P. (2014, June 10). San Quentin plans psychiatric hospital for death row inmates. *Los Angeles Times*. Retrieved from http://www.latimes.com/ local/politics/la-me-pol-ff-san-quentin-20140611-story.html

St. John, P. (2015, March 30). California's death row, with no executions in sight, runs out of room. *Los Angeles Times*. Retrieved from http://www.latimes.com/local/crime/la-me-ff-death-row-20150330-story.html

St. John, P. (2016a, January 5). A revealing look at California's death row. *Los Angeles Times*. Retrieved from http://www.latimes.com/local/lanow/la-me-ln-death-row-html-20160104-htmlstory.html

St. John, P. (2016b, June 5). On California's death row, too insane to execute. *Los Angeles Times*. Retrieved from http://www.latimes.com/projects/la-me-ln-death-row/

Stryker, A. (2016, April 13). In California death row's "adjustment center," condemned men wait in solitary confinement. Retrieved from http://

solitarywatch.com/2016/04/13/in-californias-death-rows-adjustment-center-condemned-men-wait-in-solitary-confinement/

Wagstaff, E. (2014, July 16). Here are the 13 men executed by California since 1978. *Los Angeles Times.* Retrieved from http://graphics.latimes.com/tow-ergraphic-see-13-men-executed-california-1978/

Cases Cited

California v. Anderson, 493 P.2d 880 (1972)

Furman v. Georgia, 408 U.S. 238 (1972)

Glossip v. Gross, 136 S. Ct. 20, 576 U.S. ____ (2015)

Gregg v. Georgia, 428 U.S. 153 (1976)

Lopez v. Brown, 217 Cal. App. 4th 1114 (2015)

Morales v. Tilton, 465 F. Supp. 2d 972 (2006)

Ron Briggs and John Van de Kamp v. Jerry Brown, California Supreme Court, S238309, filed November 9, 2016

Chapter 9

The Juvenile Justice System in California

Christine L. Gardiner and Jill Rosenbaum

Learning Objectives

After reading the chapter, students should be able to:

- Explain the history of juvenile justice in California.
- Demonstrate an understanding of how the juvenile justice system in California is different than the adult system.
- Present an overview of juvenile crime in California.
- Describe juvenile court processing for delinquents and dependents of the court in California.
- Explain how a juvenile can be tried in adult court in California.
- Describe two innovative programs for juvenile offenders in California.

History of Juvenile Justice in California

As was the case throughout the United States, California's juvenile justice system used to be based on the principles of discipline and structure, rather than compassion and nurturance. Their days within the institution looked strikingly similar to adult offenders'. The child saving movement criticized the dreadful conditions inflicted on these youth and, as a result, new approaches to treating youthful offenders were developed, including early prototypes of probation and foster care.

The first reform school in California, the San Francisco Industrial School, opened in 1859 (CJCJ, 2011a). It was established by the California Legislature through the Industrial School Act and was a public/private partnership (Macallair, 2003). Though this institution was seen as progressive and state of the art when it opened, it was plagued, nearly from the beginning, with a great deal of scandal.

Allegations included confinement of youth in dark cells for long periods of time and insufficient nutrition, which led to near starvation. It became known as a "nursery of crime." As philanthropic groups, such as the San Francisco Boys and Girls Aid Society, became aware of the dreadful situation inside the institution, they began developing new approaches to deal with delinquent as well as abused and neglected youth. The many charges of abuse and the dissatisfaction with the notion of institutionalizing delinquent youth led to the closing of the Industrial School in 1892 and the passage of the first Probation Act in 1883 (CJCJ, 2011a). The passage of this act created a system in which counties could pay for youth to be placed in private, philanthropic agencies, rather than solely in institutions. The first state-run reform schools were opened shortly after in Whittier in 1891 and in Ione in 1892 (CDCR, n.d.).

In 1903, California was one of the first states to identify children and youth as a distinct group for which a separate system of law existed, thus allowing the juvenile court to intervene in the lives of children. According to Schlossman (2005), youthful offenders were no longer handled in the same manner as adults. Juvenile cases were now handled in a "nonjudgmental paternalistic manner" (CJCJ, 2011, p. 5). While originally those working with juveniles were either employed by nonprofit groups or volunteers, in 1909, the California Legislature passed legislation that made juvenile probation officers agents of the state. The jobs of these probation officers were to conduct background investigations, develop individual treatment plans, and implement judicial orders, including, but not limited to, supervising youth in the community. The California Legislature also required that all counties create and maintain separate detention facilities for youth rather than confine them in adult facilities. This proved to be a costly move, which ultimately led to many youth being confined by the state by what was to become the California Youth Authority.

The implementation of a separate system led to a host of new issues. Because it was believed that juveniles were no longer being dealt with as criminals and because the court proceedings were much more informal and decisions were being made in the "best interest of the child," due process was not considered necessary. Background investigations were conducted and information was given to judges whose decisions were rendered before the child, parents, and probation officer (who was seen as an advocate). No attorneys were needed (Schlossman, 2005), and there was a great deal of inconsistency both within and between counties as to how youth were being handled. Though most youth received some combination of detention and community-based treatment throughout most of the twentieth century, inconsistency in punishment persisted as probation departments attempted to develop treatment plans geared toward the individual, as was mandated by state law (Brozek, 1985).

During the 1940s, many counties developed ranches and camps located in rural areas to detain youth at the county level. Although it was widely believed that community-based services were preferable, judges continued to commit youth to the three state juvenile institutions: Fred G. Nelles, Preston School of Industry, and the Ventura School for Girls. Though mired with problems, these facilities were maintained as a last resort. It became clear, however, that services for youth were less than adequate, and there were calls for statewide reform. As a result, the Youth Corrections Authority Act was signed by Governor Culbert Olson in 1941 (Mihailoff, 2005). This act created a new agency that was charged with developing new assessment and diagnostic tools to be utilized by county probation departments. Within a year of its creation, the three state institutions were embroiled in controversy, which led Governor Earl Warren to alter the original mandate by ordering the new agency, the *California Youth Authority*, to centrally manage all state institutions (Mihailoff, 2005; Brozek, 1985). By doing so, it was believed that there would be an end to the abuse and controversy that had existed since the inception of the state institutions.

Over the years, numerous legislative amendments gave specific mandates to the California Youth Authority (CYA), including the creation of a three-member board responsible for overseeing the CYA and directing the placement and treatment of all youth committed to the agency by the courts. This board was further mandated to hire physicians, psychiatrists, psychologists, social workers, educators, and sociologists to develop clinical assessment tools, as well as create and implement treatment plans for the youth. Although the CYA was responsible for the development and coordination of delinquency and delinquency prevention programs, probation powers remained with the county courts.

With the hiring of this multidisciplinary group of professionals, the CYA developed national and international reputations for its innovative treatment of youth and progressive experimental research agenda. The CYA was the first agency in the country to establish reception centers to diagnose offenders and to develop individual treatment programs, community treatment, forestry camps, and a system designed to handle inmate grievances. These programs were replicated by correction agencies around the country and throughout the world. As the population of California grew following World War II, the CYA population increased significantly, which led to a deterioration of conditions. Although CYA pioneered many new rehabilitative techniques, youth committed to the CYA were subject to alienation, violence, and exploitation by other wards. Still, counties continued to commit large numbers of youth to these institutions since the state, rather than the county, bore the costs of incarceration. In an attempt to halt this practice, the *Probation Subsidy Act* was launched in 1965. This legislation was enacted during a period when it was believed that delinquents would be better served in the community. It was based on the assumption that probation departments would commit fewer youth to state institutions if there were financial incentives to keep them in the local community (Lerman, 1975).

From the 1950s through the 1970s, the Research Unit at the CYA had both a national and international reputation. Researchers such as Carl Jesness, Ted Palmer, and Marguerite Warren introduced and evaluated a variety of diagnostic and treatment approaches, including guided-group interaction, therapeutic communities, behavior modification, transactional analysis, and differential treatment. They also experimented with treating delinquents in the community as opposed to institutions. The Community Treatment Project (CTP), which was directed by Marguerite Warren, examined the effectiveness of intensive, individualized psychological treatment in the community compared to the effectiveness of treatment provided in the institutions. Although the CTP was not nearly as effective as had been hoped, it did provide evidence that serious juvenile delinquents could, in fact, be treated in the community without an increase in recidivism and at a much lower cost. The experimental research conducted by the CYA showed some promising results, despite falling short of expectations. The positive achievements that were garnered, however, were quickly lost in the disillusionment of the "nothing works" attitude that prevailed from the mid-1970s.

By the 1980s, the reform efforts made by the state's progressive juvenile justice system no longer existed and were replaced by much harsher practices and a greater emphasis on security. With few exceptions, i.e., forestry camps, Free Venture (an employment experience from the private sector inside the institution), and LEAD (an intensive boot camp program), the emphasis on training and treatment within the CYA no longer existed. Without the financial incentives of the Probation Subsidy, the population of CYA's eleven institutions grew to nearly 10,000, even though design capacity was less than 6,800. To deal with the extreme overcrowding within CYA institutions, Governor Pete Wilson's administration and the state legislature enacted legislation (*SB 681*) that mandated financial penalties to counties that committed non-serious delinquent offenders to the CYA. As a result of this legislation, the CYA population began to decline. During this period (the late 1990s), an investigation by the Office of Inspector General (OIG) found that the CYA was not only severely mismanaged, but that it had become a punitive, prison-like environment that provided ineffective treatment.

These reports surfaced in 2003 when a class-action lawsuit contending that CYA failed to deliver state-mandated rehabilitation was brought against the state. It was a "system that [was] broken almost everywhere you look" (Ajmani, 2016, p. 1). Governor Schwarzenegger admitted to the failures of the system and agreed to fix the problem. Doing so, though, required "eliminating the nineteenth century training school system and replacing it with a modern system designed to be rehabilitative (CDCR, Division of Juvenile Justice, 2006)" (CJCJ, 2011, p. 9). This lawsuit, *Farrell v. Cate* (2003), led to a huge decline in the CYA population, and ultimately, the abolition of the 62-year-old CYA in 2005. All CYA functions and responsibilities were merged with the adult prison system, which became the California Department of Corrections and Rehabilitation (CDCR). The responsibilities formerly associated with CYA are now handled by the *Division of Juvenile Justice (DJJ)*, a department within CDCR. As a result of the *Farrell* case many reforms have taken place in California. For example, poorly designed and outdated facilities have been closed or are being redesigned to create small therapeutic living units. With rehabilitation in mind, the state passed *SB 81* (Juvenile Justice Realignment), which severely restricts the number of low-level offenders being committed to DJJ, increased the maximum age juveniles may be retained in local facilities, and, using the cost savings, provides monetary incentives to counties to develop additional probation services. In recognition of these efforts, an Alameda County judge found that the state had complied with "most, but not all, of the minimum requirements to reform conditions of confinement at DJJ" and officially terminated the *Farrell* lawsuit (after almost 15 years) on February 25, 2016 (Ajmani, 2016, p. 2). This was a big step for the state despite numerous monitoring reports that suggested best practices (such as cognitive behavioral therapy and motivational interviewing) are still not happening on a large scale.

How the Juvenile Justice System in California Differs from the Criminal Justice System

There are two separate and distinct justice systems in California—the criminal justice system (a.k.a. the adult system) and the juvenile justice system. Although the systems are alike in many respects, there are some key differences between the adult and juvenile justice systems. One obvious difference is that, in California, the juvenile justice system only has jurisdiction over minors (persons less than 18 at the time they committed the crime).[1, 2] Depending on a juvenile's age and

---

1. Note that individuals convicted of a serious crime as a juvenile may remain in a juvenile correctional facility up to the age of 23 (or 25, depending on when he/she was sentenced) in California.

2. The age of jurisdiction varies by state (some states automatically process juveniles as young as 15 in adult court).

alleged crime, juveniles may be processed through the juvenile court or the adult court. However, no one may be processed in the juvenile justice system for a crime they are alleged to have committed as an adult.

A second major difference between the two systems is that, in addition to delinquents, the juvenile justice system also has jurisdiction over some non-delinquents, including status offenders and children who have been abused or neglected. In practice, the juvenile justice system, which is governed by California's Welfare and Institutions Code (WIC), has jurisdiction over three categories of individuals: status offenders, delinquents, and dependents of the court. *Dependents of the court* are defined by WIC 300 as children who have been, or at risk of becoming, abused and/or neglected. *Status offenders* are defined in WIC 601(a) as, essentially, juveniles who commit an act that is deemed criminal due to their age (the five most common status offenses are: running away, truancy, incorrigibility, curfew violations, and alcohol/tobacco violations). *Delinquents*, as defined in WIC 602(a), are minors accused of violating any criminal law. In addition to the different categories of offenders that are handled by the juvenile court, the structure of the court differs from the adult criminal court system. Divisions 2 and 2.5 of the Welfare and Institutions Code define jurisdictional boundaries and set rules for juvenile justice procedures, programs, personnel, and facilities.

A third major difference is that the juvenile justice system operates under the premise of doing what is in "the child's best interest." Every decision pertaining to a juvenile, at every stage, is to be weighed and judged according to this standard, regardless of whether the juvenile is a delinquent, a status offender, or a dependent of the court. Second to the best interest of the child, but weighed heavily, is the best interest of the public. For example, WIC 202 (b) states that it is the goal of the juvenile court to provide delinquents, "in conformity with the interests of public safety and protection, [with the] care, treatment, and guidance that is consistent with their best interest, that holds them accountable for their behavior, and that is appropriate for their circum-stances." The adult system is significantly less interested in the defendant's "best interest," and much more interested in punishing the wrongdoer.

The last major difference between the two systems is that the juvenile justice system uses distinctive terminology (see Table 9.1 below). For example, an adult is "arrested" whereas a juvenile is "taken into custody." The terms are intended to provide structure for the unique populations served by the juvenile justice system (delinquents, status offenders, and dependents). As will be further explained, the differences in terminology are not trivial and, in fact, have important implications for juveniles adjudicated in the juvenile justice system.

Table 9.1. Juvenile Court Terms and Equivalent Adult Court Terms

Juvenile Court Term	Adult Court Term
Adjudicated	Convicted
Adjudication	Verdict
Adjudicatory Hearing (or Jurisdictional Hearing)	Trial
Adjustment	Plea Bargain
Aftercare	Parole
Agree to a finding	Plead guilty
Delinquent	Criminal
Delinquent Act	Crime
Deny petition	Plead not guilty
Detention Facility	Jail
Detention Hearing	Bail Hearing
Disposition	Sentence
Dispositional Hearing	Sentencing
Finding of fact (or True Finding)	Found to be guilty
Initial Appearance (or Pretrial Hearing or Preliminary Hearing)	Arraignment & Preliminary Hearing
Petition	File charges or indictment
Preventative Detention	In jail awaiting trial
Substitution	Reduction of charges
Take into custody	Arrest
Youth correctional facility	Prison

Figure 9.1. Annual Juvenile Arrests in California, 2002–2015

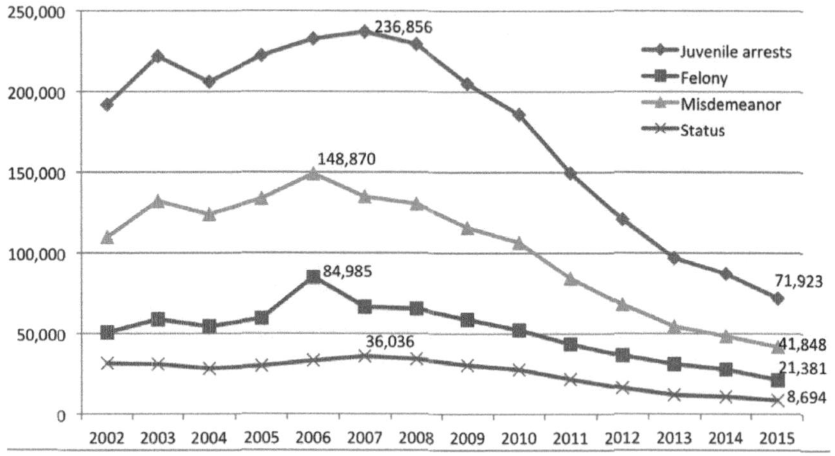

Source: California Department of Justice. (2016).

Juvenile Crime in California

Although it is difficult to know exactly how much crime in California is committed by juveniles, we do know that there were 71,923 juveniles taken into custody (arrested) by police officers in California in 2015 (California Department of Justice, 2016). This is less than half the number of juveniles arrested in 2011 (149,563) and is the lowest total arrest rate ever recorded in California (1,772 arrests for all types of crime and delinquency per 100,000 10–17-year-olds). Since 2007, the annual number of juvenile arrests has declined by 69.6%, which is almost 165,000 fewer juveniles taken into custody than eight years prior! Look at Figure 9.1 and you will notice that the number of arrests in any given category one-fourth to one-third the number of arrests in 2006–2007. Why the large drop? One big reason was likely SB 1449—the 2010 law which reduced marijuana possession from a misdemeanor to an infraction; another reason was likely Proposition 47, which reduced some felonies to misdemeanors in 2014 (Males, 2016a and 2012). Given the long downward trend of arrest rates, socioeconomic and other explanations are also probably contributing factors (Males, 2016a and 2012).

Most of the juveniles taken into custody were male (71.9%) (California Department of Justice, 2016). Three-quarters of juveniles taken into custody were between the ages of 15 and 17, one-quarter were between the ages of 12 and 14, and approximately 1% were under the age of 12. Most (58.2%) of the arrests were for misdemeanor crimes, while 29.7% were for felonies and 12.1% were for status offenses. Arrests for violent offenses accounted for 34.3% of all juvenile arrests, property offenses accounted for 31.3%, drug offenses for 7.2%, and all other offenses accounted for 27.2% of all arrests (California Department of Justice, 2016).

What happened to all these juveniles? As seen in Figure 9.2 below, about 80% of all juveniles taken into custody were referred to county probation departments for case review (California Department of Justice, 2016). Of these, just over one-half (51.0%) were petitioned in juvenile court (a little less than one-fourth of whom were detained, usually in juvenile hall). Still, 36.8% had their case dismissed (no petition was filed). Of the 44,107 juveniles petitioned in juvenile court, 64.5% were adjudicated delinquent and made a ward of the court whereas 16.7% had their petition dismissed. The vast majority of juveniles adjudicated in juvenile court received a disposition of probation (41% were sent home on supervision, 24.9% were placed in a county facility, and another 14.5% were given informal or non-ward probation).

Although we don't know exactly how many crimes were committed by juveniles, as opposed to adults, it is known that crime is disproportionately committed by young people (adolescents and young adults). Research reveals that, nationwide, more than 90% of juveniles admit to committing some minor delinquency (Agnew & Breznia, 2012; Regoli, Hewitt, & DeLisi, 2011). It also reveals that the vast majority of people desist by their early to mid-20s (on their own, without any criminal justice intervention).

Still, a small percent of individuals (often referred to as chronic, serious, or life-course persistent offenders) commit a large proportion of crimes for an extended period of time. These individuals tend to have similar traits or life circumstances in common. These traits, which increase the risk of a person committing delinquent/criminal acts, are known as *risk factors* and are often clustered in people and places. While there is not a single "key" risk factor that means someone is going to be a criminal, the accumulation of risk factors increases the *likelihood* of a person engaging in criminal behavior.

Risk factors are often classified into four categories: biological and psychological, family, social (schools and peers), and environmental (the community in which one resides). For example, evidence on the first category indicates that many antisocial individuals are *chronically under-aroused* (as diagnosed by minimal sweating, slow EEG, and low resting heart rate), have *low intelligence* (measured by verbal IQ), *lack empathy* (the ability to understand and relate to another person's thoughts/feelings), and are considered *irritable* (having a heightened sensitivity to stressors, a tendency to overreact and blame others for personal misfortune, and exhibiting overtly antagonistic behavior).

Figure 9.2. Outcomes of Juvenile Arrests in California, 2015[1]

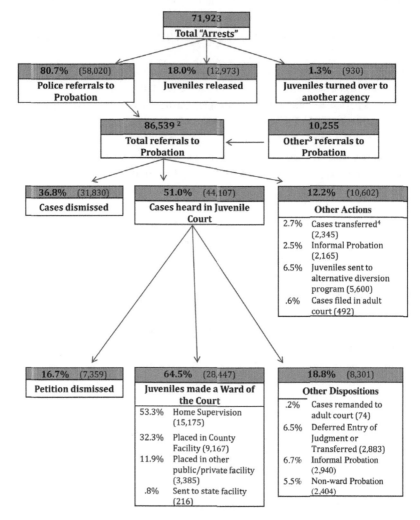

[1] Adapted from http://www.lao.gov/2007/cj_primer_013107.aspx; current data from California Department of Justice (2016).

[2] Different reporting procedures result in the number of referrals to probation by law enforcement being greater than reported in the box above.

[3] Other referral sources include: schools, other public and private agencies, guardians, and transfers from other counties.

[4] Includes traffic court and deported.

Additionally, strong evidence indicates that *impaired communication between the frontal lobes of the brain* (which regulate self-control) *and the temporal lobes of the brain* (which regulate emotions) can result in higher risk-seeking behavior and criminality (Moffitt, Ross, & Raine, 2011); which is consistent with and helps explain the higher offending levels found in youth around the world and the typical decline in offending during early adulthood (once the brain is fully developed).

Family factors are also very important, as research indicates that a small percentage of families account for a large proportion of offenders (Farrington, Barnes, & Lambert, 1996; Loeber & Stouthamer-Loeber, 1986). The strongest family risk factor for delinquency is having *antisocial parents* (for example, drug users, alcoholics, and individuals engaged in other antisocial or criminal behavior), followed by *large family size* (4+ siblings), *poor child-rearing methods*, and *high-conflict homes*. Specifically, parents who do not properly supervise their children, do not have a warm relationship with their children, use harsh and/or erratic discipline, and/or are not involved in their children's lives are more likely to raise delinquent children. The most important aspect of childrearing from a delinquency prevention viewpoint is parental supervision, as it is the risk factor that most strongly and consistently predicts future offending. The quality of home life is also very important. Although "broken homes" are often blamed for delinquency, the truth is that the amount of conflict within the family unit is much more important than the number of "parents" who reside in the house (Farrington & Welsh, 2007; McCord, 1982).

The main social risk factor for delinquency is having *delinquent friends*. Unlike adults who offend alone, juveniles tend to co-offend in small groups (usually 2–3 youth). In particular, youth who are gang members commit a lot more crimes and more serious crimes than do juveniles who are not in a gang. It is common for juveniles to increase their offending while they are active in a gang (and decrease their offending after they leave the gang). Only a small percent of youth join gangs (between 6% and 30%) but those that do commit a disproportionate amount of crime, especially violent crimes (Maxson, 2011). Schools are also correlated with delinquency. For example, the *rate of delinquents who attend a school* increases the likelihood of others engaging in crime. Other school risk factors include *dropping out of school, habitual tardiness, school misbehavior, low attachment to school, poor relations with teachers, little school involvement*, and *having low educational/occupational goals* (Agnew & Breznia, 2012).

The most potent environmental risk factor is *concentrated disadvantage* (which is a term used to describe ethnic minority communities that have high rates of poverty, unemployment, and family disruption). For example, evidence indicates that neighborhoods of concentrated disadvantage can "activate" risk factors that may have remained dormant if the child had lived in a middle-class neighborhood (possibly due to the increased presence of delinquent peers and/or opportunities for crime in disadvantaged communities) (Wikström & Loeber, 2000). As will be elaborated on later in this chapter, successful programs and policies take into account these risk factors and other facts we know about crime and criminality.

Juvenile Justice System Structure and Capacity

Just as in the adult system, the juvenile justice system exists at three levels: law enforcement, courts, and corrections. It exists both side-by-side and within the adult system. This means that in California we have separate courts and corrections systems for juveniles and adults, but only one law enforcement system. For the most part, justice in California is a function of local government. Each of California's 58 counties maintains both criminal and juvenile justice systems, and while counties differ on philosophy and available programs, the structure of the systems is very similar in each county. A flowchart of the juvenile justice system resembles closely the flowchart of the criminal justice system. Juveniles, however, have more opportunities to be diverted from formal prosecution as well as more hearings to determine fitness and jurisdictional issues to ensure the greatest chance of rehabilitation. Figure 9.3 (below) depicts juvenile justice case processing in California.

Police

With few exceptions, police officers deal with adults and juveniles in essentially the same manner. Juveniles have the same due process rights as adults (except for the rights to bail and jury trial) with few, if any, extra protections. For example, California law requires police officers to notify parents if a juvenile is taken into custody, but prior to October 11, 2017 California law did not require that juveniles consult with an attorney before waiving their *Miranda* rights (SB 395). Furthermore, police do not need to inform parents where or why their child is being held, nor do they need to allow parents' access to their child before or during questioning. On another point, the rules of search and seizure on school grounds differ from standard rules of search and seizure in that school officials and officers assigned to a K–12 school campus have a lower threshold to meet in order to be able to conduct a search. Specifically, officers and school officials only need reasonable suspicion, not probable cause, to search a student's person, backpack, locker, and/or vehicle (*New Jersey v. T.L.O.*, 1985).

Figure 9.3. Juvenile Delinquency Flowchart

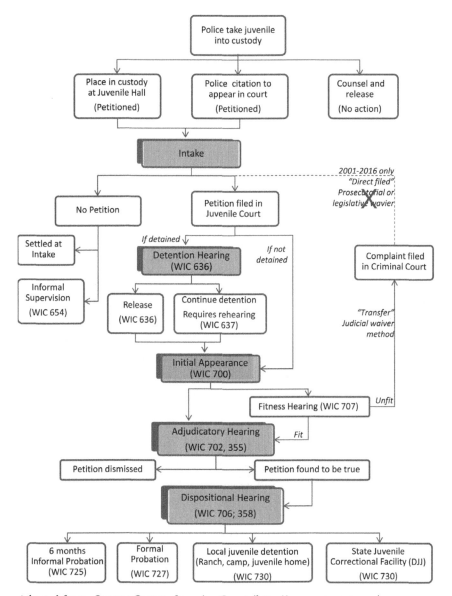

Adapted from: Orange County Superior Court (http://www.occourts.org)

Another distinction is that, whereas an officer must witness an adult committing a misdemeanor in order to arrest him/her, an officer can take a juvenile into custody for committing a misdemeanor without personally witnessing the act. In fact, a police officer can "arrest" a juvenile for a misdemeanor or felony without a warrant as long as the officer reasonably believes that the juvenile committed the crime. Additionally, a law enforcement agency can pursue consequences for a juvenile, even if she/he is *not charged* with a crime (this option does not exist for adults). This can include informal probation or other diversion programs (such as Teen Court), and means that a juvenile may be ordered to attend educational classes or perform community service by a law enforcement agency without ever being petitioned in court.[3] This option, usually available to first-time offenders caught committing a minor offense, is one method used by justice officials to admonish the offender and deter future criminal behavior while keeping the child out of the court. It is in keeping with WIC 626, which stipulates that, when taking a juvenile into temporary custody, officers "shall prefer the alternative which least restricts the minor's freedom of movement, provided that alternative is compatible with the best interests of the minor and the community."

Some, though not all, law enforcement agencies have specific units assigned to juveniles and juvenile crimes. Large agencies are most likely to have one or more specific units dedicated to juveniles. The most common units are School Resource Officers (or DARE Officers) and detectives assigned to investigate crimes committed by or against juveniles (for example, child abuse).

In 2015, law enforcement officers counseled and released 18.0% of the 71,923 juveniles they took into custody—meaning juveniles were admonished and released to a parent or guardian with no further action taken against them (California Department of Justice, 2016). Juveniles under the age of 12 were the most likely to be counseled and released (25.2% compared to 19.6% of 12–14-year-olds and 17.4% of 15–17-year-olds) and females were more likely than males to be counseled and released (22.3% vs. 16.4%). Blacks were least likely to be counseled and released (16.0% vs. 17.9% of Hispanics, 19.3% of whites, and 21.1% of offenders of other races). Most of the other juveniles (80.7%) were referred to the probation department for case review (California Department of Justice, 2016).

---

3. Juveniles taken into custody for a status offense need parental permission to participate in diversion programs.

Juvenile Court Processing: Juvenile Delinquents and Status Offenders

Once an officer takes a juvenile into custody, he/she may choose to *petition* (file charges against) the juvenile (Figure 9.3: Stage 1). At this point a probation officer reviews the case to determine whether to request that the district attorney file a petition in juvenile court, adult court, or not at all (Figure 9.3: Stage 2). If the probation officer determines that the case should be heard in court, he/she will request that the district attorney file the petition. The district attorney will then review the case and make a final decision about whether and where to file the petition. If the probation officer decides to not request that a formal petition be filed, he/she will either (1) place the juvenile on *informal probation* (WIC 654) for a period of up to six months and stipulate conditions the juvenile must meet (attending classes, community service, etc.), or (2) drop the charges completely, with no further action required. This process is known as *intake*. According to research, the factors that most impact intake decision-making are: seriousness of alleged offense, prior record, and offender demeanor (Whitehead & Lab, 2009).

If a petition is filed in juvenile court, the juvenile is subject to the rules and procedures that govern the operation of juvenile court. If a juvenile is detained in juvenile hall, the first court hearing that will take place is a *detention hearing* to determine whether the juvenile represents a threat to him/herself, to public safety, or is a flight risk (WIC 636) (Figure 9.3: Stage 3). If any of the above conditions exist, the juvenile may be remanded to custody to await further hearings and case disposition. This is known as *preventative detention* and is equivalent to being denied bail for adults (remember, juveniles do not have a right to bail). If the above conditions do not exist, the juvenile will be released to his/her parent/guardian either (1) with no conditions on his/her movement (per WIC 635) or (2) on home supervision with conditions (WIC 636). In 2015, 27.7% of juveniles were detained prior to adjudication (some on home confinement) (California Department of Justice, 2016).

The next hearing (or first hearing for non-detained juveniles) is the *initial appearance* (a.k.a. preliminary hearing or pretrial hearing) to read the petition, advise the youth of his/her rights, assign counsel (if necessary), and determine if there is enough evidence to establish the petition (Figure 9.3: Stage 4). This hearing, by law, must occur within 72 hours of petition filing (48 hours if the juvenile is detained). At this point, the judge has the option to offer youths who meet specific criteria a variety of resolutions, including informal handling and diversion pursuant to WIC 654, WIC 725, or deferred entry of judgment. After the initial appearance, there may be a *fitness hearing* (WIC 707) to

Table 9.2. Juveniles in California's Juvenile Justice System—
A Guide to JJS Shorthand

Term	Definition
300s	Juveniles who are dependents of the court
601s	Juveniles who have committed a status offense
602s	Juveniles who have committed a crime
654s	Juveniles on informal probation
707Bs	Juveniles remanded to criminal court for committing a specified felony and deemed unfit for juvenile court.

determine whether the juvenile is fit for juvenile court processing (Figure 9.3: Stage 5). The decision is based on several criteria, including age, offense seriousness, criminal sophistication, potential for rehabilitation, previous delinquent history, and success of previous attempts to rehabilitate. Juveniles deemed "not fit" are transferred to adult court for case processing (see the section on waivers in this chapter for more information).

Only some defendants have a fitness hearing, most proceed directly to the next hearing, which is the *adjudicatory hearing* (a.k.a. *jurisdictional hearing* in some counties) (Figure 9.3: Stage 6). This is equivalent to a trial in adult court. At this stage, the defendant either admits the petition (pleads guilty) or denies the petition (pleads not guilty) and both sides (prosecution and defense) present evidence to prove their case. There are no jury trials in juvenile court in California (some states do allow them). If the prosecutor fails to prove its case beyond a reasonable doubt, the judge will "find the petition to be untrue" and will dismiss the petition. If the prosecution proves its case, the judge will "find the petition to be true" and a dispositional hearing will be scheduled. Just as in adult court, the burden of proof required is "beyond a reasonable doubt." Juvenile court hearings in California are typically closed to the public, with some exceptions for unusual cases and court observers.

A *dispositional hearing* (WIC 706) is equivalent to "sentencing" in adult court (Figure 9.3: Stage 7). The judge has several options available to him/her, depending on the adjudicated offense. After adjudication but prior to disposition, the probation department prepares a *predisposition report* on the minor for the judge that recommends a disposition based on all factors known about the juvenile. After taking into account the predisposition report as well as any victim impact statements or other pertinent factors, the judge may sentence an adjudicated minor to a diversion program, six months of informal probation (WIC 725), formal probation (WIC 727), local juvenile detention (WIC 730— ranch, camp, juvenile home, forestry camp), or the Division of Juvenile Justice (WIC 730) for varying lengths of time. The judge may *not* sentence a juvenile to the death penalty (*Roper v. Simmons*, 2005); nor may she/he sentence a juvenile to "life without parole" for a crime other than first-degree murder (*Graham v. Florida*, 2010).

Juvenile Court Processing: Dependents of the Court

When it is discovered that a child has been (or may likely become) the victim of abuse or neglect by a parent or guardian, the state may need to step in to protect the child from further harm. These children, in addition to children who are left without any provision for support, are deemed "dependents of the court" by WIC 300. Some children are considered to be temporary dependents, and are only "wards of the court" during the time that family members do what is necessary to provide a stable and supportive home environment. On some occasions, however, parents lose (or forfeit) their parental rights to the state, and their children become permanent wards of the court. In this case, the juvenile court exists to protect the child and to find and maintain appropriate housing and support for the child until he/she turns 18, including adoption, when appropriate. The goal of the court is "family preservation and strengthening" (WIC 350).

The stages of the court process for dependency are essentially the same as for delinquency, with some additional reviews to accomplish family reunification, whenever possible. The difference is that the youth is the victim, not the perpetrator. It starts when a petition is filed, alleging abuse or neglect (Figure 9.3: Stage 2). There is no detention hearing, but there is an initial appearance to determine the legitimacy of the case and assign a trained *guardian ad litem* (a.k.a. *court-appointed special advocate*) to advocate on behalf of the child[4] (WIC 353 and 365.5) (Figure 9.3: Stage 4). Evidence is heard during the jurisdictional hearing (WIC 355), and the judge's decision regarding placement is made during the dispositional hearing (WIC 358) (Figure 9.3: Stage 5). Court hearings involving dependent youths are explicitly closed to members of the public (there are some specific exceptions to the rule, including judge discretion) (WIC 345-346) (Figure 9.3: Stage 6).

---

4. In special situations when there is a disagreement between the parties (i.e., parents, prosecutor, defense) the court may also appoint *guardian ad litems* in delinquency cases.

Trying Juveniles in Adult Court: Waivers and Transfers

In California, the upper age limit of juvenile court jurisdiction is 23.[5] This means that youths disposed in juvenile court must be released from incarceration (from a juvenile or adult facility) on their 23rd birthday (at the latest). For this reason, and because some juveniles are seen as not appropriate for juvenile court (due to the heinousness of their crimes and/or their past criminal history), juveniles can be waived to adult court for processing.[6] The minimum transfer age in California is 14; meaning children under the age of 14 cannot be waived to criminal court. Currently, there is only one method by which California juveniles can be waived to adult court: judicial waiver. Between 2001 and 2017, prosecutorial waiver and legislative waiver were also options and will be discussed below.

Under *judicial waiver*(a.k.a. *transfer*), the case is filed in juvenile court, and the judge decides whether or not to transfer it to adult (criminal) court. The purpose of the fitness hearing (Figure 9.3: Stage 5) is to determine whether the youth meets criteria to be adjudicated in juvenile court. As previously mentioned, there are five criteria: gravity of the offense, criminal sophistication, potential for rehabilitation, previous delinquent history, and success of previous attempts to rehabilitate. The judge can take into account any relevant factors in deciding a youth's fitness for juvenile court, including his/her maturity, intellectual capacity, and mental and emotional development, the impact of the youth's family and community environment as well as childhood trauma on offending, and the youth's potential for growth and development. The only juveniles who may be waived to criminal court are (1) those aged 14 and older who committed a 707(b) act or (2) juveniles aged 16 and older who committed a felony. As of 2017, the only time a juvenile can bypass this fitness hearing and be direct filed in criminal court is if the youth was previously deemed "unfit" for juvenile court processing, is at least 16 years old, and meets a few other criteria. Juveniles transferred to adult court are subject to the rules of adult court and sentenced to adult facilities.[7]

In 2015, there were 136 fitness hearings in California. Of these, 60 juveniles (44.1%) were found fit for juvenile court and 76 juveniles (55.9%) were found unfit and transferred to adult court (California Department of Justice, 2016).

---

5. Prior to July 1, 2012, the upper age limit was 25. This was changed to 23 when Governor Brown signed the 2012–2013 budget into law (Heller de Leon, 2012).

6. Juveniles accused of status offenses (WIC 601) may not be waived to adult court.

7. In practice, juveniles are housed in separate youth facilities run by the California Department of Corrections and Rehabilitation, Division of Juvenile Justice until they are at least 18 years old.

Only four females had a fitness hearing in 2015, and all were found fit. Of the 132 males who had a fitness hearing, 42% were found fit. As in past years, the likelihood a juvenile would be found "fit" typically declined with age (66.7% of 14-year-olds were deemed "fit" compared to 75% of 15-year-olds, 40.7% of 16-year-olds, and 38.0% of 17-year-olds).[8] The likelihood a juvenile would be found "fit" also depended on race, with "other race" and "black" juveniles being the most likely to be found "fit" (50.0% and 62.2% respectively compared to 35.2% of Hispanic and 28.6% of white juveniles) (California Department of Justice, 2016). Note, this pattern differs from previous years (this year black youth were more likely to be found fit than white youth). Also important to note is the racial distribution of fitness hearings—most offenders who had a fitness hearing identified as Hispanic (71), followed by black/African American (45), white (14), and "other" (6).

An analysis of California Department of Justice data reveals that 2015 had the smallest number of fitness hearings in California in at least two decades. Judicial waiver, once the only method of transfer to adult court, was the least utilized option in California from at least 1997 to 2016. Ironically, Proposition 57 (placed on the ballot by Governor Brown and approved by voters in November 2016) removed the direct file options, thus judicial waiver is once again the only method of waiving a juvenile to adult court in California.

Legislative waiver (a.k.a. *statutory exclusion*), previously available in California and currently available in other states, became popular in the 1990s and mandates that some cases be tried in criminal court. Prior to the passage of Proposition 57 in 2016, California laws excluded certain crimes from juvenile court jurisdiction, meaning that if a juvenile of a specified age was charged with committing one of these crimes, the case would automatically be filed in criminal court and the individual would be tried as an adult. Judges did not exercise discretion in these cases—the matter was decided by statute. For example, between 2001 and 2017, California law stipulated that juveniles aged 14 and older who committed a crime listed in WIC 707 (b) (murder and various sex crimes) were to be tried in criminal court.

Finally, *prosecutorial waivers* (a.k.a. *concurrent jurisdiction*), used to apply to those cases that could be tried in either juvenile court or adult court. California law gives both juvenile court and adult court jurisdiction over some crimes. Between July 2001 and November 2016, the law gave prosecutors the privilege of deciding where to file these cases—juvenile court or adult court. However,

---

8. These percentages should be viewed cautiously, as the cell sizes are small. For example, only four 14-year-olds and eight 15-year-olds had a fitness hearing.

Proposition 57 eliminated this "direct file" option for prosecutors and now requires these cases go through a fitness hearing with a juvenile court judge prior to being heard in criminal court.

California has two fail-safe mechanisms in place to protect juveniles from unnecessary criminal court processing/penalties (National Center for Juvenile Justice, 2008). First, California allows for *reverse waivers* from adult court to juvenile court (not all states allow this). These laws allow juveniles to be returned to juvenile court for processing if a criminal court judge determines the youth/case is not appropriate for adult court. Second, California allows *criminal blended sentences* to be given to juveniles tried in criminal court. Juveniles given a blended sentence are given both a juvenile disposition and an adult sentence (usually stayed/put on hold). The purpose of this is to mitigate the effects of the transfer to adult court and/or provide incentive for the juvenile to behave and successfully complete the imposed juvenile disposition. Notably, California also has a unique *"once an adult, always an adult"* policy that allows some juveniles to return to juvenile court in future filings. California's law is different from most states in that it stipulates that once a juvenile, aged 16 or older, has been found unfit for juvenile court or has been tried (not convicted) in adult court, subsequent offenses involving waivable crimes may be directly filed in criminal court (WIC 707.01). Importantly, juveniles tried and convicted as adults are deemed to have been "convicted of a crime" rather than "adjudicated delinquent" and therefore the conviction cannot be hidden from future employers or expunged due to age.

In 2015, there were 566 juveniles tried as adults—74 (13.1%) arrived in criminal court through a judicial waiver and the rest, 492 (86.9%), were *direct filed* through prosecutorial waiver or a statutory exclusion (California Department of Justice, 2016). Half (50.8%) of the juveniles directly filed into adult court were 17 years old; another 26.8% were 16 years old. The vast majority (95.3%) was male (California Department of Justice, 2016). Of the 416 juveniles who received adult dispositions in 2015, 366 (88.0%) were convicted, 46 (11.1%) had their cases dismissed, one was returned to juvenile court, two were acquitted (found not guilty), and one was "diversion dismissed" (California Department of Justice, 2016). Interestingly and contrary to popular belief, Males (2008) found that youths tried as adults in California typically receive shorter sentences than their counterparts tried in juvenile court.

Court Process Varies by County

As outlined above, all counties in California follow the same state laws pertaining to processing juveniles for alleged offenses. There is, however, much discretion built into our laws that allow local culture to influence procedures and routine decisions. For example, the rate of direct files (via prosecutorial waivers) in adult court per 1,000 qualifying juvenile felony arrests ranged from a low of 1.5 in San Francisco County to a high of 122.1 in Ventura County for the period 2003–2009; the statewide average was 25.4 (Teji & Males, 2011). This means that juveniles in Ventura, and other high-rate direct file counties (such as Yolo, Madera, Kings, and Napa) had a much greater likelihood of being tried and sentenced in adult court than juveniles in San Francisco and other low-rate direct file counties (such as Alameda, Los Angeles, Fresno, and Santa Clara) (Teji & Males, 2011). This is important because the consequences of an adult conviction are much greater than a juvenile adjudication. These same counties have (or in some cases, had) a history of committing a high rate of juveniles to the Department of Juvenile Justice, rather than local correctional facilities. Males (2016b) also found that direct file rates are correlated with the political affiliation of the county's district attorney. Specifically, he found that counties with a Republican district attorney direct filed a higher percentage of juvenile violent felony arrestees than did those with a Democrat district attorney (6.4% vs 2.6%) (Males, 2016b). This large proportion of direct files and the dramatic inter-county variability are part of the reason that Proposition 57 was written to return discretion to judges.

Corrections

At present, there are two levels of corrections in California—local (county) and state. The vast majority of juveniles in California serve their disposition locally, with a county probation department. A few, however, are sentenced to a state facility under the direction of the California Department of Corrections and Rehabilitation, Division of Juvenile Justice (DJJ). This section will explain both systems.

County Corrections

There are 58 county probation departments in California (one in each county) that serve both adults and juveniles.[9] Although probation departments are most commonly associated with their community supervision function, every probation department in California is also required by law to perform three other functions: (1) investigate all matters before the court for sentencing

---

9. Probation services and organization varies by state. For more information about probation functions pertaining to adults in California, see Chapter 7 in this book.

(adults and juveniles), (2) run a juvenile facility, and (3) have a case management strategy for foster care children.

Juveniles assigned to probation serve their disposition in the community. Like adults, youth on probation must adhere to a set of conditions (rules) such as: attend school, follow all laws, meet with probation officer as required, do not associate with specific people (gang members, co-defendants, other delinquents), and obey parents. In addition to meeting with their probation officer regularly and adhering to a set of specified conditions, many youth on probation are ordered to perform community service and/or pay restitution to victims as part of their probation. Informal probation lasts no longer than six months (WIC 654.2, WIC 725), while formal probation often lasts for up to three years (WIC 727). In some cases, youth may be required to wear a GPS monitor and/or remain in a small geographic area during specified hours (such as those on house arrest). Also, some juveniles are placed in a county facility for a period of time as part of their disposition.

In addition to supervising offenders in the community, county probation departments operate several types of juvenile detention facilities. All departments operate a juvenile hall but many also operate ranches, camps, or other specialized facilities. These facilities separate juveniles by age, risk profile, and stage of court processing (pre-adjudication/post-adjudication); and are intended to treat juveniles, rather than punish them. Juvenile hall houses pre-adjudication youth as well as some post-adjudication youth while ranches and camps serve only post-adjudication populations. Youths serving time in detention facilities usually have chores they must do as well as programs they must attend, including school as well as group and/or individual counseling. As a result of the passage of SB 81 in 2007, county probation departments now have the authority to retain youth in county facilities and provide services to youth up to age 21.

Approximately 36,000 California juveniles adjudicated in 2015 were supervised by county probation departments (California Department of Justice, 2016). More than 7,500 were on informal or non-ward probation (WIC 654, WIC 725) and almost 29,000 were on formal probation (WIC 727). Of the 28,447 juveniles on formal probation, 9,167 (32.2%) spent time in a county juvenile facility as part of their disposition (WIC 730). In contrast, only 216 youth sentenced in juvenile court were committed to a state facility in 2015 (California Department of Justice, 2016).

State Corrections

The Division of Juvenile Justice (DJJ), a division of the California Department of Corrections and Rehabilitation (CDCR), is responsible for treating, educating, and housing the state's most serious juvenile offenders. DJJ serves three populations of juveniles: (1) youths committed by a juvenile court, (2) youths committed to DJJ by a criminal court, and (3) youths committed to adult programs but ordered to be housed at a DJJ facility (California Department of Corrections and Rehabilitation DJJ, n.d.). Youths sent to a state facility must be at least 12 years old. Youths sentenced as juveniles can remain at a DJJ facility until their 21st or 23rd birthday[10] (depending on the seriousness of the crime they committed), while youths sentenced as adults are usually transferred to an adult facility on or after their 18th birthday to serve the remainder of their sentence. Unlike adults who receive determinate sentences, juveniles receive indeterminate dispositions and are released onto parole when they are deemed to have made sufficient "progress toward parole readiness" (California Department of Corrections and Rehabilitation DJJ, n.d.). Since Governor Schwarzenegger signed SB 81 into law in 2007, only youths who committed a serious or violent offense listed in WIC 707 (b) or a "registerable" sex offense can be sentenced to state custody. All other juveniles remain in local custody.

There are currently only three youth correctional facilities (Chaderjian, Close, Norwalk) and one youth conservation camp (Pine Grove) in operation in California; all others have been closed. Like adults, youths housed at conservation camps learn valuable firefighting skills and assist CAL Fire with wild land firefighting throughout the state. Youths in other correctional facilities attend school and/or vocational training and participate in programs.

In 1995, there were close to 10,000 youth incarcerated in state youth correctional facilities; as of December 31, 2016, there were 653 offenders in DJJ institutions, 21 in adult prisons, and 0 on juvenile parole[11] (California Department of Corrections and Rehabilitation, 2017a). This represents a drop of over 94% in the number of incarcerated youth in state facilities in California since 1995. Of the 674 youthful offenders serving time in state facilities (both youth and adult), 544 (81%) were committed by juvenile courts and the remaining 130 (19%) were committed by adult courts (California Department of Corrections and Rehabilitation, 2017b). Only 19 of the 674 offenders are females and almost all of the offenders are serving time for homicide, robbery, assault, rape, or another sex crime (California Department of Corrections and Rehabilitation, 2017b). All are serving their first DJJ commitment (California Department of Corrections and Rehabilitation, 2017b). According to the California Sentencing

10. Youths disposed prior to July 1, 2012, may remain in custody until their 25th birthday.

11. Juvenile parole was eliminated January 1, 2013. County probation departments handle post-release community supervision for juveniles (just as they do for most adults).

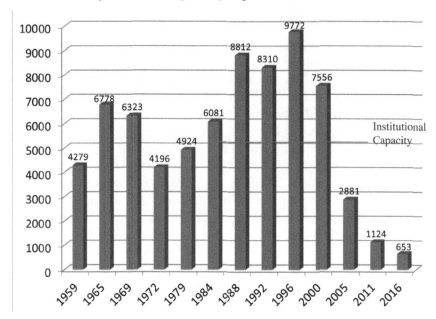

Figure 9.4. Average Daily Population of CYA/DJJ

Source: CRCR (2016) DJJ Population Overview on December 31, 2016.

Institute (2017), the juvenile state confinement rate is 31.9 per 100,000 juveniles aged 10–17; while not the absolute lowest juvenile incarceration rate in California history, it is quite a departure from the historical high of 263 per 100,000 juveniles aged 10–17 in 1995 (Males & Macallair, 2010).

Key Policies Affecting the State's Institutional Population

Historically, the state's institutional population has been very responsive to fiscally based policy changes. For example, as was noted earlier, counties committed large numbers of youth to CYA in the 1950s because the state, rather than the county, bore the costs of incarceration. The Probation Subsidy Act, launched in 1965, changed this practice and provided financial incentives to counties to house their delinquents locally (not in CYA). This move reduced CYA commitments substantially between 1965 and 1976 (see Figure 9.4). Although successful, law enforcement criticized the probation subsidy for being too lenient and referred to the subsidies as "blood money." By 1980, California switched to a direct payment system to the counties, which no longer required a reduction in correctional commitments by the county (meaning the state, not the county, would bear the brunt of the cost of incarcerating these youths).

Figure 9.5. Annual Admissions to CYA/DJJ

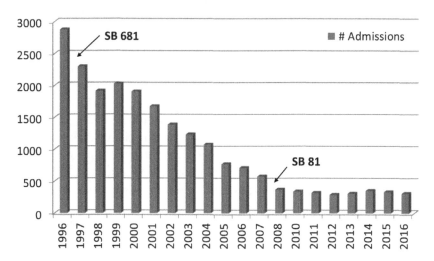

Source: CDCR (1996-2016) First Commitment Report

This caused CYA's population to swell again until it reached its peak of 9,772 juveniles in 1996. By that point, California's state juvenile institutional population exceeded its institutional capacity by more than 3,000 inmates (capacity was 6,800 at this time).

To deal with the extreme overcrowding within CYA institutions, *SB 681* was enacted in 1996, which mandated financial penalties for counties that committed non-serious delinquent offenders to the CYA. For example, a county that sentenced a serious offender would pay $2,556 per year while a county that sentenced a non-serious offender could be required to pay up to $33,096 per year to house that juvenile in a state facility. Prior to this time, counties paid $25 per offender per year, regardless of offender seriousness. The goal was to convince counties to house their non-serious offenders in county facilities, which are significantly less costly than state facilities (CYA) to operate. As a result of this legislation, the CYA population began to decline immediately (see Figure 9.5). *SB 81* (Juvenile Justice Realignment), which took effect in 2007, further reduced the state's institutional population by limiting the offenders which are allowed to be sentenced to DJJ those who committed serious, violent, and/or sexual offenses.

Current Issues Facing California's Juvenile Justice System

The key issue for juvenile justice in California in the coming years will be whether to retain dual county and state juvenile correctional systems. In addition to the *Farrell* lawsuit, which began requiring major changes to the state juvenile justice system in 2003, SB 81 and other de-incarceration initiatives served to dismantle DJJ and reduce the number of youth incarcerated in state youth facilities to today's historically low level. This is a positive development and the question now is whether California needs to retain DJJ for so few serious offenders or whether those offenders could be served locally. If DJJ were eliminated, counties would need to house and provide services for these high-risk, high-need youth or contract with another county to do so.

Interestingly, a third prison system for young offenders (ages 18–25) called the California Leadership Academy was proposed in Governor Brown's 2017–2018 budget (Washburn, 2017). This planned 250-bed facility in a remote area of the state, while technically an adult prison, is intended to serve young offenders, many of whom would have been adjudicated in juvenile court. Additionally, the governor's 2017–2018 budget proposal recommends spending $4.9 million to re-open two DJJ living units in anticipation of an estimated 10% increase in the DJJ population due to Proposition 57 (Washburn, 2017). The question is whether either of these proposals is necessary. With declining violent crime and juvenile arrest rates and most adults serving their time locally, will the state need extra bed space?

Innovative Programs in Juvenile Justice

In the mid-1990s, California started to experiment and fund wraparound services (what was then a new concept), and in 2004 *Proposition 63* added sections 18250–18258 to the Welfare and Institutions Code and required every county to implement wraparound services for youth. *Wraparound* services, as defined in WIC 18251, are "community-based intervention services that emphasize the strengths of the child and family and includes the delivery of coordinated, highly individualized unconditional services to address needs and achieve positive outcomes in their lives." It is a team-driven approach that involves numerous agencies working together to keep at-risk youth in the community (and not institutionalized). Individual plans are developed for each youth and his/her family, which utilize the formal services of social service agencies as well as the informal supports available within the family and the community.

When first proposed, wraparound services required major system change, as agencies were not accustomed to working in concert. Wraparound programs require services to be coordinated through a designated case manager so that youth and families receive fluid services. This was a large improvement over the fragmented, sometime duplicate and oftentimes missing, services from multiple agencies these multi-problem families had been receiving previously. There are two types of wraparound services in the state (funded from a variety of the same funding streams); one type utilizes only governmental agencies (for example, repeat offender prevention programs), the other type combines both private and public funding (for example EMQ Families First). Both types of wraparound services appear to be superior to the otherwise fragmented care.

EMQ Families First

EMQ (Eastfield, Ming, Quong) Families First is a private, non-profit organization. They were the first wraparound providers in California (EMQ Families First, 2012). EMQ began as a residential program based in San Jose to help orphaned and troubled children in 1867. Over nearly 150 years, they merged with a variety of other private agencies and became EMQ Families First in 1987. Their first wraparound program began in 1994 in Santa Clara County, where they partnered with the county's social services, mental health, and probation departments to work together to keep troubled youth in the community (EMQ Families First, 2012). Since its inception in 1994, 87% of youth served in the county have remained in their homes rather than juvenile halls or group homes. As a result of this early success, EMQ developed wraparound partnerships in other California counties. EMQ is a unique example of how private and public agencies can work together to achieve both change in the way we work with young troubled youth statewide as well as behavior in youth.

Repeat Offender Prevention Programs

In the late 1980s, the Probation Department in Orange County, California, realized that they were not very effective in preventing further delinquency in a specific group of juvenile offenders. At that point in time, it was believed that first-time offenders should be given a break and kept out of the system.

While this worked for 92% of delinquents, the remaining 8% went on to have a record of repeated serious offending. In fact, it turned out that 8% of the offenders were responsible for nearly 55% of all crimes committed in the county (Schumacher, 1999). This group of young, high-risk, first-time offenders shared certain characteristics upon intake that differed from youth who were arrested only once. The risk factors that they associated with continued delinquent behavior were: involved in delinquency at an early age, came from multi-problem families (abuse, neglect, criminal behavior, and lack of supervision and control), had problems at school (including truancy, suspensions or expulsions, and failing more than one class), used drugs and/or alcohol, were abused, were involved with a gang, and had previously run away (Schumacher, 1999). As a result, Orange County Probation Department decided to focus their resources on this group and developed a collaborative program to work with the youths and their families.

The program, known as the 8% Solution, featured a combination of intensive supervision and "wraparound" services (Schumacher, 1999). Various local agencies worked as a team, assessed the needs of the youth and family, devised a case plan and, together, followed the treatment plan at the Youth and Family Resource Center (YFRC). All youth were enrolled in a school located at the YFRC and transportation was provided to the center. On the premises of the YFRC, youth received drug and alcohol counseling, mental health evaluation and services, health education, health screening, job placement services and training, and life skills classes. They also were required to take part in community service endeavors. Members of these youths' families received family counseling in their home and were required to attend evening classes as well as participate in community service activities twice a month.

The early results of this program proved promising and, as a result, additional state-funded YFRC's were opened in Orange County. State funds also were provided to Los Angeles, San Diego, San Francisco, San Mateo, and Solano counties with the intention that each of these counties would develop and implement programs that served the same population of juvenile offenders with "wraparound" services. Evaluations of the various wraparound models showed that delinquents who took part in these types of programs (which became known as repeat offender prevention programs or ROPP) had better school attendance, improved their grade point averages, were less likely to fall below their grade level, were more likely to complete their court obligations, had fewer positive drug tests, had lower recidivism rates, and were less likely to run away than delinquents who received the normal probation services. Thus, while the services to these youth were more costly, they ultimately cost the state less in the long run.

Evidence-Based Practice in Juvenile Justice

Nearly twenty years ago, Elliott (1997), using scientific methods identified ten programs which met the standards of a proven "model program." At the same time, economists developed a cost-benefit model to determine the costs and benefits of utilizing these programs, which indicated that "every dollar invested in one of the more effective programs would result in $7–10 in benefits to taxpayers" (Greenwood, 2012). As a result of these findings, the use of evidence-based practices (EPB) has been encouraged. Best practices and programs (both generic and specific) which are the most cost effective and the most effective in reducing criminal behavior have been recognized, and states have been encouraged to utilize these programs.

While there are various lists of effective juvenile justice programs, the three most comprehensive sources are (1) Blueprints for Violence Prevention; (2) Mark Lipsey's meta-analysis, and (3) Washington State Institute for Public Policy publications. States are encouraged to adopt one of the "blueprint models" that have been identified and scientifically tested. While there are many programs identified as "evidence based," the best proven models include Functional Family Therapy (FFT), Multisystemic Therapy (MST), Multidimensional Treatment Foster Care (MTFC), and Nurse-Family Partnerships, which are the most likely to be implemented by the states (Greenwood, Welsh, & Rocque, 2012). These programs were all developed by one team, have gone through numerous experimental trials, and have been shown to be effective.

States have varied in their implementation of evidence-based practices. California lags sorely behind in this regard. Although the Juvenile Justice Crime Prevention Act (JJCPA) has given California counties more than 100 million dollars per year for the last nine years, with the exception of a few programs, none of the programs funded by these monies have demonstrated effectiveness through rigorous evaluation. Thus, California's juvenile justice programs fail to show up on any of the lists of evidence-based practices (Greenwood, 2013). Furthermore, in their analysis of the availability EBP family therapy teams in the population, California ranked on the low end with only two teams available per one million population, and, of those teams that did exist, nearly 80% were Functional Family Therapy teams (Greenwood, Welsh, & Rocque, 2012). While it appears that some counties have been much more effective in implementing these programs, the state, as a whole, has a very long way to go (see Figure 9.6 below).

Figure 9.6. States ranked by family therapy team availability (per million population in 2011)

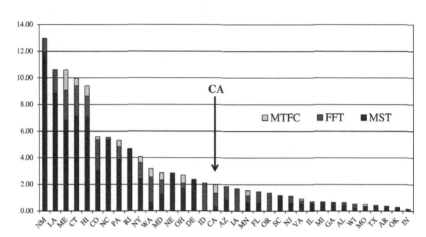

Source: Greenwood, Welsh, & Rocque, 2012. Reprinted with permission.

Conclusion

Despite several notorious missteps, California's juvenile justice system has been progressive for most of its more than 100-year history. Like other states, California's juvenile justice system was premised on, and currently operates by, a desire to do what is best for our youngest trouble-makers to dissuade them from committing future acts of mischievousness or criminality. Just like the adult system, however, policies and practices in the juvenile justice system are swayed by the punitive attitudes and beliefs held by the general public, legislators, and practitioners. The highly punitive policies that arrived in the 1990s are evidence that our system is strongly influenced by these attitudes as well as the crime trends (both real and perceived) that form them. We have turned a corner however, and today there are fewer youth held in state institutions, fewer held in county institutions, and fewer sentenced to probation than there were in 1995 (at the height of California's crime problems). There are also more programs and more incentives to serve our troubled youth locally, in our communities. We are making progress, and we are optimistic that California's juvenile justice system can once again be recognized for its accomplishments, rather than its blunders.

Key Terms and Definitions

Adjudicatory Hearing—The equivalent of a trial in adult court. Also call jurisdictional hearing.

California Youth Authority—Created in 1941 by Governor Culbert Olson, it centrally managed all state youth institutions until it was disbanded in 2005.

Dependent of the court—As defined by WIC 300, a child who has been, or is at risk of becoming abused and/or neglected.

Detention Hearing—A hearing for a juvenile detained in juvenile hall to determine if he/she is a risk to him/herself, to public safety, or is a flight risk.

Dispositional Hearing—Hearing in which the judges decides on a disposition. It is equivalent to "sentencing" in adult court.

Division of Juvenile Justice—Division with the Department of Corrections and Rehabilitation that oversees all state juvenile institutions in California. It was formed in 2005 when CYA was disbanded.

Fitness criteria—Five criteria that determine whether a juvenile is fit for juvenile court processing. They are: age of offender, offense seriousness, criminal sophistication, potential for rehabilitation, previous delinquent history, and success of previous attempts to rehabilitate.

Fitness hearing—A hearing in juvenile court to determine whether the youth meets criteria to be adjudicated in juvenile court.

Formal probation—The most common disposition given to juveniles. It involves community supervision and adhering to specified rules for a period up to three years.

Guardian ad litem—An individual appointed by the court to advocate on behalf of the child. Also called court appointed special advocate.

Informal probation—Short term probation (no more than 6 months) that is supposed to serve as a diversion for some youth.

Initial Appearance—A hearing in juvenile court in which the petition is read, the youth is advised of his/her rights and assigned counsel (if necessary), and it is determined whether there is enough evidence to establish the petition. It is the equivalent of preliminary hearing in adult court.

Intake—The process when a probation officer reviews a police officer's petition and decides whether to file a formal court petition to request that the case be heard in court.

Judicial Waiver—After a case is filed in juvenile court, a judge may decide to transfer the case to adult court based on the facts of the case and the age and criminal sophistication of the offender.

Jurisdictional Hearing—The equivalent of a trial in adult court. Also call adjudicatory hearing.

Juvenile Delinquent—As defined by WIC 602(a) a minor accused of violating any criminal law.

Legislative Waiver—The method of trying a juvenile case in adult court because state law prohibits the case from being adjudicated in juvenile court due to the crime and the age of the offender. Also called statutory exclusion. As of 2017, it is no longer available in California.

Petition—File charges against a juvenile.

Predisposition report—A report prepared by the probation department prior to disposition that recommends a disposition based on all known factors about the juvenile.

Proposition 21—Legislation passed by California voters in 2000 that redefined rules for juveniles charged with serious crimes and establishes gang enhancements.

Proposition 57—Legislation passed by California voters in 2016 that removed the options that allowed prosecutors to directly file charges against some juveniles in adult court.

Prosecutorial Waiver—A method of trying a juvenile in adult court that results from the prosecutor choosing to directly file a case in adult court instead of juvenile court at his/her discretion. As of 2017, it is no longer available in California.

Status Offender—As defined by WIC 601(a), a juvenile who commits an act that is deemed criminal due to his/her age.

Wraparound Services—Community-based intervention services that emphasize the strengths of the child and family and include the delivery of coordinated, highly individualized services.

Internet Websites

California Courts: http://www.courts.ca.gov/selfhelp-delinquency.htm

California Department of Corrections and Rehabilitation: http://www.cdcr.ca.gov/Juvenile_Justice/index.html

Center for Juvenile and Criminal Justice: http://www.cjcj.org/juvenile/justice/juvenile/justice/overview

Criminal Justice Statistics Center: http://oag.ca.gov/crime

National Center for Juvenile Justice: http://www.ncjj.org/Default.aspx

Office of Justice Programs, Crime Solutions: http://www.crimesolutions.gov/

Office of Juvenile Justice and Delinquency Prevention: http://www.ojjdp.gov/

Review Test Questions

1. How does the juvenile justice system differ from the criminal justice system?
2. Explain each stage of the juvenile justice process for juvenile delinquents and for dependents of the court.
3. Explain the three methods used to try juveniles in adult court. How frequently is each used?

Critical Thinking Questions

1. The juvenile justice system operates according to the principle "the best interest of the child." What does this mean? How does it impact the policies, procedures, and culture of juvenile court? How does this philosophy differ from the prevailing philosophies of the adult system?
2. California has had juvenile correctional facilities for more than 150 years. How has juvenile corrections changed during this time? What made the change possible? What is the significance of *Farrell v Cate*?
3. Counties differ in how frequently prosecutors' directly file juvenile cases in adult court. Some prosecutors directly file a large percent of eligible cases while other counties directly file a very small percentage. Why is this important? From an offender's perspective, which county is preferable—a high direct file county or a low direct file county? Why?

References

Agnew, R., & Breznia, A. (2012). *Juvenile delinquency: Causes and control* (4th ed.). New York, NY: Oxford University Press.
Ajmani, N. (2016, March 2). *Farrell's end gives true juvenile justice reform a chance.* Center on Juvenile and Criminal Justice. Retrieved from http://www.cjcj.org
Brozek, J. A. (1985). *History of detention in California 1850-1974.* Sacramento, CA: California State University.
California Department of Corrections and Rehabilitation (CDCR). (n.d.). *History of the Department of Juvenile Justice.* Retrieved from http://www.cdcr.ca.gov/Juvenile_Justice/DJJ_History/Index.html
California Department of Corrections and Rehabilitation (CDCR). (2017a). *Division of Juvenile Justice population overview as of December 31, 2016.* Retrieved from http://www.cdcr.ca.gov/Juvenile_Justice/Research_and_Statistics/index.html

California Department of Corrections and Rehabilitation (CDCR). (2017b). *Characteristics of the Division of Juvenile Justice population as of December 31, 2016.* Retrieved from http://www.cdcr.ca.gov/Juvenile_Justice/Research_and_Statistics/index.html

California Department of Justice. (2016). *Juvenile justice in California in 2015.* Retrieved from https://oag.ca.gov/sites/all/files/agweb/pdfs/cjsc/publications/misc/jj15/jj15.pdf

Center on Juvenile and Criminal Justice (CJCJ). (2017). *California Sentencing Institute statistics.* Retrieved from http://casi.cjcj.org/Juvenile/2015

EMQ Families First. (2012). *History: Transforming the system of care for California's children and families.* Retrieved from https://upliftfs.org/wp-content/uploads/Uplift-Family-Services-History.pdf

Farrington, D., Barnes, J., & Lambert, S. (1996). The concentration of offending in families. *Legal and Criminological Psychology, 1,* 47–63.

Farrington, D., & Welsh, B. (2007). *Saving children from a life of crime: Early risk factors and effective interventions.* New York, NY: Oxford University Press.

Greenwood, P. (2013, October 25). *Evidence-based practice in juvenile justice.* Presentation to Association of Criminal Justice Researchers, California semi-annual meeting in Irvine, CA.

Greenwood, P., Welsh, B., & Rocque, M. (2012, December). *Implementing proven programs for juvenile offenders: Assessing state progress.* Association for the Advancement of Evidence-Based Practice. Retrieved from http://www.advancingebp.org/wp-content/uploads/2012/01/AEBP-assessment.pdf

Heller de Leon, B. (2012, July 5). *Legislature, Governor Brown advance historic juvenile justice reforms.* Center on Juvenile and Criminal Justice. Retrieved from http://www.cjcj.org

Heller de Leon, B., & Teji, S. (2012). *Policy brief: Juvenile justice Realignment in 2012.* San Francisco, CA: Center on Juvenile and Criminal Justice. Retrieved from http://www.cjcj.org

Lerman, P. (1975). *Community treatment and social control.* Chicago, IL: University of Chicago Press.

Loeber, R., & Stouthamer-Loeber, M. (1986). Family factors as correlates and predictors of juvenile conduct problems and delinquency. In M. Tonry & N. Morris (Eds.), *Crime and justice* (Vol. 7). Chicago, IL: University of Chicago Press.

Macallair, D. (2003). The San Francisco Industrial School and the origins of juvenile justice in California: A glance at the great reformation. *U.C. Davis Journal of Juvenile Law and Policy, 7*(1), 1–60.

Males, M. (2008). *Myths and facts about "direct file," minorities, and adult-court sentencing*. San Francisco, CA: Center on Juvenile and Criminal Justice. Retrieved from http://www.cjcj.org

Males, M. (2012, October). *California youth crime plunges to all-time low*. San Francisco, CA: Center on Juvenile and Criminal Justice. Retrieved from http://www.cjcj.org

Males, M. (2016a, August). *California's youth and young adult arrest rates continue a historic decline*. San Francisco, CA: Center on Juvenile and Criminal Justice. Retrieved from http://www.cjcj.org

Males, M. (2016b, June). *Justice by geography: Do politics influence the prosecution of youth as adults?* San Francisco, CA: Center on Juvenile and Criminal Justice. Retrieved from http://www.cjcj.org

Males, M., & Macallair, D. (2010). *The California miracle: Drastically reduced youth incarceration, drastically reduced youth crime*. San Francisco, CA: Center on Juvenile and Criminal Justice. Retrieved from http://www.cjcj.org

Maxson, C. (2011). Street gangs. In J. Q. Wilson & J. Petersilia (Eds.), *Crime and public policy*. New York, NY: Oxford University Press.

McCord, J. (1982). A longitudinal view of the relationship between paternal absence and crime. In J. Gunn & D. Farrington (Eds.), *Abnormal offenders, delinquency, and the criminal justice system*. Chichester, England: Wiley.

Mihailoff, L. (2005). Protecting our children: A history of the California Youth Authority and juvenile justice, 1938-1968. (Unpublished dissertation). University of California, Berkeley, Department of History.

Moffitt, T., Ross, S., & Raine, A. (2011). Crime and biology. In J. Q. Wilson & J. Petersilia (Eds.), *Crime and public policy*. New York, NY: Oxford University Press.

National Center for Juvenile Justice. (2008). *Different from adults: An updated analysis of juvenile transfer and blended sentencing law, with recommendations for reform*. Retrieved from http://www.modelsforchange.net/publications/index.html

Orange County Superior Court. (n.d.). Juvenile court process. Retrieved from http://www.occourts.org/directory/juvenile/overview.html

Regoli, R., Hewitt, J., & DeLisi, M. (2011). *Delinquency in society: The essentials*. Sudbury, MA: Jones and Bartlett.

Schlossman, S. (2005). *Transforming juvenile justice*. Dekalb, IL: Northern Illinois University Press.

Schumacher, M. (1999). *The 8% solution: Preventing serious, repeat juvenile crime*. Thousand Oaks, CA: Sage.

Teji, S., & Males, M. (2011). *An analysis of direct criminal court filing 2003-2009: What has been the effect of Proposition 21?* San Francisco, CA: Center for Juvenile and Criminal Justice. Retrieved from www.cjcj.org

Washburn, M. (2017, January 20). *2017-18 budget expands youth prisons and deepens reliance on incarceration.* San Francisco, CA: Center for Juvenile and Criminal Justice. Retrieved from www.cjcj.org

Whitehead, J., & Lab, S. (2009). *Juvenile justice: An introduction* (6th ed.). LexisNexis Group.

Wikström, P., & Loeber, R. (2000). Do disadvantaged neighborhoods cause well-adjusted children to become adolescent delinquents? A study of male juvenile serious offending, individual risk and protective factors, and neighborhood context. *Criminology, 38,* 1109–1142.

Cases Cited

Farrell v. Cate (2003)
Graham v. Florida, 560 U.S. ____ (2010)
New Jersey v. T.L.O., 469 U.S. 325 (1985)
Roper v. Simmons, 543 U.S. 551 (2005)

Chapter 10

Gangs and the California Criminal Justice System

Gregory C. Brown

Learning Objectives

After reading the chapter, students should be able to:

- Define the term *gang*.
- Describe the history of gangs in California.
- Demonstrate an understanding of the different types of gangs in California.
- Describe gang crimes and approaches for dealing with gangs.
- Explain how various legislative approaches have affected gangs.

Introduction

California is called the gang capital of the United States, and there is a long history of the criminal justice system seeking to manage these groups (Howell & Griffiths, 2016). It's estimated that the state has 235,000 gang members who belong to over 6,400 street gangs (California Department of Justice, 2010). Gangs are an important criminal justice issue, because they are responsible for an inordinate amount of unlawful behavior, including loss of life, loss of personal security, and financial loss (Hagedorn, 2005; Lynskey, 1998). Some researchers estimate that gangs are responsible for 10% of all crime and one-third of violent crime nationally, and as high as half of the serious violent crime in specific gang-impacted neighborhoods (Katz, Webb, & Armstrong, 2003; O'Deane & Morreale, 2011; Spergel, 1995; Whitmer & Anker, 1997). Once considered a problem of urban areas, gangs began migrating into suburban and rural communities throughout the United States during the 1980s and 1990s. Very large cities with long histories of gang activity tend to have relatively stable patterns of serious gang crime, while the seriousness of gang problems may fluctuate more dramatically in smaller cities and towns (Howell, 2012). This chapter highlights some of the characteristics of California gangs and discusses some of the responses by the criminal justice system to their presence and activities.

What Is a Gang?

There is considerable debate about how we should define gangs (Howell, 2012; Klein, 1995; Wood & Alleyne, 2010; Curry, Decker, & Pyrooz, 2014). Klein (2000) identifies the street gang as an American product, arising from the inner city and closely associated with violence and criminal behavior. A common modern definition of a *gang* is a group of adolescents who commit delinquent acts, habitually interact face-to-face, live in the same neighborhood, and claim a territory. The group usually has a name, an identifiable leader or leaders, some form or structure, and commonly exists in lower socioeconomic areas.

The Department of Justice developed a working definition of a gang as a "group or association of three or more persons who may have a common identifying sign, symbol, or name and who are involved in criminal activity which creates an atmosphere of fear and intimidation" (2009, p. 23). In the California Penal Code, the word "gang" is defined as:

> Any organization, association or group of three or more persons, whether formal or informal, having as one of its primary activities the commission of criminal acts, having a common name or common identifying sign or symbol, and whose members individually or collectively engage in a pattern of criminal gang activity. (California Penal Code section 186.22)

According to Knox (2000, p. 1), "a gang is a group, informal or formal in nature, whose members recurrently commit crimes and where these crimes are known openly to the members, often conferring status or profit upon those members who commit the crime." Gangs are usually discussed in the context of delinquency, which is a socially unacceptable act committed by an individual or group. But many researchers believe it is important to include violence or criminality as a necessary criterion for defining a gang (Wood & Alleyne, 2010). After all, it is the criminal activity element of gangs that is of most interest to law enforcement and criminologists alike. Howell (2012) defines a gang for practical purposes as a group with five or more members, with a shared identity such as a name and other symbols, that is viewed by its own members and others as a gang, has some permanence, and is involved in an elevated level of criminal activity.

Esbensen and colleagues (2008) defined a gang as "any durable, street-oriented youth group whose involvement in illegal activity is part of its group identity" (p. 117). In Klein and Maxson's view, there are certain minimal elements of a street gang (2006, p. 4) that specifically includes delinquent, *turf-based gangs*. Delinquent, turf-based youth gang members typically "hang out" together and have identifying signs, such as clothing, styles, colors, and hand signs. They often engage in delinquent or undesirable behavior, with their offenses running the gamut from truancy, minor vandalism, and graffiti to assault and homicide. Traditional turf-based gangs are usually groups of young people (juveniles or adults), with a name, leader or leaders, identifying signs, and associated with a territory. Turf and rivalries are key identifying characteristics for these groups.

Researchers have developed a number of theories about why youth join gangs. Frederick Thrasher (1927) contributed to the development of the theory of social disorganization, also known as cultural deviance theory. *Social disorganization theory* holds that delinquency is born out of the social disorganization of immigrant groups, and the conflict between "old country" and "new world" norms. Youth become disorganized by learning American values in school and old cultural values from their parents. For example, immigrant parents encouraged their children to beg, which developed into illicit activities and the beginning of gangs. Social disorganization theory was originally developed to explain the delinquency and criminal behavior that existed in immigrant groups. More recently, it has been used to explain delinquency in African American and Hispanic communities.

Vigil (1990) describes gang formation using the concept of "*multiple marginality.*" Multiple marginality refers to macro-historical forces (i.e., racism, social and cultural oppression, and fragmented institutions) and macro-structural forces (immigration and migration, enclave settlement, and migrant poor barrio/ghetto) that prohibit youth from developing mainstream values and socialization. This results in youth holding different values than their parents, leading to a breakdown in the family. Youth instead are "street socialized" as they grow up in the hood, which eventually leads to gang participation.

History and Types of Gangs in California

Street gangs in California have developed largely along ethnic lines following the waves of immigration to the state. Racist housing covenants written into leases and deeds prevented African Americans, Hispanics, and Asians from living in white neighborhoods. These discriminatory practices led to the segregation of neighborhoods along racial and ethnic lines throughout California (the covenants were statewide), but particularly in Los Angeles (Dargis, 2009). Further, these racial and ethnic gangs also exist not only on the streets but in the prisons, and one of the more recent trends has been the development of criminal ties with transnational criminal organizations (TCO)s, especially involving Hispanic and Asian gangs.

The earliest documented gangs in California were divided along racial and ethnic lines. Mexican groups first appeared in the 1890s (Howell, 2012; Vigil, 1990) and continued to dominate through the 1930s and 1940s. African American gangs emerged in the 1940s and grew with increased immigration of African Americans in the 1950s and 1960s (Howell, 2012). Asian gangs began developing in California in the 1990s among immigrant groups of Filipinos, Koreans, Samoans, and Southeast Asians (Cambodians, Thais, and Vietnamese). Other gang types include racial supremacist groups such as the Aryan Brotherhood and Pen1 and are comprised primarily of Caucasians. White gangs primarily emerged in the 1970s.

Los Angeles is said to be home to the most street gangs in the United States (and most likely the world) (Delaney, 2014). According to the Los Angeles Police Department (LAPD) COMSTAT information, Cal Gangs Report, as of July 31, 2011, there are 427 documented gangs in the City of Los Angeles, with more than 100,000 gang members. This includes: 207 documented Hispanic gangs; 153 black gangs, 57 white gangs, and 10 Asian gangs in the city. Los Angeles County, including the City of Los Angeles, has an estimated 180,000 gang members.

Hispanic Gangs

As stated earlier, Hispanic gangs are the earliest documented gangs in California (Moore, 1978; Vigil, 1990; Howell & Moore, 2010). These gangs appear initially to have been patterned after the palomilla (meaning flock of doves), which were small groups of young Mexican men first reported in south Texas that migrated westward, eventually reaching Los Angeles in the 1920s. The first Los Angeles gangs, called "boy gangs" (Vigil, 1990), were territorial-based groups that cohered through conflicts with youth from other barrios, school officials, and police. The boy gangs became known as street gangs (Vigil, 1990; Vigil, 2004).

Two historic events are notable in the early history of Mexican American gangs in California. In 1942, a Mexican American youth was killed at Sleepy

Lagoon, a popular swimming hole in what is now East Los Angeles. Members of the 38th Street gang were arrested by the Los Angeles Police Department. Their subsequent convictions on murder charges brought together the Mexican community and increased the popularity of the 38th street gang in the community (Valdez, 2011). The *Zoot Suit Riots* of 1943 had a similar effect on the growth of Mexican street gangs. During five days of rioting, military personnel on leave and citizen groups chased and beat anyone wearing the distinctive zoot suit popular in the Mexican American community. The riots increased the cohesion of the Mexican American community and highlighted conflict with other ethnic groups in the city. Mexican immigration accelerated again in the early 1950s. Hispanic gangs continued to grow in the 1960s and 1970s, spurred by the Vietnam War, the War on Poverty, and the Chicano movement (Howell, 2012; Howell & Griffiths, 2016). The Vietnam War eliminated many positive role models from Hispanic communities (Vigil, 1990). The end of the War on Poverty increased unemployment and marginalization. The Chicano civil rights movement brought attention to suffering Hispanic barrios (Moore & Vigil, 1993).

Hispanic gangs tend to have the longest familial history of gang involvement. It is not uncommon to find three and four generations of gang participation. Unlike Hispanic gangs in New York and Chicago, which emerged from severe poverty and social disorganization and coalesced through conflict with other racial and ethnic groups, Mexican American gangs in Los Angeles drew strength from their own rich ethnic history (Howell, 2012; Howell & Griffiths, 2016). For many, this cultural link results from long-standing ties with their countries of origin. For example, the Mexican American 18th Street gang and Mara Salvatrucha, a Salvadorian Los Angeles gang, are described as transnational gangs (Howell, 2012; Franco, 2008). The 18th Street gang and Mara Salvatrucha are thought to be involved with drug cartels in Mexico and Central America.

African American Gangs

African American gangs emerged somewhat later than Hispanic gangs, starting in about the 1940s (Alonso, 1999; Perkins, 1987; Tobin, 2008; Alonso, 2014). African Americans migrated from the rural South to Los Angeles in search of better economic and social opportunities (Cureton, 2009; Howell & Moore, 2010; Perkins, 1987; Spergel, 1995; Vigil, 2002). Because of racism and housing discrimination, African Americans were confined to specific areas around Central Avenue, formerly known as South Central L.A., including the area known as Watts. The expansion of African American ghettos from the 1930s to the 1970s resulted in increased conflict between whites and African

Americans (Adamson, 2000). As the African American population increased, the KKK surfaced in Los Angeles and African Americans became the target of white violence (Cureton, 2009). As a result, African American gangs formed to protect their communities against these threats.

"White flight" began in the 1950s, as whites moved to the surrounding suburbs of Los Angeles, leaving an increased concentration of the African American population in the South Central area. The 1965 *Watts Riots* brought African American youth together for political mobilization (Alonso, 2004). These actions brought African American youth to the attention of law enforcement. As a result, key activists and leaders were incarcerated (Vigil, 2002), leading to the decimation of activist role models and a decrease in social programming, which in turn created an environment that was conducive for gang growth (Alonso, 2014). In addition, the Watts Riots accelerated the white flight to the outskirts such that very few whites remained in the Watts, Compton, and Inglewood areas. With the decreased presence of whites in the communities, African American gangs now engaged in conflict with other African American groups (Alonso, 2004), which led to the development of small gangs throughout Los Angeles for protection against the more established gangs.

The growth of African American gangs also accelerated in response to the deterioration in the labor market for young African American men beginning in the late 1970s. The dramatic rise of gangs between 1978 and 1982 in Los Angeles, Compton, and Inglewood was due in part to plant closures, which led to some 70,000 layoffs during this period. Therefore, unemployed young African American men turned to the counter-economy of drug dealing and youth crime (Davis, 1992). African American gangs also fought each other because of poverty and the lack of employment opportunities in their communities (Adamson, 2000). Of course, being a gang member with little or no education and a felony conviction made the likelihood of obtaining a legal job that much more unlikely. As a result of the high incarceration rates of men of color, these trends continue today. Presently, African American gangs tend to sell PCP, marijuana, barbiturates, amphetamines, and crack cocaine. They typically don't have a single leader, and are usually divided according to age. They can be as few as 5 to 10 members and as many as 800 to 1,000 in a specific set (Valdez, 2011).

Some of the early African American gangs were the Gladiators, the Slausons, and the Businessmen. One of the more popular early gangs was the Baby Avenues, headed by Raymond Washington. The Baby Avenues later became known as the *Crips*. Raymond Washington and Stanley Tookie Williams are recognized as the co-founders of the Crips. The Crips were initially called the Cribs. The name Crib started because "crib" referred to a person's home and the Cribs developed to protect the home turf. There are various stories as to why they later became known as the Crips. As a counter-weight to the Crips, other gangs formed that became known as the *Bloods*. Some of the early Blood sets were the Pirus, Swans, and the Brims. During the 1970s and 1980s, the Crips and Bloods grew exponentially. As a result of their rivalry, hard-core Bloods do not use the letter "c" in writing, and conversely, Crips do not use the letter "b" in writing. As a result of the many lives lost to gang violence, Tony "Bogart" Thomas, one of the main "shotcallers" for the Grape Street Crips, called a gang truce between the Crips and the Bloods after the Rodney King riots in 1992. Tony Bogart's relationship with Crips co-founder Stanley Tookie Williams and the gang truce between the Crips and the Bloods was portrayed in the film about Tookie's life, *Redemption* (Bugden & Hall, 2004). The truce was short lived.

The Blood sets have always worn red colors or some variation of red. The most notable color for Crips was blue, but the Grape Street Crips, for example, wore purple. Crips usually wear a blue handkerchief, also referred to as a "rag," while the Bloods wear red rags. Major Blood sets include Bounty Hunters, Black P Stone, Pirus, Fruit Town Pirus, Athens Park Boys, Bishops, and Leuders Park. Some of the major Crip gangs are the 83 Gangster Crips, Compton Crips, East Side Crips, Grape Street, PJ Crips, Shotgun Crips, Water Gate Crips, Pay Back Crips, Neighborhood Crips, Rolling Sixties, East Coast Crips, and Mona Park Crips.

Asian and Pacific Islander Gangs

Asian gangs developed with the influx of Asian immigrants to the U.S. As a result of the Chinese Exclusion Act of 1882 and the National Origins Act of 1924, there were few Chinese youth in the United States. Chinese gangs developed first in San Francisco (Emch, 1973; Loo, 1976). Large waves of immigration also occurred following the reign of Pol Pot and many Cambodian, Hmong, and Laotian refugees found their way to the American shores. Much of the early development of Asian gangs comes from battles between families and their youth who struggle to find their American identities while battling the cultural expectations of their parents. Unlike black and Hispanics gangs, which are generally divided along specific racial and ethnic lines, it is not uncommon for Asian gangs to include members from different ethnic groups (Chin, 2006).

Asian gangs are generally considered non-territorial gangs, with few exceptions. They are usually highly organized and are typically involved in crimes of robbery, burglary, extortion, home invasions, and auto theft, as well as victimless crimes like prostitution and opium smoking (Tracy, 1980). Asian gangs are also known to be involved in the business of human trafficking. Unlike most Asian gangs, Filipino gangs tend to be territorial. As with African American gangs, they tend to form cliques based on age. They are involved in crimes like extortion, auto theft, and drive-by shootings (Valdez, 2011). Samoan gangs often align themselves with Blood and Crip sets, mostly with Crips because of the larger representation of Crips in Los Angeles. They are involved in auto theft, assaults, and weapons violations. Several cities in southern California have been identified as hot spots for Asian gangs, including Westminster, Garden Grove, Buena Park, and Santa Ana, and hotspot regions in Northern/Central California include San Francisco, Sacramento, and Fresno.

According to the State Attorney General's Office, transnational Asian gangs are expanding in areas with large Asian American populations, especially in Fresno, Los Angeles, Orange, Sacramento, Santa Clara, and San Diego counties (Harris, 2014). Asian gangs such as the Tiny Rascal Gang and Asian Boyz are involved in human and sex trafficking, drug and weapons smuggling, marijuana cultivation, and cyber and other crimes (California Department of Justice, 2010, as cited in Harris, 2014).

White and Skinhead Gangs

White gangs are frequently associated with racist philosophies towards minorities. The *skinhead* movement started in England in the mid-1960s, and expanded to the U.S. in the 1970s due to its association with the punk-rock style of music. Considered "hate groups" and/or "terrorists" rather than traditional street gangs, racist skinhead groups have often been excluded from gang studies. It is commonly believed that skinhead groups do not typically claim territory or hang out on the street like other street gangs. They are also thought to be highly political (Simi, 2006). The communities of Huntington Beach and Hemet have been suggested as some of the breeding grounds for white racist/supremacist groups in southern California.

Southern California skinheads formed in response to "microlevel changes in the local punk rock scene and macrolevel changes in the wider social structure" (Simi, 2006, p. 149). On the micro level, punk rock music was becoming more hardcore and violent. On the macro level, increasing non-white immigration was changing California's demographic make-up, leading to a backlash against various minority groups. Scholars have noted similarities between southern California skinheads and traditional street gang members. Most skinheads reported early street socialization as they hung out with other skinheads at malls, parks, and music shows. Knox (2000, p. 6) claims that "many 'skinhead' groups and white racist groups must be considered gangs because they often engage in what is called bias crimes."

Prison Gangs

The Justice Department defines *prison gangs* as criminal organizations that originated in the penal system. These gangs typically have operations inside and outside the penal system. They consist of a select group of inmates who have an organized hierarchy and are governed by an established code of conduct. The gangs may vary in organization and composition, but generally they are highly structured. They have fewer numbers than street gangs, but like street gangs, they are usually structured along racial or ethnic lines. Like street gangs, prison gangs tend to have a creed or motto, symbols, identified leaders, and proscribed behavior, requiring absolute loyalty and secrecy (Marquart & Sorensen, 1997).

Some reasons for the development of prison gangs include the prison sub-culture, prisonization, racial issues, and violence. Prison gangs formed as a way for ethnic groups to band together to fight for control over the system. The racial divisions in prisons have given rise to gangs as a means of protection. The debate is whether gang formation is the result of importation or deprivation. The *importation model* states that the anti-social behavior was present before the inmate arrived in the institution. The *deprivation model* argues that inmate conduct is in response to institutionalization. Gang activity can be attributed to inmates adapting to the prison environment (Brown, 1990). Some researchers argue that while prisons were designed to punish or rehabilitate, they instead have become a breeding ground for more serious offenders (Brown, 1985). With a population of individuals, many of whom were street gang members, the decision becomes one of joining a prison gang or remaining on your own. As the adage goes, no one survives in prison alone. Here, race is the most important factor when it comes to prison gang membership (Brown, 1990). Given the significant size of the prison system in California, it comes as no surprise that prison gangs are alive and well in the state's penal institutions.

Inside California's prison walls there are a number of different gangs. The first prison gang in California, and the first prison gang with nationwide ties, was the *Mexican Mafia*, also known as *La Eme* for the Spanish letter "m." The Mexican Mafia emerged in 1957 at the Deuel Vocational Center in Tracy, California (Federal Bureau of Investigation, 2009; Hunt, Riegel, Morales, & Waldorf, 1993). Valdez (2011) attributes the origins of the Mexican Mafia and Nuestra Familia to a power struggle between inmates from northern and southern California. Members of the Mexican Mafia are Sureños, which means they come from geographic areas of the state south of Bakersfield. Members of the Mexican Mafia must be of Mexican descent. The gang has a "blood in, blood out" rule. A prospective member must spill blood to join. That often means attacking a rival gang member or prison guard. One can leave the Mexican Mafia only by death, so membership is for life. The number 13 represents the Mexican Mafia, because "m" is the 13th letter of the alphabet. Their color is blue and their symbol is "La Eme" or just an "M." The major source of income for the Mexican Mafia is extorting drug distributors outside of the prison. They distribute methamphetamine, cocaine, heroin, and marijuana within the prison and outside on the streets. They also control gambling and prostitution in the prisons (Valdez, 2011).

Nuestra Familia is the enemy gang of La Eme. La Nuestra Familia was created to protect its members from the Los Angeles-based Mexican Mafia. Nuestra Familia represents Norteños, or Northern Californians (north of Bakersfield), and is largely comprised of members from the Central Valley. La Nuestra Familia was also established in the 1960s, in either California's Soledad State Prison or in the Deuel Vocational Center (Landre, Miller, & Porter, 1997; Orlando-Morningstar, 1997). The symbols for Nuestra Familia include the letters "NF" and a sombrero with a knife through it. Additional Hispanic prison gangs in California include the Norteños, the Sureños, the New Structure, and the Border Brothers (Hunt et al., 1993).

The *Black Guerilla Family*, or *BGF*, was started in California's San Quentin State Prison by George Lester Jackson (Hunt et al., 1993). Jackson was a former Black Panther Party member who was killed during an attempted prison escape during the 1960s. The gang was formed to provide protection to African American members from Hispanic gangs. BGF is the largest African American prison gang in the United States (Valdez, 2011). The Black Guerilla Family is highly organized, with a paramilitary structure. It has a supreme leader and central committee. It has a national charter, code of ethics, and an oath of allegiance. The gang's primary source of income is the distribution of cocaine and marijuana. Its symbols are the letters "BGF" and a sword and rifle crossed.

The *Aryan Brotherhood*, a white supremacist gang, was started shortly after BGF in 1967. It also emerged within the walls of San Quentin State Prison, in response to the threat of African American and Hispanic inmates and gangs (Orlando-Morningstar, 1997). The Aryan Brotherhood has two factions. One is located in the California Department of Corrections and Rehabilitation (CDCR), and the other is in the Federal Bureau of Prisons. It is considered a white racist gang. However, in more recent years the Aryan Brotherhood has allied itself with La Eme. The main source of income for the Aryan Brotherhood is the distribution of cocaine, heroin, methamphetamine, and marijuana, both within the prison system and on the street. Its symbols are the letters "AB" and a shamrock with 666 in it. Oftentimes the members will display a swastika or the Nazi "SS" symbol. The Aryan Brotherhood is one of the smaller prison gangs, but it has a reputation as being one of the most violent—especially in their attacks against other gang-affiliated inmates and correctional officers.

Similar to their counterparts in the community, prison gangs are heavily involved in criminal behavior, including drug trafficking (Montgomery & Crews, 1998; Fleisher & Decker, 2001). They are more powerful within state correctional facilities than they are within the federal penal system. In addition to the drug business, prison gangs are also credited with responsibility for much of the violence inside prisons (Ingraham & Wellford, 1987). Camp and Camp (1985) estimate that prison gang members composed 3% of the prison population but accounted for 50% or more of prison violence.

Obtaining estimates of the number of prison gangs and gang membership within the prison walls is difficult for several reasons. There is little official documentation, and what is available is typically limited to internal departmental use. Outside researchers face limited access to prisons, and prison gang members are unlikely to disclose sensitive information about gang affiliation (Fleisher & Decker, 2001).

Transnational Gangs

A recent report by the California Attorney General's Office (Harris, 2014) found transnational gangs, also known as transnational criminal organizations (TCOs), or transnational organized crime, are a serious threat to the health and safety of California and its citizens. The report identified three main types of transnational criminal activity: the trafficking of drugs, weapons, and humans; money laundering; and high-technology crimes such as computer hacking and fraud. It found a TCO presence in almost every urban area in the state, as well as many smaller cities.

Transnational gangs are criminal organizations that, according to Franco (2008), have more than one of the following traits: (1) criminally active in more than one country; (2) criminal activities committed in one country are planned by gang leaders in another country; (3) criminal activities tend to be sophisticated and transcend borders; and (4) they tend to be mobile and adapt readily to new geographic areas. Some examples of TCOs are Mexican-based drug cartels, as well as Asian and Eastern European criminal groups.

As with gangs generally, there is no single definition of TCOs. The uniqueness and ambiguity of these criminal entities has been advantageous for these groups in their ability to function. Transnational criminal organizations are important to the study of gangs because of their close relationships with prison and street gangs. Transnational gangs, like most prison and street gangs, usually do business with groups of the same race or ethnicity, but have demonstrated that making money takes precedence over racial or ethnic differences. This flexibility makes them especially dangerous.

Gang Crime

A key issue in the discussion of gang violence is the definition of what counts as a gang crime (Decker & Curry, 2002). The Los Angeles Police Department defines a *gang crime* as any crime involving a gang member or a gang motive. According to a report by the California Attorney General's Office (Tita & Abrahamse, 2004), nearly 75% of the 10,000 youth gang homicides that took place in California between 1981 and 2001 occurred in Los Angeles. Howell (2012) estimated that 50.3% of all of the homicides that occurred in Los Angeles in 2009 were gang-related. The United States Government Accounting Office report (2009) concludes that LA has a "violent gang culture unlike any other gang culture in the state" (p. 16). The victimization rate among African Americans is higher than among Hispanics, which, in turn, is higher than everyone else.

The emergence of rock or crack cocaine provided unique opportunities for Los Angeles gangs (Klein, 1995). Most researchers, however, report that youth gangs are rarely involved in large-scale drug distribution activities as an organized gang function (Decker & Van Winkle, 1996; Klein, 1995). Gangs may also take a more subtle role of offering protection to drug sellers and dealers in exchange for their commitment to the gang, making the role of the gang in the distribution of drugs difficult to discern to most outsiders (Valdez & Sifaneck, 2004).

Due to the lack of prison gang studies, the relationship between crime committed by prison gangs and crime committed by gangs on the street is not well understood (Howell, 2012). Jacobs (2001) suggests that prison gangs may strengthen gangs on the street, as criminal schemes devised in prison are carried out on the street and vice versa. Adult prison gangs have influenced Mexican American communities from inside the prison (Jacobs, 1974). The influence of prison gangs in the drug market in California has increased over the last two decades (Valdez & Sifaneck, 2004).

Approaches for Dealing with Gangs

Policymakers have developed three main strategies to deal with the gang problem: prevention, intervention, and suppression (Bjerregaard, 2003; Curry,

Decker, & Pyrooz, 2014; Delaney, 2014). *Prevention programs* address factors associated with gang membership to prevent youth from joining gangs. *Intervention programs* aim to steer gang-involved youth out of gangs. *Gang suppression* programs focus on the arrest, prosecution, and incarceration of gang members. To the extent the causes of gang membership are numerous and interrelated, effectively combating gangs requires a multifaceted approach (Bjerregaard, 2003).

Gang Suppression

The gang suppression model is based on deterrence and rational choice theories, which assert that gang membership and gang crime are the result of individual choice. Gang suppression activities include police actions and gang legislation and policies that increase the certainty and/or severity of sanctions. Klein (1995) said that gang suppression became the primary focus of gang efforts in the 1980s and is the most used anti-gang strategy. Despite the focus on gang suppression, research suggests that these approaches have not been particularly successful (Klein, 1995).

Local Law Enforcement

Police agencies play a major role in gang suppression. Some police gang suppression activity proactively controls legal behavior that is connected to gang crime, such as carrying pagers, wearing colors, flashing hand signs, and congregating in problem areas (Maxson, Hennigan, & Sloane, 2005). Other gang suppression initiatives include the use of metal detectors in schools, increased surveillance, police sweeps, stake-outs, saturation patrol, curfew, truancy enforcement, and increased arrest and imprisonment of gang members (Bynum & Varano, 2003; Fearne, Decker, & Curry, 2001; Huff, 2002; Spergel & Curry, 1993). It also may include creating specialized gang police and prosecution units, follow up investigations, and intelligence gathering. Historically, the gang suppression strategy has a weak record of success. In the 1980s, the Los Angeles Police Department (LAPD) implemented a program called "Operation Hammer," a gang suppression technique aimed at reducing gang activity in South Central Los Angeles. It was determined not to be successful (Klein, 1995). Then in 1987, the LAPD established an elite gang unit called Community Response Against Street Hoodlums (CRASH). It was disbanded in 2000.

Greene (2003) suggests that police departments need to recognize that effective intervention and gang suppression efforts require external agencies' participation. Community-oriented policing strategies go beyond gang suppression to include community collaborations, social intervention, and opportunity enhancement. Some of the police assigned to gang programs also provide counseling, job development and referral, and tutoring, as well as engage in other extensive community relations and development activities. One example of an interdisciplinary strategy is LAPD's involvement with the southern California *Cease-Fire Committee*. The Cease-Fire Committee is a collaboration of former gang members who act as interventionists along with law enforcement officers, local politicians, clergy, community activists, and others. The primary goal is to stop gang violence.

Another strategy in gang suppression involves targeting the activity of gun violence rather than specifically focusing on gang affiliation. The "pulling levers" approach has been demonstrated to work in California communities such as Stockton and the Boyle Heights neighborhood of Los Angeles (United States Government Accounting Office, 2009). Thus, the message is to reduce gun violence in communities where much of the violence is committed by gang members, rather than to conduct a "war on gangs." Communities appear to be more supportive of efforts aimed at reducing the killing of their youth rather than declaring war on their youth.

Civil Gang Injunctions

Another gang suppression tool is the *civil gang injunction*. An injunction is a legal avenue to prohibit members of a designated street gang from participating in conduct or activities that are a nuisance or illegal (O'Deane & Morreale, 2011). The injunctions prohibit named gang members from participating in particular activities within a designated area (Grogger, 2002). Injunctions may be used because gangs constitute a "public nuisance" under California Civil Code (O'Deane & Morreale, 2011). The prohibited actions may include illegal activities, such as selling drugs, committing vandalism, trespassing, and drinking in public. The prohibited activities may also include normally legal activities, such as carrying a cell phone, wearing gang clothing, using gang hand signs, possessing graffiti paraphernalia, associating with other named gang members, and even with gang members that are not listed in the order (Barajas, 2007; California Department of Justice, 2003; Crawford, 2009; Grogger, 2002; O'Deane & Morreale, 2011). In addition, the injunctions may provide gang members wishing to leave the gang the impetus to denounce their membership (California Department of Justice, 2003; Crawford, 2009). In 1997, in *People v. Acuna*, the California Supreme Court upheld the constitutionality of gang injunctions.

Injunctions are enforced through a petition to the court for relief from the public nuisance caused by the named gang members. Sources of evidence against gang members may include sworn statements from community residents who have witnessed criminal acts such as drug dealing and assaults. Another primary source is police officers and informants. Prosecutors can pursue violations of the injunction either in civil or criminal court (Grogger, 2002). The maximum penalty for civil contempt is a $1,000 fine and five days in jail. Under criminal prosecution, violators face up to six months in jail and/or a fine of $1,000 (California Department of Justice, 2003; Grogger, 2002). While the civil penalties are less severe, they can be imposed without criminal due process. In addition, violators can be placed on probation for up to three years following their injunction violation arrest, thus providing police an additional measure to monitor the gang member (O'Deane & Morreale, 2011).

The primary deterrent benefit from the injunction may come from the gang member's awareness that his or her activities are being closely monitored and his or her concern over criminal charges with more serious sentences (Grogger, 2002). Civil gang injunctions are similar to community policing and "broken windows" policies in that they concentrate law enforcement resources on target neighborhoods where gangs are considered a serious problem and targeting gang members before they commit serious crimes (Barajas, 2007). Hennigan and Sloane (2013) studied gang injunctions and concluded that injunctions should target individuals rather than the gang as a group. Gang members should be held individually responsible, and forced to take steps toward strengthening the individual, thereby weakening the gang as a group.

While research on the effectiveness of gang injunctions is limited, some researchers conclude that gang injunctions yield short-term gang suppression results in the year following the injunctions (Barajas, 2007; Grogger, 2002; O'Deane & Morreale, 2011). Others find that the efficacy remains unclear (Villaraigosa, 1992). An analysis of crime data from the LAPD, the Los Angeles Sheriff's Department, the Long Beach Police Department, and the Pasadena Police Department indicated that civil gang injunctions led to a reduction in reported crime of 5% to 10% in defined injunction target areas during the year during and after injunctions were composed, compared to the five-quarter period preceding these injunctions (Grogger, 2002).

Research suggests that a reduction in crime is more apt to occur in areas that rely on information from community members to develop the case for an injunction (Maxson, Hennigan, & Sloane, 2003). In areas with less gang activity, Maxson, Hennigan, and Sloane (2005) found that injunctions were related to an increase in gang presence, greater disorder, and greater victimization. McGloin (2005) said that injunctions may be most effective against groups that have already developed cohesion. Injunctions may be more effective against smaller gangs, because it is easier to identify problem members, and they typically control a smaller area (O'Deane & Morreale, 2011). A territorial gang is likely to be affected more significantly by a gang injunction than a less territorial gang because of the injunction's tie to a specific geographic area. In southern California, Hispanic and African American gangs tend to be more territorial (Vigil, 1988; O'Deane & Morreale, 2011).

Critics of the use of civil gang injunctions cite civil liberties concerns, as they link criminal consequences to civil actions (Barajas, 2007). They restrict constitutional freedoms of association and expression without providing their subjects due process rights under criminal law. Gang injunctions need only meet the lower "preponderance of the evidence" standard of civil law rather than the higher "beyond a reasonable doubt" standard of criminal law. Further, their targets are not entitled to an attorney, unless they are already on probation, because they do not initially face criminal charges. Critics also note that gang injunctions tend to be used in economically disadvantaged areas, where few people can afford to hire attorneys, and particularly in such gang neighborhoods adjacent to affluent communities, termed by Alonso as "privileged adjacency" (Alonso, 1999; Barajas, 2007).

The courts call into question the practice of serving gang injunctions on those who have not already been found in court to be a gang member, without providing them a means to contest the allegations. In November 2013, the Ninth Circuit Court of Appeals upheld a federal court's finding that a 2009 Orange County gang injunction could not be enforced, because it violated the plaintiff's rights by not allowing them to challenge their alleged gang member status (*Vasquez v. Rackauckas*, Case No. 8:09-cv-01090-VBF-RNB, November 5, 2013).

Gang Legislation

Gang enhancement sentencing has been used as a tool to fight gang crimes and violence in California. *Proposition 21*, also known as the *Gang Violence and Juvenile Crime Prevention Act of 1998* was passed in California in 2000. The purpose of the act was to increase penalties against juvenile delinquents ages 14 and up who commit a serious crime, including but not limited to murder, arson, robbery, and rape (Sanchez, 2010). The goal is to reduce the juvenile crime rate by decreasing and preventing gang activities and crime in order to have gang-free communities (Sanchez, 2010). Proposition 21 changed the handling of juvenile offenders by extending the age juveniles could be tried in adult court to 14 (from 16) and allowing prosecutors to directly file charges in adult court for some juvenile offenders (this last aspect was rescinded by Proposition 57 in 2016). It also provided for extra prison time for crimes committed in the furtherance of a gang.

Another example of gang legislation is the *STEP Act.* Officially called the *California Street Terrorism and Prevention Act*, the STEP Act criminalizes "a person who actively participates in any street gang with knowledge that its members engage in, or have engaged in, a pattern of criminal activity, and who willfully promotes, furthers, or assists in any felonious criminal conduct by members of that gang" (California Penal Code 186.22.) As a result, gang members find themselves facing additional sentencing enhancements as a result of their affiliation. An example of this practice is when gang members use a gun in a crime; they can receive an additional five years on their sentences as a result of their gang affiliation and an additional 10 years for their use of a weapon.

Other Criminal Justice Strategies

Other jurisdictions have changed the way in which they deal with gang crimes. In an effort to increase criminal justice efficiency and effectiveness, police, prosecutors, and probation work together as a team. One example of this practice is the Tri-Agency Resource Gang Enforcement Team (TARGET). The TARGET program emphasizes implementation of vertical prosecution (Bynum & Varano, 2003). TARGET has been implemented in cities such as Fullerton, Orange, and Westminster in Orange County, California.

Gang Prevention and Intervention

Researchers, policy makers, and law enforcement have realized that suppression alone has not worked. As Leap (2013, 106) noted, "Historically, incorporating community resources and community members in a gang-membership-prevention strategy has been overlooked." There are three levels of gang prevention (Greene, 2003). *Primary gang intervention* is aimed at youth before they get involved in gangs. It provides prevention programs to selectively targeted populations of youth at risk for gang membership. Whole populations are targeted, rather than individual participants. *Secondary gang intervention* targets high-risk individuals who have risk factors for joining gangs. These youth already have an exposure to gang life. Gang intervention tries to make the youth more resistant to gang membership. It requires more intensive efforts on the part of those trying to intervene (Greene, 2003). In *tertiary gang intervention*, the focus is on rehabilitation and redirecting delinquency. This approach is more effective after a gang member has engaged in violence or is at a critical decision-making stage (Huff, 2002).

One example of a multi-faceted gang prevention and intervention program is the Los Angeles Gang Reduction and Youth Development (GRYD) Program

(Curry, Decker, & Pyrooz, 2014). GRYD includes three main components: prevention, intervention case services, and crisis intervention. The prevention component includes services for at-risk youth aimed at preventing them from joining gangs. The intervention case services and programs assist gang youth to quit their gangs and lead productive lives in the community. The crisis intervention services are outreach activities designed to reduce gang conflicts and violence, and include responses to crisis situations (Dunworth et al., 2010; Curry, Decker, & Pyrooz, 2014).

The Los Angeles Police Department (LAPD) also has a gang prevention and intervention program called the Jeopardy Program. The Jeopardy Program targets at-risk youth and their parents and offers a variety of educational and physical projects from tutoring to martial arts. The goal of the program is to offer alternatives to gangs, including safe places where young people can meet and develop. Participating children are monitored monthly for at least one year.

Another example of a gang prevention and intervention program is the Orange County, California, Gang Reduction Intervention Partnership (OC GRIP). GRIP is an award-winning law enforcement partnership composed of the Orange County District Attorney's Office, Orange County Probation, Orange County Sheriff, local schools, and police agencies. It seeks to identify at-risk youth in an effort to increase school attendance and decrease gang involvement.

One example of a gang rehabilitative program involves increasing the opportunities and resources for education, employment, and opportunities for former gang members, particularly in economically depressed areas (Office of Juvenile Justice and Delinquency Program, 2008). Homeboy Industries, located in East Los Angeles and run by Father Gregory Boyle (otherwise known among his "homies" as "G-Dog") is one example of this type of programming (Fremon, 2006). Homeboy Industries began as an employment referral and economic development program. Today, there are several entities to this business, including Homeboy Bakery, Homeboy Silk Screens, Homeboy/Homegirl Merchandise, Homeboy Maintenance, and Homeboy Landscaping.

Conclusion

As you have learned in this chapter, the gang problem is a complex issue for the state of California and its criminal justice system. Gangs, gang members, and their activities exist throughout the state, in our communities as well as our prisons. Today, one of the major changes that is occurring throughout California to solve the gang problem is the use of comprehensive programs that include prevention and intervention techniques as well as traditional suppression approaches. As one of the major hotbeds of gang activity, Los Angeles and the surrounding regions have been at the forefront of these efforts. Additionally, top commanders in police agencies statewide have supported the inclusion of community stakeholders such as clergy, community activists, business owners, and gang street workers/interventionists to help solve gang conflicts. Together, these efforts illustrate the multi-faceted approaches to the identification, prevention, intervention, rehabilitation, and suppression of gangs in our communities.

Key Terms and Definitions

California Street Terrorism and Prevention Act—California Penal Code 186.20. State legislation passed in 1988 that criminalizes participation in any street gang with the knowledge that their members engage in gang activity.

Gain-oriented gang—A gangs that is primarily focused on making money.

Gangs—Generally defined as a group of adolescents or young adults who interact face-to-face, have a name, and are involved in illegal activity. These gangs are often turf- or territory-based gangs.

Gang crime—A crime that involves a gang member, a gang motive, or is motivated by gang concerns.

Gang intervention—Activities or programs that aim to steer gang-involved youth out of gangs. These programs are for youth who are not hard-core gang members.

Gang prevention—Activities or programs that address factors associated with gang membership to prevent youth from joining gangs. These programs often focus on pre-adolescent and non-gang involved youth.

Gang suppression—The arrest, prosecution, and incarceration of gang members. These activities are the domain of law enforcement.

Gang Violence and Juvenile Crime Prevention Act—A citizen initiative, Proposition 21, passed by California voters in 2000 that increased penalties against juvenile delinquents ages 14 and up who commit a serious crime.

Multiple marginality—Explains that how macro historical and macro structural forces lead to street socialization and gang participation.

Prison gangs—Criminal organizations that exist in penal institutions. Many of them are involved in criminal activity inside and outside the penal institutions. California prisons include: the Mexican Mafia, the Black Guerilla Family, Nuestra Family, and Aryan Brotherhood.

Turf-based gangs—Also referred to as territorial gangs, these gangs defend the area they claim as their territory against other gangs. African American gangs such as the Crips and the Bloods, and many of Hispanic gangs, are turf-based gangs.

Vertical prosecution—Allows a single prosecutor to follow a criminal case from start to finish.

Internet Websites

National Criminal Justice Reference Service: https://www.ncjrs.gov/
National Gang Center: http://www.nationalgangcenter.gov/
National Gang Crime Research Center: http://www.ngcrc.com/
Street Gangs in Los Angeles: http://www.streetgangs.com/
Los Angeles Police Department: www.lapdonline.org

Review Questions

1. What criterion have researchers and policymakers used to define gangs and gang members?
2. What are the different types of gangs?
3. What approaches have been used to address the gang problem?

Critical Thinking Questions

1. Civil gang injunctions prohibit named targets from participating in legal activities. What civil rights issue does this raise?
2. How would a social disorganization theorist attempt to solve the gang problem? What would be some of the critical issues they would address?
3. How does gang legislation reinforce the suppression technique?

References

Adamson, C. (2000). Defensive localism in white and black: A comparative history of European-American and African-American youth gangs. *Ethnic and Racial Studies, 23*(2), 272–298.

Alonso, A. (1999). *Territoriality among African-American street gangs* (Unpublished master's thesis). University of Southern California.

Alonso, A. (2004). Racialized identities and the formation of black gangs in Los Angeles. *Urban Geography, 27*(7), 658–674.

Alonso, A. (2014). Racialized identities and the formation of black gangs in Los Angeles. In C. Maxson, A. Egley, J. Miller, & M. W. Klein (Eds.), *The modern gang reader* (4th ed., pp. 230–243). New York, NY: Oxford University Press.

Barajas, F. (2007). An invading army: A civil gang injunction in a southern California Chicana/o community, *Latino Studies, 5*, 393–417.

Bhimji, F. (2004). "I want you to see us as a person and not as a gang member or a thug": Young people define their identities in the public sphere. *Journal of Theory and Research, 4*(1), 39–58.

Bjerregaard, B. (2003). Antigang legislation and its potential impact: The promises and the pitfalls, *Criminal Justice Policy Review, 14*, 171.

Brown, G. C. (1985). *Overreliance on prisons: Punishment theory and practice in the United States* (Unpublished master's thesis). University of California.

Brown, G. C. (1990). *Violence in California prisons: A test of the importation and deprivation models.* (Unpublished dissertation). University of California, Irvine.

Bugden, S. (Producer), & Hall, C. V. (Director). (2004). *Redemption* [Motion picture]. U.S.: Twentieth Century Fox Film Corporation.

Bynum, T. S., & Varano, S. P. (2003). The anti-gang initiative in Detroit: An aggressive enforcement approach to gangs. In S. H. Decker (Ed.), *Policing gangs and youth violence* (pp. 214–238). Belmont, CA: Wadsworth/Thompson Learning.

California Department of Justice. (2003). *Crime and delinquency in California.*

California Department of Justice. (2010). *Organized crime in California: 2010 Annual report to the Legislature.*

Camp, G. M., & Camp, C. G. (1985). *Prison gangs: Their extent, nature, and impact on prisons.* Washington, DC: U.S. Government Printing Office.

Chin, K.-L. (2006). Chinese gangs and extortion. In A. Egley Jr., C. L. Maxson, J. Miller, & M. W. Klein (Eds.), *The modern gang reader* (3rd ed., pp. 176–184). Los Angeles, CA: Roxbury.

Crawford, L. (2009). No way out: An analysis of exit processes for gang injunctions. *California Law Review, 97*, 161–193.

Cureton, S. R. (2009). Something wicked this way comes: A historical account of black gangsterism offers wisdom and warning for African American leadership. *Journal of Black Studies, 40*, 347–361.

Curry, G. D., Decker, S. H., & Pyrooz, D. C. (2014). *Confronting gangs: Crime and community.* New York, NY: Oxford University Press.

Dargis, M. (2009, January 23). Looking for the origins of the gangs of Los Angeles. *New York Times.*

Davis, M. (1992). *City of quartz: Excavating the future in Los Angeles*. New York, NY: Vintage.

Decker, S. H., & Curry, G. D. (2002). Gangs, gang homicides, and gang loyalty: Organized crimes or disorganized criminals. *Journal of Criminal Justice, 30,* 343–352.

Decker, S., & Van Winkle, B. (1996). Slinging dope: The role of gangs and gang members in drug sales. *Justice Quarterly, 11,* 583–604.

Delaney, T. (2014). *American street gangs*, Boston, MA: Pearson.

Dunworth, T., Hayeslip, D., Lyons, M., & Denver, M. (2010, October). *Evaluation of the Los Angeles gang reduction and youth development program: Final Y1 report.* Urban Institute.

Emch, T. (1973, September 9). The Chinatown murders. *San Francisco Sunday Examiner and Chronicle.*

Esbensen, F.-A., Brick, B. T., Melde, C., Tusinski, K., & Taylor, T. J. (2008). The role of race and ethnicity in gang membership. In F. V. Genert, D. Peterson, & I. Lien (Eds.), *Street gangs, migration and ethnicity* (pp. 117–139). Portland, OR: Willan.

Fearne, N. E., Decker, S. H., & Curry, G. D. (2001). Public policy responses to gangs: Evaluating the outcomes. In A. Egley Jr., C. L. Maxson, J. Miller, & M. W. Klein (Eds.), *The modern gang reader* (3rd ed., pp. 312–324). Los Angeles, CA: Roxbury.

Federal Bureau of Investigation. (2009). *National Gang Threat Assessment: 2009.* Washington, DC: U.S. Department of Justice, Federal Bureau of Investigation.

Fleisher, M. S., & Decker, S. H. (2001). An overview of the challenge of prison gangs, *Corrections Management Quarterly, 5*(1), 1–9.

Franco, C. (2008). *Youth gangs: Background, legislation, and issues* (CRS Report RL33400, updated January 25, 2008). Washington, DC: Congressional Research Service, Library of Congress.

Fremon, C. (2006). G-Dog and the homeboys. In A. Egley Jr., C. L. Maxson, J. Miller, & M. W. Klein (Eds.), *The modern gang reader* (3rd ed., pp. 325–337). Los Angeles: Roxbury.

Greene, J. R. (2003). Gangs, community policing and problem solving. In S. H. Decker (Ed.), *Gangs and youth violence* (pp. 3–16). Belmont, CA: Wadsworth Publishing.

Grogger, J. (2002). The effects of civil gang injunctions on reported violent crime: Evidence from Los Angeles County, *Journal of Law and Economics, 45*(1), 69–90.

Hagedorn, J. (2005, May). The global impact of gangs. *Journal of Contemporary Criminal Justice, 21*(2), 153–169.

Harris, K. D. (2014). *Gangs beyond borders: California and the fight against transnational organized crime.* Sacramento, CA: California Attorney General's Office.

Hennigan, K. M., & Sloane, D. (2013). Improving civil gang injunctions. *Criminology and Public Policy, 12*(1), 7–41

Howell, J. C. (2012). *Gangs in America's communities.* Thousand Oaks, CA: Sage Publications.

Howell, J. C., & Griffiths, E. A. (2016). *Gangs in America's communities* (2nd ed.). Thousand Oaks, CA: Sage Publications

Howell, J. C., & Moore, J. P. (2010). *History of street gangs in the United States.* Tallahassee, FL: National Gang Center.

Huff, C. R. (2002). *Gangs in America III.* Thousand Oaks, CA: Sage Publications.

Hunt, G., Riegel, S., Morales, T., & Waldorf, D. (1993, August). Changes in prison culture: Prison gangs and the case of the "Pepsi" generation. *Social Problems, 40*(3), 398–409.

Ingraham, B. L., & Wellford, C. F. (1987). The totality of conditions test in Eighth-Amendment litigation. In S. D. Gottfredson & S. McConville (Eds.), *America's correctional crisis: Prison populations and public policy.* New York, NY: Greenwood Press.

Jacobs, J. B. (1974). Street gangs behind bars. *Social Problems, 21*, 395–409.

Jacobs, J. B. (2001). Focusing on prison gangs. *Correctional Management Quarterly, 5*(1), vi–vii.

Katz, C. M., Webb, V. J., & Armstrong, T. A. (2003, March). Fear of crime: A test of alternative theoretical models, *Justice Quarterly, 20*(1).

Klein, M. W. (1995). *The American street gang.* New York: Oxford University Press.

Klein, M. W. (2000). Forward. In G. W. Knox (Ed.), *An introduction to gangs.* Berrien Springs, MI: Vande Vere Publishing, Ltd.

Klein, M. S., & Maxson, C. L. (2006). *Street gang patterns and policies.* New York, NY: Oxford University Press.

Knox, G. W. (2000). *Introduction to gangs.* Peotone, IL: New Chicago Press.

Landre, R., Miller, M., & Porter, D. (1997). *Correctional contexts: Contemporary and classical readings.* Los Angeles, CA: Roxbury Pub.

Leap, J. (2013). What should be done in the community to prevent gang-joining? In T. R. Simon, N. M. Ritter, & R. R. Mahendra (Eds.), *Changing course: Preventing gang membership.* Washington, DC: U.S. Department of Justice.

Loo, C. K. (1976). *The emergence of San Francisco Chinese juvenile gangs from the 1950s to the present* (Unpublished master's thesis). San Jose State University.

Lopez, J., & Mirande, A. (1990). The gangs of Orange County: A critique and synthesis of social policy, *Aztlan: A Journal of Chicano Studies, 19*(1), 125–146.

Lynskey, D. (1998). Gangs in America. *Journal of Contemporary Criminal Justice, 14*(1), 91–93

Marquart, J. W., & Sorenson, J. R. (Eds.). (1997). *Correctional contexts: Contemporary and classical readings.* Los Angeles, CA: Roxbury Pub.

Maxson, C. L., Hennigan, K., & Sloane, D. C. (2003). For the sake of the neighborhood? Civil gang injunctions as a gang intervention tool in southern California. In A. Egley Jr., C. L. Maxson, J. Miller, & M. W. Klein (Eds.), *The modern gang reader* (2nd ed., pp. 312–324). Los Angeles: Roxbury.

Maxson, C. L., Hennigan, K. M., & Sloane, D. C. (2005). "It's getting crazy out there": Can a civil gang injunction change a community? *Criminology and Public Policy, 4*(3), 577–605.

McGloin, J. M. (2005). Policy and intervention considerations of a network analysis of street gangs, *Criminology and Public Policy, 4*(3), 607–635.

Montgomery, R. H., Jr., & Crews, G. A. (1998). *A history of correctional violence: An examination of reported causes of riots and disturbances.* Lanham, MD: American Correctional Association.

Moore, J. W. (1978). *Homeboys—Gangs, drugs and prison in the barrios of Los Angeles.* Philadelphia, PA: Temple University Press.

Moore, J. W., & Vigil, D. (1993). Barrios in transition. In J. W. Moore & R. Pinderhughes (Eds.), *In the barrios: Latinos and the underclass debate,* 27–49. New York, NY: Russell Sage Foundation.

O'Deane, M. D., & Morreale, S. A. (2011). Evaluation of the effectiveness of gang injunctions in California, *The Journal of Criminal Justice Research, 2*(1), 1–32.

Office of Juvenile Justice and Delinquency Prevention. (2008). *Best practices to address community gang problems: OJJDP's comprehensive gang model.* Washington, DC: U.S. Department of Justice.

Orlando-Morningstar, D. (1997). Prison gangs. *Special Needs Offender Bulletin, 2,* 1–13.

Perkins, U. E. (1987). *Explosion of Chicago's black street gangs: 1900 to the present.* Chicago, IL: Third World Press.

Sanchez, M. Y. (2010). *Policy analysis of the gang violence and juvenile crime prevention act of 1998: A thesis presented to the department of social work.* California State University, Long Beach.

Simi, P. (2006). Hate groups or street gangs? The emergence of racist skinheads. In J. F. Short & L. A. Hughes. (2006). *Studying youth gangs.* Lanham, MD: Alta Mira Press.

Spergel, I. A. (1984). Violent gangs in Chicago. *In search of social policy, 58,* 199–225.

Spergel, I. A. (1995). *The youth gang problem: A community approach.* New York, NY: Oxford University Press.

Spergel, I. A., & Curry, G. D. (1993). The national youth gang survey: A research and development process. In A. Goldstein & C. R. Huff (Eds.), *The gang intervention handbook,* 359–400. Champaign, IL: Research Press.

Taylor, J. (2002). California's Proposition 21: A case of juvenile injustice. *Southern California Law Review, 75,* 983–1020.

Thrasher, F. M. (1927/1963). *The gang.* (Abridged ed. 1963). Chicago, IL: University of Chicago Press.

Tita, G., & Abrahamse, A. (2004). *Gang homicide in LA, 1981-2001* (p. 3). California Attorney General's Office.

Tobin, K. S. (2008). *Gangs: An individual and group perspective.* Upper Saddle River, NJ: Prentice Hall.

Tracy, C. A. (1980). Race, crime and social policy. *Crime and Social Justice, 14,* 11–25.

United States Government Accounting Office. (2009). *Combating gangs: Better coordination and performance measurement would help clarify roles of federal agencies and strengthen assessment of efforts,* GAO-09-708.

Valdez, A. (2011). *Gangs across America: History and sociology.* San Clemente, CA: LawTech Publishing.

Valdez, A., & Sifaneck, S. J. (2004). Getting high and getting by: Dimensions of drug selling behaviors among Mexican gang members in south Texas. *Journal of Research in Crime and Delinquency, 41*(1), 82–105.

Vigil, J. D. (1988). *Barrio gangs: Street life and identity in Southern California.* Austin, TX: University of Texas Press.

Vigil, J. D. (1990). Cholos and gangs: Culture change and street youth in Los Angeles. In C. R. Huff (Ed.), *Gangs in America* (pp. 116–128). Newbury Park, CA: Sage.

Vigil, J. D. (2002). *A rainbow of gangs: Street cultures in the mega-city.* Austin: University of Texas Press.

Vigil, J. D. (2004). Street baptism: Chicano gang initiation. In F.-A. Esbensen, S. G. Tibbets, & L. Gaines (Eds.), *American youth gangs at the millennium* (pp. 218–228). Long Grove, IL: Waveland Press.

Villaraigosa, A. (1992, January 20). For safe parks, put gangs on the peace path. *Los Angeles Times.*

Whitmer, J., & Anker, D. (1997). The history of the gang injunction in California. Appendix M in *S.A.G.E.: Strategy against gang environments:*

A handbook for community prosecution. Los Angeles, CA: Office of the District Attorney, County of Los Angeles.

Wood, J., & Alleyne, E. (2010). Street gang theory and research: Where are we now and where do we go from here? *Aggression and Violent Behavior, 15*, 100–111.

Cases Cited

People v. Acuna, 14 Cal.4th 1090 (1997)

Vasquez v. Rackauckas, Case No. 8:09-cv-01090-VBF-RNB, November 5, 2013

Chapter 11

Spotlight on California Crime Policy: Guns, Drugs, and Sex

Julius Wachtel, Dixie Koo, and Heather Brown[1]

Learning Objectives

After reading the chapter, students should be able to:

- Demonstrate an understanding of California's unique firearms laws and how they compare to federal statutes and those of other states.
- Discuss why California has such conservative gun laws and such liberal drug laws.
- Explain how drug arrests and incarceration for drug crimes differ between California and the nation.
- Describe California's current drug policies and move towards harm reduction strategies.
- Demonstrate an understanding of California's various sex crimes laws.

In Chapter 1, an oft-repeated joke popular in criminology circles about the causes of crimes was offered and bears repeating here.

Q: What causes crime?

A: Law!

Now for introductory students of criminal justice, this may be confusing. To break it down a bit more, crime is socially constructed. That is to say, something does not violate the penal code (or become a crime) until the California legislature, its voters, the California courts, or all three say it does. The crime

---

1. The firearms and public policy section was authored by Julius Wachtel, the drug policy section was authored by Dixie Koo, and the sex crimes policy section was authored by Heather Brown.

cyber-harassment discussed below didn't exist until the Internet and the rise of social media, and only then *after* the state legislature passed a law declaring it a crime. Further, as discussed in Chapter 2, domestic violence was once understood as a husband's perpetration of violence against his wife that was so severe as to cause trauma. However, current California law reflects our changing societal understanding of what it means to be a perpetrator and victim of violence—therefore it is when one partner perpetrates severe physical violence, sexual violence, or combinations of these, against another partner. California's legislature and voters through the initiative process (as discussed in Chapter 3) make law to guide society towards a path that is preferred. Law serves as a form of social control—it reinforces social norms, or behaviors we believe are desirable (see Chapter 4). Guiding these laws are societal beliefs about conduct that should be rewarded and conduct that should be punished. As such, California's policies towards firearms, drugs, and sex reflect Californians' beliefs on how to best secure our state, promote liberties under the state and federal constitutions, and balance the needs of society and law enforcement. For the purposes of this chapter, the words *policy* and *law* will be used interchangeably, and the laws referred to below reflect the policy choices of Californians as well.

Firearms and Public Policy

Except in areas such as foreign relations and the national defense, where the federal government enjoys exclusive jurisdiction, states and localities are free to draft legislation that goes beyond (but does not conflict with) U.S. law. Many jurisdictions have enacted gun control measures, with California's being recently ranked as the most comprehensive in the nation.[2] Indeed, they are far more inclusive than the Gun Control Act of 1968, the federal government's effort to regulate the possession and sale of firearms. Indeed, the Golden State's approach seems particularly audacious. In addition to mandating that all gun transfers, including those between private parties, go through a records check and be perpetually recorded in a statewide database, state law addresses even the minutiae, going so far as to require that pistols imprint their serial numbers on cartridge casings to help identify those used in crimes (California Penal Code 31910).[3]

---

2. Law Center to Prevent Gun Violence, at http://smartgunlaws.org/scorecard2016/

3. Enforcement has been suspended while objections by the National Shooting Sports Foundation and other groups make their way through the courts. See *National Shooting Sports Foundation v. State of California*, 2016.

At a time when ideological quarrels make gun control a very hard sell, California seems unbowed. To find out why we will examine its firearms laws, compare them with federal statutes and those of other states and localities, and discuss the factors that have placed the Golden State on its special trajectory.

State Gun Laws: The California Model

California regulates the possession, transfer, and sale of firearms by private individuals and gun dealers. It also addresses the lethality of firearms with an assault weapons statute that limits magazine capacity and controls the characteristics of weapons that may be sold and possessed.

Gun possession by minors is strictly controlled (California Penal Code 29610-29615, 27500-27590). Persons under the age of twenty-one may not purchase handguns. With exceptions involving parental supervision and sporting events, they may not possess or be furnished a handgun. Similar restrictions govern the possession and transfer of rifles to persons under eighteen.

California prohibits convicted felons and drug addicts from having firearms. Persons convicted of certain violent misdemeanors are prohibited from possessing firearms for a period of ten years. Individuals subject to a restraining order may not have firearms for the period of its duration (California Penal Code 29800-29825).

Carrying a concealed firearm is tightly regulated (California Penal Code 26150-26225). Police chiefs and sheriffs "may" issue a permit to do so if they find "good cause." But exactly what constitutes "good cause" is undefined. For example, in the state's most populous jurisdiction, Los Angeles County, the sheriff has officially defined "good cause" as the presence of a clear and present danger to life or limb which cannot be otherwise mitigated (LASD, 2017). This broad grant of discretion has led to great variability in granting permits, which are reportedly seldom issued in the larger metropolitan areas (Maddaus, 2013). In September 2016, the governor signed a bill that seeks to make the process uniform throughout the state (California Penal Code 26175).

Open (unconcealed) carry of loaded firearms was banned in 1967 (California Penal Code 25850; Skelton, 2007). Laws passed in 2012 (relating to handguns) and 2013 (relating to long guns) extended the prohibition to include unloaded firearms. Barring a few exceptions, they may not be carried on one's person or in a vehicle in incorporated areas (California Penal Code 26350, 26400). Episodes involving the violent misuse of guns stolen from cars led to a 2016 law that requires peace officers and concealed-carry permittees who leave their guns in their vehicles to place them in the trunk or in a concealed and locked container (California Penal Code 25140).

Federal law regulates gun sales by licensed dealers. But it allows gun transactions between private parties, requiring neither record checks nor paperwork. Not so in California, where all gun transfers must go through a dealer. Buyers must present an authorized form of photo identification, and their identities are checked to ensure that they are not prohibited by federal or state law from acquiring a firearm. California (but not the federal government) also requires that ten days elapse before guns are actually delivered (California Penal Code 27540, 27545, 28050-28070). This delay is intended as a "cooling-off" period and to provide sufficient time to resolve any discrepancies uncovered during the records-check process.[4] As of January 1, 2018, ammunition may only be sold through licensed dealers; background checks for ammunition purchases will be required beginning in July 2019 (California Penal Code 16151, 30312 & 30352).

In 1924, dealers began reporting handgun sales to state authorities. This data, which is now computerized, helps identify the owners of handguns seized by police (California Penal Code 12025-12027, 12051-12053). As of January 2014, records of long gun transactions were also included (California Penal Code 11106).[5] Since California law requires that even private firearms transfers go through a dealer, the state is well on its way to creating a comprehensive registry of guns in private hands.

Handgun buyers may purchase only one handgun per month (California Penal Code 27535, 31610-31670) . Before taking delivery they must also pass an examination that covers gun laws, responsibilities of gun ownership, and the use of deadly force. Private persons may sell only five handguns each year, and long guns only occasionally and "without regularity" (California Penal Code 16730, 26525).

Gun shows, where dealers and members of the public congregate to buy and sell guns, have long been criticized by gun control advocates as providing ready opportunities for the acquisition of firearms by criminals (Henigan, 2009). As restrictive as California gun laws may seem, regulating shows is left to localities, and many such events take place each year, mostly in rural areas. Private persons face quantity and other limits on gun show activities. As they

---

4. Gun stores throughout the U.S. perform records checks by calling in buyer information to state-run centralized offices. (California gun dealers swipe buyer driver licenses through card readers.) Results are usually instantaneous. In most states guns can be immediately transferred, but should an issue arise, federal law imposes delays of up to three days before delivery. See http://www.fbi.gov/about-us/cjis/nics/general-information/fact-sheet.

5. Persons bringing guns from other states must submit equivalent information.

would otherwise, they must pay dealers to process transfers and run background checks on buyers, with many licensees attending shows for precisely this purpose.[6]

California has long outlawed machine guns (California Penal Code 32625).[7] In 1990, the state enacted an assault weapons law banning AR-15 and AK-47 type rifles as well as other semiautomatic rifles that had at least one of six named features such as a folding stock or pistol grip and could accept a detachable magazine (California Penal Code 30500-30530, 32310-32390).[8] Ammunition capacity of rifles with a fixed magazine was also limited to ten rounds. Similar provisions were applied to handguns and shotguns. Sales and transfer restrictions were imposed on magazines that could accept more than ten rounds. In 2016, the "named features" provision was dropped from the definition of an assault weapon. All lawfully possessed semiautomatic rifles with detachable (or readily detachable) magazines must be given up or registered as assault weapons by January 1, 2018 (California Penal Code 30515). As of July 1, 2017, the mere possession of high-capacity magazines became illegal (California Penal Code 32310).

These actions did not pass without notice. On April 24, 2017, the NRA announced it would back a series of federal lawsuits challenging the constitutionality of California gun laws.[9] On that day the California Rifle and Pistol Association (CRPA) and seven individuals filed the first, taking on the state's assault weapons restrictions.[10] In essence, the plaintiffs argue that neither a detachable magazine nor any of the banned features make firearms so extraordinary that it justifies removing them from the protections afforded by the Second Amendment.

A Brief History of Gun Laws

Two and a half years after the U.S. Constitution came into effect, lingering fears of overreaching by the central government led to enactment of ten amend-

---

6. Dealers often treat private-party transactions as consignment sales, taking custody of weapons and giving them to their buyers once California's ten-day waiting period has lapsed.

7. Fully automatic weapons ("machine guns") fire repeatedly with a single pull of the trigger, until the ammunition supply is exhausted. Other firearms require a separate trigger pull for each round. Those called "semi-automatic" chamber the next projectile without user intervention.

8. Rimfire rifles such as the ubiquitous .22 are exempt.

9. https://www.nraila.org/articles/20170424/lawsuit-filed-against-californias-assault-weapons-control-act

10. *Rupp v. Becerra* (U.S. District Court, Central District of California, no. 8:17-cv-007464).

ments collectively known as the Bill of Rights. Individuals were granted a number of freedoms, including to pray, speak, and assemble. The Second Amendment also guaranteed a tangible means of defending against government tyranny:

> A well regulated Militia, being necessary to the security of a free State, the right of the people to keep and bear Arms, shall not be infringed.

More than a century later, in 1911, the murder of New York City Mayor William Gaynor led to the nation's first significant firearms law, New York State's "Sullivan Act," which required that all handguns be licensed, even those kept at home (Spitzer, 1995, p. 13). Over the next two decades a few states imposed lesser restrictions on handguns (Vernick & Hepburn, 2003, p. 370–379). North Carolina required a sheriff's permit to buy a handgun, while Michigan mandated registration and background checks. California took an intermediate position, limiting handgun transactions to dealers and requiring that sales be reported to the state. To keep outsiders from circumventing local gun laws, the federal government stepped in, outlawing shipping handguns via the U.S. mails (Zimring, 1975, p. 136).

In 1934, Prohibition-era violence led Congress to pass the National Firearms Act, which imposed special taxes and registration requirements on machineguns and other "gangster-type" weapons (48 Stat. 1236).[11] To ward off threatened action against conventional firearms, the National Rifle Association helped sponsor the Federal Firearms Act of 1938 (Zimring, 1975, p. 139–141). It required that gun dealers be licensed, keep sales records, and refrain from knowingly delivering firearms to violent felons. However, no special resources were allocated for enforcement.

For the next quarter-century gun control returned to the back-burner. Then the unthinkable happened. On November 22, 1963, President John F. Kennedy was shot and killed while riding in a Dallas motorcade. His assailant, Lee Harvey Oswald, 23, had used an assumed name to obtain the murder weapon, a rifle, by mail order from a Chicago dealer (President's Commission, 1964).[12] While trying to escape, Oswald fatally wounded Dallas police officer J. D. Tippit with a handgun. He also purchased this weapon from out of state, also under an alias. (Due to the ban on mailing handguns, it was shipped by private carrier.)

---

11. 18 U.S.C. 922(o), enacted in 1986, prohibits private persons from possessing previously unregistered machine guns and rules out the manufacture of new machine guns for civilian use.

12. While a reservist Oswald defected to the Soviet Union and unofficially renounced his citizenship. He later returned to the U.S., without apparently incurring any penalty.

President Kennedy's murder did not bring on new federal gun laws. That would take another five years and two more high-profile assassinations. On April 4, 1968, one day after delivering his "mountaintop" speech, Martin Luther King, Jr. was fatally shot by James Earl Ray, 39, an escapee from the Missouri State Penitentiary, where he had been serving time for robbery. Ray had purchased the rifle used to kill Dr. King at a local gun shop, using an alias (House Select Committee, 1979, p. 287–296).

Two months later, on June 5, 1968, Robert F. Kennedy, brother of the late president, was shot and killed at a Los Angeles hotel by Sirhan Sirhan, a 24-year-old Middle Eastern immigrant with no criminal record (Moldea, 1997, p. 80). Sirhan used a .22-caliber revolver that had gone through several hands after its purchase at a gun store. Sirhan left behind a notebook filled with threats against Kennedy ("RFK must be assassinated"). At trial, Sirhan's lawyer unsuccessfully argued that his client was mentally ill (Moldea, 1997, p. 105–108, 129).

This time the legislative process moved swiftly. In October 1968, President Lyndon Johnson signed the Gun Control Act of 1968 into law (P.L. 90-618, 82 Stat. 1213). Going far beyond existing law, it regulated the distribution of firearms from manufacture through retail sale and set qualifications for gun dealers, buyers, and possessors. However, private transactions were not affected.

Individuals buying guns from dealers were required to appear in person and attest in writing that they were not prohibited from acquiring firearms. Manufacturers, distributors, and dealers had to keep records that would enable authorities to trace a recovered firearm to their buyers. Dealers were forbidden from selling long guns to persons under eighteen or handguns to those under twenty-one. Firearms could not be knowingly sold to, purchased, or possessed by felons, fugitives, illegal aliens, dishonorably discharged veterans, persons adjudicated as mentally defective, or those who had renounced their citizenship.[13] Criminal record checks were not required unless mandated by state law, so most sales effectively remained on the honor system. Dealers also retained all paperwork and no centralized sales registry was created.[14]

Concerns about gun lethality were only partially addressed. While machineguns and firearms larger than .50 caliber were essentially outlawed,

---

13. Under 18 U.S.C. §922(g), prosecution for illegal possession requires proof that a firearm affected commerce, meaning that it had crossed state lines in the past. That is usually demonstrated by citing the place of the gun's manufacture. In 1996, the list of prohibited buyers was expanded to include those subject to a restraining order or who had been convicted of misdemeanor domestic violence. See 18 U.S.C. §922(g) (8) and (9).

14. Yearly congressional appropriations typically include language barring ATF from creating a gun sales registry.

no controls were placed on the ballistics, rapid-fire capability, or magazine capacity of conventional weapons (18 U.S.C. 921-924). Enforcement was assigned to an expanded Internal Service unit that regulated the alcohol and tobacco industries. In 1972, it would become the Bureau of Alcohol, Tobacco and Firearms, a separate agency within the Treasury Department.[15]

Gun Violence and Gun Policy

America's homicide rate began a steady climb in the late 1960s. It reached 7.9 per 100,000 population in 1970 and 10.2 in 1980, then fluctuated near that peak for more than a decade (Fox & Zawitz, 2007). Most deaths were caused by a firearm. In 1993, firearms were responsible for 70% of homicides (17,075/24,530); of these, 82% (13,981) were by a handgun.

Much of the violence was fueled by drugs. Inner-city black youths were especially affected (Blumstein, 1995, p. 10–36). Between 1983 and 1993 the homicide victimization rate of white males 14–17 increased 139%, from 3.8 to 9.1 per 100,000. For blacks the jump, from 21.4 to 76.4 per 100,000, a 257% increase, reflected beginning and ending rates about eight times larger.

As the violence escalated, states previously silent on gun issues began requiring permits and/or criminal record checks, mostly for handgun sales (Vernick & Hepburn, 2003, Table 9A-3). Laws to this effect were passed in Rhode Island in 1959, Maryland in 1966, Illinois in 1968, Hawaii and New Jersey pre-1970, Minnesota in 1977, Missouri in 1981, Iowa in 1990, and Nebraska in 1991. California began requiring criminal record checks for handgun sales by licensed dealers in 1969. In 1991, it mandated checks for all types of firearms, whether acquired from dealers or private parties.[16]

Some challenges were mounted against handguns as a class. Cheap handguns known as "Saturday night specials" were banned by South Carolina in 1973, Illinois in 1974, Hawaii and Minnesota in 1975, and Maryland in 1990 (Vernick & Hepburn, 2003, Table 9A-2). Two cities beset by gun violence took it further. In 1976, the District of Columbia prohibited the possession of handguns. Six years later Chicago followed suit. Both laws were eventually annulled by the Supreme Court as violations of the Second Amendment (*District of Columbia v. Heller*, 2008; *McDonald v. Chicago*, 2010).

---

15. In 2002, ATF was placed under the Justice Department and renamed the Bureau of Alcohol, Tobacco, Firearms and Explosives.

16. Since 1991, California has required (with limited exceptions) that all firearms transfers go through a dealer.

On March 30, 1981, John Hinckley, Jr. fired six shots from a .22-caliber revolver at President Ronald Reagan as he exited a Washington, DC, hotel. His bullets wounded Reagan, Press Secretary James Brady, police officer Thomas Delahanty, and Secret Service agent Timothy McCarthy (FBI, 1981). Hinckley, a mentally troubled 25-year-old drifter, had bought the gun at a pawnshop. He was found not guilty by reason of insanity and committed to a mental hospital.

Twelve years later, on November 30, 1993, President William Clinton signed into law the Brady Handgun Violence Prevention Act (18 U.S.C. 921, et seq.) Taking a step beyond the existing honor system, it required criminal record checks of persons buying handguns from licensed dealers and, as of 1998, of long gun buyers as well. One year later came the federal assault weapons law (18 U.S.C. 922).[17] It banned the further manufacture of a host of weapons including the popular Colt AR-15, semi-automatic firearms with a detachable magazine and two or more of certain features, such as a handgrip and barrel shroud, and ammunition magazines with capacities exceeding ten rounds.

By then California had more than caught up. All firearms transactions, including those between private parties, had to go through a dealer and were subject to a criminal records check and a fifteen-day waiting period (since lowered to ten.) A comprehensive assault weapons ban, prompted by a massacre of schoolchildren in Stockton, was also in effect (Spitzer, 1995, p. 152).[18]

Between 1994 and 2005, America's homicide rate plunged 38%, from 9.0 to 5.6 per 100,000 population (Fox & Zawitz, 2007). In 2010, it was at 5.3, a number not seen since the mid-1960s (CDC, 2013, p. 14). Yet many cities continued to experience disturbing levels of gun violence. Mass shootings took place with disturbing regularity. Among these was the April 2007 gunning down of 32 and wounding of 17 at Virginia Tech, the April 2009 murder of 13 and wounding of four in Binghamton, New York, and the shooting death of six and wounding of four at a January 2011 Arizona congressional event (McFadden, 2009; Virginia Tech Review Panel, 2007; Nagourney, 2011). In each case the assailants used pistols they legally purchased at retail. They were also male and reportedly mentally disturbed.

In 2012, two bloody episodes shook the nation. In July, a graduate student used an AR-15 type rifle, a pistol, and a shotgun—all legally bought—to gun

---

17. Effective September 13, 1994, expired September 13, 2004. Available at http://www.gpo.gov/fdsys/pkg/BILLS-103hr3355enr/pdf/BILLS-103hr3355enr.pdf

18. Five children were killed and more than thirty persons were wounded. For a detailed account see www.mercurynews.com/2014/01/16/stockton-shooting-25-years-later-city-cant-forget-its-worst-day/

down 12 and wound 62 at a Colorado movie theater (Dao, 2012; Goode, 2012). That December a Connecticut man shot his mother dead with her AR-15 type rifle, then murdered 20 children and six adults at an elementary school (Kleinfield, 2013). Both perpetrators were mentally troubled. But this time their arsenals included military-style rifles. More recently, on September 16, 2013, a mentally troubled 34-year-old man shot and killed 12 and wounded three at a naval office building in Washington, DC (Shear, 2013). His weapons? A shotgun he had just purchased at a Virginia gun store and a pistol he took from one of his victims, a security guard. What the shooter lacked was the AR-15 rifle that he had practiced with, as Virginia law restricts selling those to in-state residents (Schmidt, 2013).

Political reactions have reflected long-standing positions. Democrats, who generally favor gun control, moved—so far, unsuccessfully—to revive the federal assault weapons ban and expand record checks to include private sales (Goode, 2013). In stark contrast, a host of "red" states (meaning, Republican) passed laws that, among other things, liberalized concealed carry.

What happened in Connecticut and Colorado, two states deeply affected by the violence, is especially interesting. Deeply blue Connecticut enacted universal background checks, restricted magazine capacities to ten rounds, and prohibited sale of assault weapons, including AR-15 and AK-47 type rifles (Connecticut General Statutes, Chaps. 529 and 943).[19] Barely blue Colorado introduced records checks for private gun transfers and restricted magazine capacities to fifteen rounds (Colorado Revised Statutes 18-12-112 and 18-12-301).[20] Blowback was swift. Two of the measure's backers, including the president of the Colorado Senate, were promptly recalled (Healey, 2013).

In California, one of the bluest of states, gun control seemingly picked up steam. Although there is no state gun registry *per se*, requiring that long-gun transfers be recorded in "DROS," a statewide gun sales database searchable by police, comes close. Yet for a time it seemed that the momentum was slowing. In October 2013, California Governor Jerry Brown vetoed several gun control bills. Among these was a measure to ban the sale of semiautomatic weapons that can accept detachable magazines, and another that would have allowed violence-troubled Oakland to regulate firearms, a privilege currently reserved to the state (Romney, 2013). Then in February 2014 a divided panel of the

---

19. All top state officials were Democrats, and the legislature was heavily so (22-14 Senate; 99-52 House).

20. While Colorado's governor and lieutenant governor were Democrats, three top executive positions were filled by Republicans. After the recall the Senate's democratic majority became razor-thin (18-17 Senate; 37-28 House).

Ninth Circuit Court of Appeals ruled that letting local officials deny concealed carry permits to applicants who fail to demonstrate "good cause" trespassed on the Second Amendment (*Peruta v. County of San Diego*, 2014).

Then came the December 2015 massacre in San Bernardino, California, where 14 innocent persons were killed and 22 were wounded. Six months later, on June 9, the full Ninth Circuit reversed *Peruta*, holding that "that there is no Second Amendment right for members of the general public to carry concealed firearms in public" (*Peruta v. County of San Diego*, 2016). Three days later, 49 persons were killed and 53 were wounded at an Orlando, Florida, nightclub.[21] Within a month Governor Brown signed a flurry of new gun measures. Commercially available .223-caliber semi-automatic rifles had been used by the assailants in San Bernardino and Orlando. What's more, both San Bernardino weapons, which were legal only because their magazines were purportedly "fixed," were equipped with an aftermarket "bullet button," a simple device that allows users to easily switch out magazines with the tip of a bullet.[22] In response, the law was revised to require that the removal of fixed magazines require "disassembly of the firearm action" (California Penal Code 30515). As one might expect, though, workarounds are already being marketed.[23] And thus the struggle continues.

Drug Policy

Drug-Related Offenses and the Criminal Justice System: The U.S. and California

Drug-related offenses are defined as the violation of laws regulating the possession, distribution, or manufacture of illegal drugs. This includes the possession or use, cultivation, production, and sale of illegal drugs and drug-related paraphernalia. Drug offenses can be at the felony or misdemeanor level.

Nationwide, law enforcement made an estimated 10,797,088 arrests in 2015 (FBI, 2016b). Of the 1,488,707 arrests for drug law violations, 84% were for possession of a controlled substance and only 16% were for the sale or manufacturing of a drug. Of the 84% arrested for possession, 39% were arrested

---

21. For detailed accounts see http://projects.sbsun.com/san-bernardino-terror-one-year/ and http://www.orlandosentinel.com/news/pulse-orlando-nightclub-shooting/investigation/
22. https://www.thetrace.org/2015/12/san-bernardino-shooting-bullet-button/
23. Among these is the "Patriot Mag Release." See http://www.breitbart.com/california/2016/07/06/california-gun-laws-patriot-mag-release/

Figure 11.1. U.S. Arrests for Illicit Drugs 2015

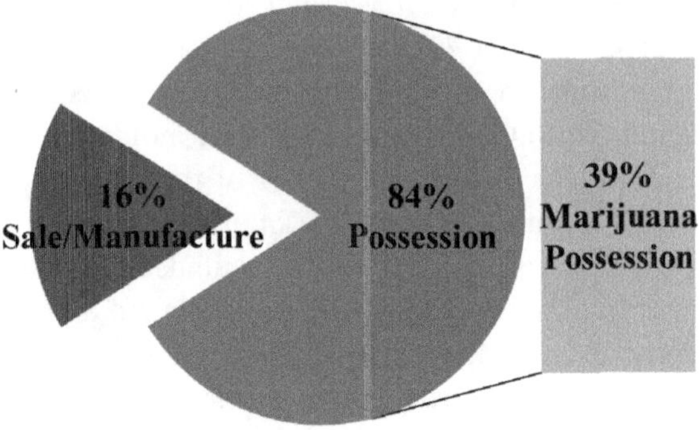

Source: Federal Bureau of Investigation, 2015

for marijuana possession (see Figure 11.1 above). Therefore, the majority of possession arrests nationwide were for marijuana. In addition, approximately 43.2% of all drug offenders were arrested for a marijuana law violation, and 89% of those charged with marijuana law violations were arrested for possession only (FBI, 2016a).

With regards to California, law enforcement made an estimated 1,158,479 arrests in 2015. Of these arrests, approximately 18% were for drug-related offenses (4% at the felony level, 14% at the misdemeanor level) (California Office of the Attorney General, 2016). Looking at it slightly differently, drug-related offenses comprised 14% of all felony arrests and 20% of all misdemeanor arrests in California in 2015. These percentages have flipped in comparison to previous years, when drug offenses were much more likely to be felonies (see Table 11.1) (California Office of the Attorney General, 2011, 2016). The significant decline in misdemeanor drug arrests following 2010 can be attributed to the marijuana decriminalization policy implemented in 2011 (further discussed in a section below). In 2015, there was a significant increase in misdemeanor drug arrests and a decrease in felony drug arrests as compared to previous years due to Proposition 47 (further discussed below). Similar to the U.S. arrest data, drug-related offenses in California comprised the largest proportion of all arrest categories (see Table 11.1 & Figure 11.2).

When comparing prisoners across all U.S. state jurisdiction levels to California, the composition of California's prisoner population by offense does significantly differ. For example, drug offenders comprised 8% of the California

Table 11.1

CALIFORNIA

Estimated Number of Felony and Misdemeanor Drug Arrests 2005–2015

	2005	2006	2007	2008	2009	2010	2011	2012	2013	2014	2015
Felony Drug Arrests of Total Arrests	10.8%	10.3%	9.6%	8.6%	8.3%	8.9%	9.3%	9.9%	11.5%	11.4%	3.9%
Misdemeanor Drug Arrests of Total Arrests	10.0%	9.8%	9.9%	9.44%	9.4%	9.5%	6.2%	6.5%	6.8%	7.7%	14.2%
All Drug Arrests of Total Arrests	20.80%	20.12%	19.35%	17.91%	17.63%	18.32%	15.44%	16.39%	18.26%	19.10%	18.06%
Drug Offense of Felony Arrests Only	29.72%	28.90%	27.46%	25.84%	25.44%	27.04%	27.47%	28.15%	30.97%	31.15%	14.18%
Drug Offense of Misdemeanor Arrests Only	15.69%	15.28%	15.08%	13.98%	13.87%	14.07%	9.32%	10.00%	10.77%	12.13%	19.52%

Sources: California Office of the Attorney General, 2011, 2016

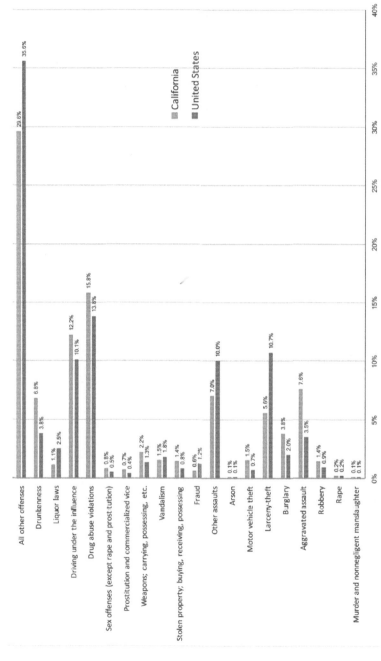

Figure 11.2. Estimated number of U.S. and California arrests, 2015

Source: Federal Bureau of Investigation, 2015b, 2015c

Figure 11.3. Prison Populations: State, Federal, & CA

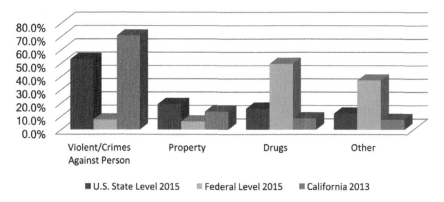

Sources: California Department of Corrections and Rehabilitation, 2014 (latest data available) & Bureau of Justice Statistics, 2016

prisoner population compared to 16% of the U.S. state level prisoner population (see Figure 11.3). Property offenders (for both California (13.5%) and all state prisoners (19%)) exceeded the number of drug offenders. The majority of prisoners in California and state prisons were violent offenders (BJS, 2016; CDCR, 2014). However, the composition of the federal prison population dramatically differs. The majority (49.5%) of this population was incarcerated for a drug-related offense, while over one-third (37%) were for other crimes such as public order offenses (Bureau of Justice Statistics, 2016).

The majority of drug offenders (78%) in California prisons were convicted of possession of a controlled substance (40%) or possession of a controlled substance for sale (38%) (see Figure 11.4). In contrast, only 14% of the drug offenders were incarcerated for the sale and/or manufacturing of a controlled substance. Marijuana-related offenders comprised 4% of the prisoners institutionalized for a drug crime (California Department of Corrections and Rehabilitation, 2014).

In addition, it is also important to highlight the changes of the California prison population by gender. According to the latest CDCR census, the majority of male (71%) and female (63%) prisoners were incarcerated for a violent/crimes against persons offense[24] followed by a property offense (13% and 21%, re-

---

24. Homicide, manslaughter, vehicular manslaughter, robbery, assault and battery, sex offenses, and kidnapping.

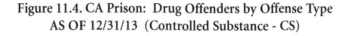

Figure 11.4. CA Prison: Drug Offenders by Offense Type
AS OF 12/31/13 (Controlled Substance - CS)

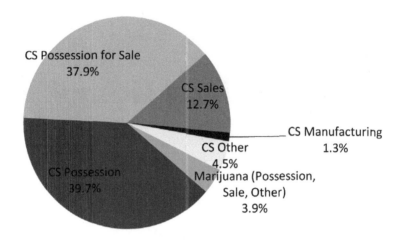

Source: California Department of Corrections and Rehabilitation, 2014 (latest data available)

spectively) (see Figures 11.5 and 11.6). Female prisoners represented a lower proportion of violent/crimes against person offenses and a higher proportion of property offenses compared to their male counterparts (see chart below). Drug offenders comprised 8% of the prison population and similar proportions of both male and female prisoners were incarcerated for a drug-related offense. This pattern between genders is a change from previous years. For the past couple of decades, a large disparity between the genders for drug-related offenses has been a consistent pattern, where a significantly larger proportion of female prisoners have been incarcerated for a drug offense. For example, in 1999, male drug offenders comprised 27% of the male prisoner population, while female drug offenders comprised 43% of the female prisoner population. As we can see in Figure 11.7, the gap between male and female drug offenders in California prisons has decreased over the past decade (California Department of Corrections and Rehabilitation, 1981, 1986, 1991, 1998, 2001, 2006, 2011, 2014). Furthermore, prisoners incarcerated for a drug-related offense have dramatically decreased in California, particularly for the women.

Figure 11.5. Male Prisoners in California (As of 12/31/13)

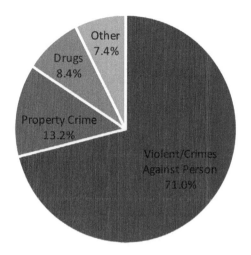

Source: California Department of Corrections and Rehabilitation, 2014 (latest data available)

Figure 11.6. Female Prisoners in California (As of 12/31/13)

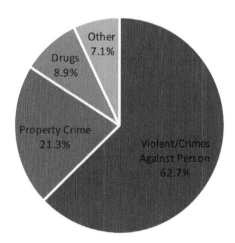

Source: California Department of Corrections and Rehabilitation, 2014 (latest data available)

Figure 11.7. California Prison Population Drug Offenders 1980–2013

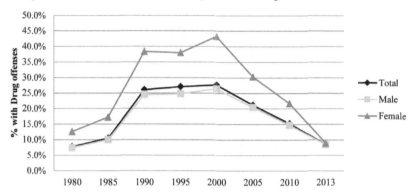

Sources: California Department of Corrections and Rehabilitation, 1981, 1986, 1991, 1998, 2001, 2006, 2011, 2014

It is important to note that the first full year in which California Public Safety Realignment (PSR) policy, also referred to as Realignment, was implemented both admissions and releases from California state prisons decreased significantly. Realignment has diverted new admissions of non-violent, non-serious, and non-sexual offenders to local jail facilities in order to reserve state prisons for people convicted of serious and violent offenses. Therefore, Realignment has significantly impacted how the criminal justice system handles and processes drug-related offenses in California. For example, in 2012, 14% of all prison admissions were for drug offenses (a decrease from 25% in 2010 and 23% in 2011) and 48% of all admissions were for violent offenses (an increase from 31% in 2010 and 32.3% in 2011) (Bureau of Justice Statistics, 2013). In addition, the majority of all prison admissions were due to new court commitments (77%) versus parole violations (23%—for example, failed drug treatment programming, failed drug tests/dirty urine, etc.). It is also important to note, that while many California counties have followed the Realignment mandate by dramatically reducing their prison commitments for low-level offenses such as drug offenders, other counties still rely on state prison facilities and continue to sentence these low-level offenders to state prison (Males & Buchen, 2013).

California's Move toward a Harm Reduction Approach: Current Policies and Legislation

Drug policies in California along with many other states have evolved throughout the past several decades. The infamous "War on Drugs" and mandatory minimum prison sentences associated with President Reagan in the 1980s have been deemed as setting the tone for one of the most punitive time periods for drug offenders. The criminal justice system was utilized as the primary response for the nation's drug issues, which resulted in an increased punishment scheme for drug offenders as well as a substantial increase of drug offenders processed throughout the criminal justice system and receiving prison sentences. Over the past decade, it is clear California has been adopting more of a harm reduction approach for drug use and abuse and has been steering away from the "War on Drugs" paradigm.

The Medicalized Use of Marijuana

While California and other states throughout the country have enacted laws to modify their drug policies, drug legislation has not changed at the federal level. The drug in particular that has created a discrepancy between many state laws and federal law is marijuana. According to the Controlled Substances Act (CSA), marijuana is a Schedule 1 drug under the federal law. There are five schedules of controlled substances, and substances listed under Schedule 1 are classified as being the most dangerous drugs due to their abuse potential, addictive quality, and lack of medical utility. For example, marijuana is deemed to have an extremely high abuse potential, as being highly addictive and having no medical utility for treatment. Therefore, Schedule 1 substances are illegal and completely banned in the U.S.; there are no circumstances where these substances are approved and/or legal. Other Schedule 1 substances include heroin, MDMA/ecstasy, LSD, peyote, and bath salts (U.S. Food and Drug Administration, 2017).

While the U.S. has been witnessing a growing trend of states approving the prescribed use of marijuana for medical purposes, the federal government has not changed its stance on marijuana. Currently (as of May 2017), marijuana has been completely legalized for medical use in 30 states and the District of Columbia, and in another 16 states with limited and/or specific provisions to use (e.g., CBD usage only or limited access) (NORML.org, 2017a) (see table below). The medical marijuana program guidelines vary by each state such as associated registration fees and possession limits. While many states have enacted marijuana laws which are in direct violation of the federal law, the federal government has allowed these states to operate without punishment and without any stated plan to reclassify marijuana to a different schedule.[25] If marijuana were reclassified into a higher schedule where the medical utility of the substance was recognized, there no longer would be a direct violation and contradiction of state laws vs. federal law.

California was the first state to legalize the use of medical marijuana. Under Proposition 215, also known as the California Compassionate Use Act of 1996, "seriously ill Californians" have the right to obtain and use marijuana for medical purposes (California Department of Public Health, 2014a). The medical use must be prescribed by a California licensed physician and eligible persons are those who would benefit from the use of marijuana to treat ailments such as cancer, AIDS, chronic pain, glaucoma, arthritis, or any other illness for which marijuana will provide relief. The Compassionate Act also indicates that patients, primary caregivers, and physicians are protected and will not be punished or face criminal prosecution or sanction. The law makes it legal for patients and their designated primary caregivers to possess and cultivate marijuana for their personal medical use. In 2004, SB420, a legislative statute, went into effect, broadening and clarifying the scope of Proposition 215, such as by extending protection to the transporting of marijuana for medical purposes, allowing patients to form medical cultivation "collectives" or "cooperatives" (dispensaries), and establishing a voluntary state ID card system run through county health departments. SB 420 also establishes guidelines or limits as to how much patients can possess and cultivate (California Department of Public Health, 2014b). For example, the possession limit for patients is two ounces. Legal patients who stay within the guidelines are supposed to be protected from arrest.

Authorized through SB 420, the Medical Marijuana Program (MMP) under the California Department of Public Health was established to create a medical marijuana identification card program and registry database for verification of medically qualified patients and their primary caregivers. Participation by patients and primary caregivers in this identification card program is voluntary. Therefore, the number of medical marijuana patients is unknown. The MMP Web-based registry allows law enforcement and the public to verify the validity of a qualified patient or primary caregiver's ID card as authorization to possess, grow, transport, and/or use medical marijuana within California. The identification program began in 2005 and 56 counties in California participate and have implemented the medical marijuana program. To date, two counties in California (Colusa and Sutter) have not adopted the program. California

---

25. This can change at any time.

medical marijuana cards are valid for one year and California does not accept other states' registry ID cards (California Department of Public Health, 2014b).

The Decriminalization and Now the Legalization of Marijuana

Another growing trend across the U.S. is the decriminalization of marijuana. Currently, 20 states and the District of Columbia have decriminalized the possession of small amounts of marijuana (NORML, 2017b) (see Table 11.2 below). While some states have not decriminalized marijuana on a state-wide basis, some counties and cities within states have institutionalized a decriminalization policy. For example, Michigan has not decriminalized marijuana, but the cities of Ann Arbor and Grand Rapids have.

Typically, decriminalization means no prison time or criminal record for first-time simple personal possession. However, decriminalization state statutes vary with the classification of offense, possession amount, as well as punishment/penalty scheme. For instance, some states classify the simple possession of marijuana as a misdemeanor, infraction, or civil offense. Also depending upon the state, simple personal possession of marijuana can be less than half an ounce, less than 1 ounce, 1 ounce or less, or less than 2.5 ounces. Some states may only require a payment of a fine (which can range from $100 to $650), while others may have conditions of performing community service, participating in a drug education program, or a combination of the above mentioned. Essentially, with decriminalizing the simple possession of marijuana, individuals will not be incarcerated and in many cases will only have to pay a fine (NORML, 2017b).

In 2010, California decriminalized simple possession of marijuana. Before the law changed, simple possession of marijuana was charged as a misdemeanor and individuals were arrested. With decriminalizing marijuana, simple possession (1 ounce/28.5 grams or less) in California became an infraction with a $100 fine, no arrest record, and no court appearance mandated. Essentially, simple marijuana possession is now treated as a minor traffic citation. Individuals possessing any amount over one ounce would be arrested for a misdemeanor or felony, depending upon the weight. With the new law enacted in 2011, the number of misdemeanor marijuana arrests in California dropped 85% from 2010 to 2011 (54,849 to 7,764). This was nearly 50,000 fewer arrests, which impacted the overall total number of drug arrests in California. More specifically, the total number of drug arrests fell 40% from 2010 to 2011 (112,085 to 69,315). The number of infraction citations is unknown; the state does not keep track of infractions (California Office of the Attorney General, 2012). It is apparent that the economic impact of decriminalizing marijuana in California had been substantial, given the fact that the individuals are no longer processed throughout the costly criminal justice system, whereby state and criminal justice resources can be diverted to more pertinent areas.

In 2014, two states (Colorado and Washington) legalized the recreational use of marijuana. More states have followed in the footsteps of Colorado and Washington, including California. As of May 2017, eight states and the District of Columbia have legalized the recreational use of marijuana (see Table 11.2 below) (NORML.org, 2017c). In November of 2016, Californians voted for the legalization of marijuana (Proposition 64—Adult Use of Marijuana Act). The legalized recreational use of marijuana is similar to how tobacco and alcohol have been regulated in the U.S. Adults, 21 years and older, are allowed to use and grow marijuana for personal use; possession of and giving up to 28.5 grams (one ounce) of cannabis and up to 8 grams of concentrated cannabis (such as hash), growing up to six cannabis plants in a private home is considered legal. Smoking cannabis in a private home or at a business licensed for on-site cannabis consumption is permitted. The sale and taxation of recreational marijuana use will go into effect January 1, 2018. Although the exact estimate of annual revenue is uncertain due to regulatory and economic factors (government actions, size of the new legal cannabis market, regulatory and administrative costs, specific allocations), revenue from the taxes is projected to be a significant amount. Proposition 64 makes specific tax revenue allocations to: (1) implement a community reinvestment grant programs that would fund certain services (e.g., job placement assistance and substance use disorder treatment) in communities most impacted by past drug policies ($10 million to $50 million annually and ongoing); (2) evaluate the effects of the measure ($10 million annually for 10 years); (3) create and adopt methods to determine whether someone is driving while impaired including cannabis ($3 million annually for 12 years); and (4) study the risks and benefits of medical cannabis ($2 million annually and ongoing). The remaining revenue will be spent on youth education, prevention, early intervention, and treatment (60%); environmental restoration and protection from illegal marijuana production (20%); and state and local government law enforcement (20%) (California Legislative Analyst's Office, 2017).

With the legalization of marijuana, the measure changes various penalties related to marijuana. For example, selling cannabis for nonmedical purposes was punishable by up to four years in prison or jails. Under Proposition 64, selling marijuana without a license is a crime punishable by up to six months in jail and/or fine up to $500. In addition, individuals serving sentences for activities that are now subject to lesser penalties are eligible for resentencing, and individuals who have completed sentences for crimes that are now reduced can apply to the courts to have their criminal records changed.

Table 11.2

United States Marijuana Laws
as of May 2017

Medical Use Legalized (in some form)				Decriminalized		Recreational Use Legalized	
1.	Alabama*	26.	Nevada	1.	Alaska	1.	Alaska
2.	Alaska	27.	New Hampshire	2.	California	2.	California
3.	Arizona	28.	New Jersey	3.	Colorado	3.	Colorado
4.	Arkansas	29.	New Mexico	4.	Connecticut	4.	District of Columbia
5.	California	30.	New York	5.	Delaware	5.	Maine
6.	Colorado	31.	North Carolina*	6.	District of Columbia	6.	Massachusetts
7.	Connecticut	32.	North Dakota	7.	Illinois	7.	Nevada
8.	Delaware	33.	Ohio	8.	Maine	8.	Oregon
9.	District of Columbia	34.	Oklahoma*	9.	Maryland	9.	Washington
10.	Florida	35.	Oregon	10.	Massachusetts		
11.	Georgia*	36.	Pennsylvania	11.	Minnesota		
12.	Hawaii	37.	Rhode Island	12.	Mississippi		
13.	Illinois	38.	South Carolina*	13.	Missouri		
14.	Indiana*	39.	Tennessee*	14.	Nebraska		
15.	Iowa*	40.	Texas*	15.	Nevada		
16.	Kentucky*	41.	Utah*	16.	New York		
17.	Louisiana	42.	Vermont	17.	North Carolina		
18.	Maine	43.	Virginia*	18.	Ohio		
19.	Maryland	44.	Washington	19.	Oregon		
20.	Massachusetts	45.	Wisconsin*	20.	Rhode Island		
21.	Michigan	46.	West Virginia	21.	Vermont		
22.	Minnesota	47.	Wyoming*				
23.	Mississippi*						
24.	Missouri*						
25.	Montana						

*Limited/Specific Provisions to the Medical Use of Marijuana

Sources: NORML.org, 2017a, 2017b, 2017c

We have seen the growing trends of more states supporting the medicalization, decriminalization, and legalization of marijuana and will continue to witness more states implementing similar policies. Public attitudes and perceptions of marijuana use have greatly evolved in the U.S. A majority of Americans support the decriminalization of marijuana and for the first time a Gallup survey (October 2013) found that 58% of Americans support nationwide legalization of marijuana (Gallup, 2013). With the trend favoring more states to legalize the recreational use of marijuana, this clearly contradicts and violates the Federal Controlled Substances Act. The previous Obama administration had been flexible on this matter, and had not interfered or challenged the states' marijuana laws as long the states maintained strict rules regarding the drug's sale and distribution. However, it is unknown how the current Trump administration will deal with the states that have legalized marijuana for recreational purposes.

Drug Treatment and Not Incarceration for Drug Offenders

As the nation's war on drugs intensified in the 1980s and 1990s, California followed national trends by relying increasingly on punishment and prisons as its primary response for handling illicit drug use. Many nonviolent drug possession offenders were arrested, convicted, and incarcerated. The concern was that too many people in California did not have the option of treatment before facing jail or prison sentences for simple drug possession. In 2000, Californians passed Proposition 36 (The Substance Abuse and Crime Prevention Act), which allows first- and second-time non-violent simple drug possession offenders the option to receive drug treatment and probation instead of incarceration (California Alcohol and Drug Programs, 2014). An underlying premise of Proposition 36 is that drug use, abuse, and addiction should be primarily viewed and treated as a public health issue rather than a criminal justice concern.

Between 2001 and 2008, approximately 50,000 offenders a year were eligible for drug treatment under Proposition 36 (Urada et al., 2008). Approximately 70% of these offenders entered treatment and over half accessed treatment for the first time. The average age of Proposition 36 participants was 35. Approximately 32% of these offenders completed treatment, which is typical for drug users who are referred to treatment by criminal justice sources. Longitudinal analyses reveal that Proposition 36 participants who completed treatment were less likely to reoffend than their counterparts who did not complete treatment, even after controlling for background factors. With regards to the economic impact of Proposition 36, it is clear that drug treatment substantially reduced incarceration costs. Cost-benefit analyses showed that diverting drug offenders to treatment instead of incarceration saved both state and local governments up to $7 for every $1 invested or allocated to treatment (Urada et al., 2008). Unfortunately, the funding for Proposition 36 was not only insufficient, which undoubtedly impacted the implementation, maintenance, evaluation, and overall effectiveness of the program, it was also unstable and Proposition 36 became an unfunded mandate in 2011 and became officially irrelevant with the passage of Proposition 47 in 2014.

Drug Sentencing Reform Efforts—Proposition 47

Prior to the passage of Proposition 47, California law mandated a felony charge for simple possession of certain types of drugs (such as heroin, crack cocaine, powder cocaine, and most other drugs), while allowing for other drugs such as LSD and methamphetamine to be "wobblers," giving local district attorneys the discretion to charge people with either a felony or a misdemeanor. Therefore, possessing certain types of drugs is automatically classified as a felony, potentially carrying a prison sentence of several years. In November 2014, Californians approved Proposition 47, The Safe Neighborhoods and Schools Act. This act reduced the classification of non-serious and non-violent property and drug crimes from a felony to a misdemeanor, unless the individual had prior convictions for murder, rape, certain sex offenses, or certain gun crimes. Proposition 47 permitted resentencing for those currently serving a prison sentence for any of the offenses that the initiative reduced to misdemeanors. It was estimated that 10,000 inmates were eligible for resentencing. The act also authorized individuals who had completed their sentences for felony convictions that would have qualified as misdemeanors under the proposition to apply for reclassification of those convictions to misdemeanors. The funds based on the saving accrued by the state are diverted to the Department of Education, Victim Compensation and Government Claims Board, and the Board of State and Community Corrections (California Courts, 2016; California Legislative Analyst's Office, 2014).

Now many offenders convicted of a drug-related misdemeanor do not have a felony on their criminal record. Simple drug possession is no longer a felony. A drug-related felony conviction can carry repercussions and collateral consequences that include being barred from receiving federal student aid, blocked from living in low-income housing or drawing food stamps, and encountering difficulty finding employment or securing home loans, thus making it more difficult for drug users to rehabilitate themselves and enter mainstream society. According to Lynn Lyman, California state director for the Drug Policy Alliance, "felony sentences don't reduce drug use and don't persuade users to seek treatment, but instead, impose tremendous barriers to housing, education, and employment after release— three things we know help keep people out of our criminal justice system and successfully reintegrating into their families and communities" (Drug Policy Alliance, 2013).

Following the implementation of Proposition 47 in late 2014, there was a significant decline in felony drug arrests (67%) in 2015, while misdemeanor drug arrests increased by 43%. The decrease in felony drug arrests exceeded the corresponding increase in misdemeanors. Total drug arrests declined about 10% from 2014 to 2015. As shown in Figure 11.8, it is clear how both the decriminalization of marijuana and Proposition 47 have significantly impacted drug arrests trends (fewer drug arrests).

Prior to the passing of California's Proposition 47, 13 states, the District of Columbia, and the federal government treated simple personal possession

Figure 11.8. Drug Offense Arrests in CA, 2005–2015

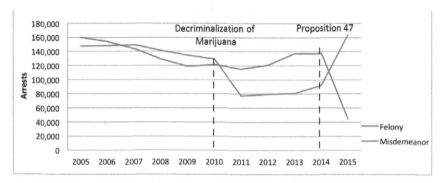

Sources: California Office of the Attorney General, 2011, 2016

as a misdemeanor. According to an analysis of U.S. Justice Department data by the Drug Policy Alliance and the American Civil Liberties Union, drug crimes were not higher in those 13 states; drug offenders were slightly less likely to use illegal drugs but were more likely to receive treatment (Drug Policy Alliance, 2013).

California's Response to the Rise in Opioid Overdoses

In September 2014, Governor Jerry Brown signed into law Assembly Bill 1535, which expanded naloxone access in California pharmacies (Drug Policy Alliance, 2014). California is among the 14 states which allow individuals to buy an opioid overdose antidote in pharmacies without a prescription. Prior to this bill, naloxone was available by prescription (since 2013), in emergency rooms, ambulances, and post-surgery recovery rooms, and to some first responders. Naloxone, also known as Narcan, reverses the effects of opioid overdoses (such as heroin, morphine, codeine, and oxycodone), restores breathing, and ultimately prevents deaths. It instantly reverses the effects of an overdose. Naloxone is non-addictive, non-toxic, and can be injected directly or sprayed intranasally into the person who is overdosing. It has no effect on a person who is not using opiates. Most opiate users who overdose do not make it to the hospital in time and/or receive immediate care. This law allows access to a drug to people such as family and friends who may be in contact with a person at risk of an opiate overdose or to an individual requesting it.

Sex Crimes Policy

Sexual assaults on adults and children have been occurring for centuries; however, society as a whole has changed its reaction to these types of crimes. California, in particular, has become less tolerant to these types of crimes as society has evolved and become more aware of the frequency in which these crimes occur as well as the long-standing detrimental effects of sexual crimes. Victims of sex crimes such as rape, child molestation, and human trafficking can suffer a whole host of long-term effects, including depression, relationship issues, drug addiction, promiscuity, loss of self-worth, fear, anxiety, isolation, and sometimes, victims in turn become sexual offenders themselves. These long-term effects of victimization in our society can lead to more crime in the form of drug abuse, thefts to support drug abuse, prostitution, child abuse, domestic violence, and various other crimes. Therefore, we as a community have a vested interest in preventing sex crimes and protecting victims of sexual abuse. As such, more resources are being expended to apprehend, prosecute, and rehabilitate perpetrators and more rights are being afforded to victims of sexual abuse.

As our attitude in society evolves and technology advances, we are not only made aware of new crimes, we are developing new ways to solve crime, identify perpetrators, and monitor and apprehend criminals. On the flipside, these advances also place our youth at risk. The Internet and various forms of social media allow children and people of all ages to have portable devices with which to communicate with strangers from all over the world with greater frequency. The ability to gain access to children and communicate with others has increased the amount of sexual crimes perpetrated upon victims. With new crimes occurring and being reported, the California legislature tries to keep up with the pace of society and routinely passes legislation and propositions to assist with the apprehension and successful prosecution of these new crimes.

Child Pornography

Child pornography is any image depicting a child under 18 years of age engaging in or simulating sexual conduct, or an image that is displaying a child's genitals in a manner that is designed to arouse the viewer (Penal Code Section 311.11). With the advent of the Internet, child pornography is easily accessible with the click of a button, and therefore, local law enforcement agencies are investigating these crimes in much greater proportion. There was a time when a purveyor of child pornography would need to order images of child pornography from a magazine mail order site. Possession of child pornography offenses were routinely investigated by the United States Postal Service; however, technology has advanced to such a degree, these mail order sites are rarely used, as criminals who want to view child pornography can subscribe to websites from their home computers, cell phones, or even access sites from the computers at their local libraries.

Local law enforcement agencies have had to keep up with technology and train more officers in computer forensics, detecting encrypted devices, and creating carbon copy images of hard drives for forensic evaluations. Computer forensic laboratories are being established for the sole purpose of searching computers and any other device used for storing information.[26] When a criminal is suspected of possessing or producing child pornography, all media seized is forensically searched, and a report is generated indicating how many images were located, where they were located, as well as information pertaining to when the images depicting children were accessed or downloaded.

Prior to September 20, 2006, possession of child pornography could only be filed as a misdemeanor, which carried a maximum punishment of one year in the county jail. The crime became a wobbler (a crime which can be filed as a misdemeanor or a felony) for a few short months. Following the passage of Jessica's Law in November 2006, the crime of possession of child pornography became a felony and the maximum punishment in jail is three years in state prison. Whether convicted of a felony or a misdemeanor for possession of child pornography, in addition to jail or prison, there is mandatory lifetime 290 registration imposed as well.

Revenge Porn

One of the newer Internet crimes is the uploading of sexually explicit media without the consent of the pictured individual. This is referred to as *"revenge porn"* as the images are often uploaded following a relationship break-up, whereby the former lover or hacker uploads the images for the purpose of humiliation or revenge to the pictured individual. On October 2, 2013, California Governor Jerry Brown signed Senate Bill 255, which criminalizes this practice and makes it a misdemeanor to intentionally cause serious emotional distress by distributing intimate images that were expected to remain private. As of January 1, 2014, Penal Code Section 653.2(a)(2) provides that any person who, with the intent to cause substantial emotional distress or humiliation, by means of an electronic device, and without the consent of the other person, publishes, e-mails, hyperlinks, or makes available for downloading nude images of another

---

26. For example, there are three Regional Computer Forensics Labs in California (Menlo Park, San Diego, and Santa Ana), which support criminal investigations from any law enforcement agency which requests assistance.

person is guilty of a misdemeanor. The maximum punishment for this crime is six months in jail and a fine of $1,000.00. This crime applies to images that were taken consensually, but only if the distributor of the image is also the photographer. Therefore "selfies," which are photos taken of oneself and sent to another, would not be protected, because arguably, once a photo was disseminated by the person in the picture, they have given up their right to privacy in that picture.

California is only the second state to have a criminal law that addresses "revenge porn." New Jersey has had a related law since 2003 that makes it a felony to post secretly recorded video or photos online. Previously, victims of "revenge porn" had only a civil remedy to sue for invasion of privacy, public disclosure of private fact, and intentional infliction of emotional distress against the individuals who uploaded the images. Forty states, including California and New York, also have anti-cyber-harassment laws that may be applicable to cases of "revenge porn."

Human Trafficking

Human trafficking is a growing criminal enterprise in which the offenders prey on the most vulnerable among us for their own personal financial gain. Once thought to exist only in the shadows with victims literally chained in basements and hidden from view, law enforcement is increasingly finding that human trafficking is almost everywhere around us. While the general public often believes sex trafficking is a foreign problem or is more prevalent among immigrant communities, the reality is quite the contrary. In California, 72% of known sex trafficking victims were born in the United States. Some would say it potentially exists anywhere there is a hotel room or an Internet connection.

Although statistics are difficult to ascertain due to under-reporting and disparate definitions of human trafficking across jurisdictions, experts estimate that as of 2012, human trafficking was a $32-billion-dollar-per-year industry (California Attorney General's Office, 2012). As such, it is the second largest criminal enterprise (drug trafficking is first). In many ways, human trafficking is easier, less risky, and more profitable than drug trafficking. However, heightened public awareness and aggressive changes to human trafficking laws are beginning to stem the tide.

Trafficking v. Smuggling

In the context of narcotics and illicit sale of firearms, the terms "trafficking" and "smuggling" are often, correctly, used interchangeably. The common use of these terms has led, however, to a widespread misunderstanding about the terms in the context of trafficking of human beings.

At its core, *smuggling* is a crime against a government perpetrated by violating its control of a border. It is essentially the movement of anything (a person, narcotics, or even otherwise lawful material such as produce) across a border without permission of the entity which controls the border. Smuggling is accomplished when the movement is complete. In the context of smuggling a person, consent of the smuggled person is irrelevant to whether the offense occurred. For example, a person in Mexico may consent, or even pay money to a "coyote," to be smuggled across the border into the United States.

In contrast, *human trafficking* involves the exploitation of a person for a particular purpose, usually coerced or forced labor or commercial sexual exploitation. The exploitation is accomplished by depriving the victim's personal liberty through use of fraud, deceit, coercion, force, or violence. If the victim is a minor, the exploitation need not be coerced or forced.

Sex Trafficking

Commercial sex trafficking generally presents in the form of a pimp/panderer/trafficker controlling and/or directing a victim to engage in acts of prostitution. The trafficker controls virtually every aspect of the victim's life, including where to "work," how much money to make, and how much and when to eat, if at all. It should be noted that commercial sex trafficking is present in virtually all areas where prostitution is present. For example, it is found in areas that are known for street-walking prostitution (known as the "track" or "blade"), motels/hotels through Internet prostitution, massage parlor brothels, and residential brothels in upscale neighborhoods.

Methods of Exploitation

Once a trafficker identifies a vulnerable target, a very strategic approach to exploitation occurs. First, the trafficker seduces the victim. Seduction can occur through flattery, making the target feel as though the trafficker cares for her (the term "her" is used because although there are male victims of trafficking, the vast majority of known cases involve female victims). This flattery is often employed by what is known as a *"Romeo" pimp*. Seduction sometimes occurs through a business proposition, where a trafficker convinces a potential victim that he is merely proposing a business relationship where they will be "partners," splitting the proceeds of prostitution. In the case of foreign victims, the seduction may involve false promises of legitimate work or travel documents to the United States.

After the victim is seduced the trafficker often isolates the victim. Isolation occurs simply by moving the victim to another jurisdiction. Isolation makes the victim dependent upon the trafficker for daily needs and decreases the chances she will flee from the trafficker or have contact with someone she knows. Isolating a sex trafficking victim by movement to the United States can be devastating for foreign victims as well. They often do not know about the protections they would have in the United States, as it is common for traffickers to teach the victims to not trust law enforcement.

Once the victim is isolated, the trafficker coerces the victim to engage in prostitution. This may be through creating a sense of desperation within the victim to get her to believe that she is doing it out of love for the trafficker and just temporarily so they can start to save money and build a life together. It is important to note that coercion may come in many forms. It can be through threats of violence or actual violence to the victim or her family. And, as noted, it may be accomplished through psychological manipulation. In some cases, coercion is accomplished through fraud or deceit. Finally, once the victim is coerced, traffickers often use some sort of violence or threat of violence to ensure the victim continues to "work" for him.

Human Trafficking Laws in California

In light of the increased awareness about human trafficking, California voters enacted the toughest anti-human trafficking laws in California history in November 2012. Californians voted by a margin of 4 to 1 to enact Proposition 35 (the CASE Act) by the largest margin of victory for a ballot measure in California's history. As a result, the penalties for human trafficking dramatically increased and additional protections for victims were enacted.

Prior to Proposition 35, in order to prove human trafficking occurred, the prosecution was required to prove that the defendant violated the personal liberty of the victim with the intent to effect or maintain forced labor (in the case of labor trafficking) or some form of commercial sexual exploitation (such as pimping, pandering, child pornography, or another offense enumerated in Penal Code section 236.1). Labor and sex trafficking were both contained in Penal Code section 236.1(a) and carried the same penalties as one another. Under the previous law, human traffickers faced a maximum of five years in prison for adult victims and eight years for minor victims.

Neither offense required registration as a sex offender. Effective November 7, 2012, when Proposition 35 went into effect, the risk for human traffickers increased exponentially. Section 236.1 was amended in a number of significant ways. First, it separated sex trafficking and labor trafficking, even as it relates to cases involving adult victims. Second, it created a new theory of human trafficking in California (consistent with the federal definition of human trafficking as contained in Title 22 of the U.S. Code, Section 7102(8)) in cases

Table 11.3. Trafficking Laws

Penal Code Section	Offense	Penalty
236.1(a)	Labor Trafficking	5–8–12 years prison
236.1(b)	Sex Trafficking (Adult Victim)	8–14–20 years prison
236.1(c)(1)	Sex Trafficking without Deprivation of Liberty	5–8–12 years prison
236.1(c)(2)	Sex Trafficking with Use of Force, Fear, Fraud, Deceit, Coercion, Violence, etc.	15–Life in prison

involving minors. If the victim is a minor, the prosecution no longer is required to prove that the trafficker deprived the minor of her personal liberty. The following are the penalties now included in section 236.1 (see Table 11.3 above).

In addition to the increase in penalties for the underlying offenses, all sex trafficking cases now require the offender to register as a sex offender. Moreover, Proposition 35 also added section 236.4(b) to the penal code, which provides for up to 10 additional years in prison if the offender inflicts great bodily injury ("GBI") upon the victim during commission of the offense. (The standard GBI enhancement for most felonies is only three additional years in prison.)

Human trafficking has long been an attractive, low-risk, high-reward endeavor for some of society's greediest criminals. Fortunately, increased public awareness and activism have given law enforcement a much-needed mandate to focus attention and resources at stemming the tide. With passage of Proposition 35, traffickers now face some of the stiffest penalties in criminal law if caught. As enforcement efforts continue, this change in the cost-benefit structure may prove to be instrumental.

Sex Offender Registration[27]

In addition to new commitment laws for sex offenders, community notification and registration statutes have been developed in an effort to inform

---

27. It is also known as 290 Registration, after the California Penal Code Section that governs the requirement.

and protect the community from sex offenders. These laws require convicted sex offenders to inform law enforcement of their current address and place of employment so law enforcement can keep track of them and monitor their whereabouts. Additionally, convicted sex offenders must provide their fingerprints, an annual photograph, the license plate of their vehicle, as well as a DNA sample. California's *Sex Offender Registration Act* was enacted in 1947 and California became the first state in the United States to have a sex offender registration program. In 1994, a federal statute called the *Jacob Wetterling Act* was passed, which required all states to pass laws requiring sex offenders to register with state sex offender registries.

Even after laws were enacted to enable law enforcement to be aware of the location of convicted sex offenders, it wasn't until 1996, when a set of New Jersey laws called "Megan's Law" was passed, that the federal government required states to pass legislation mandating *public notification* of personal information for certain sex offenders. Megan's Law is named after seven-year-old Megan Kanka, a New Jersey girl who was raped and killed by a known registered sex offender who had moved across the street from the family without their knowledge. In the wake of the tragedy, the Kankas sought to have local communities warned about sex offenders in the area. Megan's Law was met with much opposition by convicted sex offenders who argued that to publicly publish their names after conviction was a violation of their due process rights because they were not given an opportunity to a hearing to determine if they were currently "dangerous" to the community. However, the Supreme Court of the United States held in *Connecticut Dept. of Public Safety v. Doe*, 538 U.S. 1 (2003), that mere injury to reputation, even defamation, does not constitute the deprivation of a liberty interest, and even if it did, due process did not entitle the sex offender to a hearing as it was not material under the Connecticut statute dealing with registration.

The goal behind sex offender registration is to not only keep track of the location of the convicted sex offenders, but to notify the public of the location of certain sex offenders who pose a risk to the safety of the community. Since 2004, the public has been able to view information on sex offenders required to register with local law enforcement under California's *Megan's Law*. Previously, the information was available only by personally visiting police stations or by calling a 900 toll-free number. The public can view information about some designated sex offenders at the website of the Department of Justice at http://meganslaw.ca.gov. However, not all convicted sex offenders are posted on the websites that can be accessed on the Internet. In fact, only a portion of sex offenders are actually posted on the public website. Law enforcement, along with the Department of Justice, will post the full address and zip code for any registrant that California law enforcement agencies deem is currently posing a high risk to the public.

In 2007, the Adam Walsh Child Protection Safety Act became law and required states to have uniform requirements for sex offender registration across the states. Title I of the Adam Walsh Act, also known as the Sex Offender Registration and Notification Act (SORNA), has been codified in large part at 42 U.S.C. Section 16911 and is intended to be a full replacement of the Jacob Wetterling Act.

California Penal Code Section 290(a)(1) is the Penal Code section that imposes upon persons convicted of enumerated sex offenses, a lifetime obligation to register. This sex offender registration requirement applies automatically when a person is convicted of one of the enumerated offenses. Most sex offenses require a convicted offender to register, with the exception of statutory rape (Penal Code Section 261.5) (which is consensual intercourse with a minor under 18). Statutory rape is generally charged when the minor engaging in the consensual intercourse is between the ages of 14 and 18.

Penal Code Section 290 registration is mandatory, and the language within the statute states that it "shall be imposed," which leaves no discretion to the trial judge: he/she must require registration if one or more of the listed violations occur. Penal Code Section 290(a)(1)(A) requires sex offenders to register for life while residing or located in California. The registrant must appear in person to register with the police department in the city in which he or she resides or is located. A person who is a transient must register with local law enforcement and update his or her registration no less than once every 30 days (Penal Code Section 290(a)(1)(C). All 290 registrants must also register multiple addresses, and update their registration information annually, within five working days of their birthday.

Failure to register as required by Penal Code Section 290(a)(1)(A) can result in the filing of new criminal charges for Failure to Register. If the underlying offense in which a person was convicted was a felony, then the following failure to register will be filed as a felony. If the underlying offense which caused the requirement that the defendant register as a sex offender was a misdemeanor, the following failure to register would be a misdemeanor for the first offense of failing to register, but any subsequent offense would be filed as a felony. An individual could be punished in local county jail for failing to register or be sent to prison.

Statute of Limitations

Most crimes have what is called a "statute of limitations." The statute of limitations is the time in which a prosecutor has to file a case. General felonies must be filed by the prosecutor within three years of the date that the crime occurred (Penal Code Section 801). Misdemeanors must be filed within one year of the date that the crime occurred. Prosecution for any offense which is punishable by death, life imprisonment (with or without parole), or the crime of embezzlement of public money, may be commenced at any time (Penal Code 799). This means that there is no statute of limitations for crimes such as murder or embezzlement of public money.

There is a 10-year statute of limitations for felony sex crimes which require registration as a sex offender pursuant to Penal Code Section 290. Previously, the rule provided for a six-year statute of limitations for felony sex crimes which were punishable by eight or more years in prison (Penal Code Section 800). Notably, the law recognizes that most victims of sexual assault don't report right away, therefore the statute of limitations is very important in effectively prosecuting crimes which took place some time ago. Based on this recognition, exceptions to the general rule were put in place for sex crimes that are reported outside of the 10-year statute of limitation period.

Exceptions to the General Rule for Sex Crimes

As of January 1, 2006, a case may be filed involving a victim who has not yet turned 28 years old, when the crime occurred before the victim turned 18, and the conduct involves certain enumerated sexual assault crimes (Penal Code 801.1(a)). The crime must involve "substantial sexual conduct," which is defined by Penal Code Section 1203.066(B). "Substantial sexual conduct" includes oral copulation and penetration of the vagina or rectum of the victim or the offender by the penis or a foreign object. Substantial sexual conduct includes masturbation of either the victim or the offender as well. The victim must make a report to California law enforcement, and the prosecutor must file the case within one year of reporting to California law enforcement. If all of these conditions are not met, the case cannot be filed under this Penal Code Section.

In an attempt to balance the interests of the public and the victim in prosecuting sex offenses committed years ago, and the ability of a defendant to effectively defend against those allegations, certain additional evidence is required under the law before an extension of the statute of limitations is allowed.

In order to file a case falling within the parameters of Penal Code Section 801.1(a) and take advantage of the extension of the statute of limitations, there must be independent corroborating evidence, and "the independent evidence shall clearly and convincingly corroborate the victim's allegation" (Penal Code Section 803(f)(1)(C).).

Corroborating evidence is evidence which tends to support evidence that is already offered in a proceeding. For example, a child might report to law enforcement that her uncle licked her breast, and she could testify in court to this fact. That would be evidence offered that her uncle did in fact lick her breast. An example of corroborating evidence would be that DNA that matched the uncle's DNA was in fact found on the victim's breast, or a cousin who actually witnessed the sexual abuse came forward and reported having witnessed the incident years ago.

The law recognizes that most sexual assault cases do not happen in front of witnesses and most victims do not report right away. Jurors are given legal instruction that a conviction for a sexual assault crime can be based on the testimony of a complaining witness alone. This essentially means that one witness's testimony may be the basis for finding a defendant guilty beyond a reasonable doubt if the jurors believe that witness. However, in sexual assault cases where the crime occurred many years ago and where the statute of limitations needs to be extended under Penal Code Section 803 (f)(1)(C), the law requires some additional independent corroborating evidence to support the complaining witness's testimony. It can include other victims, child pornography, and admissions by the defendant. Some additional examples of independent corroborating evidence would be medical records demonstrating a sexually transmitted disease or an aborted pregnancy. Independent corroborating evidence cannot include the opinions of mental health professionals and cannot consist of inadmissible evidence; for example, a confession taken in violation of *Miranda* or evidence illegally seized from the defendant.

One Strike and You're Out!

As California's intolerance for sex offenders grows, so do the penalties that are imposed for violent sexual offenses. Since November 30, 1994, many sex laws have called for "indeterminate sentencing." An *indeterminate sentence* means the defendant serves a specified number of years until eligible for parole; however, he or she can be imprisoned for life. For example, if a defendant were to be sentenced for 15 years to life, he or she would be obligated to serve 15 years and then would come up for parole, but the California Department of Corrections and Rehabilitation could keep him or her incarcerated for his/her entire life California Department of Corrections and Rehabilitation 2011). Therefore, within indeterminate sentencing there is no set date in which the defendant is to be released and in fact, he may never get out of prison.

The "One Strike" statute provides for an alternative indeterminate sentence for certain sex crimes in specific circumstances. This applies to crimes committed on or after November 30, 1994. Further, this "One Strike Law" was substantially amended on three separate occasions and the date in which a crime occurs is very important when conducting an analysis of the One Strike sentencing law.

As the "One Strike" sentencing law stands today, for any crimes that are listed in Penal Code Section 667.61(c); such as Forcible Rape, Forcible Sodomy, Forcible Oral Copulation, and Lewd Act Upon a Minor Under 14, that were committed after September 20, 2006, if you also have one of the following factors listed below in Penal Code Section 667.61(d) present, the law will command a sentence of 25 years to life.

a. A prior conviction for a sex crime listed in the statute
b. Aggravated kidnap
c. Aggravated mayhem or torture
d. Residential burglary with intent to commit a listed forcible sex crime
e. One of the crimes listed in a.) through d.) above which were done in concert
f. Personal infliction of great bodily injury during the commission of the sexual assault (Please note: the phrase "in the commission" has been broadly construed to mean before, during, or after the completion of the sex act provided the defendant maintains control of the victim (*People v. Jones*, [2001] 25 Cal.4th 98).
g. Personal infliction of bodily harm on a victim under the age of 14 (Bodily harm is defined in subdivision (k) as any substantial physical injury resulting from the use of force that is more than the force necessary to commit the underlying offense.)

Punishment for a sex crime listed in Penal Code Section 667.61(c); such as Forcible Rape, Forcible Sodomy, Forcible Oral Copulation, or Lewd Act Upon a Child Under 14, where you have one of the following factors present is 15 years to life and if there are two of any of the following factors present, the law commands a sentence of 25 years to life:

1. Kidnap of the victim
2. During the commission of a burglary, residential or commercial
3. Personal use of a firearm or deadly weapon on the victim
4. Multiple victims; each victim must be a victim of one of the listed sex offenses (for example, if you have a defendant who commits a Lewd Act

Upon a Child (Penal Code Section 288(a)) on more than one victim, the sentence will be 15 years to life for each count of Lewd Act Upon a Child.

5. Tying or binding of the victim or another person
6. Administering a controlled substance to the victim (there is a question in the law regarding whether this administration needs to be forcible or not)
7. An in concert enumerated sex crime while committing a kidnap, burglary, or using a deadly weapon or administering a controlled substance or infliction of great bodily injury.

On September 20, 2006, two new crimes were added to the Penal Code that assisted law enforcement with obtaining indeterminate life sentences for child predators. Previous to September 20, 2006, if a defendant were to engage in sexual intercourse or oral copulation with a child under the age of 10 the penalty would be a maximum of eight years in prison as long as no force was used. Prior to September 20, 2006, in order to obtain a life sentence for having intercourse with a child under 10, force was an element that needed to be established and proved to the jury. Penal Code Section 288.7(a) was added, which commands a sentence of 25 years to life for engaging in intercourse or sodomy with a child 10 years of age or younger, without any requirement that force be used to accomplish the intercourse or sodomy. Additionally, Penal Code Section 288.7(b) was added which carries a 15-years-to-life sentence for engaging in oral copulation or sexual penetration with a child 10 years of age or younger, without any requirement that force be used to accomplish the oral copulation or sexual penetration.

Conclusion

As you have learned, society is ever changing and the California justice system needs to keep up with our evolving world and the technological advances which not only create new crimes, but allow law enforcement to more effectively track, monitor, and apprehend criminals. New legislation is being passed to keep up with the current trends, protect our citizens, and enforce our laws. As our focus on different issues in society changes, so do our laws.

Key Terms and Definitions

AK-47 rifle—Originally, a Soviet military (later, Chinese military) 7.62 cal. rifle that can fire fully automatically. Often used as a generic term for 7.62 caliber semi-automatic rifles whose design the AK-47 inspired.

AR-15 rifle—Originally, a semi-automatic .223 caliber rifle manufactured by Colt and others as a civilian version of the M-16 military rifle, which is distinguished by its ability to fire fully automatically. Often used as a generic term for .223 caliber rifles whose design was inspired by the Colt version.

Assault weapon—Definition varies according to state laws. Generally, a semi-automatic weapon, often (but not necessarily) shoulder-fired, that can accept high-capacity detachable magazines and be easily reloaded.

Brady Handgun Violence Prevention Act (18 U.S.C. 921 *et seq.*)—1993 Federal law that required criminal record checks of persons buying handguns from licensed dealers. Extended in 1998 to long gun buyers.

California Megan's Law—Passed in 2004 whereby sex offender registration was not only accessible by visiting police stations, but published on a website accessible to the public.

California Public Safety Realignment policy—Also known as Realignment, was implemented both admissions and releases from California state prisons decreased significantly. It diverted new admissions of non-violent, non-serious, and non-sexual offenders to local jail facilities in order to reserves state prisons for people convicted of serious or violent offenses.

California's Sex Offender Registration Act—In 1947, California was the first state to enact a Sex Offender Registration program.

Child Pornography—Any image depicting a child under 18 years of age engaging in or simulating sexual conduct or an image that is displaying a child's genitals in a manner that is designed to arouse the viewer.

Concealed carry (CCW)—Carrying a firearm on one's person so that its possession is unobserved by others. Generally requires a permit.

Corroborating Evidence—Evidence, which tends to support evidence that is already offered in a proceeding.

Dealer Record of Sale (DROS)—Form recording gun and purchaser information, used by dealers to report handgun sales to the California Department of Justice (and as of January 1, 2014, long guns sales as well.)

Decriminalization—Means no prison time or criminal record for first-time simple personal possession.

FFL—Federal firearms license, required to engage in the business of dealing in firearms.

Fully automatic—Firearm fires continuously with a single pull of the trigger.

Human Trafficking—The exploitation (deprivation of a person's liberty) for a particular purpose: financial gain, pleasure, revenge, etc.

Jacob Wetterling Act—A Federal Statute passed in 1994, requiring all states to pass laws requiring sex offenders to register with their state upon conviction of sexual offenses.

Long gun—Firearm fired from the shoulder; generally a shotgun or rifle.

Megan's Law—A set of laws passed in 1996 requiring public notification of personal information for certain sex offenders. These were passed in 1996 after a 7-year-old girl named Megan Kanka was raped and killed by a known registered sex offender in New Jersey.

One gun a month—Law prohibiting private persons from purchasing more than one handgun a month. Enacted to deter straw purchasing. (Also in effect in Maryland and New Jersey.)

Open carry—Carrying a firearm on one's person in plain view. Depending on gun type and whether a firearm is loaded may require a permit in some urban areas.

Possession—The use, cultivation, production, sale of illegal drugs and drug related paraphernalia.

Proposition 215—Also known as the California Compassionate Use Act of 1996, seriously ill Californians have the right to obtain and use marijuana for medical purposes.

Revenge Porn—The uploading of sexually explicit media without the consent of the pictured individual.

Romeo pimp—A pimp that uses flattery and gifts to seduce his victims.

Saturday night special—Definition varies. Generally refers to small, inexpensive, shoddily constructed, smack-caliber handguns banned in a number of states.

Semiautomatic—Gun readies cartridges without user intervention. Trigger must be released after firing each round, then pulled again to fire succeeding rounds.

Smuggling—The movement of anything (a person, narcotics, produce) across a border without the permission of the entity who controls the border. Consent of the person is irrelevant to whether the offense occurred.

Statute of Limitations—The time in which a prosecutor has to file a case.

Straw purchase—Acquisition of a firearm by a "straw" buyer on behalf of another person, who may be unqualified to buy a gun, usually because of age or criminal record.

Universal background check—State laws requiring criminal record checks of all gun buyers, including those acquiring firearms from private persons and at gun shows. (Federal law only requires records checks for persons buying guns from firearms dealers.) Default position in California, where all sales must go through a dealer.

Unlicensed dealer—A person who repetitively buys and sells guns but does not have a state or Federal gun dealer license.

Wobbler—A crime that can be filed as a misdemeanor or a felony.

Internet Websites

Brady Campaign to Prevent Gun Violence: http://www.bradycampaign.org/

Bureau of Alcohol, Tobacco, Firearms and Explosives firearms page: http://www.atf.gov/content/firearms

California Department of Public Health, Medical Marijuana Program: https://www.cdph.ca.gov/

California Coalition Against Sexual Assault: http://www.calcasa.org

California Courts Domestic Violence Self Help: http://www.courts.ca.gov/selfhelp-domesticviolence.htm

California Partnership to End Domestic Violence: http://www.cpedv.org

California State Attorney General, Bureau of Firearms: http://oag.ca.gov/firearms

Cyber Civil Rights Initiative: http://www.cybercivilrights.org

Department of Justice website: www.meganslaw.ca.gov

Drug Policy Alliance | Guiding Drug Law Reform & Advocacy: www.drugpolicy.org/

Mayors Against Illegal Guns: https://everytown.org/mayors/ http://www.mayorsagainstillegalguns.org/html/home/home.shtml

National Rifle Association, Institute for Legislative Action: http://www.nraila.org/

Office of the Attorney General: http://oag.ca.gov/human-trafficking

"The Hidden Life of Guns." A special report by *The Washington Post*: http://www.washingtonpost.com/wp-srv/special/nation/guns/?sid=ST2010121606931

"Wiped Clean." Milwaukee, Wisconsin *Journal Sentinel* series on corrupt gun dealing: http://www.jsonline.com/news/94182249.html

United States Food and Drug Administration: https://www.fda.gov/

Violence Policy Center: http://www.vpc.org/

Review Questions

1. How do California's gun laws compare with the laws of other states? With Federal firearms laws?

2. What events spurred the enactment of the 1968 Gun Control Act?

3. Why did State gun laws become more restrictive during the latter stages of the twentieth century?

4. What is the reason behind the decline in misdemeanors in relation to drug arrests?

5. What is the significance behind the fact that California was the first state to legalize marijuana for medical proposes?

6. Why is it that there is a growing trend with in the legalization of medical marijuana while at the same time the federal government has not changed its stance in marijuana?

7. Name all the states that have legalized marijuana for medical purposes or recreational use.

8. If a law was passed on September 20, 2006 making it a crime to engage in sexual intercourse with a child under 10 without the use of force, could a Defendant be charged with that law for conduct that occurred on September 19, 2006?

9. What law would be violated if a Defendant were to be prosecuted for a crime that was not in existence at the time he committed the crime?

10. What is the general statute of limitations for sex crimes?

11. What additional elements are required in order to file a sexual assault case under Penal Code Section 803(f)(1)(C), which extends the general statute of limitations?

12. How long is a sex offender required to register pursuant to Penal Code Section 290 after having been convicted of a sex crime requiring registration?

Critical Thinking Questions

1. Assuming that some firearms regulation is appropriate, how can gun laws be drawn so they comply with the letter and spirit of the Second Amendment?

2. Given the many guns in circulation—their numbers are estimated to exceed the U.S. population—can firearms laws realistically reduce their criminal misuse? If so, what kind seem the most promising?

3. In some circles California is hailed as a leader in gun regulation. In others it is heavily criticized. Explain.

4. Current law addressing drugs treats certain drug possession as felonies. How has this exacerbated problems in California's criminal justice system? How would adding discretion to judges and lawyers to be able to charge certain drug crimes as felonies or misdemeanors change the way we treat offenders?

5. Should people who abuse controlled substances be treated as criminals or patients? Why? What are the problems associated with each type of treatment? How could California better address its drug problem?

6. If a defendant who has been the victim of a sexual assault themselves as a child becomes a perpetrator of a sex crime in the future, should he/she be treated differently in our criminal justice system than a defendant who suffered no such victimization? Why or Why not?

7. What impact does technology have on the youth of America?
8. Does making the public aware of a sex offender in the neighborhood prevent or even minimize future offenses by the offender? Or, does this public notification system give people a false sense of security?

References

Adam Walsh Child Protection Safety Act, 42 U.S.C. § 16911, et seq.

Blumstein, A. (1995). Youth violence, guns and the illicit drug industry. *Journal of Criminal Law and Criminology, 86*(1), 10–36.

Bureau of Justice Statistics. (2013). *Prisoners in 2012: Trends in admission and releases, 1991-2012*. Washington, DC: U.S. Department of Justice. Retrieved from http://www.bjs.gov/content/pub/pdf/p12tar9112.pdf

Bureau of Justice Statistics. (2016). *Prisoners in 2015*. Washington, DC: U.S. Department of Justice. Retrieved from https://www.bjs.gov/content/pub/pdf/p15.pdf

California Alcohol and Drug Programs. (2014). *Criminal justice: Substance Abuse and Crime Prevention Act of 2000 (Prop. 36)*. Sacramento, CA: California Alcohol and Drug Programs. Retrieved from http://www.adp.ca.gov/sacpa/prop36.shtml

California Attorney General's Office. (2012). *The state of human trafficking in California*. Retrieved from http://oag.ca.gov/sites/all/files/pdfs/ht/human-trafficking-2012.pdf

California Courts. (2016). *Proposition 47: The Safe Neighborhood and Schools Act*. Sacramento, CA: The Judicial Branch of California. Retrieved from http://www.courts.ca.gov/prop47.htm

California Department of Corrections and Rehabilitation. (1981). *California prisoners 1980*. Sacramento, CA: Department of Corrections and Rehabilitation. Retrieved from http://www.cdcr.ca.gov/Reports_Research/Offender_Information_Services_Branch/Annual/CalPris/CALPRISd1980.pdf

California Department of Corrections and Rehabilitation. (1986). *California prisoners and civil narcotic addicts: 1983, 1984 and 1985*. Sacramento, CA: Department of Corrections and Rehabilitation. Retrieved from http://www.cdcr.ca.gov/Reports_Research/Offender_Information_Services_Branch/Annual/CalPris/CALPRISd1983_84_85.pdf

California Department of Corrections and Rehabilitation. (1991). *California prisoners and parolees 1990*. Sacramento, CA: Department of Corrections and Rehabilitation. Retrieved from http://www.cdcr.ca.gov/Reports_

Research/Offender_Information_Services_Branch/Annual/CalPris/
CALPRISd1990.pdf

California Department of Corrections and Rehabilitation. (1998). *California
prisoners and parolees 1995 & 1996.* Sacramento, CA: Department of
Corrections and Rehabilitation. Retrieved from http://www.cdcr.ca.gov/
Reports_Research/Offender_Information_Services_Branch/Annual/
CalPris/CALPRISd1996.pdf

California Department of Corrections and Rehabilitation. (2001). *California
prisoners and parolees 2001 (contains 2000 data).* Sacramento, CA: Department
of Corrections and Rehabilitation. Retrieved from http://www.cdcr.ca.gov/
Reports_Research/Offender_Information_Services_Branch/Annual/CalPris/
CALPRISd2001.pdf

California Department of Corrections and Rehabilitation. (2006). *California
prisoners and parolees 2005.* Sacramento, CA: Department of Corrections
and Rehabilitation. Retrieved from http://www.cdcr.ca.gov/Reports_
Research/Offender_Information_Services_Branch/Annual/CalPris/
CALPRISd2005.pdf

California Department of Corrections and Rehabilitation. (2011). *California
prisoners and parolees, 2010.* Sacramento, CA: Department of Corrections
and Rehabilitation. Retrieved from http://www.cdcr.ca.gov/Reports_
Research/Offender_Information_Services_Branch/Annual/CalPris/
CALPRISd2010.pdf

California Department of Corrections and Rehabilitation. (2014). *Prison
census data as of December 31, 2013.* Sacramento, CA: Department of
Corrections and Rehabilitation. Retrieved from http://www.cdcr.ca.gov/
Reports_Research/Offender_Information_Services_Branch/Annual/Census/
CENSUSd1312.pdf

California Department of Public Health. (2014a). *Proposition 215: Compassionate
Use Act of 1996.* Sacramento, CA: California Department of Public Health.
Retrieved from http://www.cdph.ca.gov/programs/mmp/pages/compas-
sionateuseact.aspx

California Department of Public Health. (2014b). *Medical marijuana program:
Facts and figures.* Sacramento, CA: California Department of Public Health.
Retrieved from http://www.cdph.ca.gov/programs/MMP

California Legislative Analyst's Office. (2014). *Proposition 47.* Sacramento, CA.
Retrieved from http://www.lao.ca.gov/ballot/2014/prop-47-110414.aspx

California Legislative Analyst's Office. (2017). *Proposition 64 revenues.* Sacramento,
CA. Retrieved from http://www.lao.ca.gov/handouts/crimjust/2017/
Proposition-64-Revenues-021617.pdf

California Office of the Attorney General. (2011). *Crime in California, 2010.* Sacramento, CA: California Department of Justice. Retrieved from http://ag.ca.gov/cjsc/publications/candd/cd10/preface.pdf

California Office of the Attorney General. (2012). *Crime in California, 2011.* Sacramento, CA: California Department of Justice. Retrieved from https://oag.ca.gov/sites/all/files/agweb/pdfs/cjsc/publications/candd/cd11/cd11.pdf

California Office of the Attorney General. (2012). *Crime in California, 2012.* Sacramento, CA: California Department of Justice. Retrieved from http://oag.ca.gov/sites/all/files/agweb/pdfs/cjsc/publications/candd/cd12/cd12.pdf

California Office of the Attorney General. (2016). *Crime in California, 2015.* Sacramento, CA: California Department of Justice. Retrieved from https://oag.ca.gov/cjsc/pubs

California Senate Bill 255. (2013). Retrieved from http://legoinfo.ca.gov/pub/13-14/bill/sen/sb.html

Dao, J. (2012, July 24). Aurora gunman's arsenal. *New York Times.* Retrieved from http://www.nytimes.com/2012/07/24/us/aurora-gunmans-lethal-arsenal.html

Drug Policy Alliance. (2013, October 15). Governor Brown vetoes bill to reduce the penalty for simple drug possession. Retrieved from http://www.drugpolicy.org/news/2013/10/governor-brown-vetoes-bill-reduce-penalty-simple-drug-possession

Drug Policy Alliance. (2014, September 16). Governor Brown signs overdose law expanding Naloxone access in California pharmacies. Retrieved from http://www.drugpolicy.org/news/2014/09/governor-jerry-brown-signs-overdose-law-expanding-naloxone-access-california-pharmacies

Federal Bureau of Investigation. (1981). *Prosecutive report: John Warnock Hinckley, Jr., attempted assassination of Ronald Reagan, President of the United States.* Washington, DC: U.S. Department of Justice. Retrieved from http://vault.fbi.gov/president-ronald-reagan-assassination-attempt/president-ronald-reagan-assassination-attempt-part-01-of-04/view

Federal Bureau of Investigation. (2016a). *Crime in the United States 2015: Arrests for drug abuse violations.* Washington, DC: U.S. Department of Justice. Retrieved from https://ucr.fbi.gov/crime-in-the-u.s/2015/crime-in-the-u.s.-2015/tables/arrest_table_arrests_for_drug_abuse_violations_percent_distribution_by_regions_2015.xls

Federal Bureau of Investigation. (2016b). *Crime in the United States 2015: Table 29: Estimated number of arrests.* Washington, DC: U.S. Department of Justice. Retrieved from https://ucr.fbi.gov/crime-in-the-u.s/2015/crime-in-the-u.s.-2015/tables/table-29

Fox, J., & Zawitz, M. (2007). *Homicide trends in the U.S.* Washington, DC: Bureau of Justice Statistics. Retrieved from http://www.bjs.gov/index.cfm?ty=pbdetail&iid=966

Gallup. (2013, October 22). *For the first time, Americans favor legalizing marijuana.* Retrieved from http://www.gallup.com/poll/165539/first-time-americans-favor-legalizing-marijuana.aspx

Goode, E. (2012, August 27). Before gunfire, hints of 'bad news.' *New York Times.* Retrieved from http://www.nytimes.com/2012/08/27/us/before-gunfire-in-colorado-theater-hints-of-bad-news-about-james-holmes.html

Goode, E. (2013, September 16). In gun debate, divide grows as both sides dig in for battle. *New York Times.* Retrieved from http://www.nytimes.com/2013/09/16/us/in-gun-debate-divide-grows-as-both-sides-dig-in-for-battle.html

Healey, J. (2013, September 11). Colorado lawmakers ousted in recall vote over gun law. *New York Times.* Retrieved from http://www.nytimes.com/2013/09/11/us/colorado-lawmaker-concedes-defeat-in-recall-over-gun-law.html

Henigan, D. (2009). *Lethal logic.* Washington, DC: Potomac Books.

House Select Committee on Assassinations. (1979). *Report* (pp. 287–96). Washington, DC: Government Printing Office. Retrieved from http://www.archives.gov/research/jfk/select-committee-report/part-2a.html#ray

Jacob Wetterling Act, 42 U.S.C.A. § 14071.

Kleinfield, N. (2013, March 29). Newtown killer's obsessions, in chilling detail. *New York Times.* Retrieved from http://www.nytimes.com/2013/03/29/nyregion/search-warrants-reveal-items-seized-at-adam-lanzas-home.html

Law Center to Prevent Gun Violence (LCPGV). (2011). *Gun laws matter.* Retrieved from http://smartgunlaws.org/wp-content/uploads/2010/07/Gun_Laws_Matter_Brochure.pdf

Los Angeles County Sheriff's Department (LASD). (2017). *Concealed weapon licensing policy.* Retrieved from http://shq.lasdnews.net/content/uoa/SHQ/ConcealedWeaponLicensePolicy.pdf

Maddaus, G. (2013, February 14). Sheriff Lee Baca and the gun-gift connection. *L.A. Weekly.* Retrieved from http://www.laweekly.com/2013-02-14/news/sheriff-lee-baca-concealed-weapons-permit/

Males, M., & Buchen, L. (2013). *Beyond Realignment: Counties' large disparities in imprisonment underlie ongoing prison crisis.* Center on Juvenile and Criminal Justice. Retrieved from http://www.cjcj.org/uploads/cjcj/documents/beyond_realignment_march_2013.pdf

McFadden, R. (2009, April 4). Upstate gunman kills 13 at citizenship class. *New York Times,* Retrieved from http://www.nytimes.com/2009/04/04/nyregion/04hostage.html

Moldea, D. (1997). *The killing of Robert F. Kennedy* (p. 80). New York: Norton.

Nagourney, A. (2011, January 10). A single, terrifying moment: Shots fired, a scuffle and some luck. *New York Times*. Retrieved from http://www.nytimes.com/2011/01/10/us/10reconstruct.html

NORML. (2017a). *Medical marijuana laws by state as of 5/10/2017*. Retrieved from http://norml.org/legal/medical-marijuana-2

NORML. (2017b). *States that have decriminalized as of 5/10/2017*. Retrieved from http://norml.org/aboutmarijuana/item/states-that-have-decriminalized

NORML. (2017c). *States that have legalized as of 5/10/2017*. Retrieved from http://norml.org/legal/legalization

President's Commission. (1964). *Report on the assassination of President Kennedy* (pp. 118–121, 689, 693–710). Washington, DC: U.S. Government Printing Office. Retrieved from http://www.archives.gov/research/jfk/warren-commission-report/

Romney, L. (2013, September 13). Oakland, reeling from gun violence, aims for unprecedented solution. *Los Angeles Times*. Retrieved from http://www.latimes.com/local/la-me-oakland-gun-law-20130914,0,7851727,full.story

Schmidt, M. (2013, September 18). State law prevented sale of assault rifle to suspect last week, officials say. *New York Times*. Retrieved from http://www.nytimes.com/2013/09/18/us/state-law-stopped-gunman-from-buying-rifle-officials-say.html

Shear, M. (2013, September 17). 12 shot to death by lone gunman at a naval base. *New York Times*. Retrieved from http://www.nytimes.com/2013/09/17/us/shooting-reported-at-washington-navy-yard.html

Skelton, G. (2007, May 3). A seminal event remembered. *Los Angeles Times*. Retrieved from http://articles.latimes.com/2007/may/03/local/me-cap3

Spitzer, R. (1995). *The politics of gun control*. London: Chatham House.

Urada, D., Hawken, A., Conner, B. T., Evans, E., Anglin, D., Yang, J., Teruya, C., Herbeck, D., Fan, J., Rutkowski, B., Gonzales, R., Rawson, R., Grella, C., Prendergast, M., Hser, Y., Hunter, J., & Poe, A. (2008). *Evaluation of Proposition 36: The Substance Abuse and Crime Prevention Act of 2000: 2008 report*. Department of Alcohol and Drug Programs: California Health and Human Services Agency. Retrieved from http://www.adp.ca.gov/SACPA/PDF/2008_Final_Report.pdf

U.S. Food and Drug Administration. (2017). Controlled Substances Act. Washington, DC: U.S. Department of Health & Human Services. Retrieved from https://www.fda.gov/regulatoryinformation/lawsenforcedbyfda/ucm148726.htm

Vernick, J., & Hepburn, L. (2003). State and federal gun laws: Trends for 1970-99. In J. Ludwig & P. J. Cook (Eds.), *Evaluating gun policy* (pp. 370–379). Washington, DC: Brookings Institution.

Virginia Tech Review Panel. (2007). *Mass shootings at Virginia Tech*. Richmond, VA: Commonwealth of Virginia. Retrieved from http://www.governor. virginia.gov/TempContent/techPanelReport.cfm

Zimring, F. (1975). Firearms and federal law: The Gun Control Act of 1968. *Journal of Legal Studies, 4*(1), 136, 139–141.

Cases Cited

Connecticut Dept. of Public Safety v. Doe, 38 U.S. 1 (2003)

District of Columbia v. Heller, no. 07-290 (2008). Retrieved from http://www.supremecourt.gov/opinions/07pdf/07-290.pdf

McDonald v. Chicago, no. 08-1521 (2010). Retrieved from http://www.supremecourt.gov/opinions/09pdf/08-1521.pdf

National Shooting Sports Foundation v. State of California, no. F072310 (2016). Retrieved from http://www.courts.ca.gov/opinions/documents/F072310.pdf

People v. Jones, 25 Cal.4th 98 (2001)

Peruta v. County of San Diego, no. 10-56971 (2014 and 2016). Retrieved from https://www.ca9.uscourts.gov/content/view.php?pk_id=0000000722

Rupp v. Becerra, no. 8:17-cv-007464 (2017). Retrieved from https://www.supremecourt.gov/opinions/07pdf/07-290.pdf

Chapter 12

Victims' Rights and Services in California

Christine L. Gardiner, Stacy L. Mallicoat,
Veronica M. Herrera, and Monisha Miller

Learning Objectives

After reading the chapter, students should be able to:

- Demonstrate an understanding of the history of the victims' movement in California and the nation.
- Explain Marsy's Law and the rights victims have in the state of California.
- Describe the intricate network of victim services and available support, including the agencies responsible.

This chapter provides an overview of victim's rights and services in California. It begins with a brief history of the victim's movement in California and the nation. Next it provides detailed information on victims' rights in California. Following the discussion of victims' rights, the chapter explains the intricate network of victim services and support in the state. Finally, it describes restorative justice and the role it plays in the California criminal justice system.

Brief History of the Victims' Movement

Victims have always been a part of the criminal justice system. After all, the majority of crimes involve someone who has been victimized as a result of the actions of an offender. However, victims have historically played a minor role in the system. In chapter 4, you learned that in the criminal court, it is the state that files charges against the offender (The State of California v. John/Jane Doe) rather the victim (John/Jane Smith v. John/Jane Doe). Generally speaking, victims were reduced to a piece of evidence in a case, assuming that any charges were filed against a defendant. Throughout the criminal justice process, victims received few, if any rights to information about the case nor were they able to participate in the process.

The *1967 Commission on Law Enforcement and Administration of Justice* was the first systematic evaluation of the criminal justice system in the United States. In their over 1,000-page report to Congress, the commission devoted only two pages to discussions about victims or victims' rights (Knepper, 1999). In 1972, there were only three victim assistance programs in the United States. One of these programs, a rape crisis center, was located in the San Francisco Bay Area (Young & Stein, 2004). In response to the treatment that crime victims received by the criminal justice system, victims' groups began to emerge throughout the country during the mid-1970s to provide support to victims and victims' families, to bring attention to certain crimes, and to advocate on behalf of victims. Examples of these efforts include Families and Friends of Missing Persons (FFMH), Mothers Against Drunk Driving (MADD), National Center for Victims of Crime (NCVC), and Parents of Murdered Children (PMC). The majority of these programs grew from community-based grassroots efforts. In 1975, the *National Organization for Victim Assistance (NOVA)* was created. Not only did NOVA serve to unify the discrete grassroots groups around a shared voice and purpose, its creation represented a turning point for the victims' rights movement (Young & Stein, 2004).

Partially aided by the Law Enforcement Assistance Agency in the 1970s as well as increased public awareness of the issue early in the 1980s, the Victims' Movement gained momentum and lobbied for the creation of victims' rights and victim programs (Young & Stein, 2004). A key moment came in 1981 when the Violent Crime Task Force, appointed by President Ronald Reagan, "recommended that the attorney general lead the way 'in ensuring that the victims of crime are accorded proper status by the criminal justice system'" (Gest, 2001, p. 50). This recommendation led to the creation of President Reagan's *Task Force on Victims of Crime* in 1982. The task force was headed by the infamous Oakland, CA, prosecutor and champion of victims' rights, Lois Herrington. In their report, the task force offered 68 recommendations aimed at improving victims' assistance, including the recommendation for a federal constitutional amendment for victims' rights. Although the federal government never did adopt a constitutional amendment guaranteeing victims' rights, the U.S. Congress did pass the *Victim and Witness Protection Act of 1982* (which created the Office for Victims of Crime within the Department of Justice) and the Victims of Crime Act (VOCA) in 1984 (Gest, 2001; Young & Stein, 2004).

Victims' Rights in California

Since the beginning of the victims' rights movement, California has been a leader in championing for the needs of victims. In 1965, California was the first state in the nation to establish a victims' compensation fund. In 1982, they were the first state to enact a constitutional amendment governing victims' rights. According to Steve Twist (general counsel for National Victims' Constitutional Amendment Network), California currently has the "most comprehensive victim's bill of rights in the nation" (NVCAP, n.d.). *Marsy's Law (California Victims' Bill of Rights Act of 2008)*, replaced the 1982 Constitutional Victims' Bill of Rights Amendment and provides victims the right to a voice, compensation, and due process among other things (Victims' Bill of Rights Act of 2008).

Marsy's Law: Victims' Bill of Rights Act of 2008

Marsy's Law amended the California Constitution to provide victims with meaningful and enforceable rights within the criminal justice system. As defined in Marsy's Law, a victim is

> a person who suffers direct or threatened physical, psychological, or financial harm as a result of the commission or attempted commission of a crime or delinquent act. The term "victim" also includes the person's spouse, parents, children, siblings, or guardian, and includes a lawful representative of a crime victim who is deceased, a minor, or physically or psychologically incapacitated. The term "victim" does not include a person in custody for an offense, the accused, or a person whom the court finds who would not act in the best interests of a minor victim (California Constitution Article 1, Section 28(b)(17)(e)).

The Victim's Bill of Rights, which includes the following 16 specific rights, can be found in Article 1, Section 28 of the California Constitution and provides for the following rights for victims of crime:

1. Fairness and respect
2. Protection from the defendant
3. Victim safety considerations in setting bail and release conditions
4. Prevention of the disclosure of confidential information
5. Refusal to be interviewed by the defense
6. Conference with the prosecution and notice of pretrial disposition
7. Notice of and presence at public proceedings
8. Appearance at court proceedings and expression of views

9. Speedy trial and prompt conclusion of the case
10. Provision of information to the probation department
11. Receipt of pre-sentence report
12. Information about conviction, sentence, incarceration, release, and escape
13. Restitution
14. Prompt return of property
15. Notice of parole procedures and release on parole
16. Safety of victim and public are factors in parole release

As can be seen, victims' rights are not limited to restitution and compensation—though much of the case law revolves around these essential issues, and they are critical rights for many victims. California recognized that victims' needs often are centered on the need to feel safe and secure, to have a voice in the criminal justice process, and to be protected from additional harm. Under Marsy's Law, victims have the right to be notified of all court proceedings and to be present at all proceedings, including parole board hearings. Furthermore, victims have the right to confer with the prosecutor and to be heard, if so requested, at *any* public court proceeding. Conversely, victims have the right to *not* talk to the defense attorney about their experience. Finally, victims have the right to receive the pre-sentence report and information about all decisions regarding conviction, sentence, incarceration, release, death, and escape. Victims can register with the California State Victim Notification Service (VINE), a free anonymous service, that allows them to use the telephone or internet to search for information regarding their offender's custody status and register to receive telephone and email notification when their offender's custody status changes (to register call 1-877-411-5588 or visit www.thevinelink.com).

In all, 16 of California's 29 legal codes have sections specifically pertaining to victims' rights. These rights can be found on the California attorney general's website at www.ag.ca.gov/victimservices. In addition to the California Constitution and the attorney general's web page, many counties also provide victims' rights information on their websites (often on the district attorney's webpage). Individuals interested in case law should visit the National Center for Victims of Crime website, which maintains a database of victims' rights laws in all 50 states (www.victimlaw.info).

Services and Support for Victims

Not only is California a leader in victims' rights, it is also a leader in victim services. As home to one of the first victim services programs in the United

States—a rape crisis center in the San Francisco Bay Area—California has long been an advocate for victim services (Young & Stein, 2004). For example, in response to the growth in victim service agencies and the need for trained personnel, California State University, Fresno offered the first Victim Services Certificate program in the country beginning in the mid-1980s (Young & Stein, 2004). Additionally, though not exclusively for victims, the statewide 2-1-1 system has a wide variety of service providers ready to assist crime victims in crisis (or non-crisis) situations. Staffers can provide referrals to temporary shelters, suicide hotlines, counseling, medical care, and a multitude of other services to individuals and families in need.

As might be expected, victims' services in California are well coordinated and victim service programs exist in all 58 counties to provide information and referrals to crime victims. State agencies and programs that provide services and assistance to victims of crime include the California Office of the Attorney General, Victims Service Unit; the California Department of Corrections and Rehabilitation, Office of Victim and Survivor Rights and Services (OVSRS); California Victims Compensation Board (CalVCP); the California Victim/Witness Assistance Program (VWAP); and the Victims of Crime Resource Center. In addition, rape crisis organizations and domestic violence shelters provide specialized services for victims and their families.

California Office of the Attorney General Victims' Services Unit

The California Office of the Attorney General Victims Services Unit offers crime victims and their families support and information at every stage of the criminal process. The Victims' Services Unit provides appeal notification to victims and their families, as well as assistance and outreach when the attorney general's office is prosecuting a case (State of California, Department of Justice, n.d.). Victims and their families can also track the status of appeals and recusal cases. These updates allow victims and their families to exercise their rights to testify or otherwise participate in parole, clemency, and execution proceedings. In addition to working with victims involved in indicted cases, the Victim Service Unit staff members also work closely with Victim/Witness Assistance staff from county programs as well as various federal agencies, such as the Federal Bureau of Investigation, U.S. Postal Inspection Service, or U.S. Immigration and Customs Enforcement, who also provide services to federal victims for cases under investigation.

CDCR Office of Victim and Survivor Rights and Services

The California Department of Corrections and Rehabilitation's (CDCR) Office of Victim and Survivor Rights and Services (OVSRS) offers information and assistance to victims and survivors of criminal activity where the offender has been sentenced to a CDCR facility. With the mission of giving crime victims and their families a voice, OVSRS was formed in 1988. "OVSRS is responsible for providing information, notification, restitution, outreach, training, referral and support services to crime victims and their next of kin" (California Department of Corrections & Rehabilitation, n.d.). Services the OVSRS provides include notification to victims, family members of the victim, or witnesses who testified against the offender about the offender's release, death, or escape; the opportunity to provide input regarding special conditions of parole for the offender; notification of an impending Parole Suitability Hearing of the offender; collection of restitution from offenders who are in the custody of the CDCR; and assistance with writing victim impact statements for CDCR-related proceedings. In order to receive services from the OVSRS, a victim or family member of the victim may be required to fill out the appropriate form for a specific service (a list of the forms can be found at http://www.cdcr.ca.gov/Victim_Services/publications.html).

California Victims Compensation Program (CalVCP)

As previously mentioned, California was the first state to establish a Victim Compensation Program (CalVCP) in 1965. CalVCP was established to provide financial reimbursement to victims of violent crime who suffer unreimbursed financial losses due to physical/emotional injury, threat of physical injury, or death as a direct result of a crime. The CalVCP program can provide economic assistance with such things as medical/dental and hospital expenses, counseling/therapy services, income/support loss, relocation expenses, rehabilitation/job retraining, funeral/burial expenses, crime scene clean up, and home security, among other costs. Property damage or loss is not a covered expense. California law limits reimbursements, not to exceed $63,000. This program is funded by fines and penalties assessed by the courts and deposited in the Restitution Fund. CalVCP covers victims of crime that occur in California or residents of California victimized out of the state or country.

The CalVCP can help victims and family members of victims of crimes such as domestic violence, child abuse, assault, sexual assault, elder abuse, molestation, homicide, robbery, hate crimes, drunk driving, vehicular manslaughter, human trafficking, stalking, and online harassment (State of California, n.d.). CalVCP also reimburses "good Samaritans," people who go out of their way to rescue someone else, apprehend a criminal, or prevent a crime from taking place. A private citizen (not a law enforcement officer or rescue worker) who is injured or who suffers financial loss while helping others this way is eligible for compensation of up to $10,000 through the Good Samaritan Program.

California Victim/Witness Assistance Program (VWAP)

California Victim/Witness Assistance Program (VWAP) was established in 1977 and funded by the California Office of Emergency Services (CalOES). In the aftermath of crime, a victim may experience emotional, financial, and legal difficulties. These difficulties can lead to feelings of anger, helplessness, hopelessness, guilt, and frustration. The role of the Victim Witness Assistance Program is to ensure that victims of crimes who have suffered physical, financial, or emotional trauma, are informed of their rights and receive the assistance and protection to which they are entitled under the law. There are 59 VWAPs in California: 43 in district attorney's offices, 13 in probation departments, 2 in community-based organizations, and 1 in a city administration office (Los Angeles). Each county has several branch offices located throughout the county to be more accessible to victims. For example, Los Angeles county has 32 VWAP branch offices.

Victims are assigned victim advocates who provide support and act as a liaison between families and court officials and law enforcement. They empower crime victims by informing them of their rights. Victim advocates work in courthouses and police stations, providing services and referrals to assist crime victims and their families to become survivors. Some victim advocates work in specialized units within the district attorney office, focusing on helping victims of specific types crimes such as gang crimes, sex crimes, family violence, elder abuse, and human trafficking. Victim advocates are available to assist victims in several languages. Program services are provided free of charge and there is no legal residency or citizenship requirement.

The VWAP provides a variety services and assistance to victims and witnesses. VWAP mandated services include non-court related assistance such as crisis intervention and follow-up counseling for emotional, personal, and financial problems resulting from the crime; emergency financial assistance; resources and referral to social service agencies, counselors, and others who can assist with personal problems; property recovery of personal items that are being held as evidence; employer notification; and assistance filing claims with CalVCP. Mandated court related assistance includes orientation to the criminal justice system and information about the status of the court case and victims' rights in court, court escort to attend court with victims and provide emotional support, helping victims prepare victim impact statements during sentencing and parole board hearings, restitution assistance, and temporary restraining order assistance in family court (Halcon, n.d.).

Victims of Crime Resource Center (VCRC)

The Victims of Crime Resource Center (VCRC) is also funded through CalOES and run by the Pacific McGeorge School of Law in Sacramento (VCRC, n.d.). The center is mandated by California Penal Code section 13897 and exists to provide information and referrals to crime victims, family members of crime victims, victim advocates, and victim service providers. The center uses volunteer lawyers and law students enrolled in crime victims' assistance legal clinic programs to counsel crime victims throughout California. Victims can contact the center by a single state-wide toll-free phone number (1-800-VICTIMS). It also maintains an extensive website for victims (http://www.1800victims.org). Not only is the center a clearinghouse of victims' rights information, the center also provides legal research on victims' issues for service providers. The center also offers limited representation to victims of crime, determined on a case-by-case basis. Through this service, victims are able to receive assistance from attorneys in exercising their rights at various stages in the criminal justice process.

Rape Crisis Organizations

Rape crisis organizations in California (and throughout the United States) began as small community-based movements seeking to provide assistance for victims of sexual assault. Within these organizations, the goals were "to change the society that permitted and encouraged the oppression of women and sexual violence against them" (Collins & Whalen, 1989, p. 61). While today's rape crisis organizations are staffed with clinical mental health professionals, these early centers were primarily run by volunteers, many of whom had their own experiences with rape and sexual assault. During the 1980s, rape crisis centers began to link up with other community and government agencies, such as hospital and police departments. They also began to link up to other community service agencies, largely due to the need to share funding sources in a time where state and local budgets were strained. While the shift from a grassroots to a professional organization changed the way in which these organizations functioned on a day-to-day basis, the fundamental philosophy aimed at eliminating sexual assault remained. Despite the professionalization of the rape crisis movement, volunteers continue to serve a vital role in rape crisis organizations as crisis line responders and victim support services throughout the criminal justice process.

Victims' services can vary significantly in the types of direct services provided, the levels of community support and action, and their levels of social activism. In addition, programs vary in terms of their connectivity to other services, such as hospitals and police agencies. For example, Community Service Programs (CSP) is a victim service agency in Orange County, California. The organization provides services for victims of all different types of victimization, including rape and sexual assault. As the only rape crisis organization in the county, CSP provides direct services for teen and adult victims of these crimes.[1] When a case of rape or sexual assault is reported to the police and physical evidence is to be collected, victims are transported to Anaheim Regional Medical Center where a CSP advocate meets with the victim to provide crisis services. Specially trained nurse practitioners are on hand to collect samples for a rape kit. CSP also provides victims' services for the victim throughout the criminal justice process. Regardless of the status of the case in the system (whether the victim decides to make a report to the police or if charges are filed), CSP also provides mental health and therapeutic resources for victims.

Interviews with rape crisis workers illustrate that victims' services workers view their work as a way to advocate and empower victims of crime. Here, rape crisis workers serve as a source of support for victims. In addition, victims' advocates hope to reduce the trauma of their victimization experience by providing information on available services and to empower victims about their available choices (Mallicoat, Marquez, & Rosenbaum, 2007).

Domestic Violence Shelters and Services

Another example of a victims' services agency is a shelter for victims of intimate partner violence. While the term "shelter" refers specifically to housing assistance (often in confidential locations to protect victims from their batterers), many are tied to larger community agencies designed to provide community education and therapeutic resources for victims. However, many of these organizations are either closing their doors or have significantly limited their services due to the limited availability of funds. California's Department of Public Health *Domestic Violence Program* was created following the deaths of Nicole Brown Simpson (the ex-wife of O.J. Simpson) and Ronald Goldman and has funded over 94 different domestic agencies statewide. In 2009, Governor Schwarzenegger removed the state funding for this program ($20.4 million),

---

1. Under California statutory law, rape or sexual assault of a child under the age of 14 is handled by a separate organization that provides investigative and wraparound services for child victims.

leaving organizations to survive on funding from the federal government, grants from foundations, and donations from private citizens (AP, 2009). Such cuts have a significant effect on victims, a group whose numbers are staggering. According to the National Network to End Domestic Violence (2016), 5,568 victims in California received domestic violence services by 111 participating programs in California during a 24-hour period on September 14, 2016. On the same day, 1,083 victim requests for services were denied due to insufficient resources (76% were for shelter). Given that many victims never reach out for help from police and other criminal justice authorities, these services provide a valuable resource for victims. Without funding, the lives of many victims may be in jeopardy.

Although rape and domestic violence represent a large portion of victimizations, there are other types of victimizations as well and services exist for victims of every type of crime in California. Victim service organizations, though not as well funded as they once were, are plentiful in the state. For example, human trafficking is a crime in that has been increasing in California and which has special laws and programs aimed to protect the victims and prosecute the criminals. These cases are complex and difficult to detect and prosecute, because the immigration status of most victims discourages them from reporting and seeking help.

Restorative Justice

Over the past two decades, there has been a growing interest in new approaches to justice that involve the community and focus on restoring victims back to their normal lives after being victimized. In recent years, a new goal of sentencing has emerged with a focus that is based on the belief that sentencing should involve restoration and justice for all of the parties that are affected by the crime committed. Restorative justice is this alternative model of sentencing, which focuses on the restoration of the victim, and society, with the involvement of the offender. Traditionally, victims have been left out of the justice process, and it has only been recently that programs have emerged to help victims make sure that their voices are heard.

According to John Braithwaite (2004, p. 28), restorative justice is: "a process where all stakeholders affected by an injustice have an opportunity to discuss how they have been affected by the injustice and to decide what should be done to repair the harm."

In a restorative justice process, the citizens who have been affected by a crime must take an active role in addressing that crime (Braithwaite, 2004).

While victims are taking an active role in the process, offenders are encouraged to take responsibility for their actions. It is based on a concept of justice that considers crime and wrongdoing to be an offense against an individual or community, rather than the state(Judicial Council of California, 2006). The guiding principles of restorative justice are (National Institute of Justice, 2007):

- Crime is an offense against human relationships.
- Victims and the community are central to justice processes.
- The first priority of justice processes is to assist victims.
- The second priority is to restore the community, to the degree possible.
- The offender has personal responsibility to victims and to the community for crimes committed.
- Stakeholders share responsibilities for restorative justice through partnerships for action.
- The offender will develop improved competency and understanding as a result of the restorative justice experience.

Restorative Justice Policy in California

California's history as it relates to restorative justice is unique. Prior to 1850, California was part of Mexico and under the Mexican California legal system, which encouraged parties to solve their disputes among each other rather than filing a lawsuit. This system, which placed community healing at the forefront, worked most of the time and 85% of civil litigation cases were resolved through this "conciliation" process (Judicial Council of California, 2006). When California joined the United Sates, it adopted the traditional U.S. legal system, which was not concerned with the breach in community caused by crime (Judicial Council of California, 2006).

In its modern context, restorative justice originated in the 1970s as mediation or reconciliation between victims and offenders. In 1974, a probation officer in Elmira, Ontario, walked door-to-door with two teenagers, to meet directly with their victims following a vandalism spree to agree to restitution. The officer's actions were regarded as successful in connecting the fields of conflict resolution and victim–offender reconciliation and are credited with the initiation of the restorative justice movement in North America (OJJDP, 2006). Forty years later, the restorative justice model is still gaining traction and momentum in justice systems across the county.

Despite numerous attempts to incorporate restorative justice into California's legal system, statewide efforts have mostly failed (Judicial Council of California, 2006). It wasn't until 1999 that we saw some successes at the state level, including

AB 637, which shifted the focus of the California Youth Authority from retributive punishment to community and victim restoration, offender training, and treatment (Judicial Council of California, 2006). Senate Bill 334, also passed in 1999 and which contained specific restorative justice language, gave victims the right to be notified of all judicial proceedings and to provide victim impact statements in all juvenile court hearings (Judicial Council of California, 2006). There has been no statewide effort to incorporate restorative justice into the criminal (adult) justice system. Although there is interest in restorative justice in California, the state has seen more success at the local (county) level.

Victim-Offender Reconciliation Programs in California

There are several types of victim-offender reconciliation programs (VORPs), all of which are in existence in California in some form, including: (1) victim-offender mediation, (2) victim-impact panels, (3) restorative justice panels, (4) community reparative boards, (5) community-based courts, (6) family-group counseling, (7) circle sentencing, (8) court diversion programs, and (9) peer mediation (Judicial Council of California, 2006; Schmalleger & Ortiz Smykla, 2011). These methods both supplement and provide an alternative to traditional justice processing. Research indicates that victim satisfaction with these programs is generally very high and one of the main strengths of this approach (Evje & Cushman, 2000). In 2004 (latest available data) there were 24 victim-offender reconciliation programs (VORP) throughout the state of California (Fresno Pacific University, 2004); though it is highly likely that this number has increased in the past decade. The first VORP was started in Fresno in 1982 (Judicial Council of California, 2006).

Conclusion

As can be seen, California has a long history of advocating for victims. This history began with grassroots victim services agencies advocating on behalf of victims beginning in the 1970s and eventually grew into Marsy's Law (Victims' Bill of Rights Act of 2000), possibly the strongest victims' rights law in the nation. Through this law, which amended the California Constitution, the state enumerated strong, unequivocal rights for victims, provided victims with a voice in the criminal justice process, coordinated services to help victims heal, and established victim centers to inform victims of their rights and benefits.

Key Terms and Definitions

1967 Commission on Law Enforcement and Administration of Justice— First systematic evaluation of the criminal justice system in the United States.

California Office of the Attorney General Victims Services Unit— This unit provides appeal notification to victims and their families, as well as assistance and outreach when the Attorney General's Office is prosecuting a case.

California Victim Compensation Program (CalVCP)— This program provides financial reimbursement to victims of crime who suffer unreimbursed financial losses due to injury, threat of injury, or death as a direct result of a crime.

California Victim/Witness Assistance Program (VWAP)— This program ensures that victims of crimes who have suffered physical, financial, or emotional trauma, are informed of their rights, receive the assistance and protection to which they are entitled under the law.

Marsy's Law (California Victims' Bill of Rights Act of 2008)— Provided California crime victims with 16 meaningful and enforceable rights within the criminal justice system. These rights are found in Article 1, Section 28 of the California Constitution.

National Organization for Victim Assistance (NOVA)— This organization unifies grassroots victims' rights groups around a share voice and purpose. Its creation in 1975 represented a turning point in the victims' rights movement.

Office of Victim and Survivor Rights and Services (OVSRS)— This program offers information and assistance to victims and survivors of criminal activity where the offender has been sentenced to a CDCR facility.

Restorative Justice— An alternative model of sentencing which focuses on restoring the harm done to the victim and society. It involves the offender trying to make amends with individuals affected by his/her crimes and encourages stakeholders affected by the injustice to discuss the incident and participate in the restoration process.

Task Force on Victims of Crime— Created by President Reagan in 1982 to recommend and improve victims' rights and services in the United States.

Victim and Witness Protection Act of 1982 (VWPA)— Major legislation that increased protection of victims and witnesses in the United States, including restitution.

Victims of Crime Resource Center (VCRC)— Legally mandated center that provide information and referrals to crime victims, family members of crime victims, victim advocates, and victim service providers.

Internet Websites

California 211: http://www.211california.org/

California Attorney General's Office, Marsy's Law: http://oag.ca.gov/victimservices/marsys_law

California Department of Corrections and Rehabilitation, Victims Rights: http://www.cdcr.ca.gov/victim_services/victim_rights.html

California Victims Compensation: http://vcgcb.ca.gov/victims/

California Victims of Crime Resource Center: http://www.1800victims.org/

Fresno Pacific University Restorative Justice Project: https://www.fresno.edu/programs-majors/graduate/restorative-justice

International Institute of Restorative Practices: http://www.realjustice.org/

Jerry Lee Center of Criminology at Cambridge: http://www.crim.cam.ac.uk/research/experiments/

National Institute of Justice: http://www.nij.gov/

Office of Justice Programs: https://www.victimlaw.org/

Restorative Justice Online (Prison Fellowship International): http://www.restorativejustice.org/

Restorative Justice Research Network: http://www.iars.org.uk/content/RJRN

Victims' Rights Law Center: http://www.victimrights.org/

Review Questions

1. What resources exist in the state of California for crime victims?
2. What are the specific rights afforded to crime victims in California? What is the name of the law that establishes these rights?
3. Explain the main steps in the national victims' rights movement in chronological order from the 1967 Commission on Law Enforcement to the passage of the 1982 Victim and Witness Protection Act.
4. What services does the California Victim/Witness Assistance Program provide to victims and witnesses?
5. What is restorative justice? How is it implemented in California?

Critical Thinking Questions

1. What impact did the victim's rights movement have on the criminal justice system in California?

2. Criminal justice policy debates are often framed as a dichotomy between victims and perpetrators. In other words, a person is either "for the victim" or they are "for the offender." Why does framing the debate this way almost always result in "tougher" criminal justice policies?
3. Why did the civil right movement, and specifically the women's right movement, need to precede the victims' rights movement? Is it coincidental that the victims' rights movement followed almost immediately after the women's rights movement?

References

Associated Press (AP). (2009, September 9). California violence shelters closing amid budget cuts. *MSNBC*. Retrieved from http://www.msnbc.msn.com/id/ 32742820/ns/us_news-life/t/calif-violence-shelters-closing-amid-budget- cuts/#.T2jzpxySeT0

Braithwaite, J. (2004). Restorative justice and de-professionalization. *Good Society Journal, 13*(1), 28–31.

California Department of Corrections and Rehabilitation. (n.d.) Victim & survivor rights & services. Retrieved from http://www.cdcr.ca.gov/Victim_Services/

California Department of Justice. (n.d.) Victim Services Unit. Retrieved from https://oag.ca.gov/victimservices/

Collins, B. G., & Whalen, M. B. (1989). The rape crisis movement: Radical or reformist? *Social Work, 34*, 61–63.

Evje, A., & Cushman, R. (2000). *A summary of the evaluations of six California victim offender reconciliation programs*. A report to the California Legislature submitted by the Judicial Council of California. Retrieved from http://www.courts.ca.gov/documents/vorp.pdf

Fresno Pacific University. (2004). *Restorative justice project: Directory of California victim offender programs*. Retrieved from http://peace.fresno.edu/rjp/vomdir.pdf

Gest, T. (2001). *Crime and politics*. New York, NY: Oxford University Press.

Halcon, K. (n.d.). Victim Witness Assistance Program of Santa Clara County. Retrieved from http://law.scu.edu/wp-content/uploads/VWAP-PPT_KHal-con-PDF.pdf

Judicial Council of California. (2006). *Balanced and restorative justice: An information manual for California*. Retrieved from http://www.courts.ca.gov/documents/BARJManual3.pdf

Knepper, P. (1999). *North Carolina's criminal justice system*. Durham, NC: Carolina Academic Press.

Mallicoat, S. L., Marquez, S. A., & Rosenbaum, J. L. (2007). Guiding philosophies for rape crisis centers. In R. Muraskin (Ed.), *It's a crime: Women and criminal justice* (4th ed., pp. 217–225). Upper Saddle River, NJ: Prentice-Hall.

National Institute of Justice. (2007). Restorative justice. Retrieved from https://www.nij.gov/topics/courts/restorative-justice/Pages/welcome.aspx#note1

National Network to End Domestic Violence. (2016.) *Domestic violence counts California summary.* Retrieved from http://nnedv.org/downloads/Census/DVCounts2016/California.pdf

National Organization for Victim Assistance. (n.d.). Retrieved from http://www.trynova.org/about/

National Victims' Constitutional Amendment Passage (NVCAP). (n.d.). *Marsy's Law—California's new VRA—Passes.* Retrieved from http://www.nvcap.org/

Office of Juvenile Justice and Delinquency Prevention (OJJDP). (2006). *Balanced and restorative justice: Program summary.* NCJ 149727. Retrieved from https://www.ncjrs.gov/pdffiles/bal.pdf

Schmalleger, F., & Ortiz Smykla, J. (2011). *Corrections in the 21st century,* (6th ed., pp. 64–66). New York, NY: McGraw Hill.

The State of California. (n.d.). The California Victim Compensation Board. Retrieved from http://www.victims.ca.gov/victims/eligibility.aspx/

The United States Attorney's Office, Central District of California. (n.d.). Victim/Witness Assistance Program. Retrieved from https://www.justice.gov/usao-cdca/victimwitness-assistance-program/

Victims' Bill of Rights Act of 2008. (2008). Retrieved from https://oag.ca.gov/victimservices/marsys_law

Victims of Crime Resource Center (VCRC). (n.d.). Retrieved from http://www.1800victims.org/

Young, M., & Stein, J. (2004). *The history of the crime victims' movement in the United States: A component of the Office for Victims of Crime Oral History Project.* Washington, DC: U.S. Department of Justice. Retrieved from https://www.ncjrs.gov/ovc_archives/ncvrw/2005/pdf/historyofcrime.pdf

Chapter 13

Employment Trends for California's Criminal Justice System

Sigrid Williams, Stacy Mallicoat, and Christine Gardiner

Learning Objectives

After reading the chapter, students should be able to:

- Demonstrate an ability to research the scope of career opportunities available and the requirements for education, training, certification, and licensure in a variety of criminal justice professions.
- State the major types of occupations found in the public safety field.
- Demonstrate an understanding of the initial entry requirements of public service (physical, educational, and legal).
- Describe the various types of law and of legal practices within the legal profession.
- Become familiar with educational and experiential requirements needed to establish and maintain successful careers in each practice area.

Introduction

Over the past three decades, the criminal justice system has provided significant opportunities for employment. Many of these opportunities have come as a result of the dramatic growth in the state's prison population, as well as increased funding opportunities from the federal government to police agencies to provide additional officers in the community. While many cities and counties have seen a recent reduction in the number of available jobs as a result of budgetary challenges throughout the state, employment in the criminal justice system remains a stable growth opportunity for those seeking opportunities to work within the system.

This chapter highlights some of the major areas of employment in the criminal justice system. First, we begin with a discussion of law enforcement as a career. Second, we highlight some of the different occupations within the court system. Third, we look at the occupation of correctional officers. We end this chapter with a review of community supervision positions, such as probation and parole.

Law Enforcement as a Career

There are more people employed in law enforcement careers than are employed in any other area of the criminal justice system. When most people think of "law enforcement," they think of police officers; however, there are many other career opportunities available in this segment of the criminal justice system. For example, the following positions exist in most law enforcement agencies in the state: crime analyst, records clerk, crime prevention officer,

Table 13.1. California Law Enforcement Employment and Salary Statistics

Description	National Average Salary	California Average Salary
Correctional Officers and Jailers	$46,750	$70,020
Detectives and Criminal Investigators	$78,120	$100,360
Police and Sheriff's Patrol Officers	$59,680	$98,250
Private Investigators and Detectives	$48,190	$61,610
State Level—Fish and Game Wardens	$51,730	$74,560
Security Guards	$25,770	$30,760
Emergency Dispatcher	$38,870	$60,040
Forensic Science Technician	$56,750	$80,150

Source: U.S. Department of Labor, Bureau of Labor Statistics, 2016. http://www.bls.gov/oes/EDD/LMID Occupational Employment Statistics Survey, 2016

community service officer, parking enforcement officer, and, of course, crime scene investigator. First, we will discuss what it takes to become a sworn police officer/deputy sheriff.

Police Officer/Deputy Sheriff

California Government Code Section 1031(a-f) requires that individuals vested with the powers of a peace officer need to meet the state minimum selection standards, which include:

- U.S. citizen or permanent resident who has applied for U.S. citizenship
- High school graduate or GED equivalent
- Minimum age of 18 at date of hire
- No felony convictions and/or no misdemeanor convictions that would prevent the applicant from carrying a gun
- Good moral character
- Free of any physical, emotional, or mental condition that might adversely affect one's ability to exercise the powers of a peace officer

As mentioned in chapter five, the California Peace Officer Standards and Training Commission (POST) sets the training standards for all sworn law enforcement officers in the state. According to POST Regulations (Commission Regulations 9050–9055), the minimum entrance requirements for most law enforcement agencies in the state also include:

- Good physical condition and excellent health
- Weight appropriate to height and build
- Possession of a valid CDL
- Clean driving record
- No poor employment history
- Clean and responsible financial history

POST regulations are intended to set the minimum standards for the field, and local agencies often create requirements that exceed these minimums, such as a minimum age requirement of 21 years old and/or requiring a two-year college degree. Candidates who meet the above requirements also undergo a battery of tests, including a written exam to measure the reading and writing abilities of prospective officers, a physical abilities test, an oral interview, a background check to ensure good moral character [per GC § 1031(e)], a complete medical exam, a polygraph test, and a psychological exam (POST, 2011).

There are several basic issues that often disqualify applicants for law enforcement positions: Failure to meet minimum physical standards, inability to meet the mental and psychological standards, and failure to pass the criminal background check. Police and sheriff's departments throughout California have all stated the primary reason applicants are failing their backgrounds is lying. Applicants are being disqualified for failing to disclose information in their personal history statement, failing to own up to mistakes, and failing to disclose embarrassing situations. Background detectives/investigators throughout California all agree applicants must have honesty, integrity, and credibility.

In 2016, the U.S. Bureau of Labor Statistics (BLS) estimated that peace officers throughout the nation earned an annual average salary of $59,680. California is ranked highest in the United States with an annual average salary of $96,660, followed by New Jersey ($87,490), Alaska ($79,510), Washington ($76,340), and the District of Columbia ($73,250). Officers in California are very well paid, as evidenced by the fact that nine of the top ten highest paying metropolitan areas are in California (BLS, 2016).

Table 13.2. Police and Detectives jobs according to the
U.S. Department of Labor

Industry	Employment	Percent of industry employment	Hourly mean wage	Annual mean wage
Local Government	560,590	10.42	$30.13	$62,680
State Government	60,380	2.76	$33.27	$69,190
Colleges, Universities, and Professional Schools	14,440	0.48	$25.44	$52,920
Federal Executive Branch	12,060	0.60	$26.43	$54,980
Elementary and Secondary Schools	4,500	0.05	$24.65	$51,260

Source: U.S. Department of Labor, Bureau of Labor Statistics, 2016

Benefits packages for police officers usually include medical insurance, dental insurance, life insurance, vacation, sick leave, family leave, and long-term disability pay. Many departments also include educational incentives, bilingual allowances, uniform and equipment allowances, and lucrative retirement eligibility packages at age 50. Many sworn officers in California receive a retirement package which equals 3% for each year of service at the highest yearly income, up to 90% of a police officer's final pay for officers who are employed for thirty years. This has recently changed in many jurisdictions, wherein new legislation regarding public service is offering retirement benefits of 2% at age 55 for each year of service at the highest yearly income.

Police and detectives held about 657,690 jobs nationwide in 2016 (BLS, 2016). About 85% of these positions were found with local government agencies. Job opportunities in most local police departments will be favorable for qualified individuals for the near future (BLS, 2016).

According to the Career and Technical Education of Orange County (CTEoc) Public Safety Regional Advisory Board, law enforcement agencies are looking for mature, seasoned individuals to work in law enforcement. "The younger generation will be challenged" as they will be competing against older, educated, and military-trained candidates. To get hired, candidates in the future will need to demonstrate responsibility and life experience. They will need to be stable, be able to sell themselves, and will need to be diverse—not merely developed in one specific field (V. Anderson, personal communication, December 2, 2011). Departments are also looking for individuals with knowledge in technology, the willingness to continue one's education (professional development), and strong "soft" skills (integrity and morals). Agencies value diversity and place a high value on hiring women and minorities, as well as individuals who speak multiple languages. California's Employment Development Department (EDD) (2012) is projecting that California law enforcement agencies will have on an annual basis 2,670 job openings through 2020.

Private Investigator

Private detectives and investigators generally perform specialized work that requires follow-up. Some may work as computer forensic investigators, legal investigators, corporate investigators, or store detectives, also known as loss prevention agents (BLS, 2011). While there is no formal educational requirement for most private detectives and investigators, some have post-secondary degrees and many were law enforcement officers in a previous career. In California, private investigators must be licensed with the Bureau of Security and Investigative Services of the California Department of Consumer Affairs (BSIS) and meet minimal eligibility

Table 13.3. Estimated Employment and Projected Growth for Police and Sheriffs

Geographic Area (Estimated Year-Projected Year) 2014–2024	Median Annual Wages (2014)	Estimated Employment	Projected Employment	Numeric Change	Percent Change	Add'l. Openings Due to Net Replacements
United States	59,680	680,000	714,200	34,200	5.0	Unknown
California	96,660	70,790	73,700	5,000	7.3	22,600
East Bay Area	100,985	4,670	4,590	-80	-1.7	1,540
Fresno County	68,740	1,050	1,220	170	16.2	350
Inland Empire Area	91,878	4,330	4,810	480	11.1	1,430
Kern County	69,934	1,570	1,730	160	10.2	520
Los Angeles County	99,940	24,690	26,270	1,580	6.4	8,140
Northern Coast Region	89,247	560	660	100	17.9	180
Orange County	100,440	3,910	N/A	N/A	N/A	N/A
Sacramento Metro Area	92,837	3,970	4,310	340	8.6	1,310
San Benito and Santa Clara Co.	117,647	3,700	3,790	90	2.4	1,220
San Diego County	77,510	4,720	N/A	N/A	N/A	N/A
San Francisco Bay Area	109,642	4,580	4,640	60	1.3	1,510
Santa Barbara County	96,530	600	630	30	5.0	200
Santa Cruz County	104,452	420	420	0	0	140
Ventura County	108,439	1,320	N/A	N/A	N/A	N/A

Source: U.S. Department of Labor, Bureau of Labor Statistics, 2016

criteria, including: be 18 years of age or older, have a combination of education in police science, criminal law, or justice experience equaling three years or 6,000 hours, pass a criminal history background check, and receive a qualifying score on a two-hour written exam covering laws and regulations (BLS, 2016). Many universities in California offer a Private Investigator Certificate Program to train and prepare aspiring investigators for the state exam. Private investigators in California can expect to earn approximately $61,610 annually (BLS, 2016).

Security Guard

Unlike private investigators who spend most of their time investigating past crimes (or tracking down information for a client), security guards spend most of their time patrolling, monitoring, or guarding a given space in order to prevent crime. Most guards in California work for a large private security company. They are primarily employed in restaurant industries, followed by elementary and secondary schools as well as department and specialty stores, accommodation industries (e.g., hotels), bars and other establishments which serve alcohol, and medical facilities (California Employment Development Department [EDD], 2017). Security guards are required to possess a license through the Department of Consumer Affairs, Bureau of Security and Investigative Services (which includes passing a background check and participating in 40 hours of training). Security guards make significantly less than other positions in this sector. Currently the United States has more than 1 million security guards and surveillance officers, whose average annual salary across the nation is $25,770. The occupational job outlook shows a 12% increase and employment changes are estimated to increase by more than 30,760 jobs over the next ten years (BLS, 2016).

Crime Analyst

Crime analysts collect, track, analyze, and disseminate information within an agency and between agencies. Crime analysts utilize a variety of technologies to identify criminals and hotspots of criminal activity, predict crime trends, investigate sophisticated crimes, profile criminals, and report on the use of department resources. Intelligence analysts perform similar functions, but spend more time learning about and analyzing sophisticated criminal relationships, networks, and organizations. Most analysts are civilian employees. Both positions require a bachelor's degree, and often a certificate in Crime and Intelligence Analysis approved by the California Department of Justice (EDD, n.d.). This is a relatively new field and little information exists about compensation; the information that does exist suggests that analysts earn between $35,000 and $60,000 annually (EDD, n.d.).

Forensic Science Technician

As you might guess from television, crime scene investigators (a.k.a. forensic science technicians) "collect, identify, classify, and analyze physical evidence related to criminal investigations" (EDD, 2011). Unlike on television, most crime scene investigators (CSI's) do not wear high heels and/or tight or revealing clothes. This field has progressed rapidly in the past decade and as a result, investigators are required to wear gloves and sometimes special suits and/or booties at crime scenes so as to not contaminate any evidence. Students interested in this career need to have at least an associate's degree and often a Bachelor's degree. There is also a certificate program for Forensic Science Technology that many agencies require. Forensic science technicians make approximately $80,150 per year in California (BLS, 2016).

Emergency Dispatcher

Police dispatchers receive emergency and non-emergency calls from citizens and then dispatch officers to locations where individuals need assistance. Dispatchers must make important decisions very quickly, multi-task effectively, and manage a lot of information simultaneously. At times, it is a very fast-paced job and, depending on the agency, it can also be a very slow-paced job. Dispatchers often work 8–12-hour shifts sitting at a console answering public service calls, complaints, and emergency services requests. Overtime is very common in this field. Most agencies require dispatchers to have a high school diploma and complete a California Department of Justice certificate course (often provided by the agency, post-hire). Dispatchers usually make between $25,100 and $61,270 in California (EDD, 2017). The national average is $38,870 (BLS, 2016).

Although many agencies slowed or halted their hiring between 2008 and 2015 (during the Great Recession), many agencies are again hiring. According to the U.S. Bureau of Labor Statistics (2016), a career in California law enforcement will be in demand through 2024 and we are expecting to see about 5% growth over the next decade. Individuals who are multi-lingual, have a bachelor's degree, and/or have military experience are particularly attractive to agencies.

Working in the Courts System

As you learned in chapter six, there are a variety of different actors that make up our courts system. From prominent positions such as judges and attorneys, to the behind-the-scenes actors such as file and courtroom clerks, interpreters, and court reporters, California's courtrooms (both within the criminal justice system as well as civil divisions) require a number of individuals to ensure that the system runs smoothly.

Judge

In chapter six, you learned that in order to be considered for a judicial position, you have to be licensed by the State Bar of California as an attorney for at least ten years prior to your appointment or election. In California, there are seven judges who sit on the California Supreme Court, and 105 judges who hear cases in the California Court of Appeals. As the largest division of the courts, there are approximately 2,175 judges and commissioners at the trial level (California Judicial Branch, 2012). According to the National Center for State Courts (2016), California's Supreme Court judges have the highest salary of all state supreme court judges in the nation ($233,888). California's Court of Appeals judges also have the highest salaries compared to judges in other state appellate courts at $219,272. Likewise, trial judges are highly ranked and well compensated, receiving a yearly salary of $191,612, a dramatic increase over the nationwide average salary of $149,609 (NCSC, 2017). Given the competitive nature of these positions, job growth in this field is slower compared to other legal fields (BLS, 2016).

Attorney/Lawyer

Within the criminal courts system, there are several types of attorneys. First, the district attorney, or prosecutor, is hired by the state to file and present cases against criminal defendants who have allegedly violated the law. Given the nature of the position, prosecutors have a high degree of discretion in determining when and what charges should be filed, based on the information collected by the police. In contrast, the job of a defense attorney is to represent individuals accused of a crime. As a result of the U.S. Supreme Court ruling in *Gideon v. Wainwright* (1963), all defendants must be provided with an attorney in their defense, regardless of their ability to pay. Here, the public defender's office steps in to provide legal counsel for indigent offenders. Like prosecuting attorneys, public defenders are paid out of state funds. Despite similar budgetary constraints that have faced other court employees in the state, deputy district attorneys in California are well compensated. For example, the average annual salary for attorneys (prosecutors and public defenders) in the San Francisco Bay area is $161,172, in comparison to attorneys in Los Angeles who make on average $160,909 annually. In California, the average salary range is $102,454–$145,600 with employment projections of more than an additional 13,400 lawyers needed through 2024.

Other Court Personnel

Perhaps the area with the greatest number of employees in the courts system is the administrative support branch of the courts. For example, Orange County courts employ more than 1,600 individuals in a variety of positions within the courtrooms and related divisions.[1] An example of one position found in the courts system is an interpreter. Given the multicultural diversity of the state of California, there is often a need to provide translation or interpreter services to non-English speaking individuals in the courtroom. For example, interpreters may be provided to translate court proceedings into Spanish, Vietnamese, Chinese, or Korean, just to name a few. In order to be employed as a court interpreter, individuals must hold a certificate from the Judicial Council of California. These positions can be highly competitive and usually require applicants to pass an exam focusing on the translations of legal terminology. The salary for a court interpreter in the Los Angeles metro area is on average $77,010 a year while the state median annual salary is $51,320 (BLS, 2017). In northern California, the metropolitan area of Oakland, Hayward, and Berkley pays on average $102,340 a year to their court interpreters (BLS, 2017).

Another example of a position within the courts system is a court reporter. The court reporter is responsible for maintaining a transcript, or record of all court proceedings. In order to be considered for this position, applicants must either have an associate's degree or have completed specialized training in court reporting. In addition, applicants need to possess current certification by the California Department of Consumer Affairs Certified Shorthand Reporters Board. They also need to have a working knowledge of legal terminology, be familiar with the practices and procedures of the courts, and have basic English language skills. The median annual salary for a court reporter in Fresno is $87,110 and in Riverside/San Bernardino Counties $79,800. The outlook for this type of employment is very good, as the field is expected to increase nationwide by 29% by 2024, a faster than average growth compared to most occupations. It is expected that the number of positions will continue to outnumber the number of jobseekers in this field (BLS, 2016).

---

1. www.oc.gov

A third example of a position within the courts system is a legal research assistant, or judicial law clerk. In many jurisdictions, a law clerk must be a member of the Bar Association. In other regions, students currently pursuing an advanced education in the study of law are eligible to apply. As a legal research assistant, you might find yourself briefing memos to the court or providing legal research on a case. The position of a legal assistant in Sacramento County receives compensation of $64,410 and in San Diego $65,690 annually. With over 37,700 positions nationwide, opportunities for growth in this field are greater than average.

Beyond these positions, there are many other support positions within the court system (see Table 13.4 below). For example, every court room has a court clerk, whose job it is to schedule the court's calendar, perform clerical duties, gather information for the judge, and ensure everything runs smoothly. Also,

Table 13.4. California Court and Legal Careers—
Employment and Salary Statistics 2014–2024

Description	National Average Salary[1]	California Average Salary[2]	Estimated CA Employment[2]	Additional CA Openings Expected[2]
Arbitrators	$59,770	$77,396	1,200	200
Court Clerks	$32,920	$45,219	8,900	700
Court Reporter	$51,320	$71,510	NA	NA
Interpreter	$46,120	$47,361	9,300	3,400
Judges	$109,940	$123,156	1,600	100
Lawyers	$118,160	$148,167	91,900	10,800
Legal Secretary	$49,500	$51,700	29,300	3,100
Legal Support Workers	$34,050	$55,681	6,700	500
Paralegal, Legal Assistant	$49,500	$57,441	29,500	3,900

[1] Source: U.S. Department of Labor, Bureau of Labor Statistics, 2016. http://www.bls.gov/oes/
[2] Source: Employment Development Department, Labor Market Information Division https://www.labormarketinfo.edd.ca.gov/

lawyers and law firms have many assistants, with varying degrees of education. Paralegals, which only need an associate's degree, help prepare legal documents, research legal precedent, and investigate the facts of a particular case. Additionally, arbitrators help resolve cases outside of the court system by negotiating and mediating conflicts through dialogue between the two (or more) parties at disagreement. As you can see, there are many varied career opportunities in California courts.

Correctional Officers

With one of the largest prison systems in the United States, employment opportunities for correctional officers in California have grown significantly in recent decades. Correctional officers are responsible for maintaining the safety and security of the inmates and staff for our state penal institutions. Like policing, there is a risk of danger in this occupation. As an officer at one of California's state prisons, workers are represented by one of the strongest union organizations in the state, the California Correctional Peace Officers Association (CCPOA). In addition to fighting for higher wages, healthcare benefits, and retirement benefits, the CCPOA is actively involved in working for increased on-the-job safety for its workers. One of the unique characteristics of the CCPOA is their activity related to lobbying for increased penalties for offenders. Some might argue that their tough on crime stance is another way of insuring job security for their workers. Their efforts have paid off as, California's prison guards represent some of the highest paid correctional officers in the nation, with a median salary of $70,020 (BLS, 2016). Madera County offers their correctional officers an average annual salary of $75,860 while those in southern California earn an annual salary of $71,460 (BLS, 2016). Given that facilities are open 24 hours a day, 365 days a week, officers can often benefit from opportunities for overtime shifts, which can significantly increase their salaries. While most employees consider anything over a 40-hour work-week to be overtime, California's correctional officers receive overtime pay for any work over 160 hours in a 28-day pay period. For example, while one Californian prison guard indicated that his salary is $81,683 annually, in one year he collected $114,334 in overtime pay (Finley, 2011).

In order to be considered to work as a correctional officer in the state of California, minimum requirements state that you must be at least 21 years old, possess a high school diploma or GED, be in good physical health, and have a clean criminal record. While there are over 30,000 correctional officers'

Table 13.5. Estimated Employment and Projected Growth for Correctional Officers

Geographic Area (Estimated Year-Projected Year) (2014–2024)	Median Annual Wages (2016)	Estimated Employment	Projected Employment	Numeric Change	Percent Change	Addl. Openings Due to Net Replacements
United States	42,820	457,600	474,700	17,100	4	Unknown
California	77,378	35,100	43,300	600	1.4	7,500
Inland Empire	78,754	4,070	4,460	390	9.6	1,120
Los Angeles County	60,705	3,400	3,470	70	2.1	930
Monterey County		1,340	1,490	150	11.2	370
Mother Lode Region	80,355	880	1030	150	17	240
North Coast Region	72,870	820	910	90	11	230
Sacramento Metro Area	76,623	2,260	2,510	250	11	620
San Diego County	80,345	2,630	2,880	250	9.5	460
Santa Barbara County	62,965	540	580	40	7.4	150

Source: U.S. Department of Labor, Bureau of Labor Statistics, 2016
Source: Employment Development Department, Labor Market Information Division https://www.labormarketinfo.edd.ca.gov/

positions in California, the competition for these jobs is high. Each year, the state receives over 130,000 applications—that means only one person out of every 140 applicants will be selected for the position (Hill, 2008). Due to anticipated retirements, job vacancies, and job growth, BLS (2016) estimates that there will be over 17,900 available positions through 2024. While recent legislative changes will alter the business of corrections throughout the state, the next decade will still see moderate growth in the field (4% increase).

Community Supervision: Probation and Parole

While probation and parole officers historically work with different populations, the duties of these two positions are similar. Both provide social services for offenders in the community. Here, their supervision of offenders is done to provide rehabilitative options and support for offenders while maintaining the safety of their communities. Probation and parole officers can also function like police officers, as they have the ability to revoke an offender's community sentence and return them to a secure, locked environment (such as jail or prison) if the individual violates the terms and conditions of their discretionary release. In California, there are 11,760 people employed in these positions. The average annual wage for these positions is $83,350. This is significantly higher than the national average, where the median annual salary is $50,160 (BLS, 2014).

In order to apply for a position as a probation or parole officer, candidates need to have a bachelor's degree from a college or university with a focus on the social sciences (social work, criminal justice, sociology, or psychology, for example). In some cases, agencies may prefer an advanced degree (master's) or related experience. As part of the application process, interested employees will undergo written and oral assessments as well as psychological and criminal background investigations. While employment in this field has always been relatively positive, changing sentencing practices (such as the amendment of mandatory sentencing and the de-incarceration of low-level offenders) may mean increased opportunities for employment in the future. Nationwide, this career field is expected to see a 4% increase in available jobs as a result of job growth and job replacement. In California, interested applicants can expect to see opportunities, with a 16.2% growth in the field over the next decade (EDD, 2013).

Table 13.6. Estimated Employment and Projected Growth for Probation Officers and Treatment Specialists

Geographic Area (Estimated Year-Projected Year) 2014–2024	Median Annual Wages 2013	Estimated Employment	Projected Employment	Numeric Change	Percent Change	Additional Openings Due to Net Replacements
California	85,592	10,900	11,800	900	8.3	300
Fresno County	76,128	350	410	60	17.1	70
Inland Empire Area	78,197	950	1,060	110	11.6	190
Kern County	85,846	600	750	150	25	120
Los Angeles County	83,584	3,100	3,270	170	5.5	610
Sacramento Metro Area	98,741	840	920	80	9.5	160
San Francisco Bay Area	82,707	350	370	20	5.7	70

Source: Employment Development Department, Labor Market Information Division, https://www.labormarketinfo.edd.ca.gov/

Conclusion

As you can see, there is significant diversity in the opportunities for employment within California's criminal justice system, both in terms of the types of job duties as well as the educational requirements and compensation. While recent years have slowed the growth of some occupational recruitment for new employees as well as fewer salary increases for those currently employed, the historical presence of the criminal justice system in the state provides opportunities for relatively stable employment compared to the traditional job market. Based on projected job growth in these fields nationwide and the significant presence that the criminal justice system has in the state of California, it appears that the projected growth and maintenance in these related fields will continue to rise over the next decade.

Internet Websites

California Attorney General's Office: https://oag.ca.gov/careers
California Department of Corrections and Rehabilitation: http://www.cdcr.ca.gov/Career_Opportunities/
California Employment Development Department: http://www.labormarket info.edd.ca.gov
California POST: https://post.ca.gov/law-enforcement-jobs.aspx
Chief Probation Officers of California: http://www.cpoc.org/employment
Criminal Justice Profiles: http://www.criminaljusticeprofiles.org/california-criminal-justice-jobs.html
International Association of Chiefs of Police: http://discoverpolicing.org/
United States Bureau of Labor Statistics: https://www.bls.gov/ooh/protective-service/home.htm

References

Bureau of Labor Statistics, U.S. Department of Labor. (n.d.). *Occupational outlook handbook, 2016-2017 edition, police and detectives.* Retrieved from http://www.bls.gov/ooh/protective-service/police-and-detectives.htm
California Commission on Peace Officer Standards and Training (POST). (2011). *Employment.* Retrieved from http://www.post.ca.gov
Employment Development Department (EDD). (n.d.). *Labor market information: Crime and intelligence analysts.* Retrieved from http://www.calmis.ca.gov/file/occguide/crimanlt.htm

Employment Development Department (EDD). (2016).*Labor market information*. Retrieved from https://www.labormarketinfo.edd.ca.gov/

Finley, A. (2011, April 30). California prison academy: Better than a Harvard degree. *Wall Street Journal*. Retrieved from http://online.wsj.com/"article/SB10001424052748704132204576285471510530398.html?KEYWORDS=ALLYSIA+FINLEY

Hill, E. G. (2008, February 7). *Correctional officer pay, benefits and labor relations*. Legislative Analyst Office, State of California. Retrieved from http://www.lao.ca.gov/2008/stadm/ccpoa_pay_020708/ccpoa_pay_020708.pdf

Judicial Council of California. (2012). *Court FAQ*. Retrieved from http://www.courts.ca.gov/2954.htm

Judicial Salary Tracker. (2017). Retrieved from http://www.ncsc.org/salarytracker

National Center for State Courts (NCSC). (2017). *Survey of judicial salaries*. Retrieved from http://contentdm.ncsconline.org/cgi-bin/showfile.exe?CISOROOT=/judicial&CISOPTR=288

Cases Cited

Gideon v. Wainwright, 372 U.S. 335 (1963)

Index